SCHOLASTIC

2016 BOOK OF WORLD RECORDS SPECIAL EDITION: EPIC WINS AND FAILS

BY JENNIFER CORR MORSE • A GEORGIAN BAY BOOK • SCHOLASTIC INC.

To Isabelle Nicole—May you always find wonder in the world.
—JCM

CREATED AND PRODUCED BY GEORGIAN BAY LLC

GEORGIAN BAY STAFF
Bruce S. Glassman, Executive Editor
Jenifer Corr Morse, Author
Joe Bernier, Designer

ISBN 978-0-545-82623-5

10 9 8 7 6 5 4 3 2 1 15 16 17 18 19

Printed in the U.S.A. 40
First edition, November 2015

Cover design by David DeWitt
Emily Teresa, Photo Editor

In most cases, the graphs in this book represent the top five record holders in each category. However, in some graphs, we have chosen to list well-known or common people, places, animals, or things that will help you better understand how extraordinary the record holder is. These may not be the top five in the category. Additionally, some graphs have fewer than five entries because so few people or objects reflect the necessary criteria.

Due to the publication date, the majority of statistics are current as of June 2015.

Contents

5:13 PM
Social
Facebook
Twitter
Instagram
Messenger
Pinterest
YouTube
Tumblr
LinkedIn
Google+

SCIENCE AND TECHNOLOGY RECORDS

- EPIC FAILS
- VIDEO GAMES
- INTERNET
- TECHNOLOGY
- VEHICLES
- STRUCTURES
- TRANSPORTATION
- ENVIRONMENT

EPIC FAIL

CAR WITH THE WORST GAS MILEAGE

The Nissan Armada Platinum has the worst fuel economy of any production car on the road, averaging just 13 miles per gallon (5.5 km/liter). It gets 9 miles per gallon (3.2 km/liter) in the city, and 18 miles per gallon (7.6 km/liter) on the highway.

10:20
DELAYED
10:40
DELAYED
10:45
DELAYED
11:15
DELAYED
DELAYED
DELAYED

ON-TIME FLIGHT FAILURES

American Airlines has the worst on-time performance of all the major North American airlines. Only 74% of all flights are on time, with an average delay of 58 minutes. Worldwide, Pakistan International Airlines has the worst record with just 37% of flights departing on time.

EPIC FAIL

AIRLINE THAT LOSES THE MOST LUGGAGE

Envoy Air, formerly known as American Eagle, loses approximately 9 bags per every 1,000 passengers. Express Jet comes in second with about 6 bags, and AirTran is third with about 5 bags lost for every 1,000 passengers.

EPIC FAIL

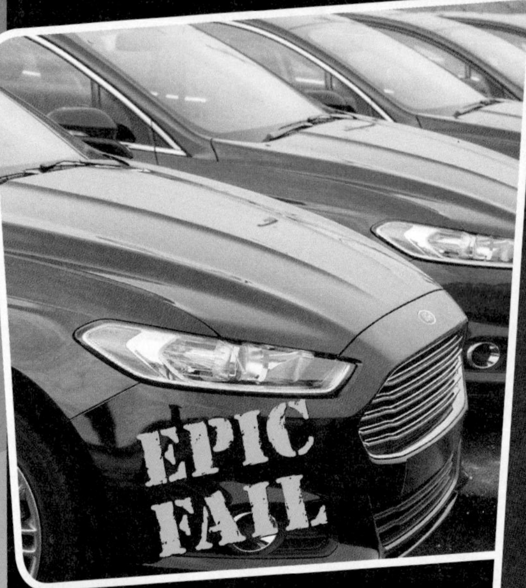
EPIC
FAIL

MOST AUTOMOBILE RECALLS

2014 saw more car recalls than any year in history. More than 800 recalls were made on nearly 64 million vehicles in the United States, shattering the previously held record, set in 2004, of 30.8 million cars recalled. Automobiles were recalled for a variety of issues, from faulty ignition switches and airbags to problems with hood latches.

WORST USE OF SOCIAL MEDIA

EPIC
FAIL

A Montana man on the run from the police took the time to like his mug shot on Facebook. Before he could unlike it, the media got a hold of it, and the liked mug shot went viral. The man was soon arrested and went to court to face charges of theft and forgery.

WORST TRAFFIC AREA

Los Angeles, California, ranks first in traffic throughout the United States. During peak commuting times, drivers are delayed about 40 minutes per hour of driving. The second-place spot belongs to San Francisco, California, where commuting drivers will waste about 83 hours stuck in traffic each year.

EPIC FAIL

MOST POLLUTED CITY

New Delhi, India, is the most polluted city in the world, according to the World Health Organization. The pollution levels are especially bad on major streets, where hundreds of thousands of cars travel each week. In an effort to improve air quality, the government is working on banning cars older than 15 years.

EPIC FAIL

MINNESOTA
EPIC FAIL
50

SMALLEST NFL STADIUM

TCF Bank Stadium is the smallest arena in the NFL with 52,525 seats. Ordinarily the home of the University of Minnesota's Golden Gophers, the stadium is currently the temporary home to the Minnesota Vikings for the 2015 season while their official stadium is built. It's located in Minneapolis, Minnesota. It was opened in 2009 and has a field turf playing surface and an open roof.

WORLD'S SMALLEST SKYSCRAPER

The Newby-McMahon building in Wichita Falls, Texas, is known as the world's smallest skyscraper—it's just 39.4 feet (12 m) tall. The architect drew up plans and collected $200,000 from investors in 1912 because they didn't notice that McMahon's tower wasn't 480 feet (146.3 m) tall, but was actually 480 inches (12 m). Once McMahon completed the tiny project, he skipped town with the cash.

EPIC FAIL

Welcome
Bienvenue
EPIC FAIL

DISNEY ATTENDANCE DROP

Disneyland Park and Walt Disney Studios Park at Disneyland Paris saw the biggest drop in attendance of any major theme park in 2013, with visitor levels at both parks dropping 6.9%. Despite the decline, Disneyland Paris is the most-visited theme park in Europe. About 14.1 million people visited the park between September 2013 and September 2014.

WATER PARK ATTENDANCE FALLS

Sunway Lagoon—a large water park located in Kuala Lumpur, Malaysia—saw the biggest drop in water park attendance in 2013 at 8.3%. About 100,000 fewer people showed up compared to the previous year. The park has a man-made surf beach, a giant wave pool, and one of the world's longest water rides.

EPIC
FAIL

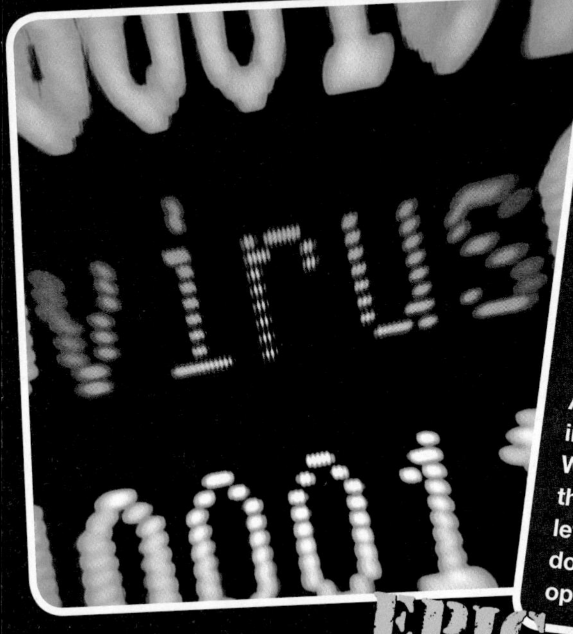
virus

COSTLIEST COMPUTER VIRUS

The costliest computer virus was known as MyDoom and caused more than $38 billion in damages. About 25% of all emails were infected with this virus in 2004. When a computer was infected, the virus opened networks to let others access the files and documents. The virus could also open additional programs.

EPIC FAIL

BUILDING MATERIAL BLUNDER

The Aon Center—Chicago's third-tallest building at 1,136 feet (346 m)—was an amazing sight when it was built in 1973 using an exterior layer of Italian Carrara marble. However, since this marble is much thinner than building marble, slabs would slide off the building and crash into the roof of the Prudential Center below. The fancy exterior marble had to be stripped off and replaced with granite at a cost of $80 million in 1973—that's $430 million today!

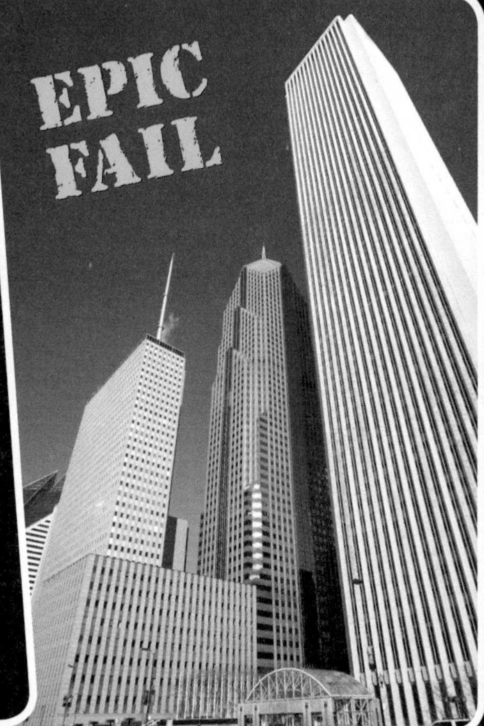
EPIC FAIL

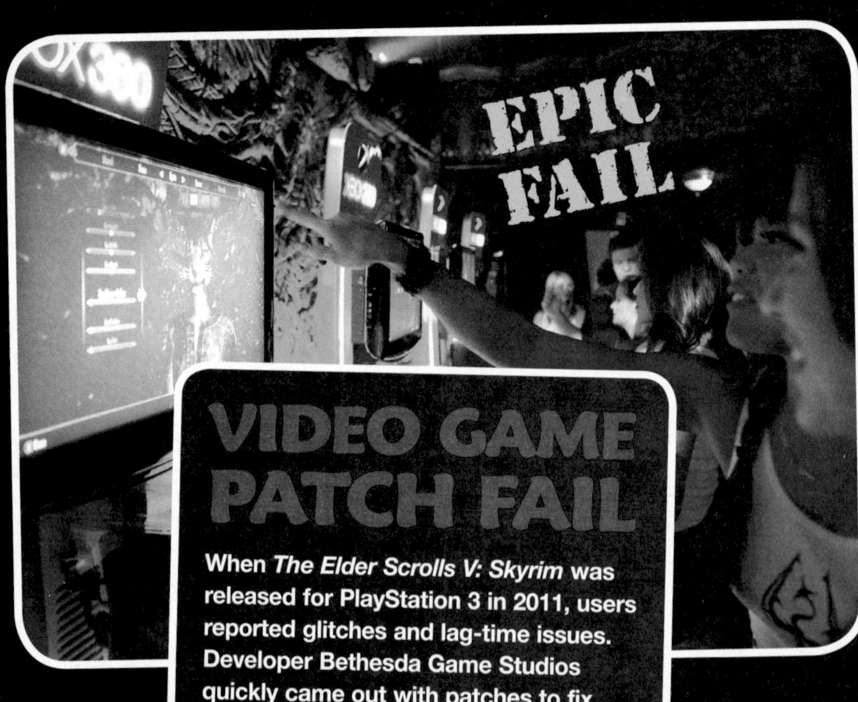
EPIC FAIL

VIDEO GAME PATCH FAIL

When *The Elder Scrolls V: Skyrim* was released for PlayStation 3 in 2011, users reported glitches and lag-time issues. Developer Bethesda Game Studios quickly came out with patches to fix some issues, but they accidentally resulted in dragons flying backward.

UK Border

AIRPORT GLITCHES CAUSE CHAOS

EPIC FAIL

In April 2014, London's Heathrow and Gatwick airports suffered computer glitches that prevented immigration officials from checking arriving passengers' passports electronically. Since they had to be checked by hand, long lines formed, and some people waited up to 4 hours to exit the airport. Some joked that their flights were shorter than the immigration process.

Sprint

EPIC FAIL

WORST CELL PHONE SERVICE

The 2014 US Wireless Network Quality Performance study found that Sprint Nextel and T-Mobile ranked the lowest among the major carriers. Sprint Nextel had the most trouble in the Northeast and Southeast regions of the US, dropping between 18 to 19 calls per 100 network connections. T-Mobile averaged about 15 dropped calls per 100 connections throughout the country.

SAMSUNG CELL SALES SLIPPING

Although Samsung is the bestselling cell phone brand, the company had the biggest decline in sales between 2013 and 2014 because of increased competition in the smartphone market. Their market share went down 5.1%, resulting in 23,000 fewer phones sold worldwide. The decline occurred mostly in Europe and Asia—Samsung's smartphone sales slipped 28.6% in China alone.

EPIC FAIL

CRUISE INDUSTRY PROBLEMS

Between 2009 and 2013, there were 203 major mishaps reported in the cruise ship industry. The most common problem was technical failure—such as broken engines or loss of electricity—which was reported 92 times. However, not all mishaps were due to technical failures. In 2013, the Carnival *Triumph* was stranded at sea for five days with no working toilets because of an engine-room fire. The voyage later became known as the "poop cruise."

EPIC FAIL

SONY PICTURES ENTERTAINMENT
SONY

EPIC FAIL

HACKERS ATTACK SONY

In November 2014, Sony Pictures Entertainment's computer system was hacked, resulting in a website takeover, as well as days of employees' computers, emails, and voicemails being frozen. Five Sony films—four of which had not yet been released—were made available online, and millions of copies were illegally downloaded. Hundreds of confidential documents were also released, including salary and budget information and celebrity contact information.

EriTel

NATION WITH LOWEST CELL PHONE AND INTERNET USAGE

Eritrea, in Africa, has the fewest cell phone subscriptions in the world, with just 6 cell subscriptions per 100 people. It also has the lowest percentage of Internet users with 0.9 per 100 people. This developing country has a population of about 6.3 million, with some 69% of the population at or below the poverty line.

EPIC FAIL

EA SPORTS
MADDEN NFL 15
EPIC FAIL

MADDEN NFL 15 GLITCH

When EA Sports created *Madden NFL 15*, they inadvertently included a glitch that turned out to be a big hit with gamers. Rookie linebacker Christian Kirksey—who is 6 feet 2 inches (1.9 m) tall—transforms into a 1-foot-tall (0.3 m) player when he puts on a Tennessee Titans uniform. The game plays normally otherwise, and the tiny linebacker can still take down the normal-sized players.

STREAMING STOPPED

Aereo seemed like a great idea for subscribers who wanted to stream shows from major broadcasters onto their phones, tablets, and laptops for a few bucks a month by renting a special antenna. However, the Supreme Court ruled that Aereo was stealing programs by doing this. The company went out of business in June 2014 after just 5 months in operation.

EPIC FAIL

ROLLER COASTER PROBLEMS

Fury 325 may be the fastest and tallest giga-coaster in the world, but it keeps getting stuck mid-ride. When it opened in North Carolina in April 2015, it routinely malfunctioned. It stalled three times in its first three weeks, stranding riders at the top of the steep incline and dangling them 150 feet (45.7 m) in midair.

EPIC FAIL

CHINA'S GIANT GHOST TOWN

The largest ghost town in the world is Ordos in the autonomous region of Inner Mongolia in China. The city was created to be home to a million people, but construction was stopped before completion after loans weren't paid and investors pulled out. Only 2% of its buildings were ever occupied, because the finished buildings became useless when streets and other common areas weren't completed.

EPIC
FAIL

EPIC
FAIL

AQUARIUM SPRUNG A LEAK

The Dubai Aquarium was built in 2008 in one of the world's largest shopping centers—The Dubai Mall. The 2.5-million-gallon aquarium houses about 400 sharks and 33,000 fish. Just two years after opening, the aquarium sprung a leak and the mall had to be evacuated while six divers patched up the hole. Luckily, no fish were hurt during the disaster.

EPIC FAIL

REPLACEMENT WINDOWS

The John Hancock Tower is a 60-story skyscraper in Boston that was completed in 1976. It was praised for its appearance and style, but it had one major flaw: The windows would fall out and crash to the pavement. Eventually, all 10,000 windows had to be replaced at a cost of $5 million in 1976, which is the equivalent of $21 million in 2015.

Wii U
SONIC BOOM
RISE OF LYRIC
NINTENDO NETWORK
EVERYONE 10+
ESRB
SEGA

SONIC'S LOWEST-SELLING GAME

Sonic Boom: Rise of Lyric is the worst-selling video game in the series, moving just 490,000 copies worldwide across WiiU and 3DS. By comparison, *Sonic Colors* sold 2.18 million copies in 2010, and *Sonic Lost World* sold 710,000 copies in 2013.

EPIC FAIL

Shop
amazon
Amazon Fire TV and Kindle Fire Tablets
Amazon Fire TV
Amazon
$99.00
Kindle Fire HDX 8.9", HDX Di...
Kindle
$379.00
Kindle Fire HDX 7", HDX Disp...
Kindle
Phone
Messaging
Email
Silk Browser
EPIC FAIL

AMAZON'S FIRE PHONE FADES OUT

Amazon's Fire Phone, the retail giant's attempt at entering the smartphone market, did not perform nearly as well as expected in 2014. After dismal sales, Amazon cut the price from $200 to 99 cents with a contract. The technology could not compete against other well-known smartphones that had a good history in the market. At the end of 2014, Amazon was stuck with $83 million worth of unsold Fire Phones.

Facebook

EPIC FAIL

FACEBOOK'S COSTLY VIDEO SWITCH UP

In 2014, Facebook inadvertently started costing cell phone users a lot of money. The site automatically started playing videos in its users' newsfeeds, running up big bills as the continuously playing content quickly used up data plans. Luckily, users just had to change the video setting to go back to normal.

ON TO THE EPIC WINS!

bestselling family video game

Pokemon Omega Ruby and *Alpha Sapphire*

Pokemon Omega Ruby and *Alpha Sapphire* sold more than 7 million units for Nintendo 3DS during 2014. The two games, which are updated versions of the originals that were released for Game Boy in 2003, generally feature the same storyline and characters as the originals. However, they have been updated to include the newest generation of Pokemon. A new story—the "Delta Episode"—has been added as well. The story takes place in Hoenn, and as players journey through the game looking for new Pokemon, they meet new trainers and Professor Birch. The professor runs the Pokemon Lab, and he becomes a valuable partner throughout the game.

bestselling family video games

units sold in 2014, in millions

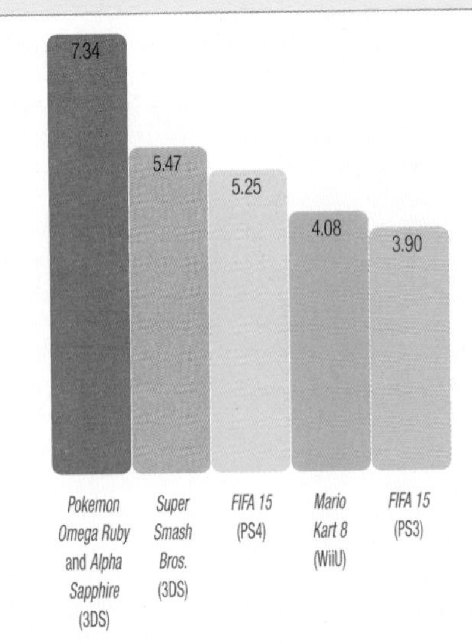
7.34
5.47
5.25
4.08
3.90
Pokemon Omega Ruby and Alpha Sapphire (3DS)
Super Smash Bros. (3DS)
FIFA 15 (PS4)
Mario Kart 8 (WiiU)
FIFA 15 (PS3)

bestselling video game console

PlayStation 4

During 2014, more than 13.6 million units of the PlayStation 4 console were sold. The console is made by Sony and launched in the United States in November 2013. Since its debut, it has sold a total of 18.5 million units. PlayStation4, or PS4, has powerful graphics and allows for many different players. It features 500 GB of storage and a wireless DualShock 4 controller, which includes a jack so a headset can be plugged directly into it. Users can stream gameplay footage and create videos. The PS4 includes a web browser, so players can surf the Internet when connected. There is also a Blu-ray player in the console for watching movies.

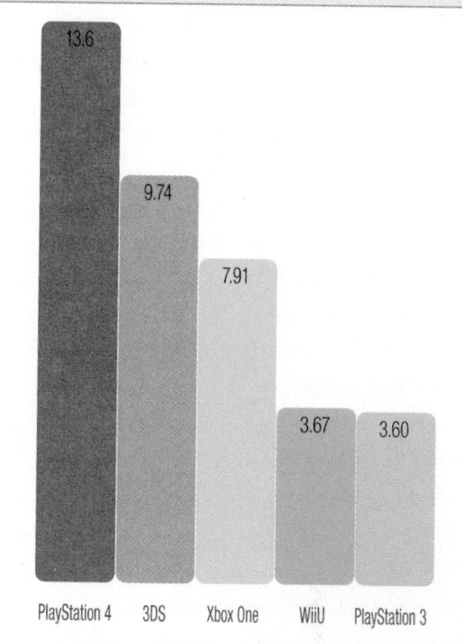
bestselling video game consoles
sales in 2014, in millions of units
13.6
9.74
7.91
3.67
3.60
PlayStation 4
3DS
Xbox One
WiiU
PlayStation 3

most popular tweet per minute

Ellen's Oscar Selfie

After Ellen DeGeneres—the comedian who hosted the 2014 Academy Awards—tweeted a photo of herself with several movie stars, it generated 254,644 tweets per minute. The photo was taken by Bradley Cooper on Ellen's phone and included Jennifer Lawrence, Meryl Streep, Julia Roberts, Kevin Spacey, Brad Pitt, Channing Tatum, and several others. It was retweeted in 151 different countries, and more than 2 million people marked it as a favorite. Later in the Oscars broadcast, Ellen shared a pizza delivery with the celebrity audience, creating another top retweet-able moment.

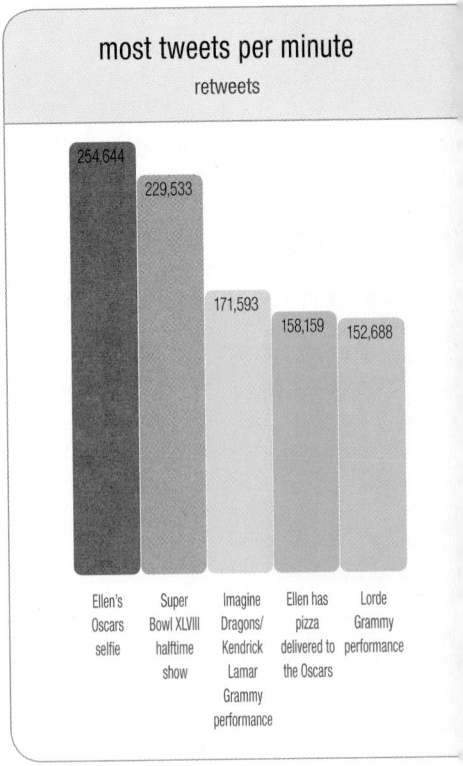

most tweets per minute

retweets

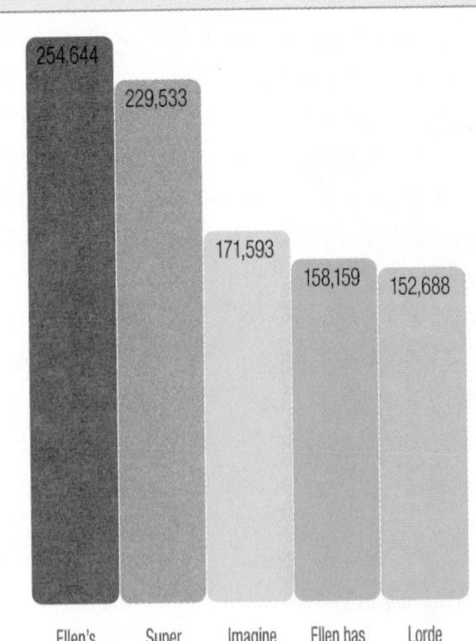
254,644
229,533
171,593
158,159
152,688
Ellen's Oscars selfie
Super Bowl XLVIII halftime show
Imagine Dragons/ Kendrick Lamar Grammy performance
Ellen has pizza delivered to the Oscars
Lorde Grammy performance

most popular social media site

Facebook

More than 1.3 billion active users visit the Facebook website on a regular basis. That's more than the next three social sites combined. Facebook was founded by Mark Zuckerberg in 2004 as a way for Harvard students to keep in touch. Ten years later, Facebook has about 1.28 billion registered users and about 757 million log-ons every day. Every minute of the day, about 4.75 billion pieces of content are shared. People spend an average of 8.3 hours on Facebook each month. There are around 150 billion friend connections, and 4.5 billion "likes" per day.

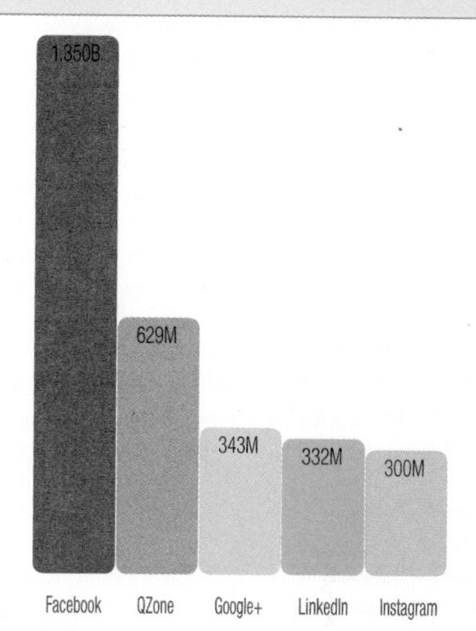
most popular social media sites
number of active users worldwide, in millions and billions
1.350B
629M
343M
332M
300M
Facebook
QZone
Google+
LinkedIn
Instagram

most-used search engine

Google

About 67 percent of people browsing the Internet choose Google as their search engine. Google is the world's largest online index of websites. In addition, Google offers email, maps, news, and financial services, among others. Headquartered in California's Silicon Valley, the company runs hundreds of thousands of servers around the globe. A "googol" is a 1 followed by 100 zeros, and the site was named after the term to indicate its mission to organize the virtually infinite amount of information on the Web.

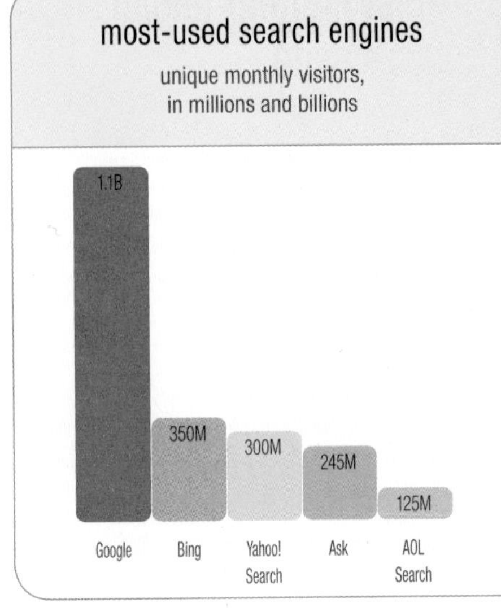
most-used search engines
unique monthly visitors, in millions and billions
1.1B
350M
300M
245M
125M
Google
Bing
Yahoo! Search
Ask
AOL Search

most-visited website

Google

The most-visited website in the world is Google, which gets more than 164 million unique page views per month. Created by Stanford grad students Larry Page and Sergey Brin in 1998, Google has indexed 30 trillion pages. Google performs about 100 billion searches each month. There are more than 425 million people using Gmail, the website's email feature. Over the years, Google has acquired many impressive companies, including YouTube, Android, DoubleClick, and Blogger. Google employs more than 50,000 people worldwide.

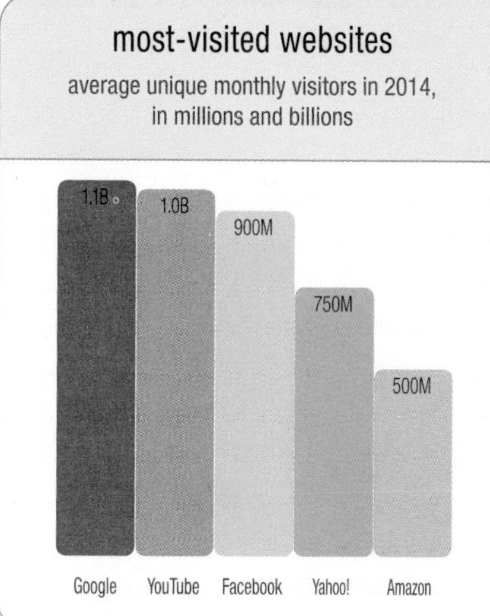
most-visited websites
average unique monthly visitors in 2014, in millions and billions
1.1B
1.0B
900M
750M
500M
Google
YouTube
Facebook
Yahoo!
Amazon

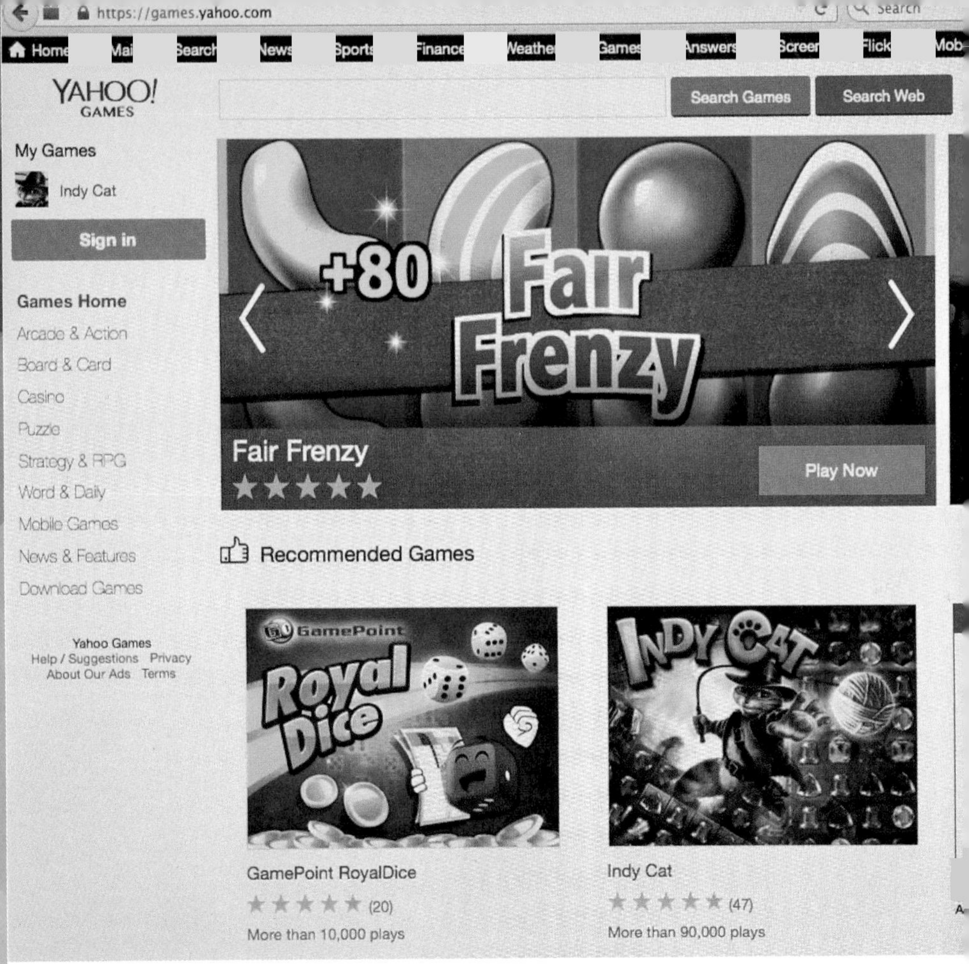

most popular game website

Yahoo! Games

Yahoo! Games is the most popular gaming website on the Internet with about 25 million unique visitors each month. Most games can be played on the site, but some need to be downloaded. The main game categories include Arcade & Action, Board & Card, Puzzle, Strategy & RPG (for role playing), and several others. Yahoo! no longer develops its own games—it only offers games from third parties. Some of the games found on the site include *Super Bingo*, *Daily Crosswords*, *Mahjongg*, *Sudoku Daily*, *Monster Match*, and *Klondike*.

most popular game websites

unique monthly visitors, in millions

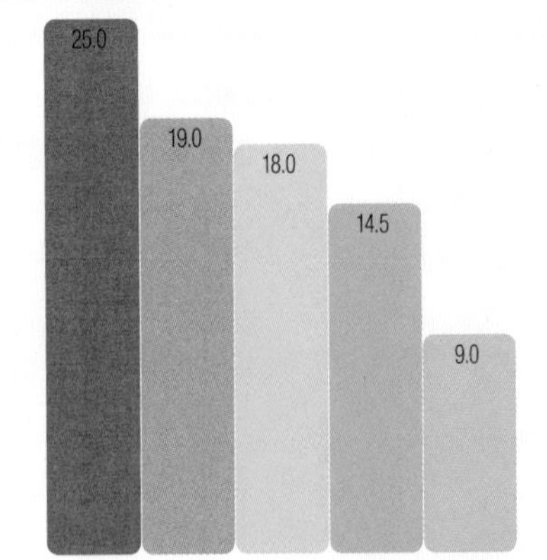
25.0
19.0
18.0
14.5
9.0
Yahoo! Games
Y8
Pogo
MiniClip
Big Fish Games

most popular kids website

nick

The nick.com website is tops among kids, with about 7 million unique visitors each month. Run by Nickelodeon, the site offers games, videos, and TV episodes of some of the network's most popular series. Shows featured on the site include *The Thundermans*, *SpongeBob SquarePants*, *Every Witch Way*, *Henry Danger*, *Haunted Hathaways*, and several others. There's also a radio station on the site that plays the latest kid-friendly hits and lets listeners vote on favorites. Fans can stream their favorite artists 24 hours a day.

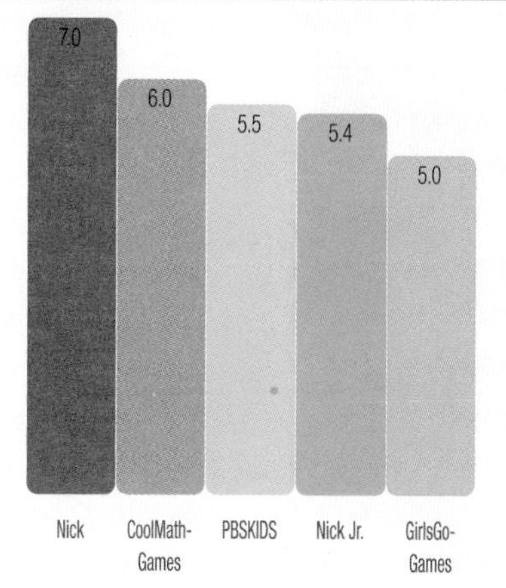
most popular kids websites
unique monthly visitors, in millions
7.0
6.0
5.5
5.4
5.0
Nick
CoolMath-Games
PBSKIDS
Nick Jr.
GirlsGo-Games

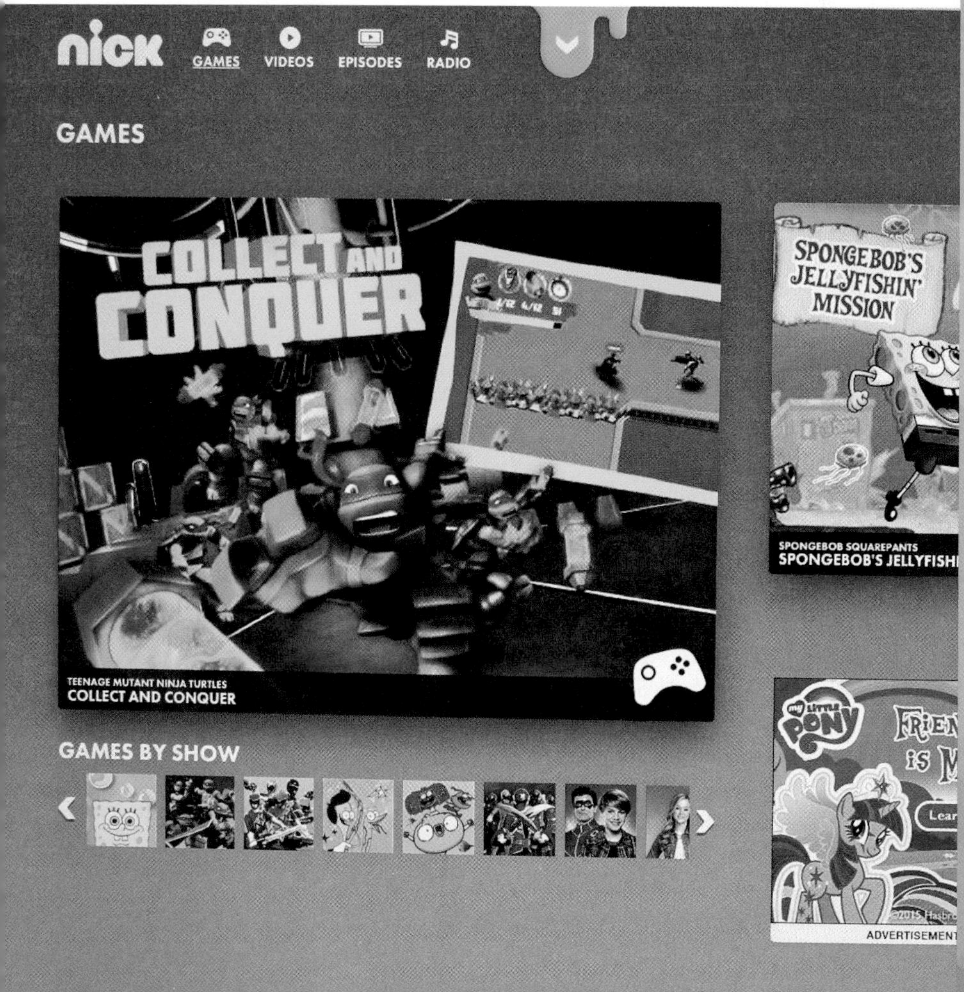

nick GAMES VIDEOS EPISODES RADIO

GAMES

COLLECT AND CONQUER

TEENAGE MUTANT NINJA TURTLES
COLLECT AND CONQUER

SPONGEBOB'S JELLYFISHIN' MISSION

SPONGEBOB SQUAREPANTS
SPONGEBOB'S JELLYFISH

GAMES BY SHOW

ADVERTISEMENT

most-viewed YouTube video

"Dark Horse"

Katy Perry's "Dark Horse" video was viewed more than 715 million times on YouTube during 2014. That's enough for every person in the United States to see it 2.2 times. The song, which also features rapper Juicy J, was released from Perry's fourth studio album, *Prism*, in September 2013. She first performed the song for the iHeartRadio Music Festival, and later at the 56th Grammy Awards. The video combines ancient Egyptian culture and Memphis hip-hop. "Dark Horse" won Best Female Video at the MTV Video Music Awards and Single of the Year at the American Music Awards.

most-viewed YouTube videos

views, in millions

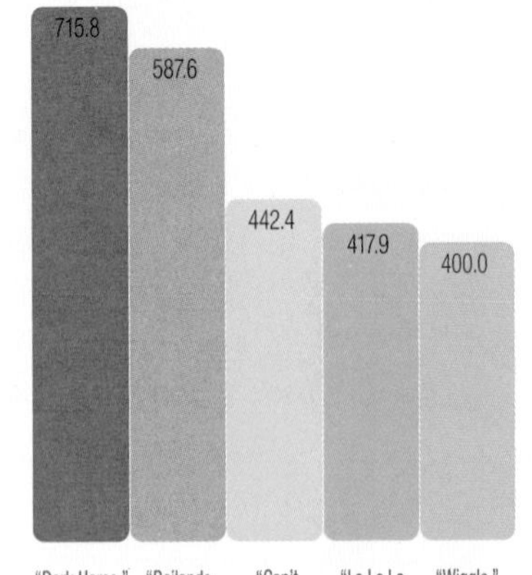
715.8
587.6
442.4
417.9
400.0
"Dark Horse," Katy Perry
"Bailando (Español)," Enrique Iglesias
"Can't Remember to Forget You," Shakira
"La La La (Brazil 2014)," Shakira
"Wiggle," Jason Derulo

top-grossing iOS mobile game

Clash of Clans

Each day, the mobile game *Clash of Clans* rakes in about $1.38 million! That totals more than half a billion dollars a year. Players of this strategy game construct and expand their villages, acquire more powerful warriors, raid other people's villages, and create and join clans. The game is free to play, but players can buy extras as in-app purchases, including green gems to use as currency. Finnish mobile game developer Supercell created the game, and it debuted on iTunes in August 2012, and later on Google Play in October 2013.

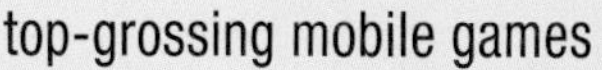
top-grossing mobile games

daily revenue, in US dollars

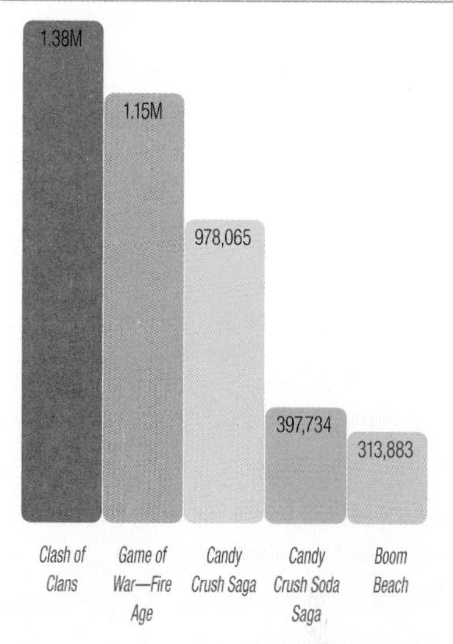
1.38M
1.15M
978,065
397,734
313,883
Clash of Clans
Game of War—Fire Age
Candy Crush Saga
Candy Crush Soda Saga
Boom Beach

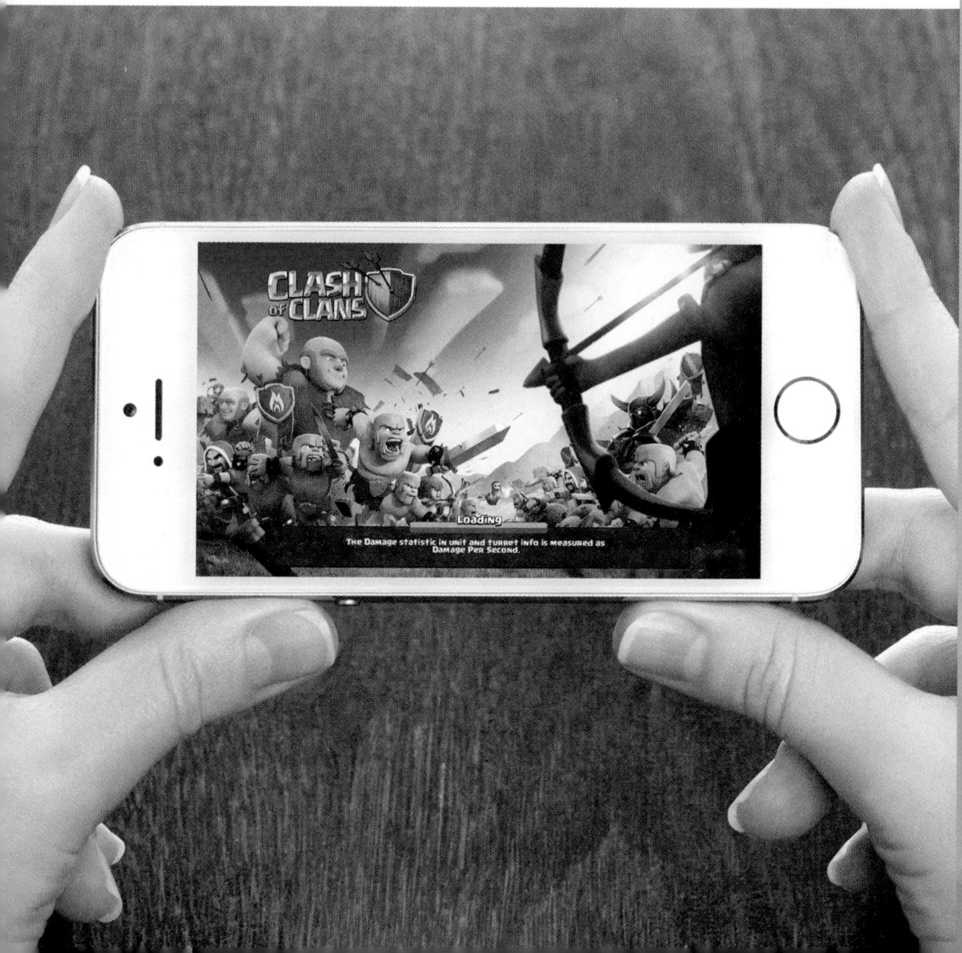

product with the most Facebook fans

Coca-Cola

Coca-Cola is the most popular product on Facebook, with more than 90 million fans. On the page, fans can post and read stories, explore products, and check out the latest photos. The company has acquired some impressive statistics during its 128 years in business. Coca-Cola produces more than 3,500 different types of beverages, which are sold in 200 countries throughout the world. Each day, about 1.7 billion servings of Coca-Cola products are enjoyed. In addition to its cola products, the company also produces A&W, Crush, Dasani, Hi-C, Minute Maid, Nestea, and many others.

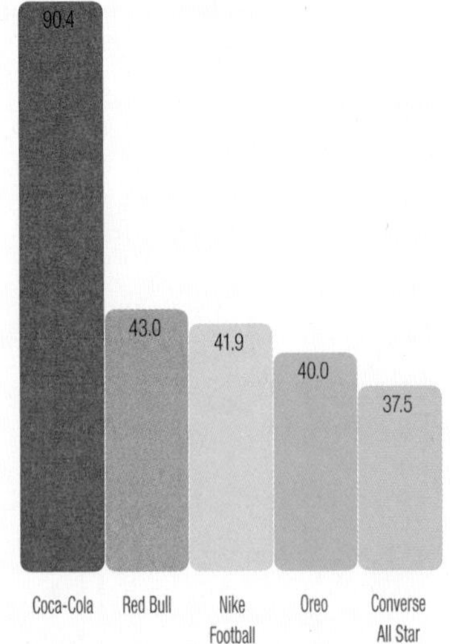
products with the most Facebook fans
number of fans, in millions*
90.4
43.0
41.9
40.0
37.5
Coca-Cola
Red Bull
Nike Football
Oreo
Converse All Star
*As of May 2015

INTERNET

top-trending person on Google

Jennifer Lawrence

Jennifer Lawrence is a popular lady on Google, ranking number one on Google's Top Trending People list for all of 2014. The Oscar-winning actress became the face of the *Hunger Games* when the first movie debuted in 2012, and had a busy year in 2014. She reprised her role as Katniss Everdeen in *Catching Fire* and enjoyed the popularity from the previous year's blockbuster *American Hustle*. Lawrence played Rosalyn Rosenfeld in the movie and received an Academy Award nomination for Best Supporting Actress. In May 2014, Lawrence appeared as Mystique in *X-Men: Days of Future Past*, which earned over $233 million at the box office.

top-trending celebrities on Google

ranking according to Google

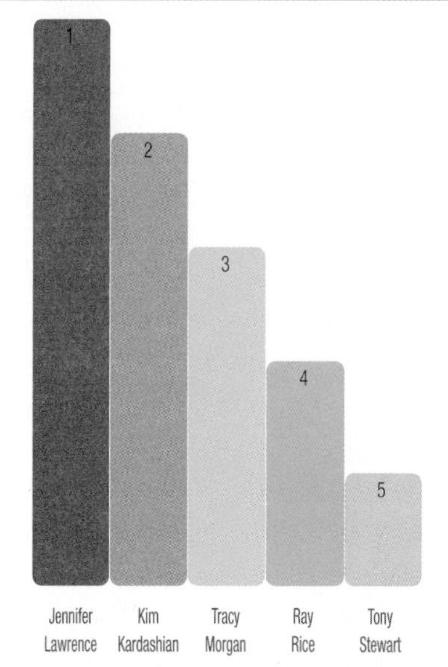
1
2
3
4
5
Jennifer Lawrence
Kim Kardashian
Tracy Morgan
Ray Rice
Tony Stewart

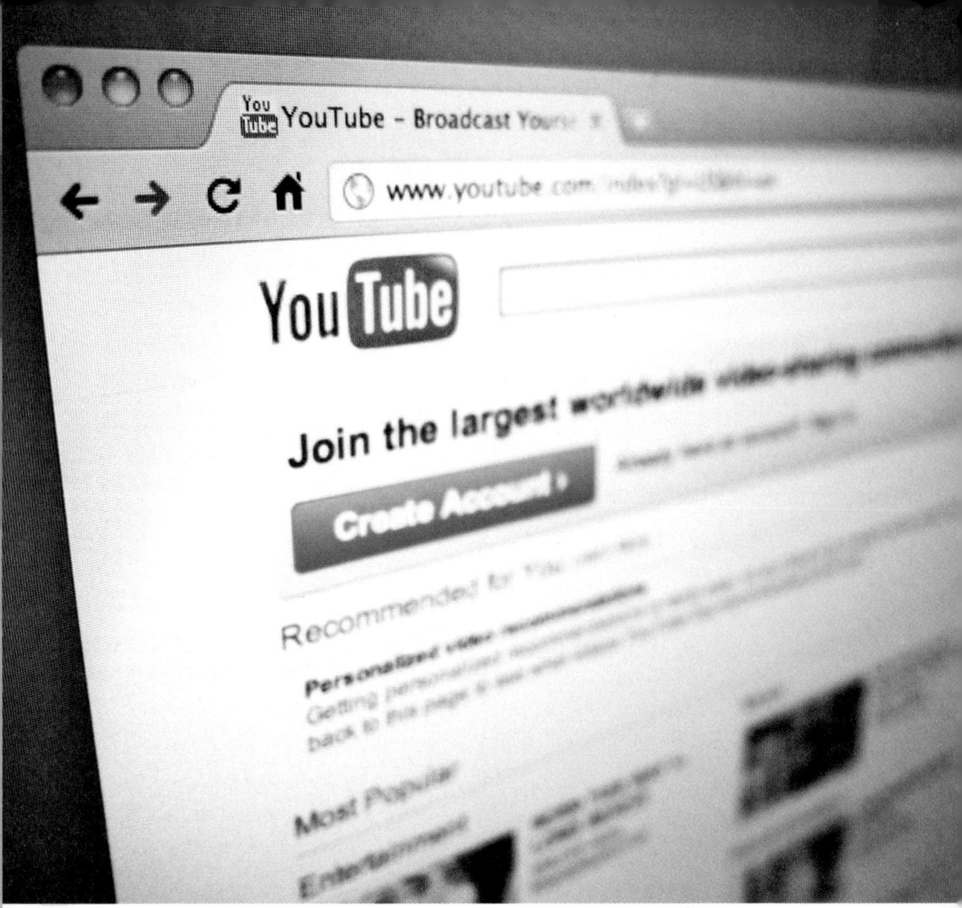

most-visited video site

YouTube

When Web surfers are looking for videos, the majority log on to YouTube. With more than 1 billion unique visitors per month, YouTube can turn everyday people into Internet stars. Each minute, about 300 hours of video is uploaded to the site, and people watch hundreds of millions of hours of YouTube each day. About half of all YouTube views happen on mobile devices. The company is available in about 75 countries, and in 61 languages. Approximately 60% of a video's views come from outside the creator's home country. In fact, in 2014 the ALS ice bucket challenge captivated users and registered more than 1 billion views worldwide.

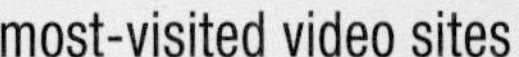

most-visited video sites

unique visitors per month, in millions and billions

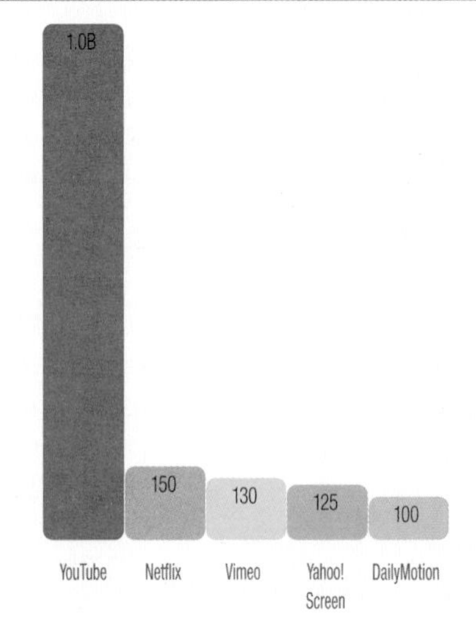
1.0B
150
130
125
100
YouTube
Netflix
Vimeo
Yahoo! Screen
DailyMotion

most popular mobile chat app

WhatsApp

More than 700 million active users chat with friends and family using WhatsApp each month. The app lets iPhone, Android, Blackberry, Nokia, and Windows phone users share unlimited messages for free. Users can download the app for free for a year and then pay a low annual price. WhatsApp has become one of the bestselling paid apps across all platforms. It's used in 250 countries on 750 networks. On any given day, about 30 billion messages are sent using the app. The company, founded by former Yahoo! employees Jan Koum and Brian Acton, launched in 2009.

most popular mobile chat apps
monthly active users, in millions

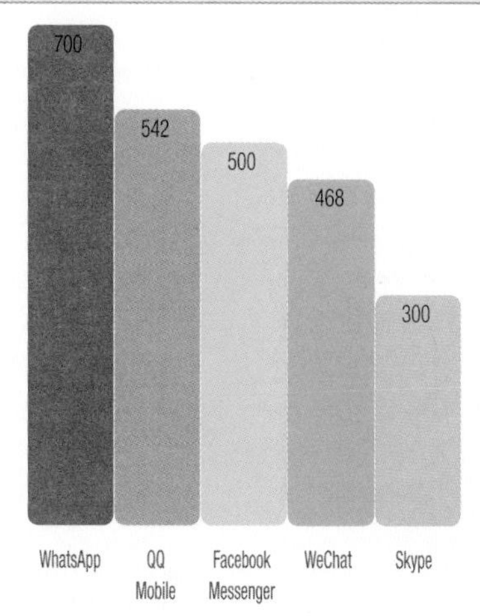
700
542
500
468
300
WhatsApp
QQ Mobile
Facebook Messenger
WeChat
Skype

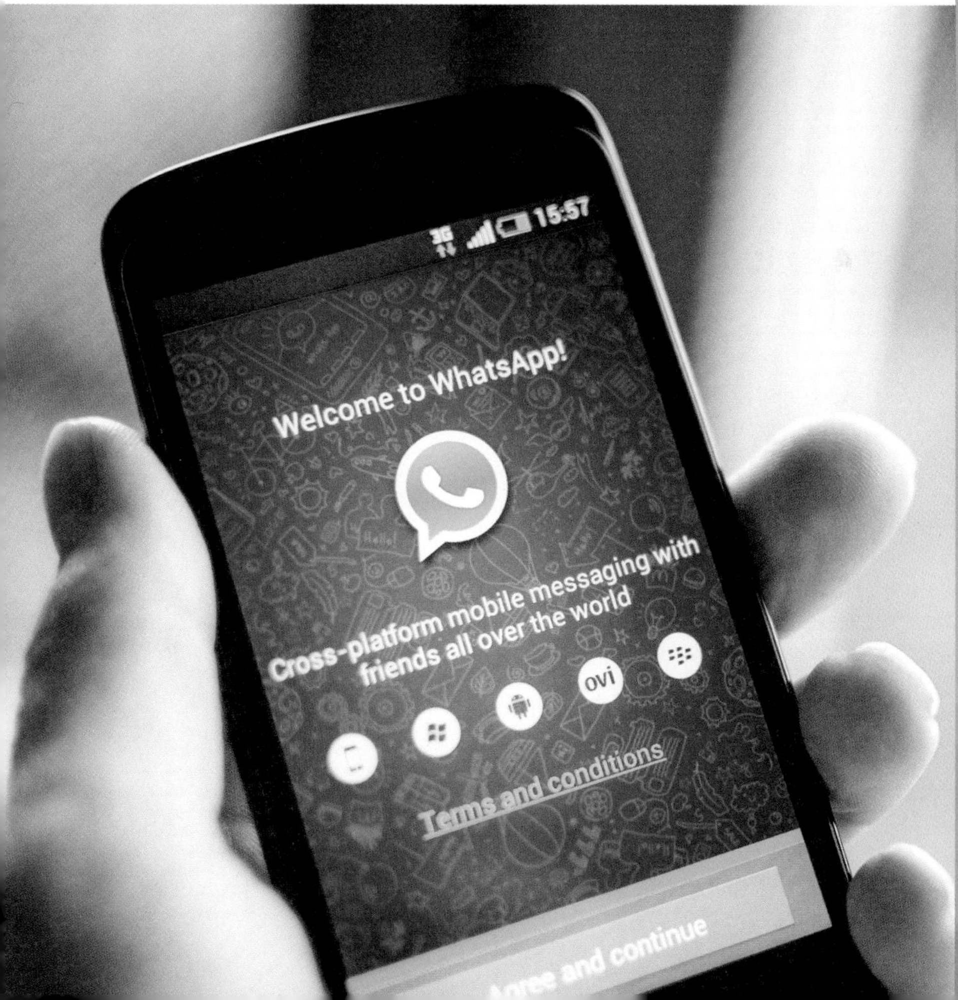

celebrity with the most Twitter followers

Katy Perry

More than 70 million fans follow Katy Perry on Twitter since she joined the site in February 2009. The singer has sent out about 5,400 tweets since joining and averages 2 per day. In November 2013, @katyperry became the most popular celebrity Twitter handle. Three months later, Perry tweeted to her "Katycats" to celebrate becoming the first person to surpass 50 million followers. Perry owes some of her popularity to the 2014 Grammy Awards, where she performed her hit "Dark Horse." After the show aired, she picked up an additional 800,000 followers!

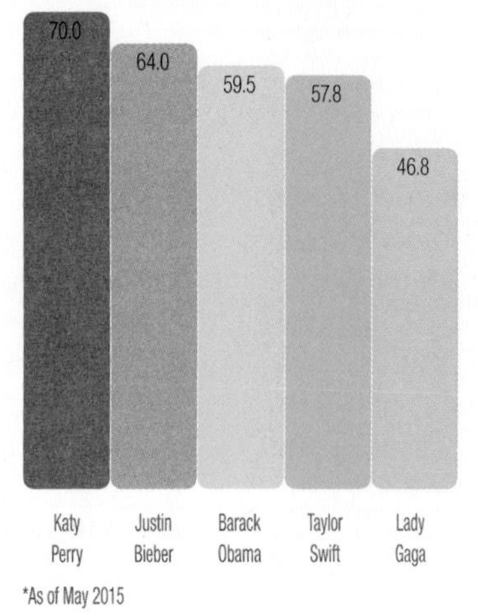
celebrities with the most Twitter followers
followers, in millions*
70.0
64.0
59.5
57.8
46.8
Katy Perry
Justin Bieber
Barack Obama
Taylor Swift
Lady Gaga
*As of May 2015

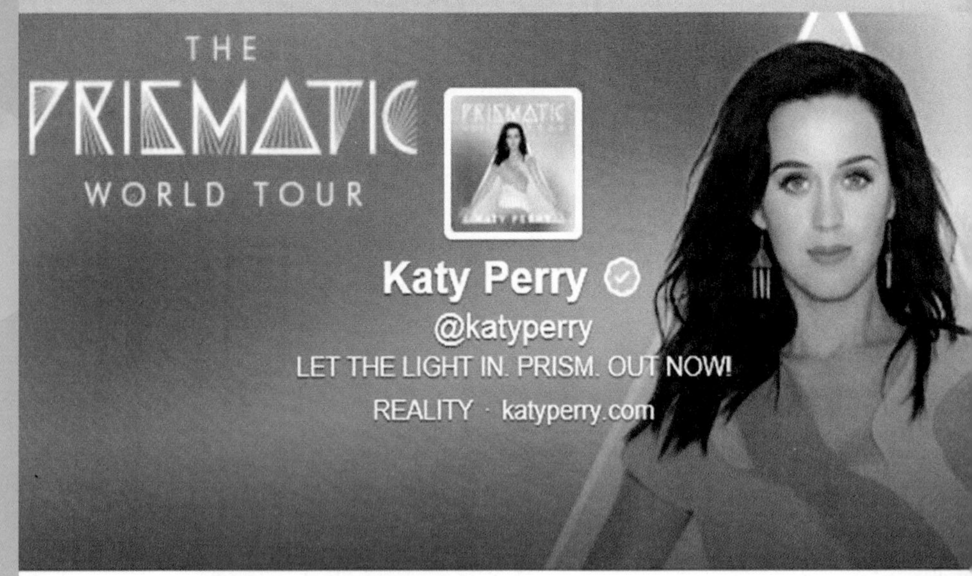
THE
PRISMATIC
WORLD TOUR
Katy Perry
@katyperry
LET THE LIGHT IN. PRISM. OUT NOW!
REALITY · katyperry.com

TWEETS 5,486 FOLLOWING 136 FOLLOWERS 52.2M Follow

Tweets All / No replies

Katy Perry @katyperry · Apr 13
Sand is the new dry shampoo. #coachella
Expand Reply Retweet Favorite

city with the most Instagram selfies per day

Makati City, the Philippines

Time magazine studied which world city posted the most Instagram selfies, and Makati City, the Philippines, won with 258 Instagram selfies posted in a 24-hour period for every 100,000 people who live there. This photo-happy Filipino city is the financial center of the country and is one of 16 cities that make up the Manila area. It has earned the nickname "Wall Street of the Philippines" because of all of the banks and corporations located there. Makati City's population almost doubles during the day, when commuters travel in to work and shop, but returns to about 600,000 at night. The city also offers lots of entertainment, including fancy hotels and restaurants, and upscale department stores and boutiques. To be counted in *Time*'s study, a photo had to be tagged "selfie" and include a geographic coordinate.

cities with the most Instagram selfies per day

selfies per 100,000 people

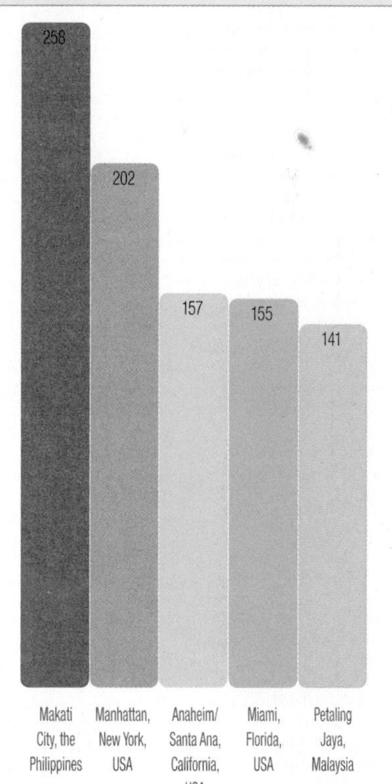
258
202
157
155
141
Makati City, the Philippines
Manhattan, New York, USA
Anaheim/ Santa Ana, California, USA
Miami, Florida, USA
Petaling Jaya, Malaysia

most popular blog

The Huffington Post

The Huffington Post blog pulls in about 110 million unique visitors each month—more than the next top four blogs combined! *The Huffington Post* website includes current events and news stories from around the world, and its blogs have similar content. Some of their content categories include comedy, college, style, technology, and politics. They also have a blogger dedicated to teens and teen interests. Sometimes even celebrities, athletes, and politicians contribute a blog. *The Huffington Post* has won two Webby Awards for the Best Political Blog, and in 2012, it picked up a Pulitzer Prize.

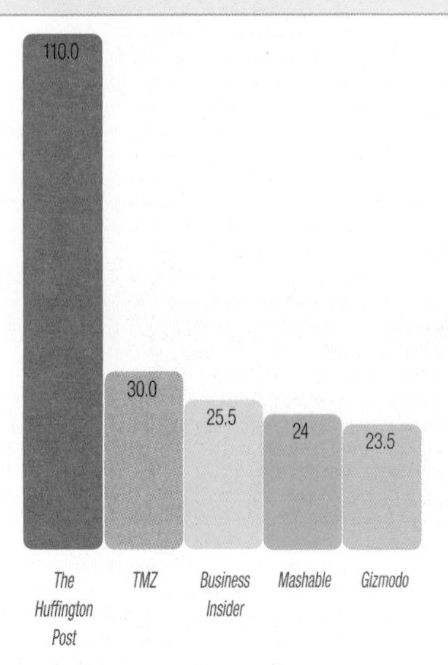
most popular blogs
estimated unique monthly visitors, in millions
110.0
30.0
25.5
24
23.5
The Huffington Post
TMZ
Business Insider
Mashable
Gizmodo

country with the most internet users

China

China dominates the world in Internet usage, with more than 649 million people—or almost half of the country—browsing the World Wide Web under government censorship. China's "Great Firewall" denies or severely restricts access to sites such as Google, Twitter, and Facebook because they are not deemed appropriate. Some search terms are also banned by the government. About 80% of China's internet population—or about 557 million people—surfs the web on mobile devices, using smartphones and tablets to log on. However, internet user growth seems to be slowing. In 2013, about 54 million new users logged online, but there were only 31 million new users in 2014.

countries with the most internet users

users, in millions

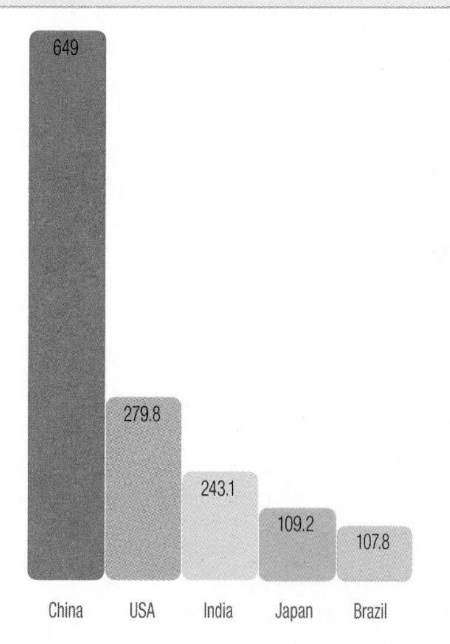
649
279.8
243.1
109.2
107.8
China
USA
India
Japan
Brazil

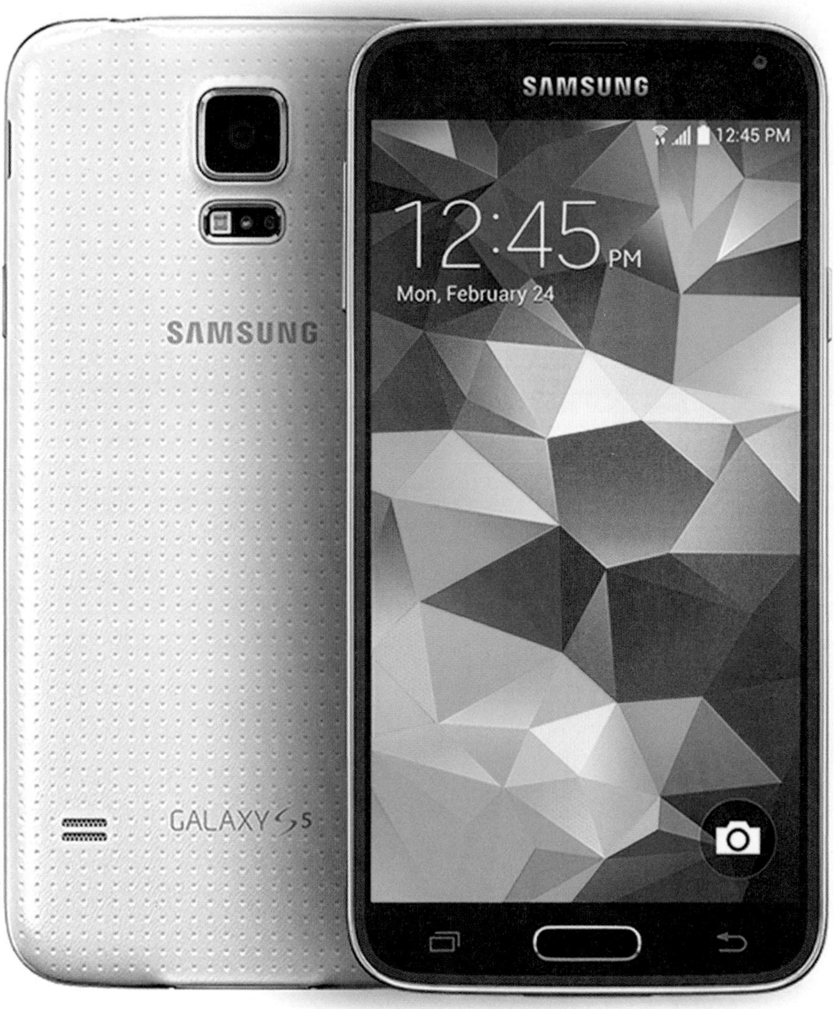

bestselling cell phone brand

Samsung

Samsung commands more than 20 percent of the cell phone market, meaning that 1 in every 5 phones sold is made by that company. Samsung leads the smartphone market as well, with about 32 percent of all sales. In 2014, Samsung sold more than 307.5 million smartphones worldwide. One of Samsung's most popular phone brands is the Galaxy. There are five different types of these smartphones, and all are Android devices. The less-expensive models are in demand and sell very quickly in developing countries.

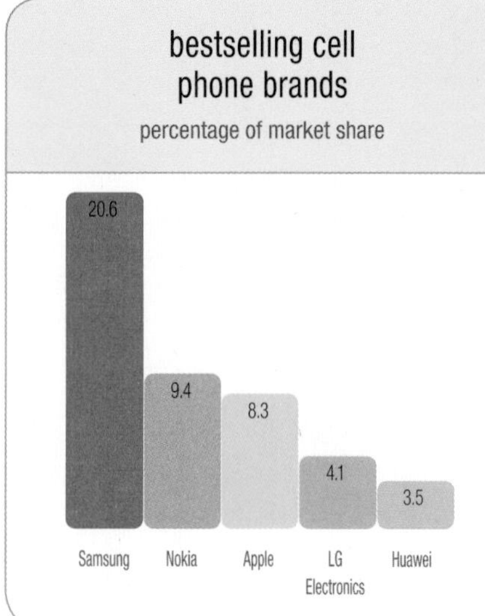
bestselling cell phone brands
percentage of market share
20.6
9.4
8.3
4.1
3.5
Samsung
Nokia
Apple
LG Electronics
Huawei

United States' bestselling smartphones

Android

The Android maintains the lead in the American smartphone race, with 52% of the market share. Android devices accounted for almost 85% of worldwide phone shipments during 2014. Some 76 million Americans use Android apps, and the average user spends about 55 hours per month using apps. Some of the most popular apps include Facebook, MyFitnessPal, Candy Crush Saga, Pandora, and NFL Mobile. More than 53% of Android users are under the age of 45.

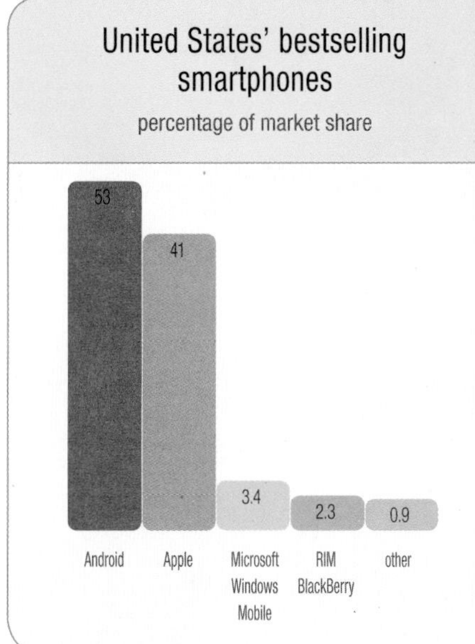
United States' bestselling smartphones
percentage of market share
53
41
3.4
2.3
0.9
Android
Apple
Microsoft Windows Mobile
RIM BlackBerry
other

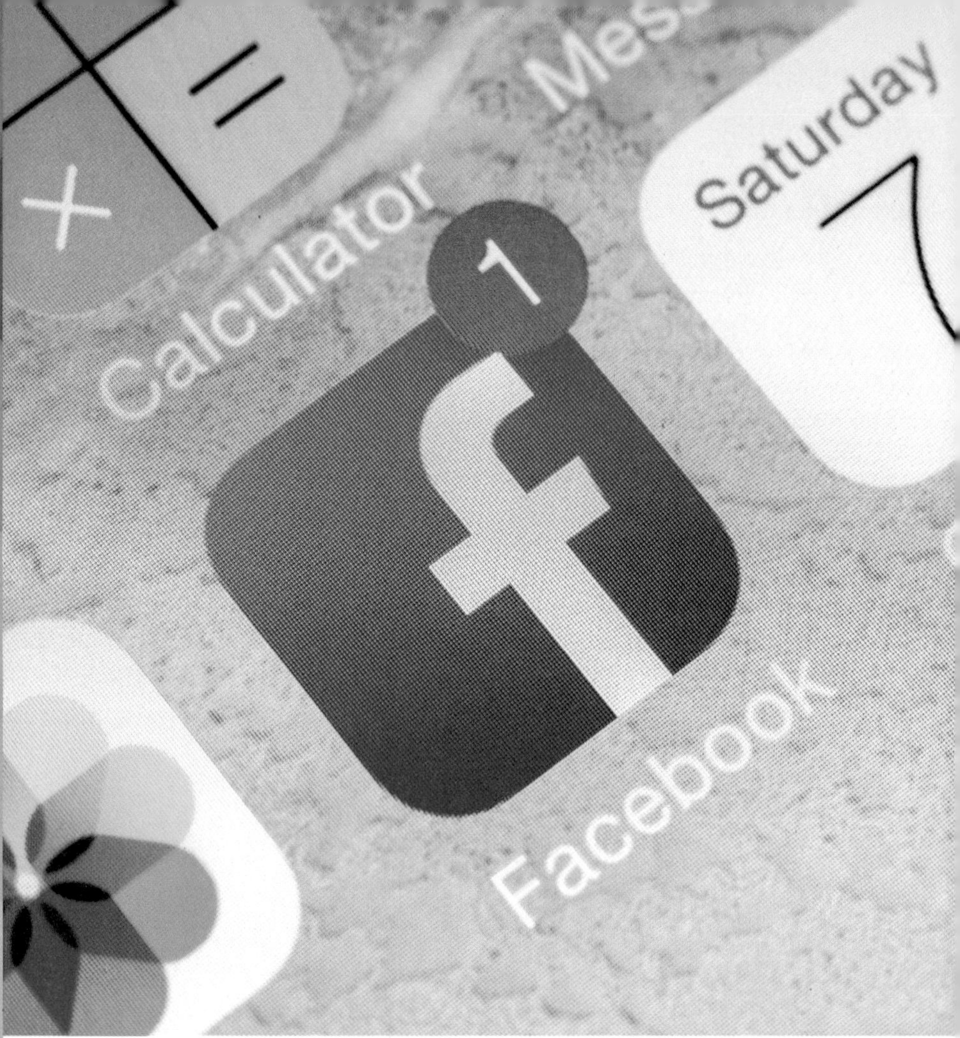

most popular mobile app

Facebook

Smartphone users check their Facebook app most, with 115.3 million unique users each month. In fact, about 30% of all Facebook users only use their smartphones to login. About 800 million people use Facebook Messenger to communicate with friends and family. Some 65% of users turn to Facebook mobile to watch videos. Businesses are recognizing the growing mobile audience as well, with some 19 million companies optimizing their Facebook pages to be smartphone friendly.

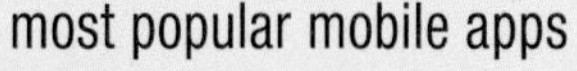
most popular mobile apps

average unique users, in millions

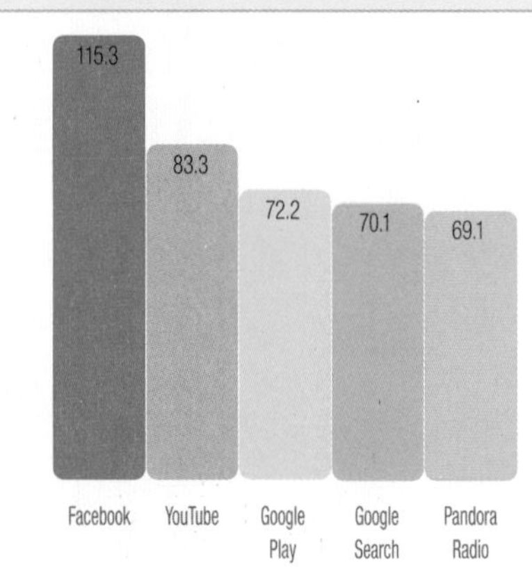
115.3
83.3
72.2
70.1
69.1
Facebook
YouTube
Google Play
Google Search
Pandora Radio

most popular mobile app activity

Social Media

When people use their mobile apps, about 25% of their time is spent on social media. Some familiar favorites include Facebook, Twitter, YouTube, and Instagram. In fact, users spend more than 114 billion mobile minutes on Facebook and 8 billion mobile minutes on Instagram each month. But some newer apps—such as What'sApp, Yik Yak, Snapchat, and Tumblr—are quickly gaining popularity. Users totaled about 68 million mobile minutes on What'sApp and 62 million mobile minutes on Snapchat monthly. About 79% of smartphone users say they use at least one social media app each day.

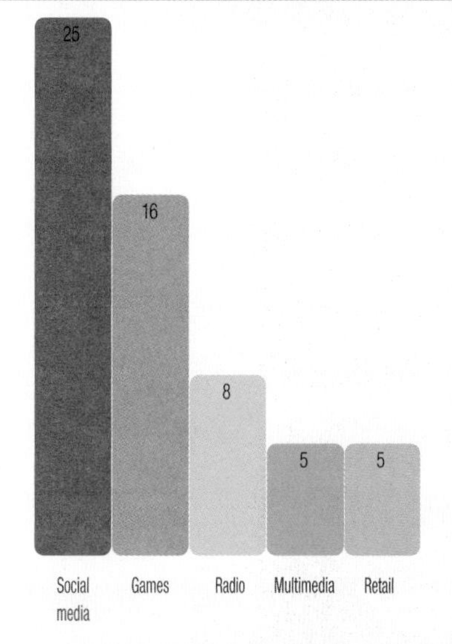
most popular mobile app activities
percentage of time spent
25
16
8
5
5
Social media
Games
Radio
Multimedia
Retail

most popular e-reader service

Amazon.com

Amazon.com is the most popular e-reader service, making up more than 51% of the market. Users can purchase all types of books and magazines to read on Amazon's two types of e-readers: the Kindle and the Kindle Fire HD. Since the original Kindle launched in 2007, more than 60 million Kindle units have been sold. The online bookseller exceeds 270 million accounts worldwide. Most e-books are priced between $4 and $10, and Amazon keeps about 30% of all sales.

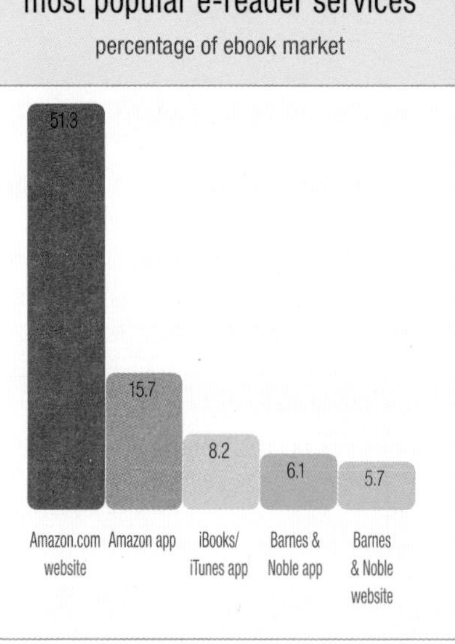
most popular e-reader services
percentage of ebook market
51.3
15.7
8.2
6.1
5.7
Amazon.com website
Amazon app
iBooks/ iTunes app
Barnes & Noble app
Barnes & Noble website

fastest growing social media site

Tumblr

Tumblr's active users have grown 120% in the last year, making it the fastest-growing social media site. This versatile site lets users post texts, links, photos, music, and videos from their phones, browsers, desktops, or emails. Tumblr was founded by David Karp in 2007, and has since seen more than 104 billion posts and 218 million blogs. The company employs about 310 people and has its headquarters in New York City. The average Tumblr user visits 67 pages every month, and about a third of all users are from the United States. Each Tumblr visit lasts about 14 minutes.

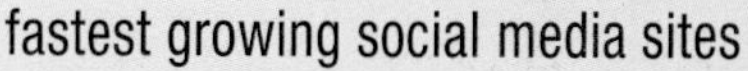
fastest growing social media sites
growth percentage in active users

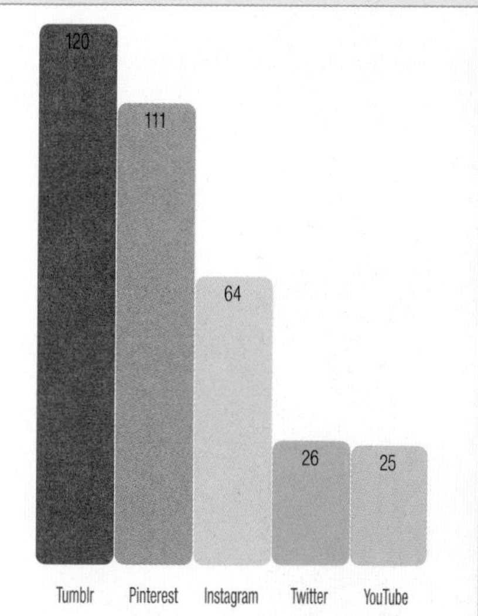
120
111
64
26
25
Tumblr
Pinterest
Instagram
Twitter
YouTube

largest cruise ships

Oasis of the Seas & Allure of the Seas

Royal Caribbean's sister cruise ships—*Oasis of the Seas* and *Allure of the Seas*—weigh in at 225,282 gross tons (228,897 t) each! These giant ships are more like floating cities with seven different themed neighborhoods: Central Park, Boardwalk, Royal Promenade, Pool and Sports Zone, Vitality at Sea Spa and Fitness Center, Entertainment Place, and Youth Zone. *Oasis of the Seas* and *Allure of the Seas* each feature 16 decks and include more than 20 eateries, 3 pools, a water park, and a zip-line ride. Both ships have 2,700 staterooms and can accommodate a whopping 5,400 guests.

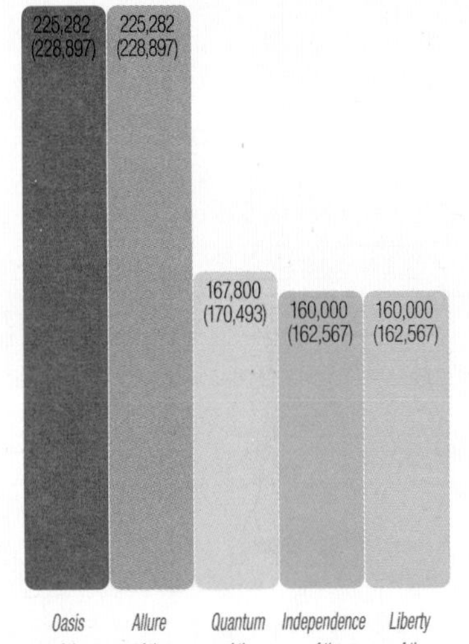
largest cruise ships
weight, in gross tons (tonnes)
225,282 (228,897)
225,282 (228,897)
167,800 (170,493)
160,000 (162,567)
160,000 (162,567)
Oasis of the Seas
Allure of the Seas
Quantum of the Seas
Independence of the Seas
Liberty of the Seas

RoyalCaribbean
INTERNATIONAL

Oasis of the Seas

fastest passenger train

CRH380AL

When China unveiled the CRH380AL commercial passenger train in 2010, it cruised into the record books with a top speed of 302 miles (486 km) per hour. The train reached its top speed in just 22 minutes. Its lightweight aluminum body and streamlined head help the CRH380AL travel that fast.The train's route connects Beijing and Shanghai, and reduced the average travel time from 10 hours to 4 hours. The train is part of China's $313 billion program to develop the world's most advanced train system by 2020.

fastest passenger trains

maximum speed, in miles (kilometers) per hour

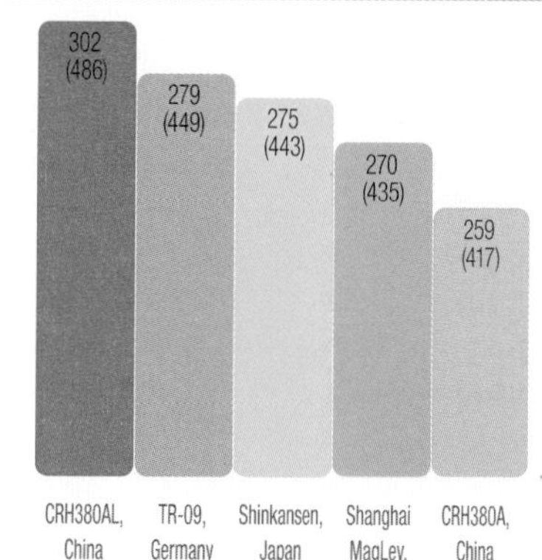
302 (486)
279 (449)
275 (443)
270 (435)
259 (417)
CRH380AL, China
TR-09, Germany
Shinkansen, Japan
Shanghai MagLev, China
CRH380A, China

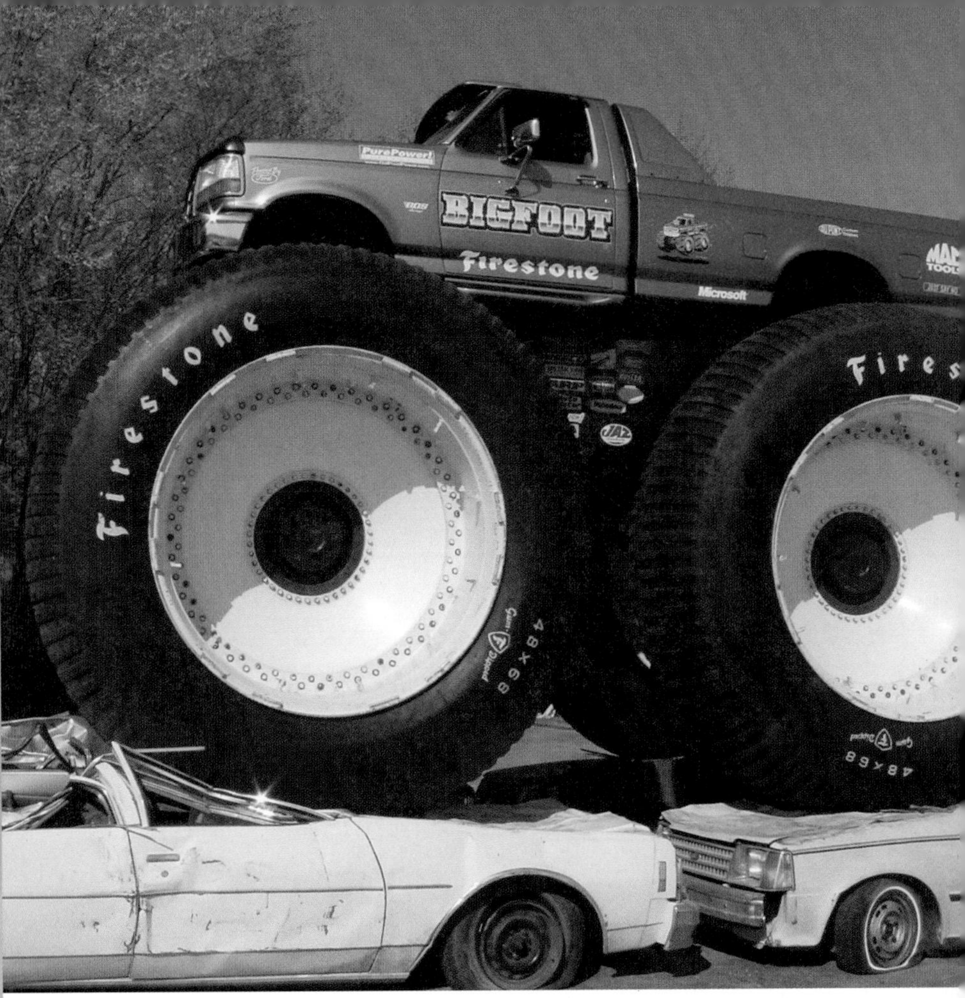

biggest monster truck

Bigfoot 5

The Bigfoot 5 truly is a monster—it measures 15.4 feet (4.7 m) high! That's about three times the height of an average car. Bigfoot 5 has 10-foot (3 m) Firestone Tundra tires, each weighing 2,400 pounds (1,088 kg), giving the truck a total weight of about 38,000 pounds (17,236 kg). The giant wheels were from an arctic snow train operated in Alaska by the US Army in the 1950s. This modified 1996 Ford F250 pickup truck is owned by Bob Chandler of St. Louis, Missouri. The great weight of this monster truck makes it too large to race.

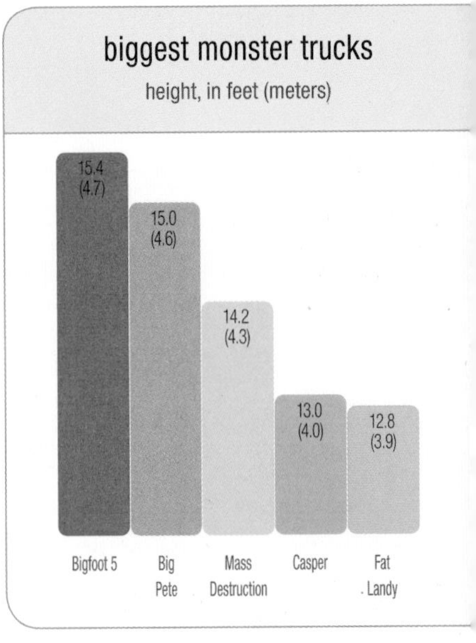

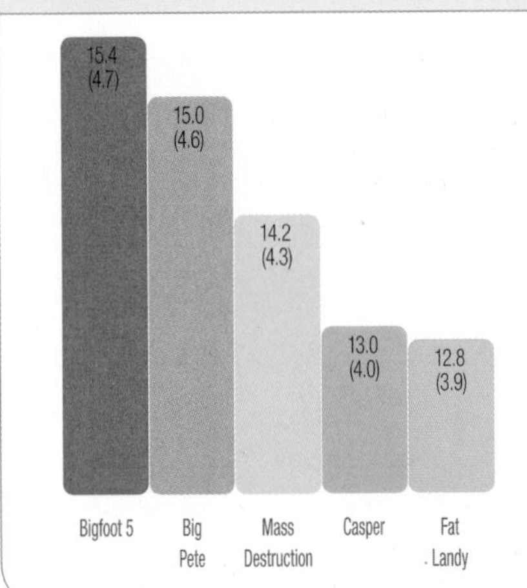
biggest monster trucks
height, in feet (meters)
15.4 (4.7)
15.0 (4.6)
14.2 (4.3)
13.0 (4.0)
12.8 (3.9)
Bigfoot 5
Big Pete
Mass Destruction
Casper
Fat Landy

smallest production car

Peel P50

The Peel P50 is the smallest production car ever made, measuring just 4.5 feet (1.4 m) long. That's not much longer than the average adult bicycle! The Peel P50 was originally produced on the Isle of Man between 1962 and 1965, and only 46 cars were made. However, the company began production again in 2012. The Peel P50 has three wheels, one door, one windshield wiper, and one headlight. The microcar weighs just 130 pounds (58.9 kg) and measures about 4 feet (1.2 m) tall. With its three-speed manual transmission, it can reach a top speed of 38 miles (61 km) an hour. It cannot, however, go in reverse.

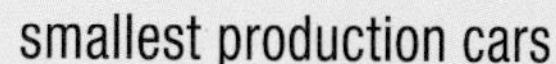
smallest production cars

length, in feet (meters)

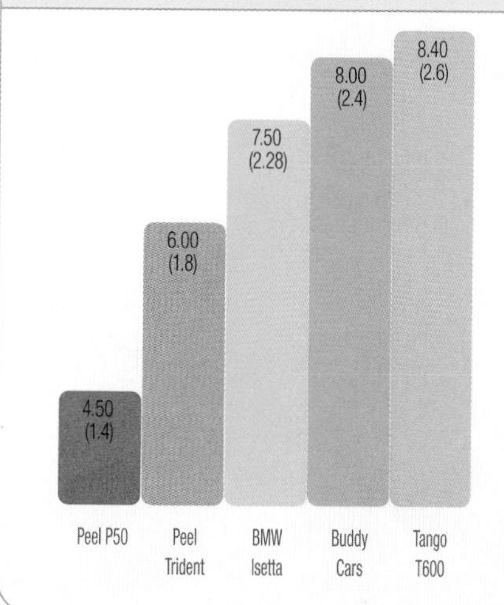
4.50 (1.4)
6.00 (1.8)
7.50 (2.28)
8.00 (2.4)
8.40 (2.6)
Peel P50
Peel Trident
BMW Isetta
Buddy Cars
Tango T600

fastest land vehicle

Thrust SSC

The Thrust SSC, which stands for Supersonic Car, reached a speed of 763 miles (1,228 km) per hour on October 15, 1997. At that speed, a car could make it from San Francisco to New York City in less than four hours. The Thrust SSC is propelled by two jet engines capable of 110,000 horsepower. It has the same power as 1,000 Ford Escorts or 145 Formula One race cars. The Thrust SSC runs on jet fuel, using about 5 gallons (19 L) per second. It takes only approximately five seconds for this supersonic car to reach its top speed. It is 54 feet (16.5 m) long and weighs 7 tons (6.4 t).

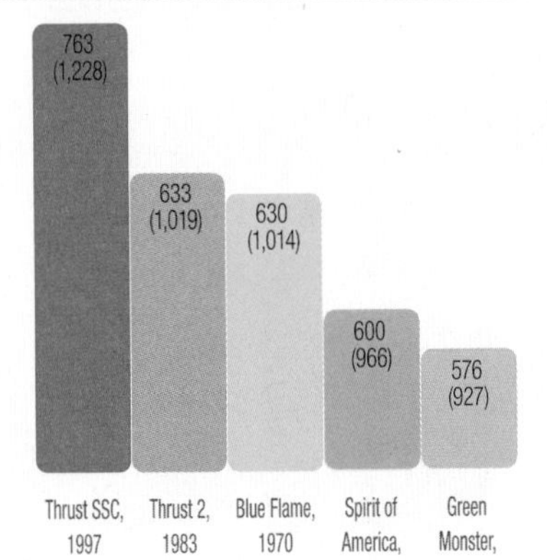
fastest land vehicles
maximum speed, in miles (kilometers) per hour
763 (1,228)
633 (1,019)
630 (1,014)
600 (966)
576 (927)
Thrust SSC, 1997
Thrust 2, 1983
Blue Flame, 1970
Spirit of America, 1965
Green Monster, 1965

fastest production motorcycle

Kawasaki Ninja H2R

The Kawasaki Ninja H2R has an estimated top speed of 260 miles (km) per hour. This impressive speed claim is based on a calculation that focuses on the huge 300-horsepower supercharged engine. The bike is expected to go from 0 to 60 miles (100 km) per hour in just 2.5 seconds. It has the same power as a sports car, but at one fifth the weight. Although the top speed is above one of a street-legal bike, it is still considered a production motorcycle. The manufacturer recommends it only be used on a closed course. The bike sells for about $50,000.

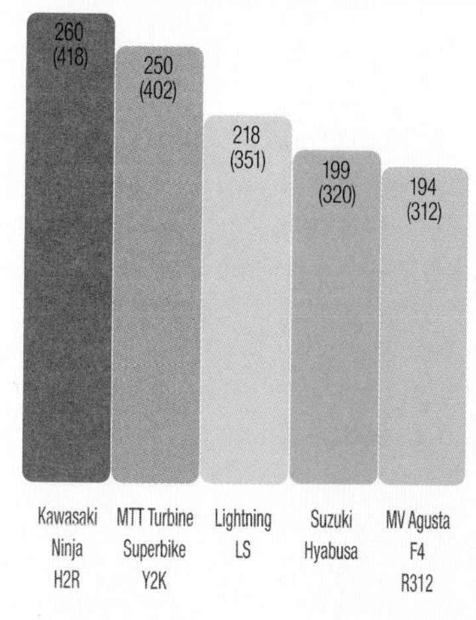
fastest production motorcycles
maximum speed, in miles (kilometers) per hour
260 (418)
250 (402)
218 (351)
199 (320)
194 (312)
Kawasaki Ninja H2R
MTT Turbine Superbike Y2K
Lightning LS
Suzuki Hyabusa
MV Agusta F4 R312

fastest production car

Hennessey Venom GT

The Hennessey Venom GT can reach a top speed of 270 miles (435 km) per hour. The 1,244 horsepower twin turbocharged V8 engine accelerates the supercar from 0–60 miles (96 km) per hour in just 2.7 seconds and can complete a quarter mile in just under 10 seconds. The Venom GT can also go from 0 to 200 miles (322 km) per hour in a record-breaking 14.5 seconds! Just 29 of these sports cars will be built and delivered to buyers around the world. It takes about 6 months to customize the car, which costs $1.25 million.

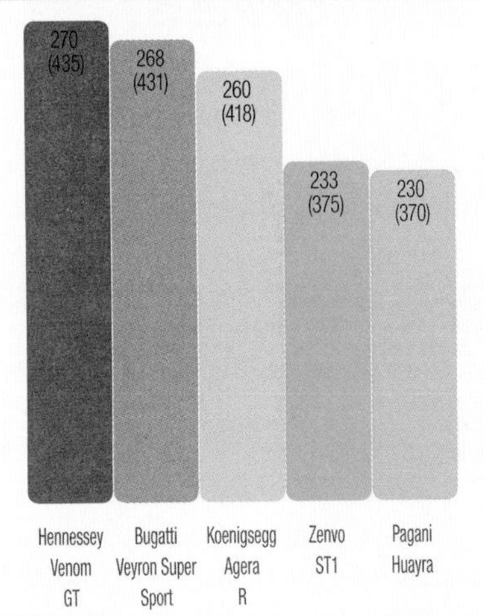
fastest production cars
maximum speed, in miles (kilometers) per hour
270 (435)
268 (431)
260 (418)
233 (375)
230 (370)
Hennessey Venom GT
Bugatti Veyron Super Sport
Koenigsegg Agera R
Zenvo ST1
Pagani Huayra

fastest helicopter

Eurocopter x3

The Eurocopter X3 can fly up to 302 miles (486 km) per hour. That's the same speed as the fastest train on Earth! The X3 uses three different rotating blades—one large blade on the roof and two smaller blades on each side of the helicopter. It's powered by 2 Rolls-Royce Turbomeca RTM322 engines, and each engine can produce 2,270 horsepower. The aircraft can fly at about 12,500 feet (3,810 m). Although it is still in the experimental stages, the X3 will probably be used for military missions as well as civilian search and rescue.

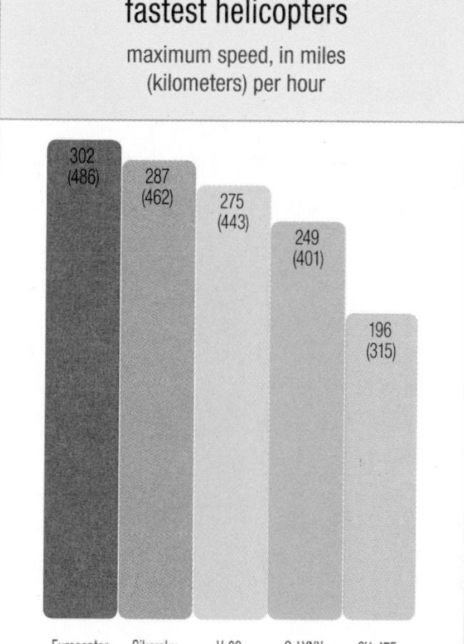
fastest helicopters
maximum speed, in miles (kilometers) per hour
302 (486)
287 (462)
275 (443)
249 (401)
196 (315)
Eurocopter X3
Sikorsky X-2
V-22 Osprey
G-LYNX
CH-47F Chinook

lightest jet

BD-5J Microjet

The BD-5J Microjet weighs only 358.8 pounds (162.7 kg), making it the lightest jet in the world. At only 12 feet (3.7 m) in length, it is one of the smallest as well. This tiny jet has a height of 5.6 feet (1.7 m) and a wingspan of 17 feet (5.2 m). The Microjet uses a TRS-18 turbojet engine. It can reach a top speed of 320 miles (514.9 km) per hour, but can carry only 32 gallons (121 L) of fuel at a time. A new BD-5J costs around $200,000. This high-tech gadget was flown by James Bond in the movie *Octopussy*, and it is also occasionally used by the US military.

lightest jets

weight, in pounds (kilograms)

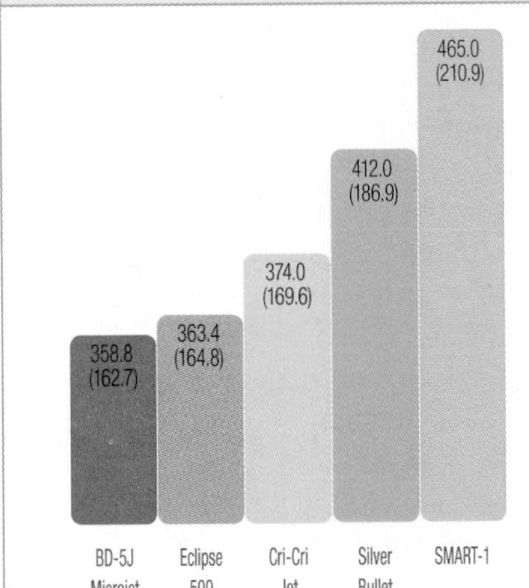
358.8
(162.7)
363.4
(164.8)
374.0
(169.6)
412.0
(186.9)
465.0
(210.9)
BD-5J Microjet
Eclipse 500
Cri-Cri Jet
Silver Bullet
SMART-1

fastest plane

X-43A

NASA's experimental X-43A plane reached a top speed of Mach 9.8—or more than nine times the speed of sound—on a test flight over the Pacific Ocean in November 2004. The X-43A was mounted on top of a Pegasus rocket booster and was carried into the sky by a B-52 aircraft. The booster was then fired, taking the X-43A about 110,000 feet (33,530 m) above the ground. The rocket was detached from the unmanned X-43A, and the plane flew unassisted for several minutes. At this rate of 7,459 miles (12,004 km) per hour, a plane could circle Earth in just over three and a half hours!

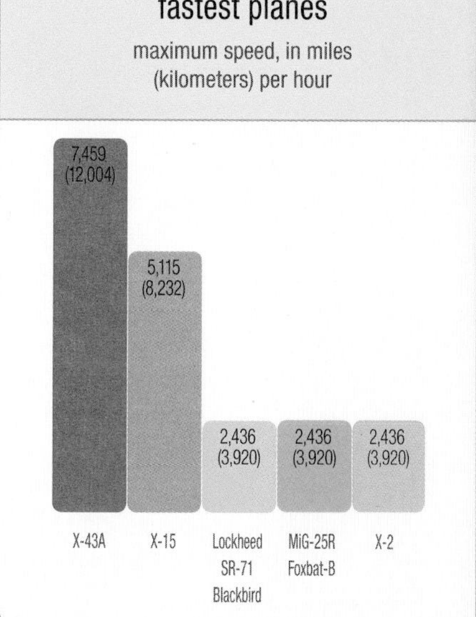
fastest planes
maximum speed, in miles (kilometers) per hour
7,459 (12,004)
5,115 (8,232)
2,436 (3,920)
2,436 (3,920)
2,436 (3,920)
X-43A
X-15
Lockheed SR-71 Blackbird
MiG-25R Foxbat-B
X-2

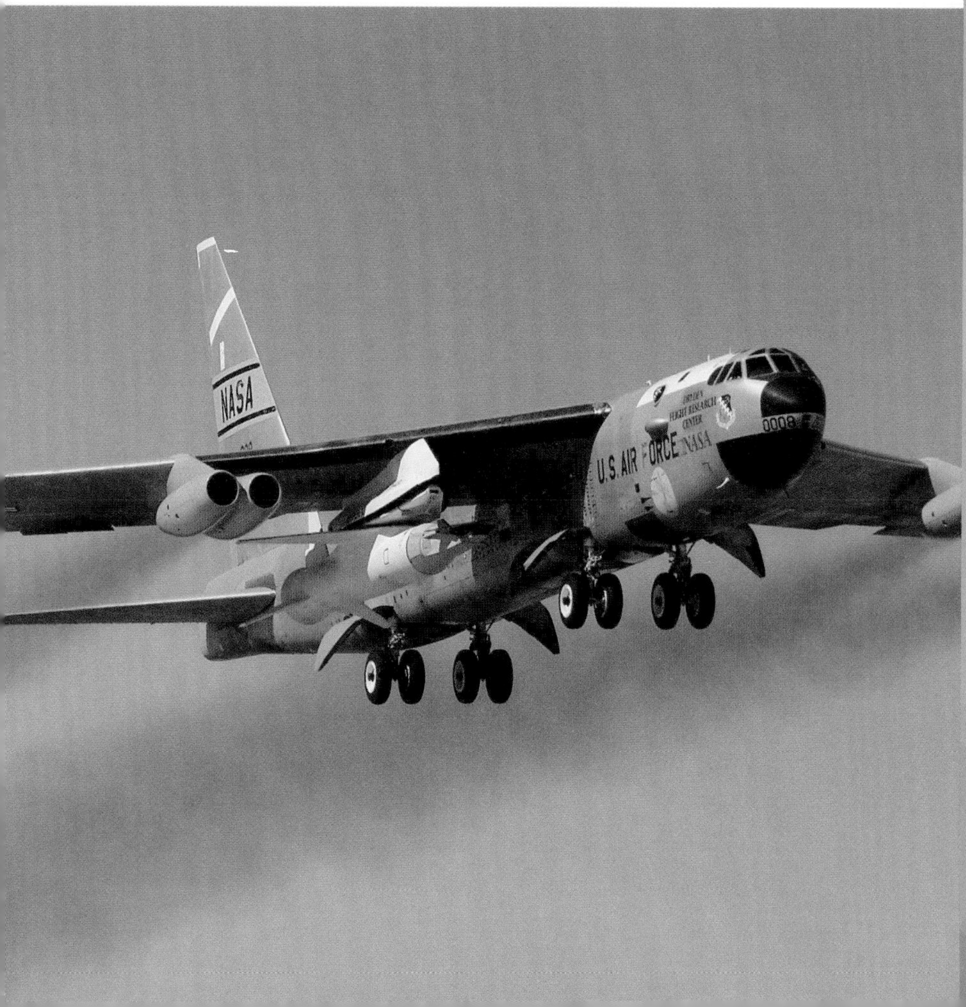

tallest roller coaster

Kingda Ka

Kingda Ka towers over Six Flags Great Adventure in Jackson, New Jersey, at a height of 456 feet (139 m). Its highest drop plummets riders down 418 feet (127 m). The steel coaster can reach a top speed of 128 miles (206 km) per hour in just 3.5 seconds, and it was the fastest coaster in the world when it opened in 2005. The entire 3,118-foot (950 m) ride is over in just 28 seconds. The hydraulic launch coaster is located in the Golden Kingdom section of the park. It can accommodate about 1,400 riders per hour.

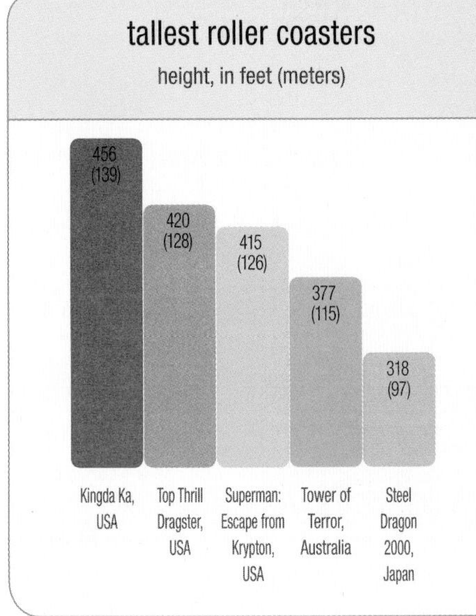
tallest roller coasters
height, in feet (meters)
456 (139)
420 (128)
415 (126)
377 (115)
318 (97)
Kingda Ka, USA
Top Thrill Dragster, USA
Superman: Escape from Krypton, USA
Tower of Terror, Australia
Steel Dragon 2000, Japan

amusement park with the most rides

Cedar Point

Located in Sandusky, Ohio, Cedar Point offers park visitors 71 rides to enjoy. GateKeeper—one of the park's newest rides—is the fastest and longest-running winged roller coaster in the world. Top Thrill Dragster roller coaster is the second tallest in the world at 420 feet (128 m). And with 17 roller coasters, Cedar Point also has the most coasters of any theme park in the world. Over 53,963 feet (16,448 m) of coaster track—more than 10 miles (16.1 km)—run through the park. The park is also the second-oldest continually operating amusement park in North America and celebrated its 146th season in 2015.

amusement parks with the most rides

number of rides

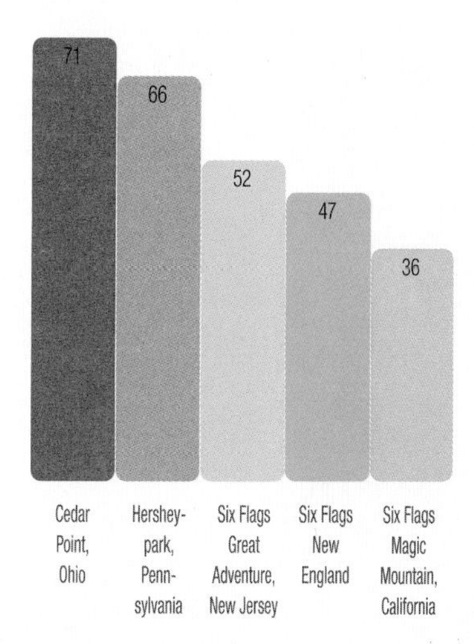
71
66
52
47
36
Cedar Point, Ohio
Hershey-park, Penn-sylvania
Six Flags Great Adventure, New Jersey
Six Flags New England
Six Flags Magic Mountain, California

fastest roller coaster

Formula Rossa

The Formula Rossa coaster in the United Arab Emirates speeds past the competition with a top speed of 149 miles (240 km) per hour. Located at Ferrari World in Dubai, riders climb into the F1 race car cockpits and can experience what 4.8 g-force actually feels like. The coaster's hydraulic launch system rockets the coaster to its top speed in just 4.9 seconds. The track is about 1.4 miles (2.2 km) long, with the sharpest turn measuring 70 degrees.

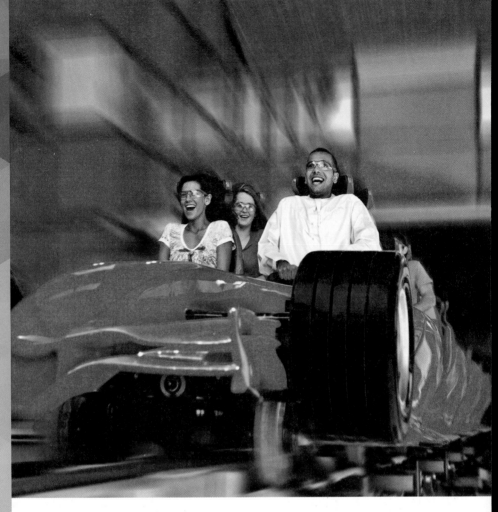

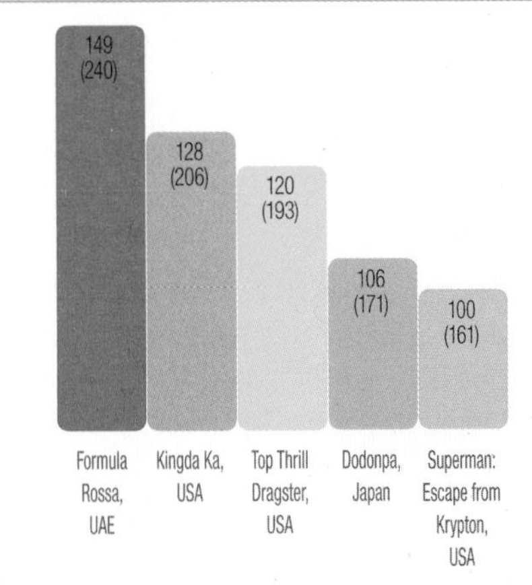
fastest roller coasters
speed, in miles (kilometers) per hour
149 (240)
128 (206)
120 (193)
106 (171)
100 (161)
Formula Rossa, UAE
Kingda Ka, USA
Top Thrill Dragster, USA
Dodonpa, Japan
Superman: Escape from Krypton, USA

city with the most skyscrapers

Hong Kong

There are 233 skyscrapers soaring above the streets of Hong Kong, a major financial center and business sector in China. The skyscrapers measure at least 500 feet (152 m) tall. The three tallest buildings in the city include International Commerce Centre at 1,588 feet (484 m), Two International Finance Centre at 1,352 feet (412 m), and Central Plaza at 1,227 feet (3,874 m). The flat, buildable land in the area only measures about 77 square miles (200 sq km), so architects have to build up instead of out to keep pace with the increasing population.

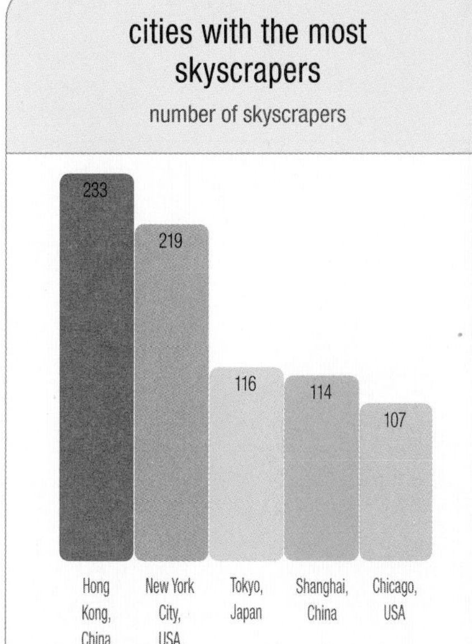
cities with the most skyscrapers
number of skyscrapers
233
219
116
114
107
Hong Kong, China
New York City, USA
Tokyo, Japan
Shanghai, China
Chicago, USA

tallest habitable building

Burj Khalifa

Burj Khalifa in the United Arab Emirates towers 2,717 feet (828 m) above the ground. With more than 160 floors, the building cost about $4.1 billion to construct. Both a hotel and apartments are housed inside the luxury building, which covers 500 acres (202 ha). The building features high-speed elevators that travel at 40 miles (64 km) per hour. The tower supplies its occupants with about 66,043 gallons (250,000 liters) of water a day, and delivers enough electricity to power 360,000 100-watt lightbulbs.

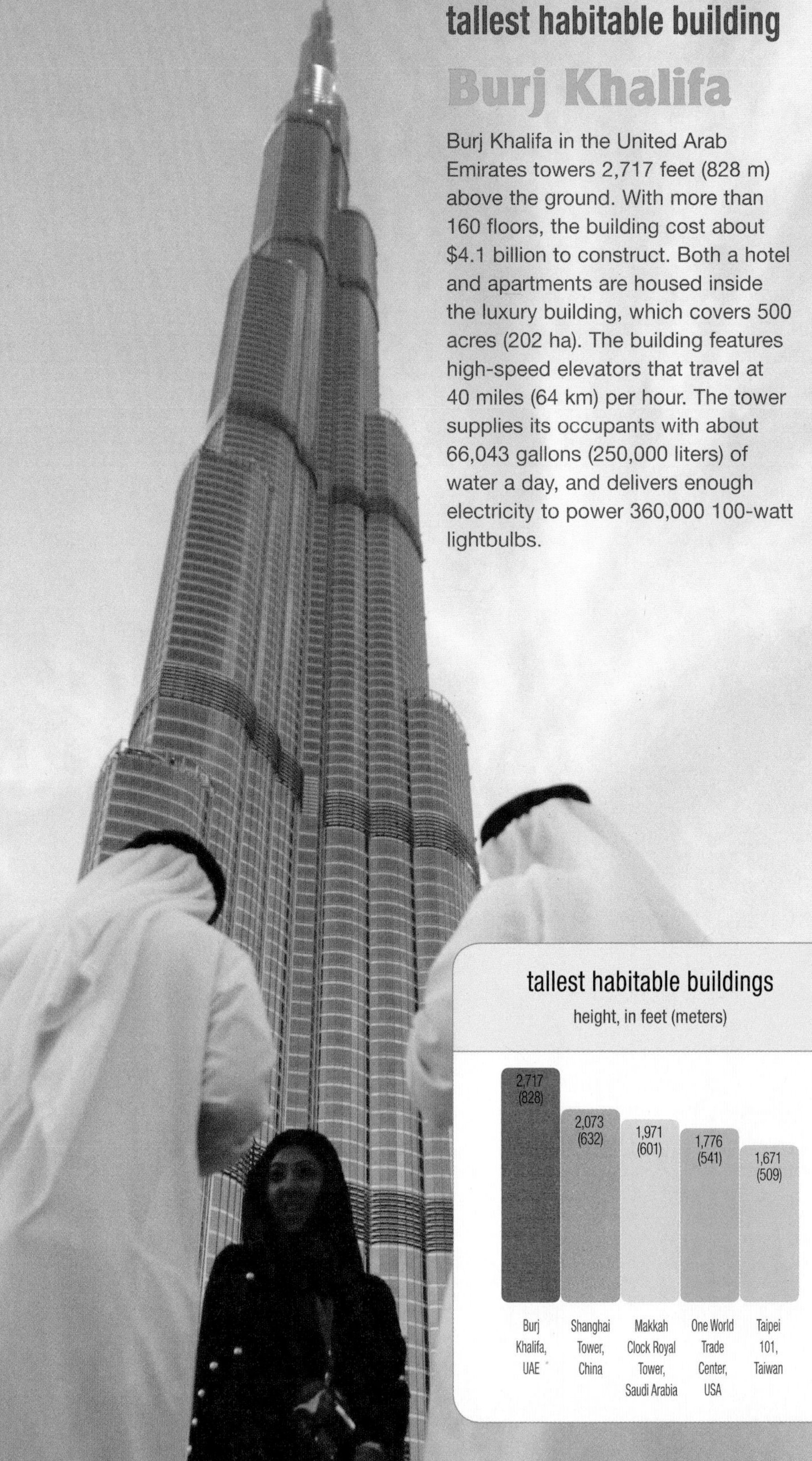
tallest habitable buildings
height, in feet (meters)
2,717 (828)
2,073 (632)
1,971 (601)
1,776 (541)
1,671 (509)
Burj Khalifa, UAE
Shanghai Tower, China
Makkah Clock Royal Tower, Saudi Arabia
One World Trade Center, USA
Taipei 101, Taiwan

largest swimming pool

San Alfonso Del Mar

The gigantic swimming pool at this resort in Chile spreads over 19.7 acres (8 ha). The humongous pool is the equivalent to 6,000 standard swimming pools and holds 66 million gallons (250 million L) of water. In addition to swimming, guests can sail and scuba dive in the saltwater lagoon, which is surrounded by white sand beaches. And there's no diving for pennies here—the deep end measures 115 feet (35 m). The pool took five years to complete and first opened in December 2006. The project cost $2 billion, and it costs about $4 million annually to maintain.

largest swimming pools

size, in acres (hectares)

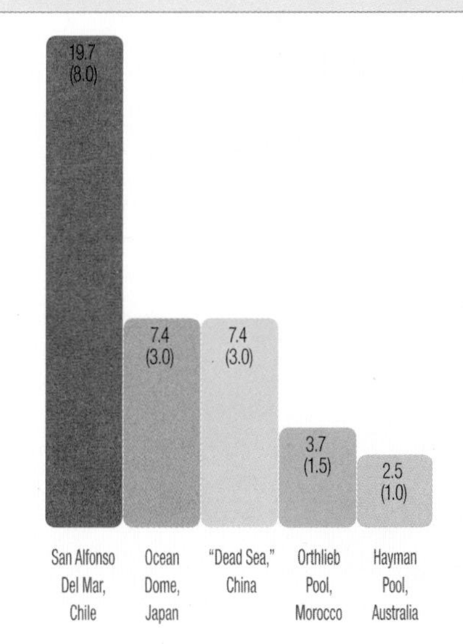
19.7 (8.0)
7.4 (3.0)
7.4 (3.0)
3.7 (1.5)
2.5 (1.0)
San Alfonso Del Mar, Chile
Ocean Dome, Japan
"Dead Sea," China
Orthlieb Pool, Morocco
Hayman Pool, Australia

largest sports stadium

Rungrado May First Stadium

The Rungrado May First Stadium, also known as the May Day Stadium, can seat up to 150,000 people. The interior of the stadium covers 2.2 million square feet (204,386 sq m). Located in Pyongyang, North Korea, this venue is mostly used for soccer matches and other athletic contests. It is named after Rungra Island, on which the stadium is located, in the middle of the Taedong River. When it is not being used for sporting events, the stadium is used for a two-month gymnastics and artistic festival known as Arirang.

largest sports stadiums

number of seats

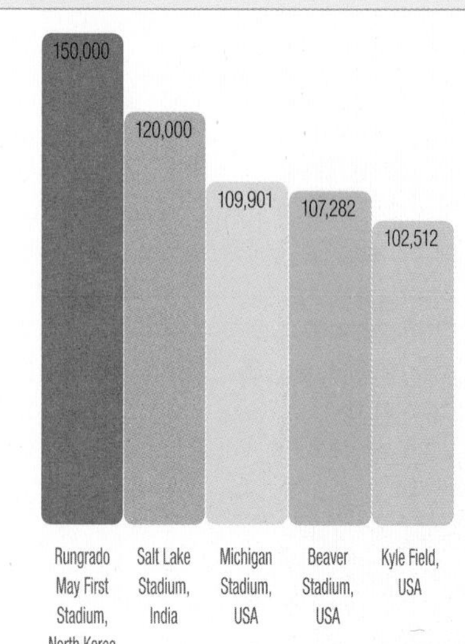
150,000
120,000
109,901
107,282
102,512
Rungrado May First Stadium, North Korea
Salt Lake Stadium, India
Michigan Stadium, USA
Beaver Stadium, USA
Kyle Field, USA

busiest airport

Hartsfield-Jackson Atlanta International Airport

The Hartsfield-Jackson Atlanta International Airport has about 94.4 million people land or depart from its gates each year. Approximately 2,500 planes depart and arrive at this airport every day. With parking lots, runways, maintenance facilities, and other buildings, the Hartsfield terminal complex covers about 130 acres (53 ha). Hartsfield-Jackson Atlanta International Airport has a north and a south terminal, an underground train, and seven concourses, with a total of 167 domestic and 40 international gates.

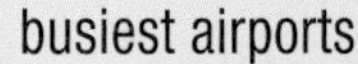
busiest airports
passenger traffic, in millions

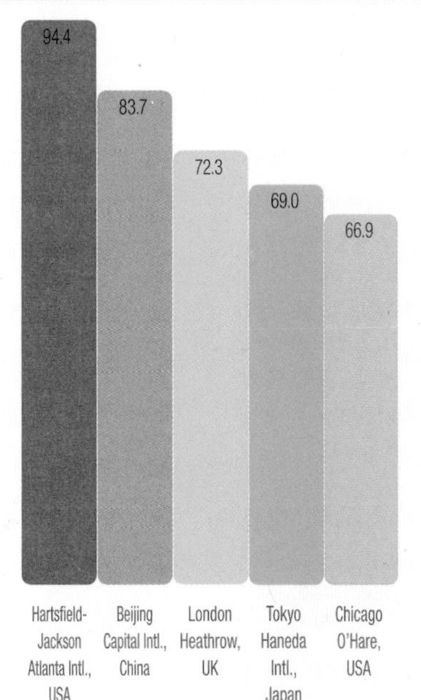
94.4
83.7
72.3
69.0
66.9
Hartsfield-Jackson Atlanta Intl., USA
Beijing Capital Intl., China
London Heathrow, UK
Tokyo Haneda Intl., Japan
Chicago O'Hare, USA

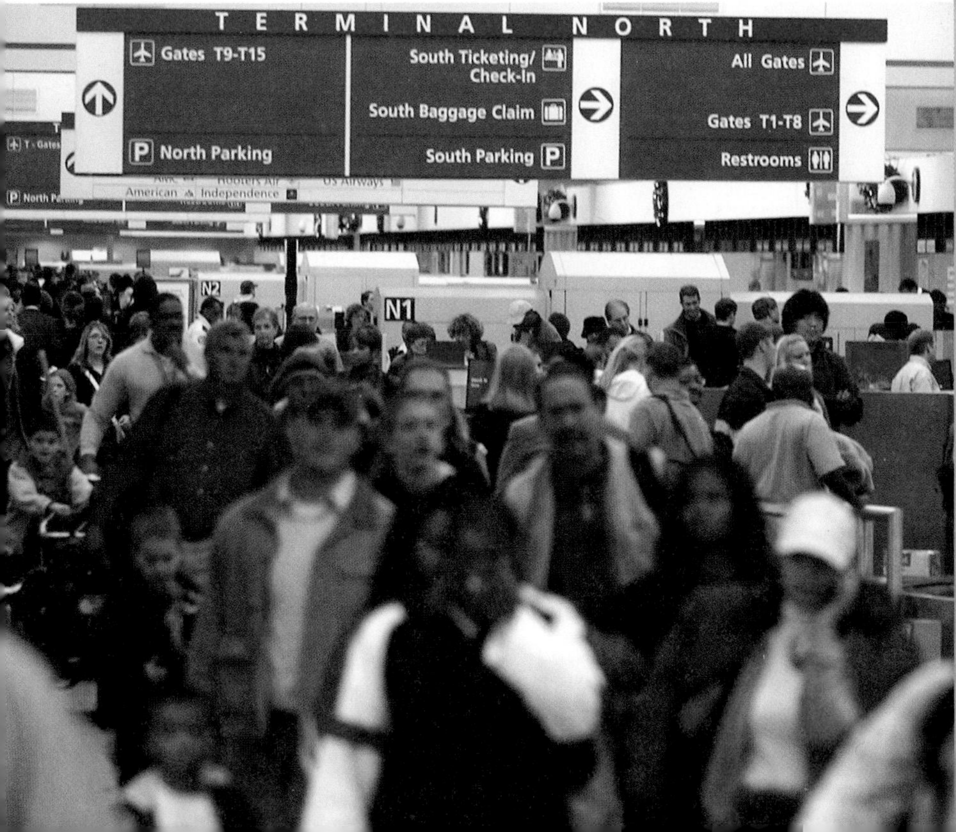

country that produces the most cars

China

China leads the world in car and commercial vehicle production, accounting for 25.4% of vehicles annually. Some of China's most popular car brands include Chery, Great Wall, Gely, and Chang'an. International brands with factories in China include Volkswagen, General Motors, and Honda. Most of the cars that are produced in China are also sold there. Approximately 1 million cars are exported annually. China's growth in the car production industry is fairly recent. Since the country joined the World Trade Organization in 2001, China's car production has grown by about 2.5 million vehicles annually.

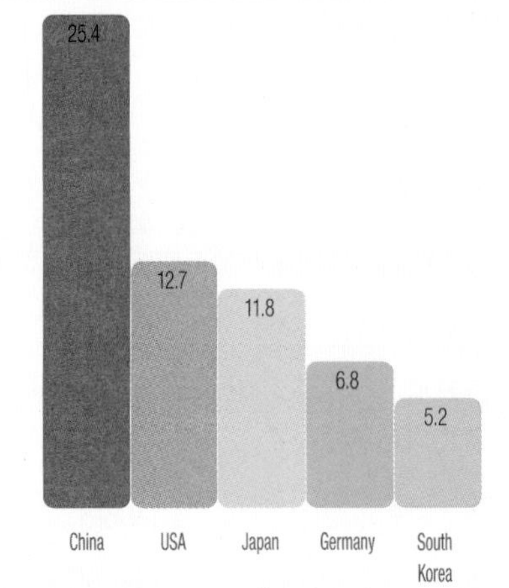
countries that produce the most cars
percentage of cars and commercial vehicles produced
25.4
12.7
11.8
6.8
5.2
China
USA
Japan
Germany
South Korea

world's greenest country

Sweden

Sweden was ranked as the greenest country in the world in 2014. It was among the first countries to tax carbon dioxide emissions, and was also one of the first to meet the European Union's climate goals on renewable energy. About 75% of Swedes recycle, and only about 4% of the country's garbage goes to landfills. Dual Citizen, which publishes the Global Green Economy Index, ranks countries according to their efforts to create and maintain an environmentally friendly economy. Some of the factors considered include leadership and climate change, efficiency, and environmental investment.

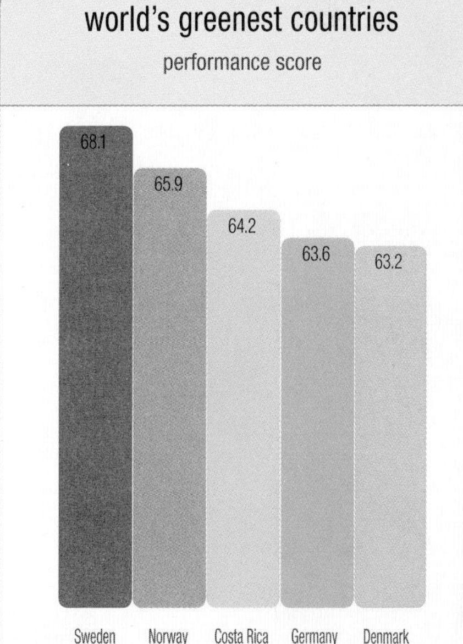
world's greenest countries
performance score
68.1
65.9
64.2
63.6
63.2
Sweden
Norway
Costa Rica
Germany
Denmark

MONEY RECORDS

- EPIC FAILS
- MOST EXPENSIVE
- WEALTHIEST
- MOST VALUABLE
- BIG BUSINESS

EPIC FAIL

LEAST VALUABLE CURRENCY

The Iranian rial is the world's least valuable currency, with nearly 30,000 rial equaling just 1 US dollar. The US-led economic sanctions against Iran are probably the leading cause for the extremely low value.

EPIC
FAIL

LOWEST-PAYING COLLEGE MAJOR

The website College Factual used recent grad surveys to determine that animal science is the least profitable college major, with entry-level jobs starting at an average of just $31,100 annually. Students with this degree often find work on farms or ranches, or in agriculture.

EPIC
FAIL

LARGEST FCC FINE

The Federal Communications Commission (FCC) issued the largest fine in history against Chinese online retailer CTS Technology. The company was selling illegal signal jammers in the United States in 2014 and was fined $34.9 million. Signal jammers can interfere with 911 and cell phone calls, Wi-Fi networks, and GPS systems.

EPIC FAIL

NBA CONTRACT WITH SMALLEST RETURN

In 2014, as a free agent, Lance Stephenson signed a $27.4-million, three-year contract with the Charlotte Hornets. However, he managed to make an average of just 8.2 points, 4.5 rebounds, and 3.9 assists per game. The Hornets actually scored more per possession when he was on the bench! After one year with the Hornets Stephenson was traded to the Los Angeles Clippers.

LEAST VALUABLE NFL TEAM

The St. Louis Rams were at the bottom of the NFL in 2014 with a franchise value of $930 million. That's quite a bit below the league average of $1.43 billion. In fact, they come in about $2.3 billion behind the Dallas Cowboys, which topped the most valuable chart.

EPIC FAIL
27

EPIC FAIL
BUCKS
19

LEAST VALUABLE NBA TEAM

The Milwaukee Bucks are the least valuable team in the NBA with a current value of $600 million. They have the fewest season ticket holders with 4,000, but things may be looking up. After finishing the 2013–2014 season with a franchise-worst 15 wins, the Bucks advanced to the playoffs in 2015 for the first time in 14 years under new head coach Jason Kidd.

bp
BP
Centre
EPIC
FAIL

BIGGEST CRIMINAL FINES

Oil giant BP had to pay the largest criminal fine in US history for its massive oil spill in the Gulf of Mexico in 2010. The overall payout totaled $42 billion, which covered cleanup, fines, and payment to the victims.

RAYS
EPIC
FAIL

LEAST VALUABLE MLB TEAM

Worth $625 million, the Tampa Bay Rays are the least valuable team in Major League Baseball. Fans can find some of the least expensive seats in professional baseball at Tropicana Field—an average of just $22 a seat! Yet the Rays had the lowest seasonal attendance for the third year in a row in 2014. Some criticize the stadium for being difficult to get to. The Rays have made four postseason appearances since 2008.

CCM
Ford

EPIC FAIL

LEAST VALUABLE NHL TEAM

The Florida Panthers are the least valuable team in the NHL with a total worth of $190 million. That's about $1.1 billion less than the top team in the league (Toronto Maple Leafs). The Panthers suffer from low attendance and only generate $9 of revenue per fan. The hockey club loses about $20 million each year.

EPIC FAIL

LOWEST-EARNING NASCAR TEAM

Worth just $22 million, Front Row Motorsports lags way behind all of the other NASCAR driving teams worth just $22 million. Those earnings are 16 times less than the organization's top team, Hendrick Motorsports. The team was established in 2005 and has only three cars. They bring in about $15 million in annual revenue and $8 million in prize money.

GILLILAND
Love's
Fast. Clean. Frien
GOODYEAR
MOOG
MAHLE

EPIC FAIL

SUPERHERO WITH SUPER-LOW PAY

One of the lowest-paid superheroes in the Marvel Avengers film universe is Chris Evans. He was paid just $300,000 for his role as Captain America in 2011. When he reprised his role for *The Avengers* in 2012, his salary bumped way up to between $2 and $3 million.

DELTA
EPIC FAIL

HIGHEST AIRLINE FEES

American, Delta, United, and US Airways charge the highest fees in the US airline industry. These airlines charge $200 to change a non-refundable ticket, but fees can reach as high as $450 for international flights. Delta, United, and US Airways also charge $200 per additional suitcase once a traveler has paid between $185 and $210 to check his or her first three bags.

EPIC FAIL

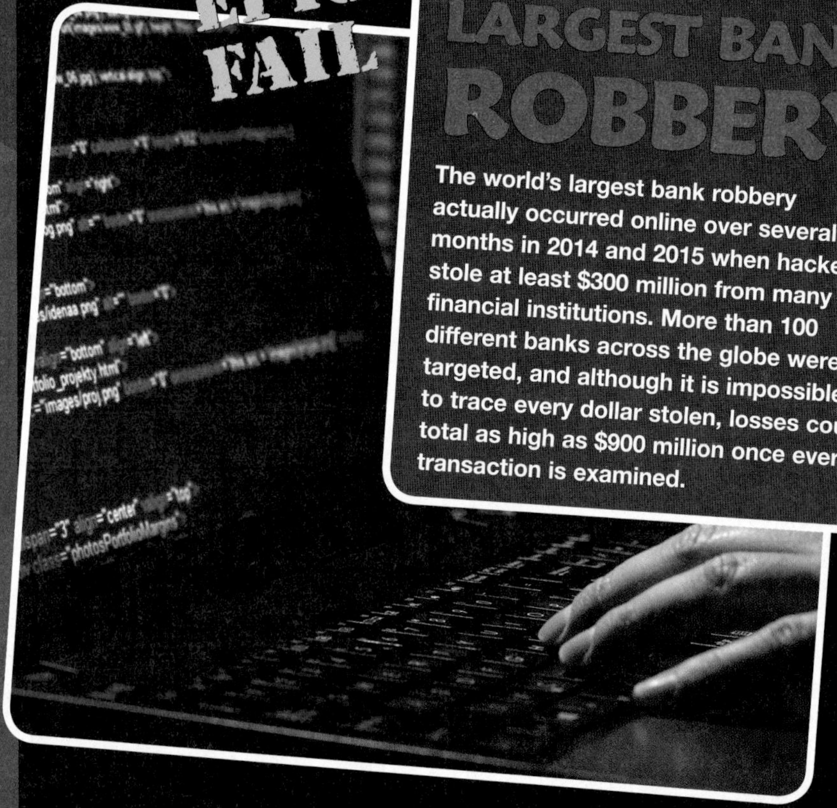

LARGEST BANK ROBBERY

The world's largest bank robbery actually occurred online over several months in 2014 and 2015 when hackers stole at least $300 million from many financial institutions. More than 100 different banks across the globe were targeted, and although it is impossible to trace every dollar stolen, losses could total as high as $900 million once every transaction is examined.

MOST-CLOSED FRANCHISES

Quiznos—a once-popular sub sandwich shop—has closed more than 44% of its locations in the last few years. At its most successful, in 2006, Quiznos had more than 5,000 stores open, but by late 2014, less than 1,500 remained open. The franchise filed for Chapter 11 bankruptcy in 2014 when it couldn't pay its debt.

Quizno's
SUBS
OVEN TOASTED TASTES BETTER
WE CATER

EPIC FAIL

Comcast
EPIC FAIL

LEAST-TRUSTED COMPANY

According to a recent study, the least trusted company in the United States is Comcast. The TV and Internet service provider came in last out of 293 companies, with only 19% of those surveyed expressing their confidence in the business.

US COMPANY WITH THE BIGGEST MONETARY LOSS

Apache Corp.—a US company that produces oil and natural gas—lost the most money in 2014. The company had a $5.4 billion net loss that year, and saw its stock price drop 21.6%. The severe losses were due to falling oil prices.

EPIC FAIL
RIG 298

EPIC FAIL

LOWEST-PAYING INDUSTRY

The lowest-paying industry in the United States is food service, which has an average annual salary range of $18,870 to $21,160. Squeaking in just above food service is the beauty industry, with beauty professionals making about $18,910 each year, according to the Bureau of Labor Statistics.

LOWEST-EARNING TENNIS PRO

During his first year on the ATP, Lithuanian tennis player Lukas Zvikas bottomed out on the 2014 prize money list. He earned $36 for the only doubles match he competed in that year. That's just enough to buy about four cans of tennis balls. Zvikas was only seventeen years old at the time—he was born in 1997.

EPIC FAIL

PING

LOWEST-PAID GOLFER

Golfer Chris DiMarco ranked last, at 377th, on the PGA money list with $6,370 in earnings for 2014. He played in seven events that year, averaging just $910 per outing. He only made the cut in one event during his 24th year on the tour. His last PGA victory was at the Phoenix Open in 2002.

EPIC FAIL

EPIC FAIL

BILLIONAIRE WHO LOST THE MOST MONEY

In one year, Nigerian sugar and cement tycoon Aliko Dangote lost $10.3 billion, topping *Forbes*'s list of people who have seen their fortunes decline the most in 2014. Dangote's losses are mostly due to the lowered Nigerian currency value and the lower demand for cement.

LEAST VALUABLE COIN

Uzbekistan—a landlocked country in central Asia—has a one-cent tiyin, which holds the title of the least valuable coin in the world. It would take about 2,546 tiyin to equal just one US penny. The coin is becoming rare because of its very low value, however, and is seldom seen in circulation.

EPIC FAIL

MOST FREQUENTLY STOLEN VEHICLE

The most frequently stolen car is the Honda Accord, boosted 53,995 times in 2013. This is followed by the Honda Civic, with 45,001 thefts in that year. The Accords and Civics stolen were mostly older model years. The most frequently stolen new car is the Nissan Altima, with 810 new 2013 models getting stolen during that year.

Twelve Oaks
EPIC FAIL

VOGUE'S COVER WITH THE LOWEST SALES

Olympians Ryan Lochte, Hope Solo, and Serena Williams were the cover models for the lowest-selling issue in *Vogue*'s history with 202,000 copies sold in June 2012. Rihanna was another low seller when her November 2012 issue sold just 227,000 copies.

1
STEVENS
EPIC FAIL
Hope Solo

EPIC
FAIL

MUSHROOM DISAPPOINTS AT AUCTION

On December 5, 2014, the world's largest white truffle mushroom was expected to sell for around $1 million at a Sotheby's New York auction. However, the truffle only fetched $61,250. The mushroom was found in Italy and weighed about 4.1 pounds (1.86 kg)! More common truffles grow from the size of a walnut to the size of an apple, weigh between 1 and 2 ounces (30 and 60 g), and sell for up to $450 a pound.

EPIC
FAIL

EXTREMELY OVERDUE LIBRARY BOOK

Beginning in August 2012, the Chicago Public Library held a three-week amnesty period where any person who returned a late book would not have to pay a fine. A woman named Harlean Hoffman Vision took advantage of this, and returned a book that was 78 years overdue—Oscar Wilde's *The Picture of Dorian Gray*. It was originally checked out in 1934. Without amnesty—and the library's $10 cap on overdue fines—Vision would have owed almost $6,000.

EPIC FAIL

THE PRICE OF *STAR WARS* AUTOGRAPHS

Bargain-shopping *Star Wars* fans can pick up an autograph at Anaheim's *Star Wars* Celebration for just $20 from Tim Rose, who played Admiral Ackbar in *Return of the Jedi*. Fans with deeper pockets can get something autographed by Carrie Fisher, who played Princess Leia, for $70. The highest-priced autograph belongs to Luke Skywalker actor Mark Hamill, who charges $125.

COIN PRODUCTION COSTS

Some US money actually costs more than it's worth to produce. It costs 2.41 cents to make a penny, and it costs 11.18 cents to make a nickel. It actually costs less to make a dime than it does to make a nickel, since a dime can be produced for 5.65 cents.

EPIC FAIL

TOP COUNTERFEITED BILLS

The $20 bill is the type of money most likely to be counterfeited within the US, and the $100 bill is most likely to be copied in other countries. Counterfeiters producing $20 bills usually produce smaller amounts of fake bills, but international counterfeiters generally produce $100 bills totaling millions.

EPIC
FAIL

pepsi
KINGS
pepsi

EPIC FAIL

LOWEST NBA SALARY

David Stockton was at the bottom of the NBA salary list for the 2014-2015 season, taking home $29,483. This low paycheck was actually for a special 10-day contract with the Sacramento Kings. During that time, Stockton played in one NBA game and scored 1 point. Sacramento eventually signed Stockton—son of NBA legend John Stockton—under a two-year contract worth just over $850,000, beginning the 2015–2016 season.

EPIC FAIL

PRICEY SPEEDING TICKETS

Although the average US speeding ticket costs drivers $110 to $150, residents of Virginia have to pay a lot more. On top of the basic $200 ticket, Virginians have a $1,050 surcharge, bringing the ticket total to $1,350. Each year, US drivers pay about $6.2 billion in speeding tickets. However, other countries issue even higher fines. In Canada, some speeding tickets can reach more than $10,000, or about $9,300 in US dollars.

ON TO THE EPIC WINS!

most expensive music video

"Scream"

Siblings Michael and Janet Jackson teamed up to create "Scream," the most expensive music video of all time. Adjusted for inflation, the video cost a whopping $10.8 million. The video was directed by Mark Romanek and shows the Jacksons in a spacecraft escaping the media on Earth. There were 13 different parts of the set built. The lighting cost about $175,000, and the computer-generated spaceship cost another $65,000. "Scream" won Best Dance Video at the MTV Video Music Awards in 1995, as well as a Grammy for Best Music Video, and a Billboard Music Award for Best Pop/Rock Video. The song was the first single off Michael Jackson's ninth studio album—*HIStory: Past, Present, and Future, Book I.*

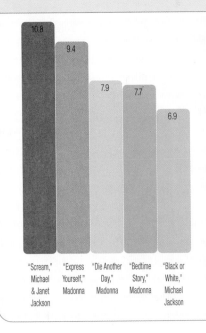

most expensive music videos

production cost, in millions of US dollars

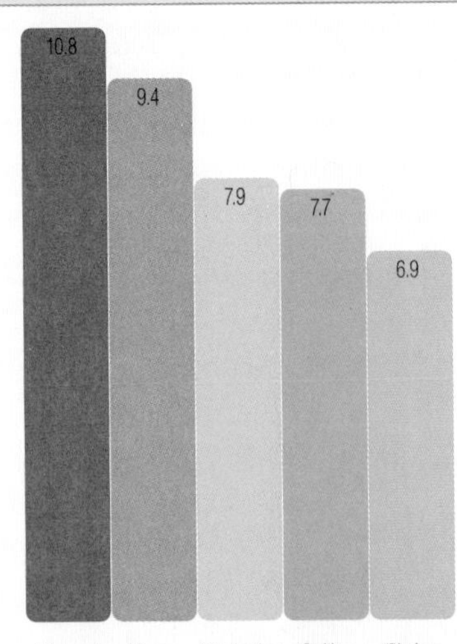
10.8
9.4
7.9
7.7
6.9
"Scream," Michael & Janet Jackson
"Express Yourself," Madonna
"Die Another Day," Madonna
"Bedtime Story," Madonna
"Black or White," Michael Jackson

most expensive hotel

Royal Penthouse Suite

Guests better bring their wallets to the President Wilson Hotel in Geneva, Switzerland—the Royal Penthouse Suite costs $83,200 a night! That means a weeklong stay would total $469,000, which is almost twice the price of the average house in the US. The suite is often booked by heads of state and celebrities, and offers beautiful views of the Alps and Lake Geneva. The 18,082-square-foot (1,680 sq m) twelve-bedroom luxury suite has a private elevator and marble bathrooms. The state-of-the-art security system includes bulletproof doors and windows.

most expensive hotel
price per night, in US dollars

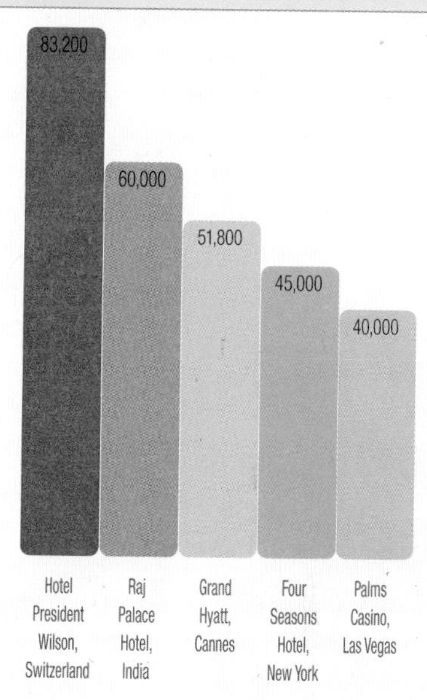
83,200
60,000
51,800
45,000
40,000
Hotel President Wilson, Switzerland
Raj Palace Hotel, India
Grand Hyatt, Cannes
Four Seasons Hotel, New York
Palms Casino, Las Vegas

most expensive painting ever sold

When Will You Marry?

Paul Gauguin's 1892 oil painting *When Will You Marry? (Nafea Faa Ipoipo?)* sold for an estimated 300 million dollars—the most expensive painting ever sold in a private sale or at auction! Paul Gauguin, a French artist, traveled twice to Tahiti to paint his romanticized versions of the natives, but to no critical success. It wasn't until after his death that his paintings began to gain recognition. The most expensive painting ever sold at auction happened in May 2015 at Christie's Auction house with Pablo Picasso's *Women of Algiers (Version O)* when it sold for 179.4 million dollars!

most expensive paintings ever sold

sale price, in millions of US dollars

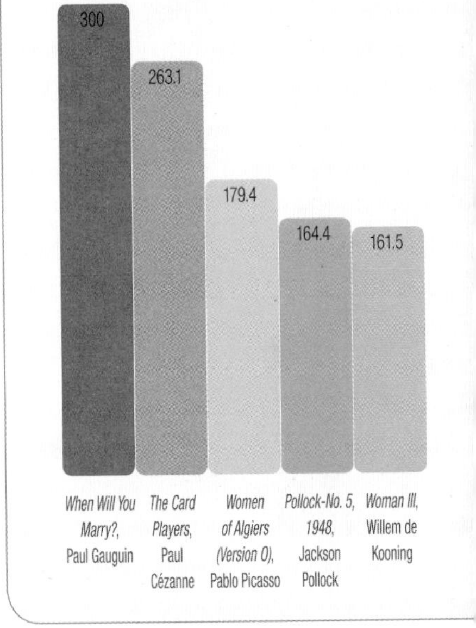

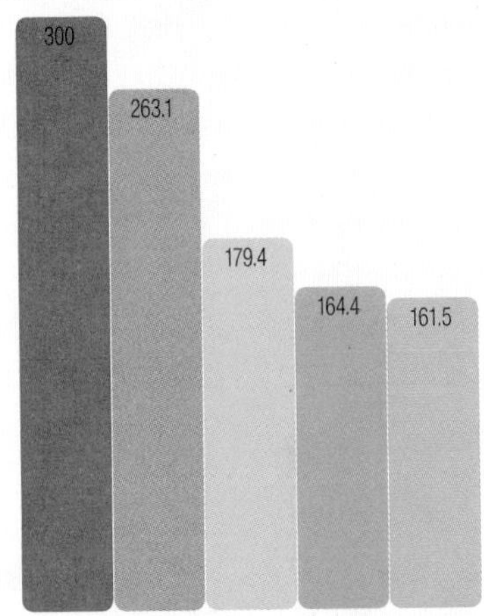
300
263.1
179.4
164.4
161.5
When Will You Marry?, Paul Gauguin
The Card Players, Paul Cézanne
Women of Algiers (Version O), Pablo Picasso
Pollock-No. 5, 1948, Jackson Pollock
Woman III, Willem de Kooning

most expensive TV series ad slot in 2014

Sunday Night Football

For every 30-second commercial shown during *Sunday Night Football* in 2014, advertisers had to pay a whopping $623,425. That breaks down to 20,781 per second! That's also the same cost as 27,105 footballs. *Sunday Night Football*—which was also the second-highest-rated show in 2014—is seen by about 21 million people each week, and advertisers want to capture their attention.

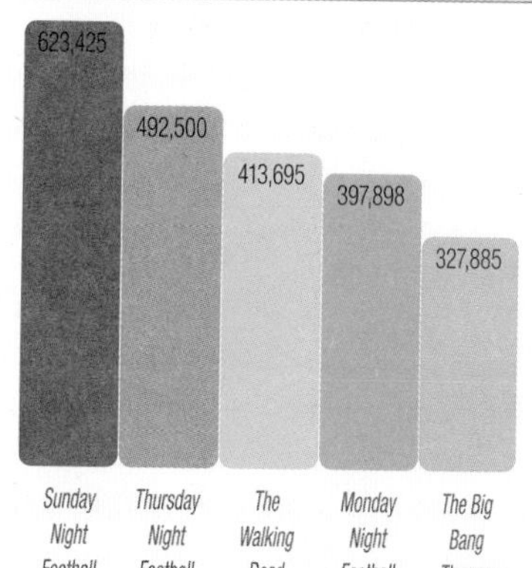
most expensive TV series ad slots in 2014
cost per commercial, in US dollars
623,425
492,500
413,695
397,898
327,885
Sunday Night Football
Thursday Night Football
The Walking Dead
Monday Night Football
The Big Bang Therory

Cris Collinsworth and Al Michaels of *Sunday Night Football*

richest tech billionaire

Bill Gates

In 2014, Bill Gates had a net worth of $79.2 billion—enough to give every person in the United States about $240. Gates became a self-made billionaire after his brainchild, Microsoft, rocketed to international success. The computer tycoon is very generous with his money. The Bill and Melinda Gates Foundation funds many worthy causes both domestically and internationally. Since it was formed in 2000, the foundation has given away more than $30 billion to aid such causes as eliminating polio, malaria, and Ebola, and creating education scholarships in the United States.

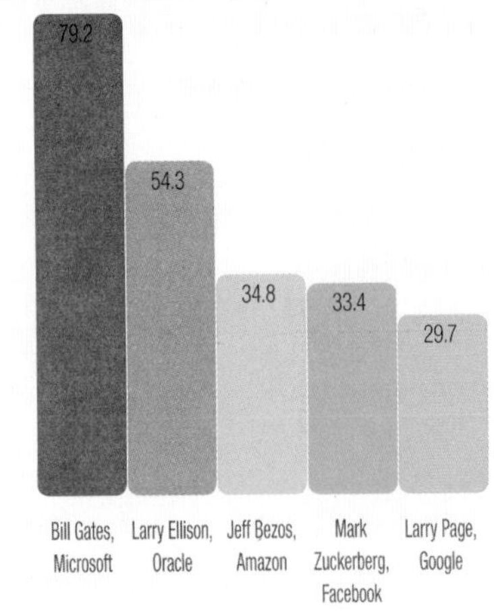
richest tech billionaires
net worth, in billions of US dollars
79.2
54.3
34.8
33.4
29.7
Bill Gates, Microsoft
Larry Ellison, Oracle
Jeff Bezos, Amazon
Mark Zuckerberg, Facebook
Larry Page, Google

most valuable production car

Lamborghini Veneno Roadster

The Lamborghini Veneno costs a whopping $4.5 million—about 88 times the median income ($52,000) in the United States! The open-roof super sportscar boasts a 750-horsepower, V-12 engine and a 7-speed manual transmission. The Veneno can reach a top speed of 221 miles per hour (354 km/hr) and can accelerate from 0 to 60 in about 2.9 seconds. The car was created to celebrate Lamborghini's 50th anniversary. Only nine cars were produced and sold.

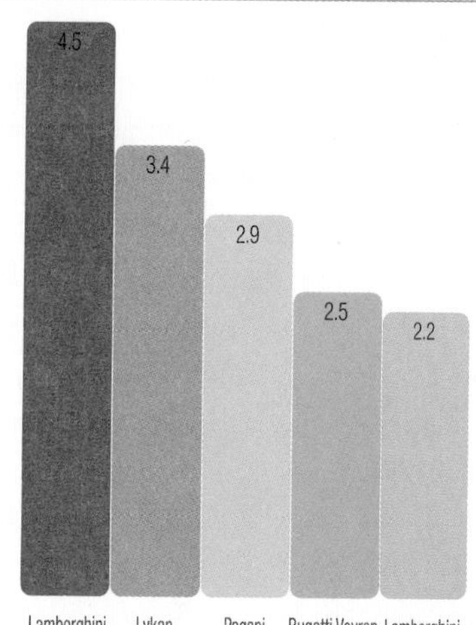
most valuable production cars
cost, in millions of US dollars
4.5
3.4
2.9
2.5
2.2
Lamborghini Veneno Roadster
Lykan HyperSport
Pagani Zonda Revolucion
Bugatti Veyron 16.4 Grand Sport
Lamborghini Sesto Elemento

world's most valuable brand

Apple

Apple—the computer company founded in 1976—is worth a staggering $124.2 billion. That's enough money to give every person living in the company's home state of California about $2,736. The company has sold more than 72 million Macs to date, and nearly 1 million people visit its more than 400 retail stores in 14 countries daily. Apple has also sold more than 700 million iPads, iPhones, and iPod-touches. About 900,000 iOS apps are available in the App Store. There are 300 million iCloud users across the globe, and this service has handled about 7.4 trillion push messages since it began.

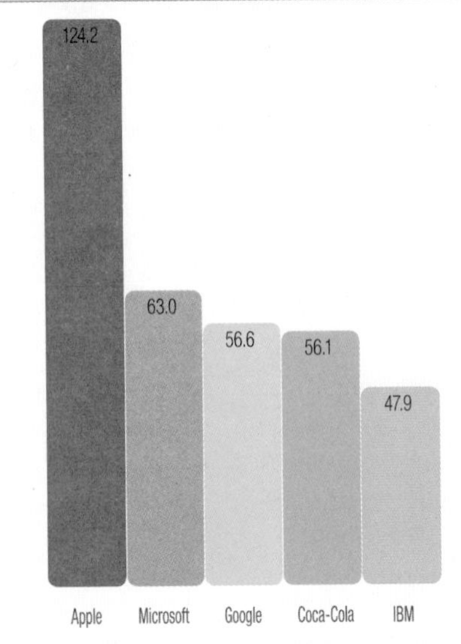
world's most valuable brands
brand value, in billions of US dollars
124.2
63.0
56.6
56.1
47.9
Apple
Microsoft
Google
Coca-Cola
IBM

most valuable football team

Dallas Cowboys

Worth $3.2 billion, the Dallas Cowboys are the most valuable team in the National Football League for the eighth year in a row. In addition to ticket sales, the Cowboys have several side businesses that bring in the cash. In 2008, they launched Legends Hospitality Management, a company that consults with other team owners to maximize earnings. They also started Silver Star Merchandising to make and distribute team apparel. Cowboys Stadium has 320 suites and 15,000 club seats, and generates $500 million in revenue annually. The team and its loyal fans have enjoyed 22 division championships, 10 conference championships, and 5 Super Bowl championships since the franchise began in 1960.

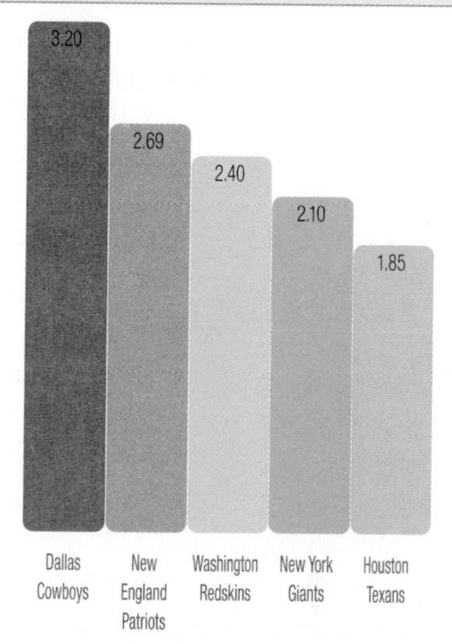
most valuable
football teams
value, in billions of US dollars
3.20
2.69
2.40
2.10
1.85
Dallas Cowboys
New England Patriots
Washington Redskins
New York Giants
Houston Texans

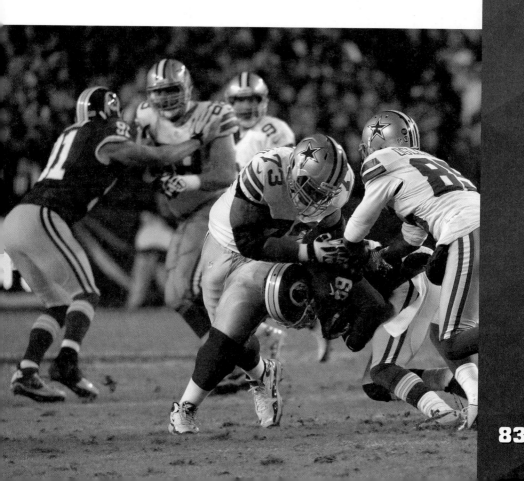

most valuable hockey team

Toronto Maple Leafs

The Toronto Maple Leafs are worth $1.30 billion, which is more than twice the average pro hockey team's value. The team's top ranking is largely due to strong ticket sales and television deals. Although Toronto won 13 Stanley Cups between 1917 and 1967, they have not won a cup in 47 years, which is the longest losing streak in the league. Toronto was one of the six teams that formed the National Hockey League in 1917. Their home arena is called Air Canada Centre.

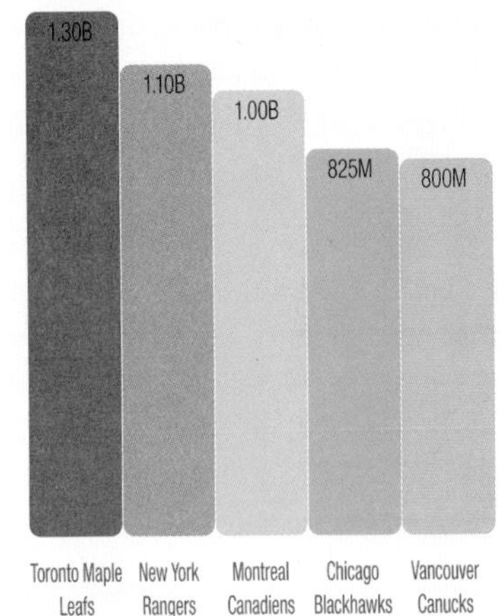
most valuable hockey teams
value, in millions and billions of US dollars
1.30B
1.10B
1.00B
825M
800M
Toronto Maple Leafs
New York Rangers
Montreal Canadiens
Chicago Blackhawks
Vancouver Canucks

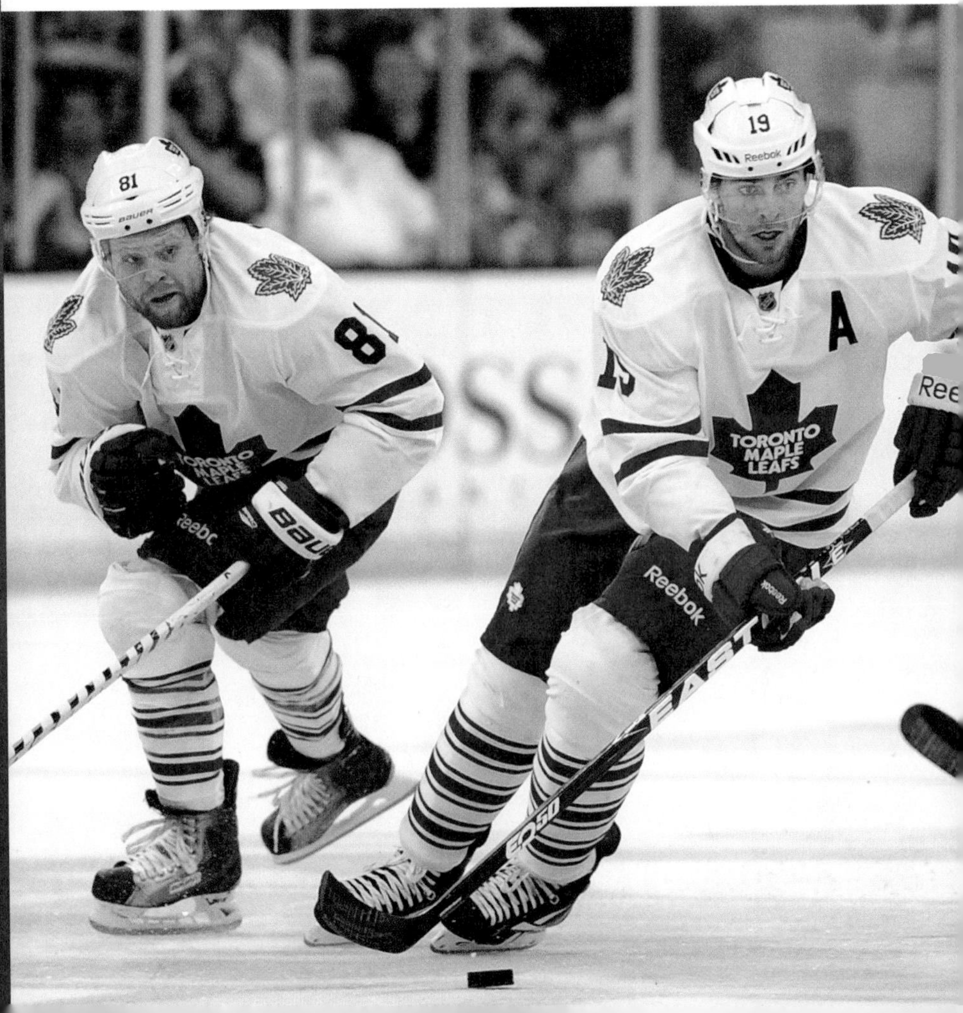

most valuable soccer team

Real Madrid

Spain's Real Madrid is valued at more than $3.4 billion. The team is also known as Los Merengues or Los Blancos (for their white uniforms). During the 2011–2012 season, Real Madrid won the La Liga league. This was the club's 32nd win—a La Liga record. In 2015, Real Madrid finished the season in second place. The team has also won 10 European Cup/UEFA Championship League titles. The club has been home to some of the world's best-known players, including Cristiano Ronaldo and Raúl. Real Madrid was founded in 1902 and plays in the 85,454-seat Estadio Santiago Bernabeu.

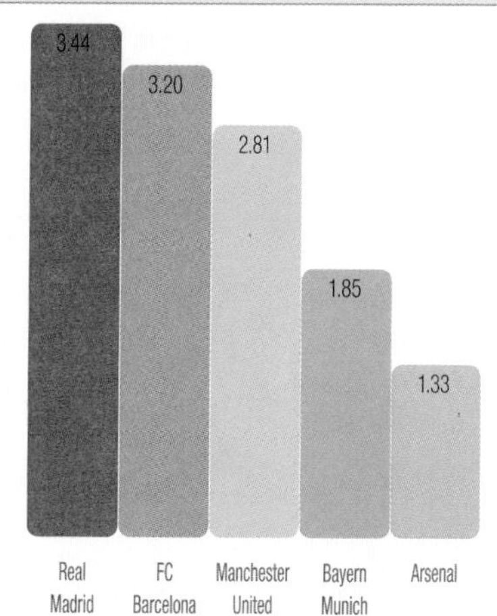
most valuable soccer teams
value in billions of US dollars
3.44
3.20
2.81
1.85
1.33
Real Madrid
FC Barcelona
Manchester United
Bayern Munich
Arsenal

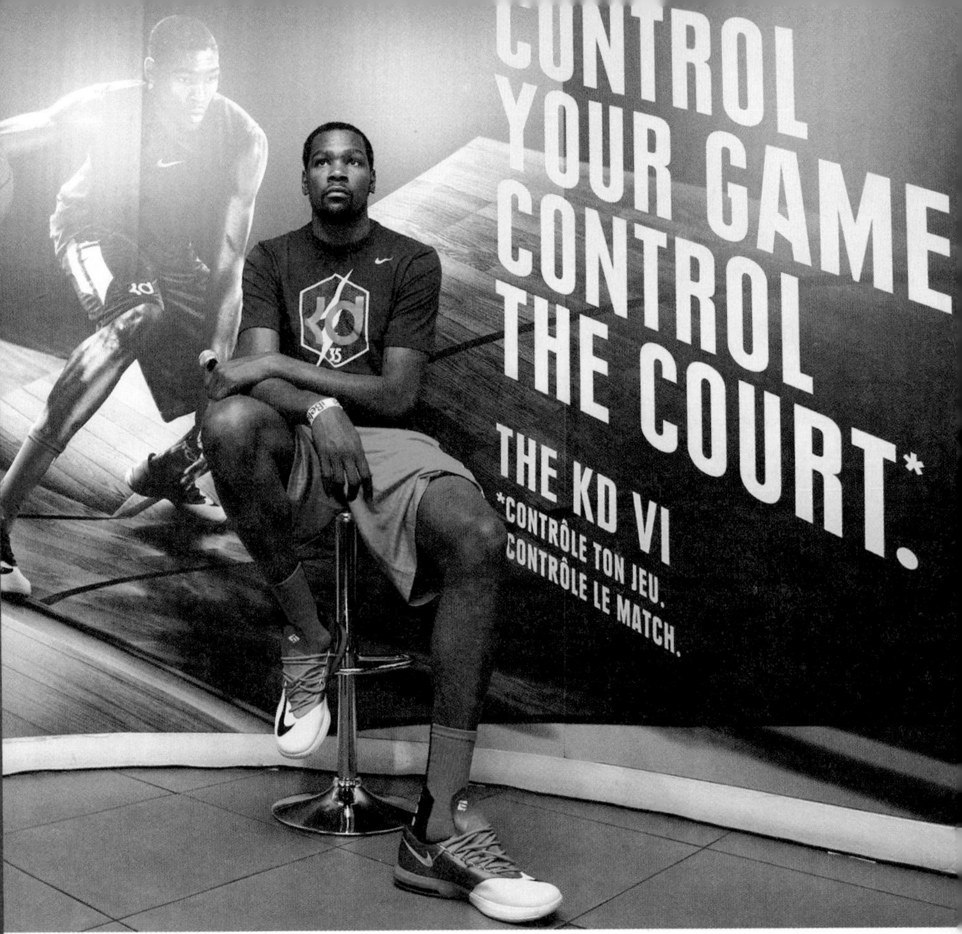

most valuable endorsement contract

Kevin Durant

In 2014, Kevin Durant inked a contract with sportswear manufacturer Nike worth an estimated $300 million over 10 years. Durant, who was a spokesperson for the company in the past, already has a Nike sneaker line, which brings in about $175 million annually. The basketball superstar is represented by Roc Nation, a newly formed company which is owned by Jay-Z. Roc Nation was able to drive up the contract value by starting a bidding war between Nike and Under Armour, which was hoping to work with Durant to increase its presence in the basketball market.

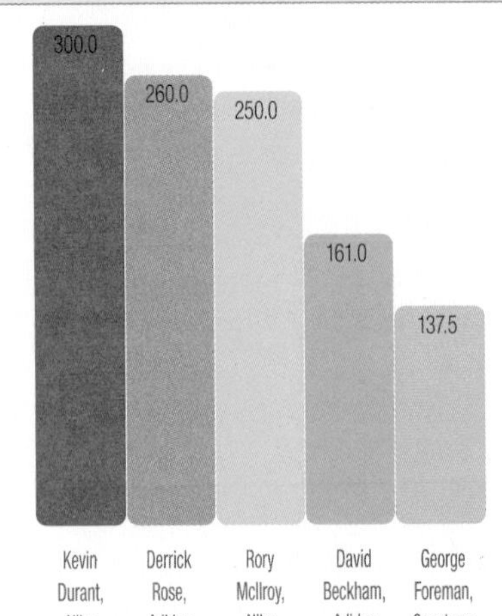
most valuable endorsement contracts
value, in millions of US dollars
300.0
260.0
250.0
161.0
137.5
Kevin Durant, Nike
Derrick Rose, Adidas
Rory McIlroy, Nike
David Beckham, Adidas
George Foreman, Spectrum

most valuable NBA team

Los Angeles Lakers

The Los Angeles Lakers are worth a whopping $2.6 billion! Although the team had a tough year with a record of 21-61, much of their profit was a result of the $4 billion contract they signed with Time Warner in 2012. Some of the top players on the roster include Kobe Bryant, Jordan Hill, and Jeremy Lin. The Lakers won 16 NBA Championships between 1949 and 2010. Between 2006 and 2013, the team sold out 320 consecutive games at the 18,997-seat Staples Center.

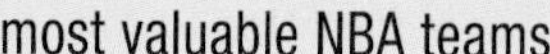
most valuable NBA teams

value, in billions of US dollars

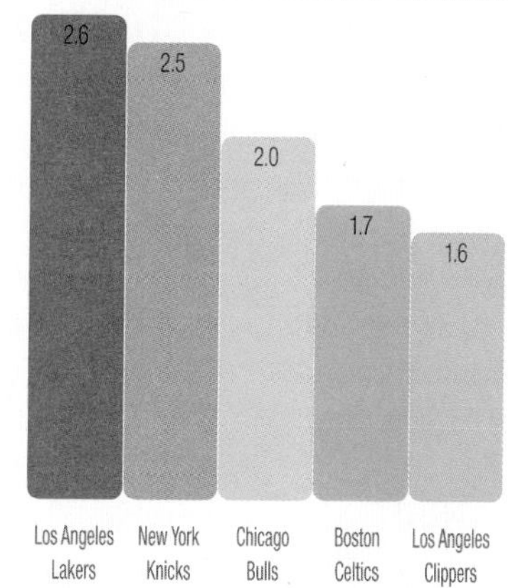
2.6
2.5
2.0
1.7
1.6
Los Angeles Lakers
New York Knicks
Chicago Bulls
Boston Celtics
Los Angeles Clippers

*As of Jan. 2015

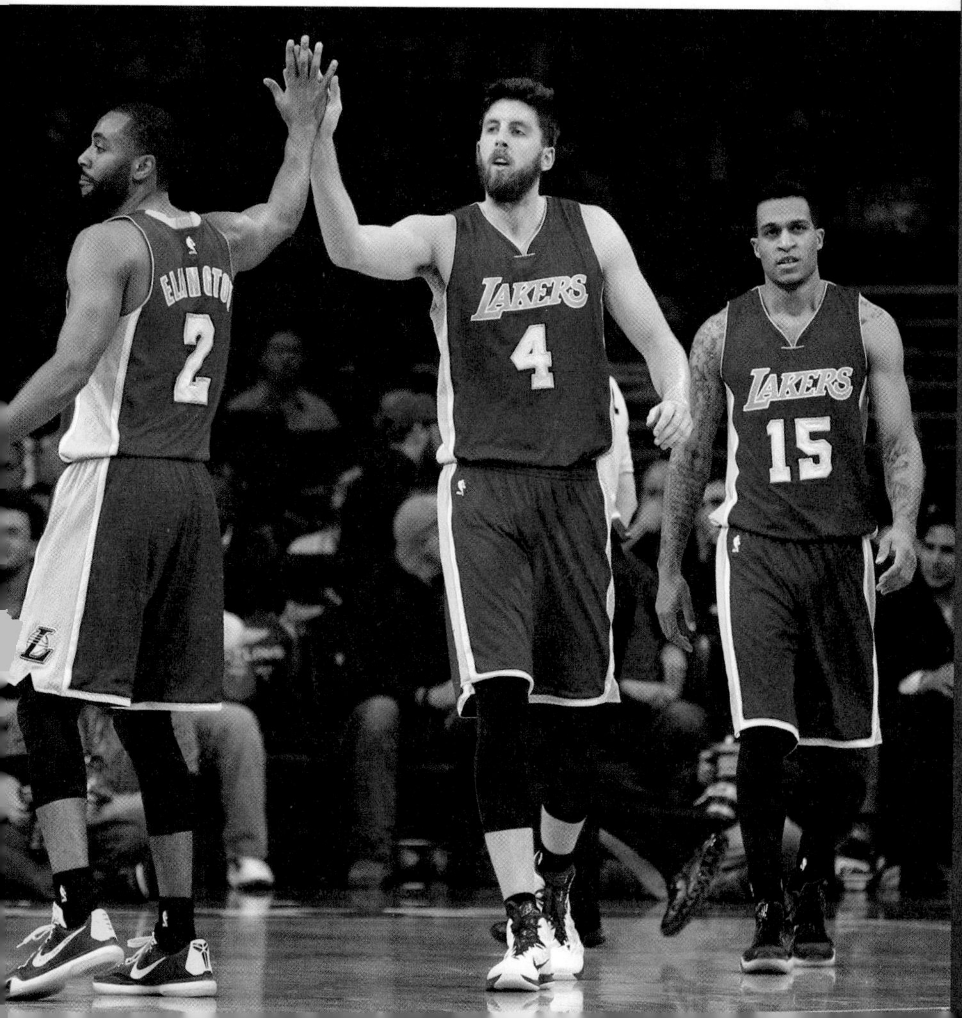

United States' bestselling automobiles

Ford F-Series

Ford sold 753,851 F-Series trucks during 2014. The F-Series originated in 1948, when the F-1 (half ton), the F-2 (three-quarter ton), and the F-3 (Heavy Duty) were introduced. Since then, many modifications and new editions have been introduced, including the F-150. The modern F-150 sports a V-6 or V-8 engine and the option of a regular, extended, or crew cab. The bed size ranges from 5.5 feet (1.6 m) to 8 feet (2.4 km). The Platinum F-150—the top-of-the-line version—features platinum chrome wheels, a fancy grille design, leather upholstery, and heated seats.

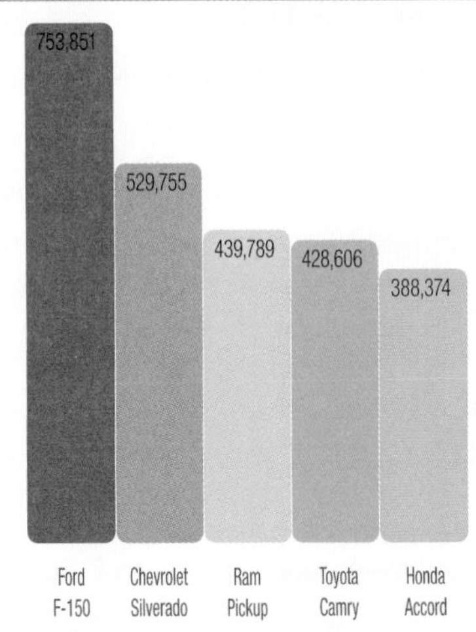
United States' bestselling automobiles
number of automobiles sold in 2014
753,851
529,755
439,789
428,606
388,374
Ford F-150
Chevrolet Silverado
Ram Pickup
Toyota Camry
Honda Accord

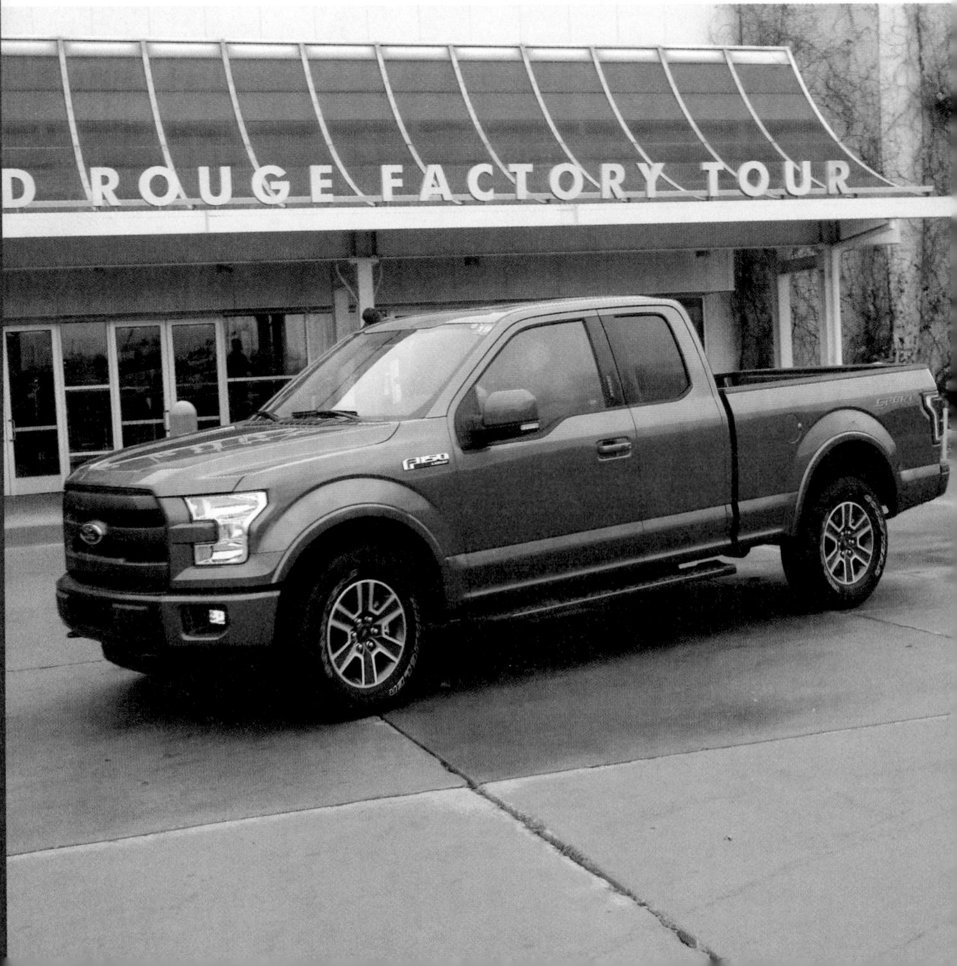

largest global food franchise

Subway

There are 42,296 Subway restaurants located throughout the world. There are 26,690 franchises in the United States, and another 15,606 international locations. Subway, which is owned by Doctor's Associates, Inc., had global sales totaling $18.8 billion in 2014. They had a brand value of $5.7 billion. The sandwich company was started by Fred DeLuca in 1965 and began franchising in 1974. Start-up fees run between $84,000 and $258,000, and 100 percent of the company is franchised. About 65 percent of franchisees own more than one location.

largest global food franchises

number of franchises

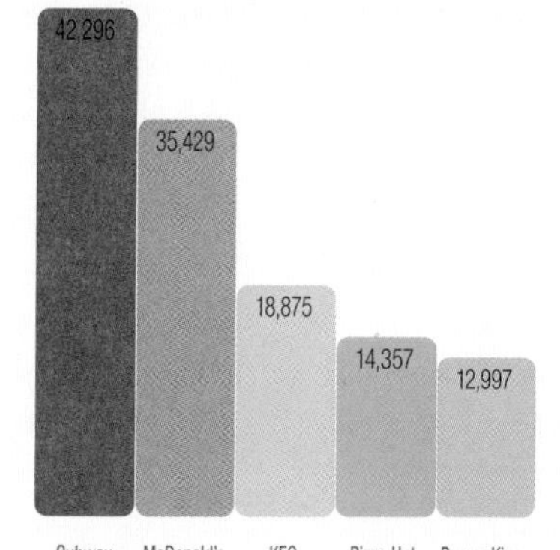
42,296
35,429
18,875
14,357
12,997
Subway
McDonald's
KFC
Pizza Hut
Burger King

largest retail franchise

7-Eleven

There are 53,856 7-Eleven convenience stores located around the world. Out of these, there are 8,160 locations in the United States and 45,696 locations internationally. The store chain is ranked number two on the *Forbes* Top 20 Franchises for the Buck list, meaning that investors have a very good chance of making a profit on their stores. The stores sell about 320 baked goods every minute, 13 million Slurpee beverages each month, and more than 100 million hot dogs each year. Approximately 25 percent of Americans live within a mile (1.6 km) of a 7-Eleven store.

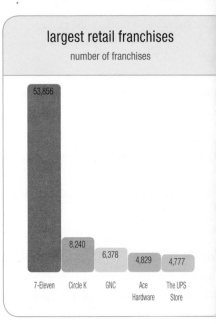

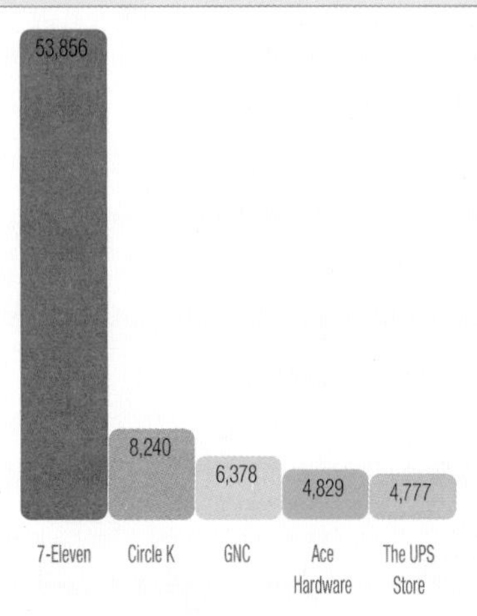
largest retail franchises
number of franchises
53,856
8,240
6,378
4,829
4,777
7-Eleven
Circle K
GNC
Ace Hardware
The UPS Store

POP CULTURE RECORDS

- EPIC FAILS
- ENTERTAINMENT
- TELEVISION
- MOVIES
- MUSIC
- THEATER

NSGATE
THEEXP
15

EPIC FAIL

ACTOR WITH THE MOST GOLDEN RASPBERRY AWARDS

Sylvester Stallone holds the record for the actor with the most Golden Raspberry nominations with 32 nods. These awards, also known as Razzies, honor the worst movies of the year and are given out the day before the Academy Awards. Stallone has won 10 Razzies, including 6 for Worst Actor and 1 each for Worst Director and Worst Screenplay. His most recent Razzie win was for Worst Supporting Actor in *Spy Kids 3-D: Game Over* in 2003. The runner up is Adam Sandler with 22 nominations and 7 wins.

ACTRESS WITH THE MOST GOLDEN RASPBERRY AWARDS

Madonna leads all other actresses in Golden Raspberry Awards with 15 nominations and 9 wins. She won 6 awards for Worst Actress, another 2 for Worst Supporting Actress, and 1 for Worst Screen Couple. Her most recent award came in 2002 for *Die Another Day*. Bo Derek comes in second with 11 nominations and 6 wins.

EPIC FAIL

JILL
EPIC FAIL

MOVIE WITH THE MOST GOLDEN RASPBERRY AWARDS

In 2011, *Jack & Jill* became the Golden Raspberry's all-time worst movie when it won all 10 awards for which it was nominated. This is the first time a movie accomplished this, and it was also the first time the same actor won for Worst Actor and Worst Actress. Adam Sandler took this honor because he played both the male and female of a pair of twins.

EPIC FAIL

DISMAL ALBUM DEBUT

Robin Thicke's 2014 album, *Paula*, sold just 25,000 copies in its first week. In fact, it sold less than 55 copies in Australia that week. In the UK, the album debuted at number 200 and sold 530 copies. By comparison, Thicke's previous album, *Blurred Lines*, sold 177,000 copies during its first week.

NBA PLAYER'S RAP ALBUM UNDERWHELMS

Ron Artest, who was an NBA forward at the time, decided to try his hand at music in 2006 and released his debut album, *My World*. In its first month it sold just 343 copies. The rap album was released by Cash Money Records. Artest has played for the Indiana Pacers, the Chicago Bulls, the Sacramento Kings, the Houston Rockets, the LA Lakers, and the NY Knicks. In 2011, he changed his name to Metta World Peace.

EPIC FAIL

EPIC FAIL

MORE RAP ALBUM WOES

Kevin Federline—best known as Britney Spears's former husband—decided to be a rapper in 2006 and released an album. Entitled *Playing With Fire*, it sold a total of 18,000 copies. Spears was the executive producer of the record, and the first single was "Lose Control."

EPIC FAIL

MADONNA'S WORST-SELLING ALBUM

Music icon Madonna has released 13 studio albums, and this last one has proven to be unlucky. *Rebel Heart* came out in March 2015 and sold just 116,000 copies in its first week—her lowest sales since 1994. Even worse, sales in the second week plummeted to just 22,800—an 80% drop!

EPIC FAIL
TI

JAY-Z'S APP FAILURE

In March 2015, Jay-Z launched Tidal, a streaming service with subscriptions priced at $10 to $20 a month. The higher-than-average price point was set in order to pay musicians more for their work and attract top artists. Digital downloads, streaming, and piracy have cut into artists' earnings in recent years. Music lovers seem unwilling to pay up, though. In less than a month, the app dropped off the iPhone top 700 download chart, while its competition—Spotify and Pandora—shot up to the top five.

TAYLOR SWIFT'S FAILED JOB

One of Taylor Swift's first jobs was on her family's Christmas tree farm in Pennsylvania. She was too young to cut down the trees or attach them to cars, but she could knock praying mantis cocoons out of the branches. One time, she forgot to check, and people unknowingly bought trees that had cocoons. A bunch of the insects hatched and crawled out of the trees on Christmas, invading people's homes.

EPIC FAIL

KATY PERRY STRIKES OUT AT THE GRAMMYS

Katy Perry has been nominated for 13 Grammy Awards but has yet to actually win one. In fact, she's lost at least one award each year since 2009. Her most frequent Grammy losses include Best Female Pop Vocal Performance and Best Pop Solo Performance.

EPIC FAIL

AMERICAN IDOL HITS A LOW NOTE

During the 14th season finale of *American Idol* in May 2015, the show scored a rating of only 1.6—the lowest in the show's history. Only about 7.7 million viewers watched as Nick Fradiani was crowned champion. That's down about 27% from last year's audience. *American Idol* is scheduled to end after the 15th season.

EPIC
FAIL

EPIC
FAIL

KIDS' CHOICE AWARDS CREEPIEST COSTUME

When viewers tuned in to see Nickelodeon's Kids' Choice Awards in March 2015, they expected to watch Nick Jonas host the event. However, viewers also got to see a surprise as well: his older brother, Joe Jonas, dressed up like a scary grandma. Luckily, Joe avoided being slimed.

LEO KEEPS LOSING OSCARS

Leonardo DiCaprio is one of the most nominated actors never to win an Academy Award, despite a successful 20-year career in Hollywood. He has been nominated five times, including two nominations for *The Wolf of Wall Street* (2014) and one nomination each for *Blood Diamond* (2007), *The Aviator* (2005), and *What's Eating Gilbert Grape* (1994).

EPIC
FAIL

EPIC
FAIL

WAITING 10 YEARS FOR AN EMMY

After 33 nominations, talk show host Bill Maher finally won his first Emmy in 2014. The monumental win came for his work as a producer on HBO's *Vice*. Maher was first nominated for an Emmy in 2004 and has been nominated every year since for his work on *Real Time with Bill Maher*. However, he has yet to win a statue for that show.

EPIC
FAIL

SEVEN GRAMMY LOSSES IN ONE NIGHT

In 2014, Kendrick Lamar was nominated for 7 Grammys, including Song of the Year and Album of the Year for *good kid, m.A.A.d. city*, but he left empty-handed. In 2002, India.Arie was nominated for 7 Grammy Awards, including Best New Artist and Album of the Year for *Acoustic Soul*, but she also took home nothing.

GRAMMY'S BIGGEST LOSERS

Hip-hop artist Snoop Dogg—now called Snoop Lion—and R&B singer-songwriter Brian McKnight have each been nominated for 16 Grammy Awards, but neither has won a statue. Among others, Snoop Dogg was nominated with Katy Perry for "California Gurls" and with Bruno Mars and Wiz Khalifa for "Young, Wild & Free."

EPIC
FAIL
BOB MARLEY

EPIC
FAIL

MOST GOLDEN GLOBE LOSSES

Meryl Streep has been nominated for 29 Golden Globe Awards but lost a record 21 of them. Her most recent loss came in 2015 for her role in *Into the Woods*. However, she also holds the record for the most wins.

LOWEST OSCAR AUDIENCE

In 2008, the Oscars drew the smallest audience ever with 32 million viewers. Jon Stewart hosted the show and drew good reviews from critics. However, the show continued to lose viewers as the night went on, ending with just 25.4 million people watching.

EPIC
FAIL

EPIC
FAIL
Optimus
Prime
says
stay
in

QUICK BROADWAY CANCELLATIONS

Glory Days and *Teaneck Tanzi: The Venus Flytrap* were two Broadway shows that closed after just one performance. *Glory Days*—a play about four friends reuniting after college—had its single performance on May 6, 2008. *Teaneck Tanzi: The Venus Flytrap* opened and closed on April 20, 1983, and told the story about a family that settled disputes through wrestling.

LOW EARNINGS FOR A BIG VOICE

When Spencer Lacey Ganus spent the day recording the voice of teenage Elsa in Disney's *Frozen*, she was paid just $926. The movie went on to earn $1.27 billion worldwide. However, after the film's success, her earnings were raised to about $10,000.

EPIC
FAIL

EPIC
FAIL

ANIMATED MOVIE BOMBS

The animated Disney film *Mars Needs Moms* cost about $170 million to create but brought in just $26.1 million at the box office in March 2011. This resulted in a loss of $144 million—or roughly the cost of 16 million movie tickets!

Carl Hiaasen
HOOT
Carl Hiaasen
HOOT
Carl Hiaasen
HOOT

SUPER LOW WEEKEND BOX OFFICE RESULTS

In May 2006, *Hoot* was released in 3,018 theaters but only brought in $3.36 million for the weekend. That's an average of $1,116 per theater. The movie starred Brie Larson, Logan Lerman, Cody Linley, and Luke Wilson (not shown), and told the story of a family who fought to save a group of endangered owls.

EPIC FAIL

EPIC
FAIL

WORST MOVIE EVER?

IMDb—International Movie Database—has a section of the website devoted to fans' reactions to movies. The worst ever, according to fans, is 80s actor Kirk Cameron's TV movie *Saving Christmas*, which debuted in 2014. The movie scored just 1.3 stars out of a possible 10.

SONY'S MOVIE HACK

In November 2014, hackers got into Sony Picture's email and computers, stealing important information. Five major movies were also stolen and posted on the Internet. *Fury*, a film starring Brad Pitt, was already in theaters, but was downloaded illegally more than 1 million times. *Annie*, *Mr. Turner*, *Still Alice*, and *To Write Love on Her Arms* were also posted online, and early viewing probably took a chunk out of box office revenue once the movies were actually released in theaters.

SONY PICTURES
EPIC
FAIL

EPIC
FAIL

FANTASY MOVIE FLOP

The 2013 fantasy adventure film *Jack and the Giant Slayer* cost $195 million to make. However, it brought in just $27.2 million in its opening week and eventually $197 million worldwide, making it one of the biggest disappointments of the year. The movie starred Nicholas Hoult, Ewan McGregor, and Stanley Tucci.

SNL'S LOWEST RATINGS IN 39 YEARS

In 2014, late-night comedy show *Saturday Night Live* saw its two lowest ratings since the show began in 1975. On May 10, actress Charlize Theron pulled in a rating of just 3.8, which was then match by the October 11 show hosted by Bill Hader.

EPIC
FAIL

EPIC FAIL

WORST TV SHOW DEBUT

NBC's *Do No Harm* holds the record for the worst in-season debut of a scripted show on the major networks with just 3.1 million viewers. The show ran on January 31, 2013, and was quickly canceled after the second episode. The show starred Steven Pasquale and Phylicia Rashad.

EPIC FAIL

DANCING WITH THE STARS LOWEST SCORE

During the season 18 finale of *Dancing with the Stars* in 2014, dance pro Mark Ballas and actress Candace Cameron Bure (DJ from *Full House*) earned the lowest freestyle score ever given in the finals with just 24 points. The couple came in third place, 11 points behind the next couple, Derek Hough and Amy Purdy.

WORST-SELLING PEOPLE COVER

In 2014, Hillary Rodham Clinton graced the cover of the worst-selling *People* magazine issue of the year. The June 16 issue, with Clinton's cover image, sold just over 500,000 copies. By comparison, *People*'s best-selling cover featured Robin Williams, with just over 1.1 million copies sold.

EPIC FAIL

ON TO THE EPIC WINS!

top TV special on twitter

The Oscars

More than 13.9 million people viewed one or more of the 11.2 million tweets sent out about the 2014 Academy Awards shown on TV on ABC. The top winner at the 86th annual Oscars was *Gravity* with seven wins, including Best Director, Cinematography, Visual Effects, and Original Score. Best Picture went to *12 Years a Slave*, and one of the film's actresses, Lupita Nyong'o, won for Best Supporting Actress. *Dallas Buyers Club*, *Frozen*, and *The Great Gatsby* each picked up multiple statues. The show was hosted by Ellen DeGeneres—who also sent out a record-breaking tweet during the telecast—and drew a television audience of 43.7 million people.

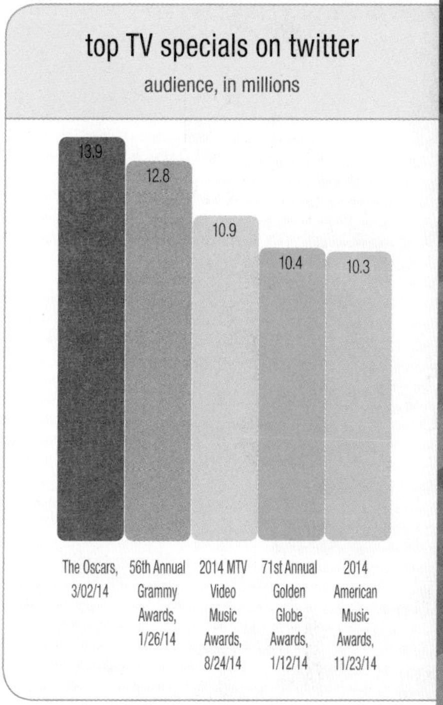

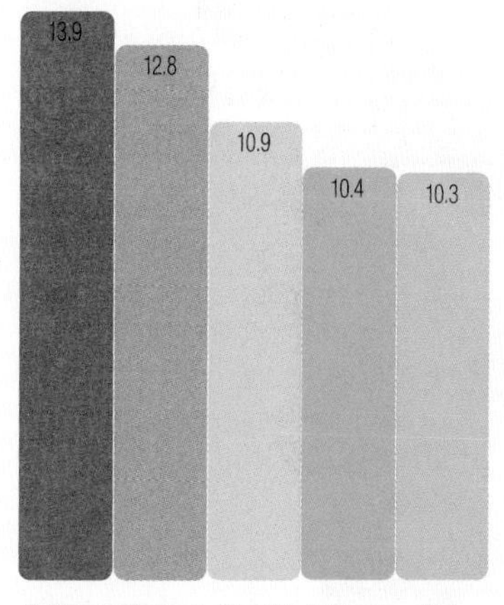

top TV specials on twitter
audience, in millions
13.9
12.8
10.9
10.4
10.3
The Oscars, 3/02/14
56th Annual Grammy Awards, 1/26/14
2014 MTV Video Music Awards, 8/24/14
71st Annual Golden Globe Awards, 1/12/14
2014 American Music Awards, 11/23/14

ENTERTAINMENT

top-paid celebrity under 30

Justin Bieber

In 2014, at the age of twenty, pop star Justin Bieber earned a staggering $80 million. Most of Bieber's impressive income came from his last world tour—*Believe*—which wrapped up in late 2013. The 7-leg, 162-show tour made the singer more than $86.6 million and sold more than 1.1 million tickets. In October 2013, Bieber announced that he would release a new "Music Monday" song each week to count down to the release of his film, *Justin Bieber's Believe*. These ten songs, plus another five previously unreleased tracks, were combined to create the collection, *Journals*. The complete *Journals* was available only on iTunes beginning January 2014.

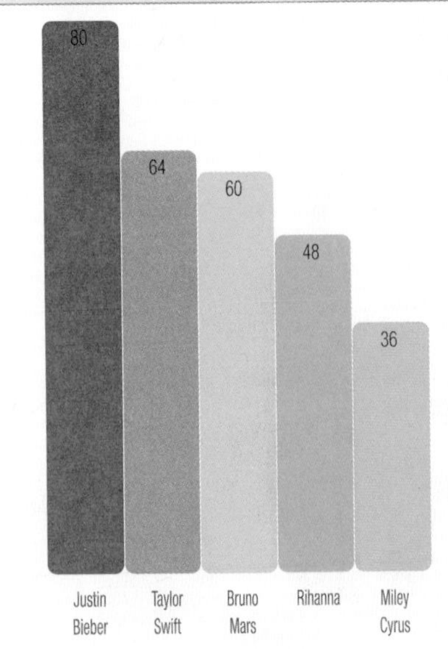
top-paid celebrities under 30
2014 earnings, in millions of US dollars
80
64
60
48
36
Justin Bieber
Taylor Swift
Bruno Mars
Rihanna
Miley Cyrus

highest-paid talk show host

Howard Stern

Talk show host Howard Stern earned $95 million in 2014. Stern can only be heard on Sirius XM Satellite Radio, and he has two stations—Howard 100 and Howard 101. Howard 100 features *The Howard Stern Show* live on Mondays, Tuesdays, and Wednesdays. Howard 101 features several other independent talk shows. Stern is also a judge on the television variety show *America's Got Talent*. He was inducted into the National Radio Hall of Fame in 2012.

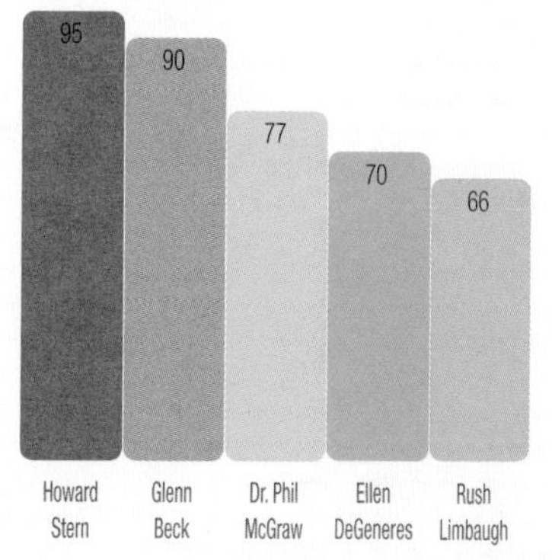
highest-paid talk show hosts
2014 earnings, in millions of US dollars
95
90
77
70
66
Howard Stern
Glenn Beck
Dr. Phil McGraw
Ellen DeGeneres
Rush Limbaugh

ENTERTAINMENT

TV show with the most Emmy awards

Saturday Night Live

The comedy sketch show *Saturday Night Live* has earned 40 Emmy Awards since it picked up its first four statues in 1976. Some of the categories that *SNL* has won awards for include Outstanding Variety, Music, or Comedy Series, Outstanding Guest Actor in a Comedy Series, Outstanding Original Music and Lyrics, and Outstanding Writing for a Variety, Musical, or Comedy Program. The show has launched the careers of many comedians that went on to be big stars, such as Kristin Wiig, Will Ferrell, Dana Carvey, Adam Sandler, Mike Myers, Tina Fey, and Andy Samberg.

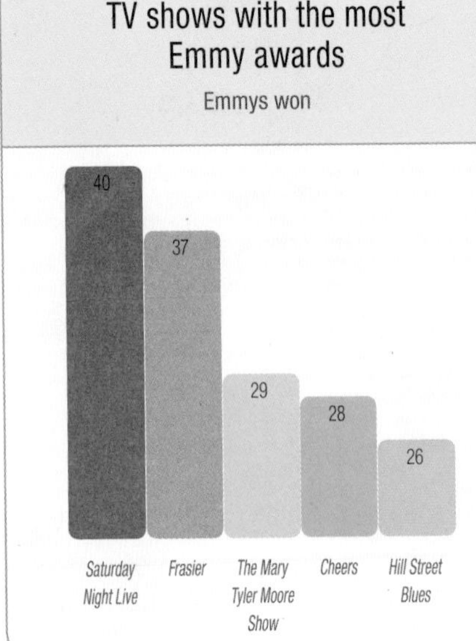
TV shows with the most Emmy awards
Emmys won
40
37
29
28
26
Saturday Night Live
Frasier
The Mary Tyler Moore Show
Cheers
Hill Street Blues

TV show with the most consecutive Emmy awards

The Daily Show with Jon Stewart

The Daily Show with Jon Stewart has won an Emmy Award for Outstanding Variety, Music, or Comedy Series for ten consecutive seasons between 2003 and 2012. In total, the show has received 27 Emmy nominations and has won 18 of them. Although it is considered a fake news show, the program often uses actual recent news stories and delivers them with a funny or sarcastic spin. The show began in 1996, and it is the longest-running program on Comedy Central. *The Daily Show* was hosted by Craig Kilborn until 1998, when Kilborn was replaced by Stewart. On August 6, 2015, Stewart left the show, and was replaced by Trevor Noah on September 28.

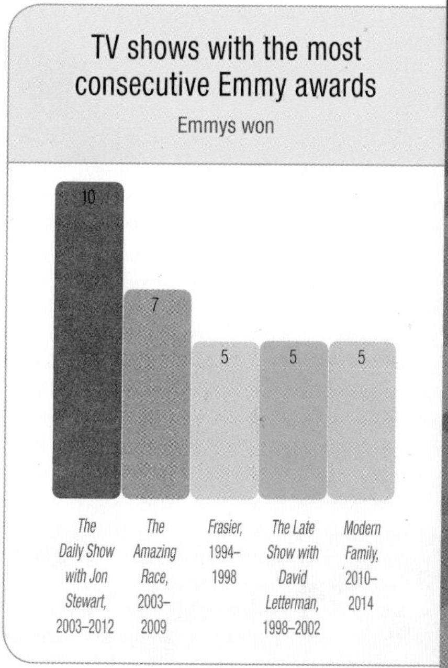

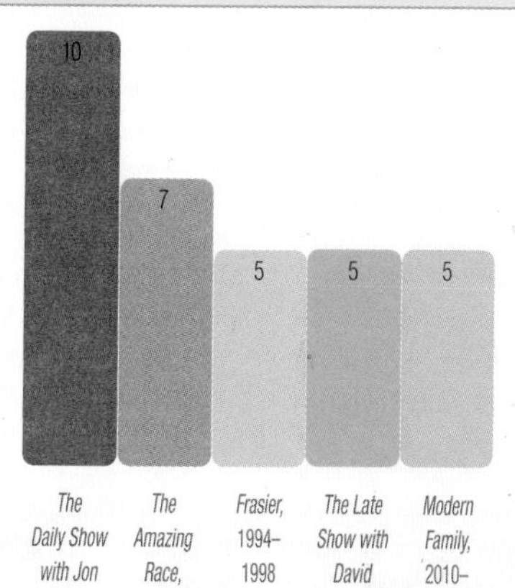
TV shows with the most consecutive Emmy awards
Emmys won
10
7
5
5
5
The Daily Show with Jon Stewart, 2003–2012
The Amazing Race, 2003–2009
Frasier, 1994–1998
The Late Show with David Letterman, 1998–2002
Modern Family, 2010–2014

most popular TV show

Sunday Night Football

Sunday Night Football pulls in about 21 million viewers each week. Hosts Al Michaels and Cris Collinsworth offer commentary on the game, players, and teams throughout the night. The show kicks off with Carrie Underwood's theme song. The 2014 season included seventeen games running from September to December. NBC first aired *Sunday Night Football* in 2006.

most popular TV shows

average viewers per week, in millions

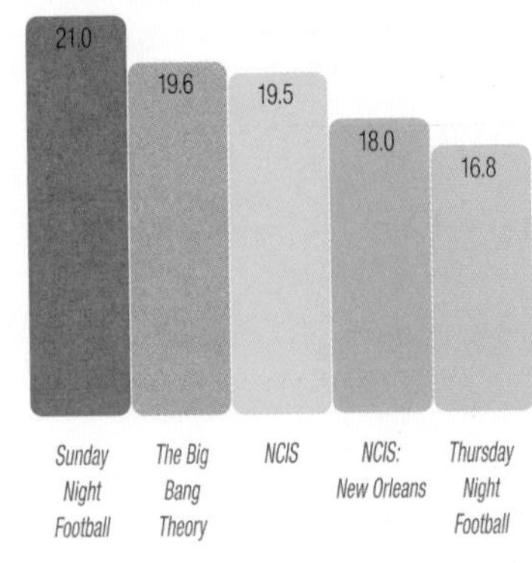
21.0
19.6
19.5
18.0
16.8
Sunday Night Football
The Big Bang Theory
NCIS
NCIS: New Orleans
Thursday Night Football

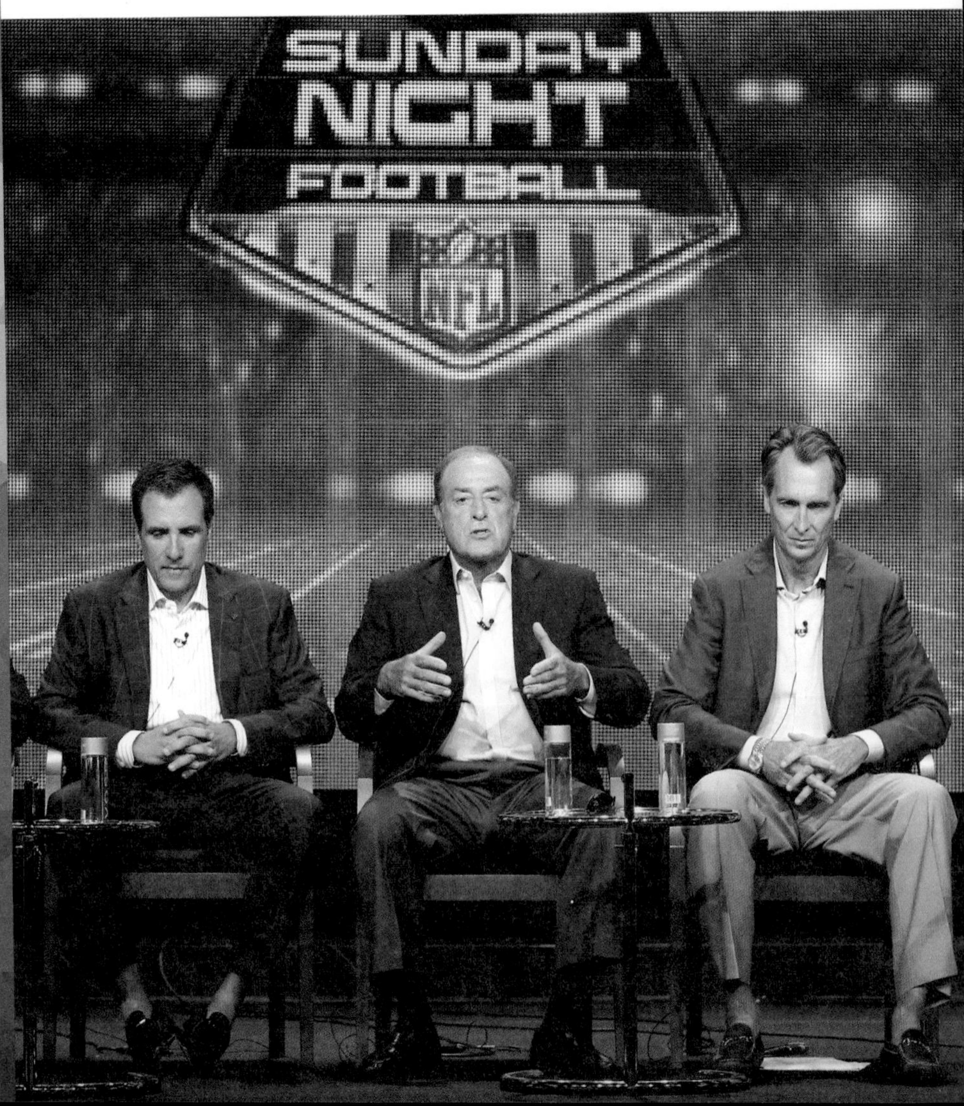

highest-paid TV actress

Kaley Cuoco-Sweeting

Kaley Cuoco-Sweeting—star of CBS's hit comedy *The Big Bang Theory*—makes $1 million per episode. This is a huge increase from the $60,000 she was making during the first three seasons on the show. Cuoco-Sweeting, who began her role as Penny in 2007, plays a waitress-turned-pharmaceutical-rep. She lives across the hall from Sheldon Cooper (Jim Parsons) and Leonard Hofstadter (Johnny Galecki), and she befriends the two super-smart neighbors even though their social skills are lacking. By the end of season 7, Penny and Leonard are engaged. Cuoco-Sweeting has won two People's Choice Awards and one Critics' Choice Television Award for the role.

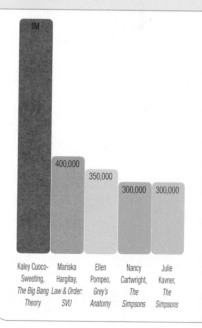

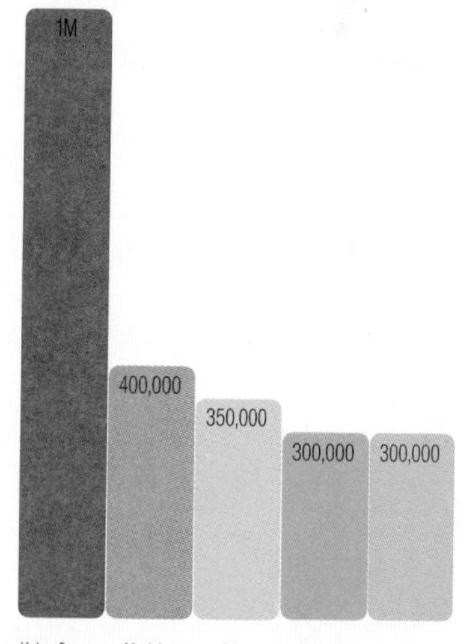
highest-paid TV actresses
2014 per episode earnings, in US dollars
1M
400,000
350,000
300,000
300,000
Kaley Cuoco-Sweeting, The Big Bang Theory
Mariska Hargitay, Law & Order: SVU
Ellen Pompeo, Grey's Anatomy
Nancy Cartwright, The Simpsons
Julie Kavner, The Simpsons

highest-paid TV actor

Johnny Galecki & Jim Parsons

Johnny Galecki and Jim Parsons, also known as Leonard Hofstadter and Sheldon Cooper on CBS's *The Big Bang Theory*, each earn $1 million per episode. Both actors play physicists with very high IQs but impaired social skills. They share an apartment in Pasadena, California, and much of the show takes place in their apartment with their friends and less educated but street-smart neighbor Penny (Kaley Cuoco-Sweeting). Since the show began in 2007, Parsons has picked up four Emmy Awards; Galecki has yet to pick up a statue, though he has been nominated for both an Emmy and a Golden Globe Award.

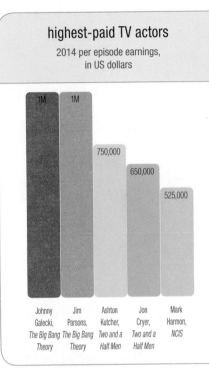

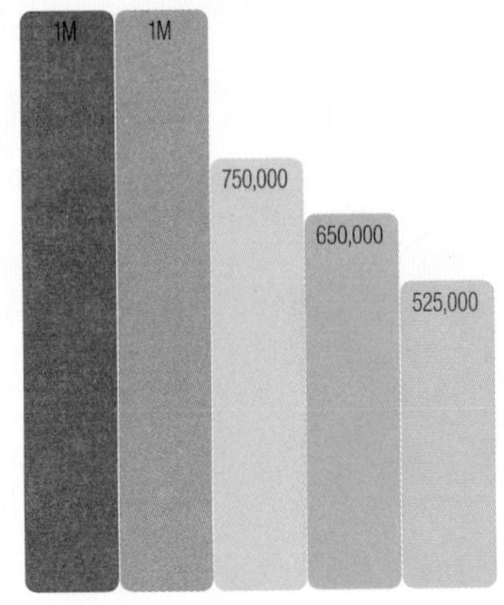
highest-paid TV actors
2014 per episode earnings, in US dollars
1M
1M
750,000
650,000
525,000
Johnny Galecki, *The Big Bang Theory*
Jim Parsons, *The Big Bang Theory*
Ashton Kutcher, *Two and a Half Men*
Jon Cryer, *Two and a Half Men*
Mark Harmon, *NCIS*

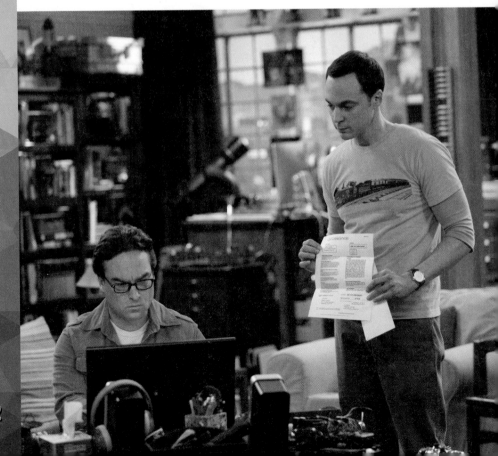

celebrities with the most Kids' Choice Awards

Adam Sandler

Kids love funny actors! With their votes, Adam Sandler has won 10 Nickelodeon Kids' Choice Awards since the show began in 1988. Sandler's awards include Favorite Movie Actor (1999, 2000, 2003, 2005, 2007, 2012, 2014), Favorite Voice From an Animated Movie (2003, 2013), and a Wannabe Award (2004). Some of Sandler's most popular recent movies include *Bedtime Stories* (2008), *Hotel Transylvania* (2012), *Grown Ups* (2010), and *Click* (2006). In addition to his Kids' Choice Awards, Sandler has also won two Teen Choice Awards, three People's Choice Awards, and five MTV Movie Awards.

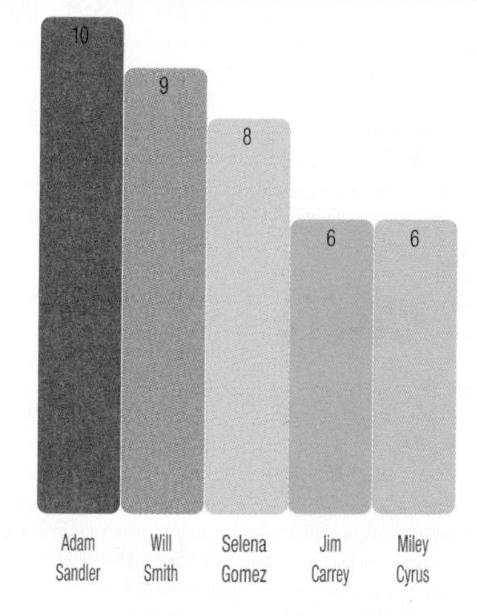
celebrities with the most Kids' Choice Awards
awards won
10
9
8
6
6
Adam Sandler
Will Smith
Selena Gomez
Jim Carrey
Miley Cyrus

highest-paid producer

Steven Spielberg

Legendary producer Steven Spielberg earned $100 million in 2014. Although Spielberg is best known for his films, he spent much of the year producing the television series *Under the Dome, Falling Skies,* and *Extant*. *Under the Dome* is a drama that follows the lives of people in a small town that is trapped under an invisible force field. The sci-fi thriller *Falling Skies* follows survivors of an alien attack. *Extant* stars Halle Berry as an astronaut who finds herself entangled in a mystery as she adjusts to life back on Earth. Spielberg also spent the year producing *Jurassic World*, the fourth installment of the extremely popular dinosaur franchise.

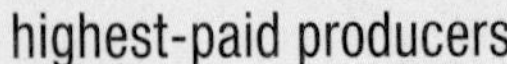
highest-paid producers
2014 earnings, in millions of US dollars

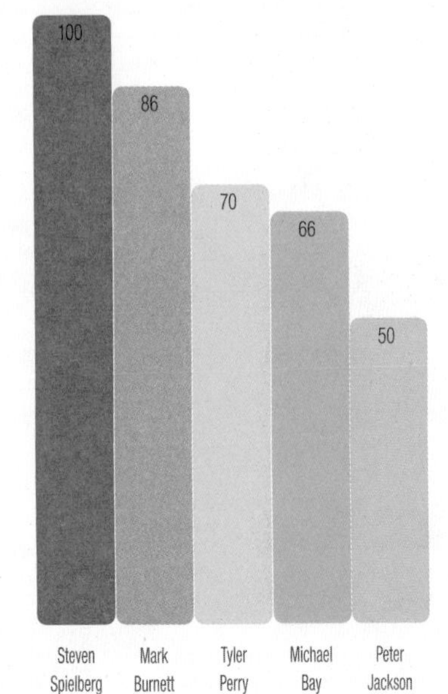
100
86
70
66
50
Steven Spielberg
Mark Burnett
Tyler Perry
Michael Bay
Peter Jackson

MOVIES

actor with the lowest returns per salary dollar

Adam Sandler

For every dollar that Adam Sandler gets paid, his movies bring in just $3.20. Sandler has had a tough few years at the box office as a leading man, bringing his career earning average way down. *That's My Boy* (2012), in which Sandler starred as Donny, had a production budget of $67 million but earned just $58 million worldwide. During his career, Sandler has starred in 24 movies, and his box office average earnings are $77.5 million per film. While that may not sound too low, Sandler usually commands about $20 million per role.

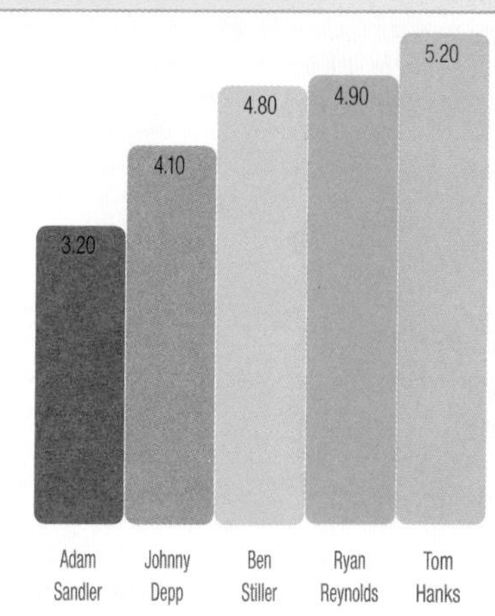
actors with the lowest returns per salary dollar
return for every dollar paid, in US dollars
3.20
4.10
4.80
4.90
5.20
Adam Sandler
Johnny Depp
Ben Stiller
Ryan Reynolds
Tom Hanks

actors with the highest returns per salary dollar

Emma Stone

For every dollar that actress Emma Stone is paid, her movies generate $61.45 in box office earnings. Through 2013, Stone starred in six films, and each earned an average of $191.5 million. Her most successful movie was *The Amazing Spider-Man* (2012) in which she played Gwen Stacy. It earned $757 million worldwide. She also lent her voice to Eep in *The Croods* (2013), which earned $573 million, and played Skeeter in *The Help* (2011), which earned $213 million. Stone reprised her role as Gwen in *The Amazing Spider-Man 2* in 2014. Stone has won two MTV Movie Awards, three Teen Choice Awards, and one People's Choice Award.

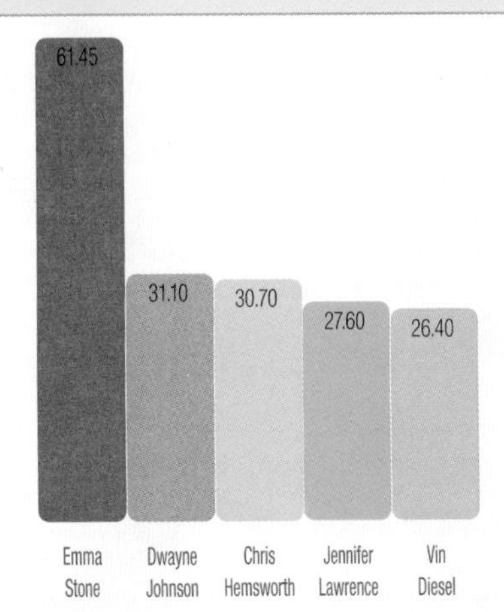
actors with the highest returns per salary dollar
return for every dollar paid, in US dollars
61.45
31.10
30.70
27.60
26.40
Emma Stone
Dwayne Johnson
Chris Hemsworth
Jennifer Lawrence
Vin Diesel

actress with the most Oscar nominations

Meryl Streep

Meryl Streep is the most-nominated actress in the history of the Academy Awards, with 19 chances to win a statue. Her first nomination came in 1979 for *The Deer Hunter* and was followed by *Kramer vs. Kramer* (1980), *The French Lieutenant's Woman* (1981), *Sophie's Choice* (1982), *Silkwood* (1983), *Out of Africa* (1985), *Ironweed* (1987), *A Cry in the Dark* (1988), *Postcards From the Edge* (1990), *The Bridges of Madison County* (1995), *One True Thing* (1998), *Music of the Heart* (1999), *Adaptation* (2002), *The Devil Wears Prada* (2006), *Doubt* (2008), *Julie and Julia* (2009), *The Iron Lady* (2012), *August: Osage County* (2013), and *Into the Woods* (2015). Streep won her first Academy Award for *Kramer vs. Kramer,* her second for *Sophie's Choice*, and her third for *The Iron Lady.*

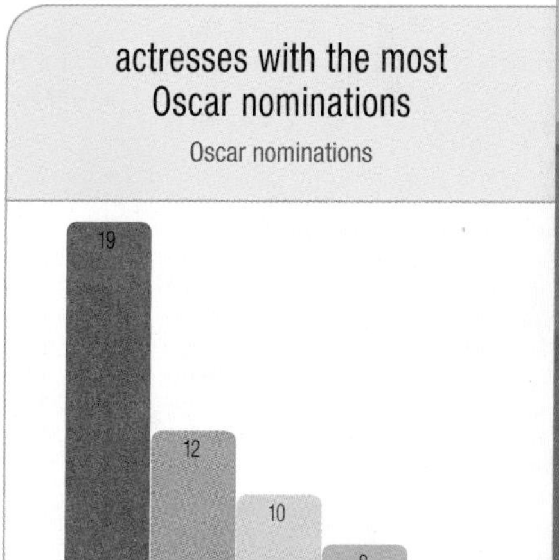

actresses with the most Oscar nominations

Oscar nominations

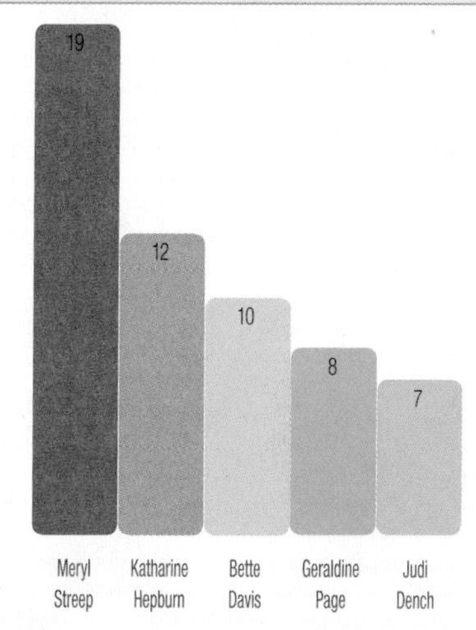
19
12
10
8
7
Meryl Streep
Katharine Hepburn
Bette Davis
Geraldine Page
Judi Dench

actor with the most Oscar nominations

Jack Nicholson

Jack Nicholson has been nominated for a record 12 Oscars during his distinguished career. He is one of only three men to have been nominated for an acting Academy Award at least once every decade for five decades. He was nominated for eight Best Actor awards for his roles in *Five Easy Pieces* (1970), *The Last Detail* (1973), *Chinatown* (1974), *One Flew Over the Cuckoo's Nest* (1975), *Prizzi's Honor* (1985), *Ironweed* (1987), *As Good As It Gets* (1997), and *About Schmidt* (2002). He was nominated for Best Supporting Actor for *Easy Rider* (1969), *Reds* (1981), *Terms of Endearment* (1983), and *A Few Good Men* (1992). Nicholson picked up statues for *One Flew Over the Cuckoo's Nest*, *Terms of Endearment*, and *As Good As It Gets*.

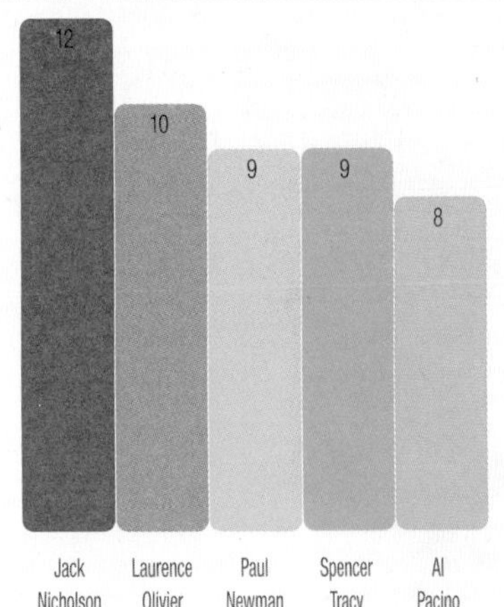
actors with the most Oscar nominations
Oscar nominations
12
10
9
9
8
Jack Nicholson
Laurence Olivier
Paul Newman
Spencer Tracy
Al Pacino

actor with the most MTV Movie Awards

Jim Carrey

Jim Carrey has won 11 MTV Movie Awards since the television station began awarding them in 1992. He has won the award for Best Comedic Performance five times for his roles in *Dumb & Dumber* (1995), *Ace Ventura II: When Nature Calls* (1996), *The Cable Guy* (1997), *Liar Liar* (1998), and *Yes Man* (2009). Carrey won the award for Best Male Performance twice for *Ace Ventura II: When Nature Call*s and *The Truman Show* (1999). He also won awards for Best Kiss for *Dumb & Dumber*, Best Villain for *The Cable Guy*, and the MTV Generation Award in 2006.

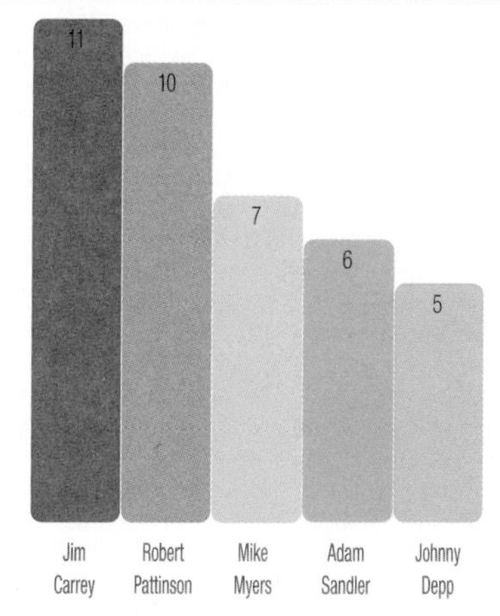
actors with the most
MTV Movie Awards
awards won
11
10
7
6
5
Jim Carrey
Robert Pattinson
Mike Myers
Adam Sandler
Johnny Depp

actress with the most MTV Movie Awards

Kristen Stewart

Kristen Stewart, who rose to fame playing Bella Swan in the Twilight saga, won seven MTV Movie Awards for her role. She picked up her first two awards—Best Female Performance and Best Kiss—in 2009 for *Twilight*. She shared the Best Kiss award with costar Robert Pattinson. A year later, she picked up the same two awards for *New Moon*. In 2011, Stewart nabbed the same two again for *Eclipse*. Stewart's most recent award win came in 2012, when she once again shared the Best Kiss award with Robert Pattinson for the 2011 Twilight film, *Breaking Dawn: Part One*.

actresses with the most MTV Movie Awards

awards won

	Awards won
Kristen Stewart	7
Jennifer Lawrence	5
Uma Thurman	4
Sandra Bullock	4
Shailene Woodley	4

Presenters and the cast of *The Lord of the Rings* (Peter Jackson in front)

movies with the most Oscars

Ben-Hur, Titanic, and The Lord of the Rings: The Return of the King

The only three films in Hollywood history to win 11 Academy Awards are *Ben-Hur*, *Titanic*, and *The Lord of the Rings: The Return of the King*. Some of the Oscar wins for *Ben-Hur*—a biblical epic based on an 1880 novel by General Lew Wallace—include Best Actor (Charlton Heston) and Director (William Wyler). Some of *Titanic*'s Oscars include Best Cinematography, Visual Effects, and Costume Design. *The Lord of the Rings: The Return of the King* is the final film in the epic trilogy based on the works of J.R.R. Tolkien. With 11 awards, it is the most successful movie in Academy Awards history because it won every category in which it was nominated. Some of these wins include Best Picture, Director (Peter Jackson), and Costume Design.

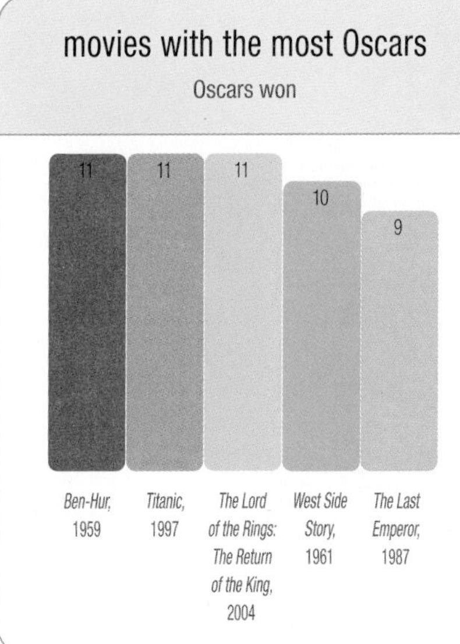
movies with the most Oscars
Oscars won
11
11
11
10
9
Ben-Hur, 1959
Titanic, 1997
The Lord of the Rings: The Return of the King, 2004
West Side Story, 1961
The Last Emperor, 1987

actor with the highest career box-office gross

Samuel L. Jackson

Samuel L. Jackson's movies have a combined total gross of $7.11 billion. Jackson, who has appeared in more than 115 films, has starred in several extremely successful movie franchises which helped to boost his total box office receipts. Most recently, Jackson has starred as Nick Fury in the Avengers movies. Between 1999 and 2008, Jackson appeared in several Star Wars films. And earlier in his career, he had roles in several movie classics, including *Goodfellas* (1990), *Patriot Games* (1992), *Jurassic Park* (1993), and *Pulp Fiction* (1994).

actors with the highest career box-office gross

total gross, in billions of US dollars*

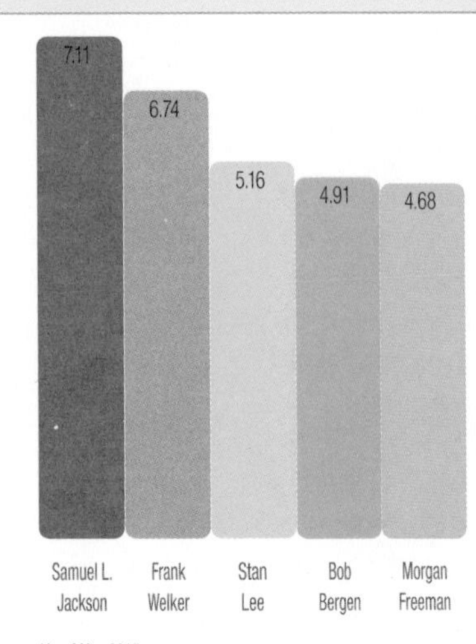
7.11
6.74
5.16
4.91
4.68
Samuel L. Jackson
Frank Welker
Stan Lee
Bob Bergen
Morgan Freeman
*As of May 2015

top-grossing animated movie

Frozen

Disney's animated adventure *Frozen* has earned more than $1.27 billion worldwide since it opened in November 2013. It's one of the ten highest-grossing films of all time. The story centers on sisters Elsa and Anna, and how Elsa's special powers keep the sisters apart. Anna—voiced by Kristen Bell—is a free spirit, while Elsa—voiced by Idina Menzel—is a bit more reserved. Together with ice salesman Kristoff (Jonathan Groff), Olaf the snowman (Josh Gad), and a helpful reindeer named Sven, the sisters battle to overcome their differences and be a family again. The movie won Academy Awards for Best Animated Feature and Best Original Song.

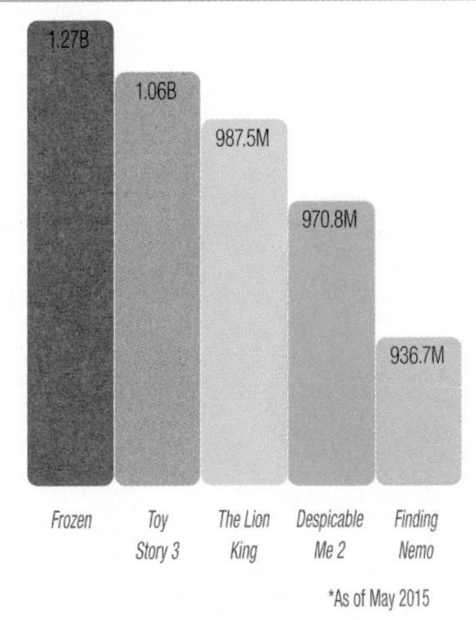
top-grossing animated movies
worldwide gross earnings, in millions and billions of US dollars*
1.27B
1.06B
987.5M
970.8M
936.7M
Frozen
Toy Story 3
The Lion King
Despicable Me 2
Finding Nemo
*As of May 2015

Kristen Bell, the voice of Anna.

movie with the most successful domestic opening weekend

Jurassic World

Jurassic World—the fourth installment of the dinosaur thriller—dominated the box office on June 12, 2015, bringing in $208.8 million for the weekend. Produced by Steven Spielberg, the movie focuses on what happens 22 years after the original Jurassic Park experiment failed terribly. Now, the dinosaur theme park has been open for about 10 years, and is looking for a new attraction to revive the public's interest and draw in more visitors. *Jurassic World* stars Chris Pratt and Bryce Dallas Howard.

movies with the most successful domestic opening weekend

weekend earnings, in millions of US dollars

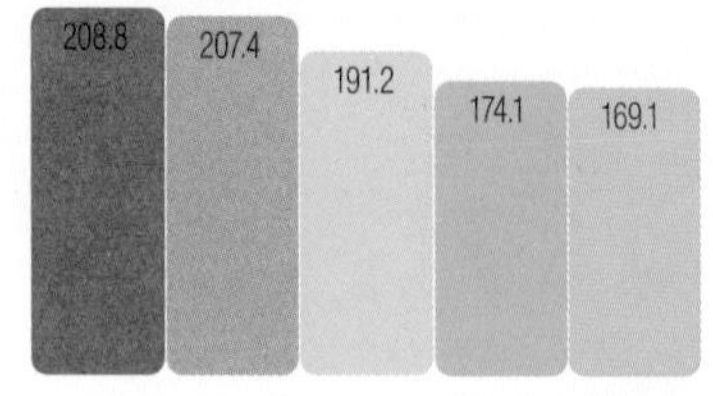
208.8
207.4
191.2
174.1
169.1

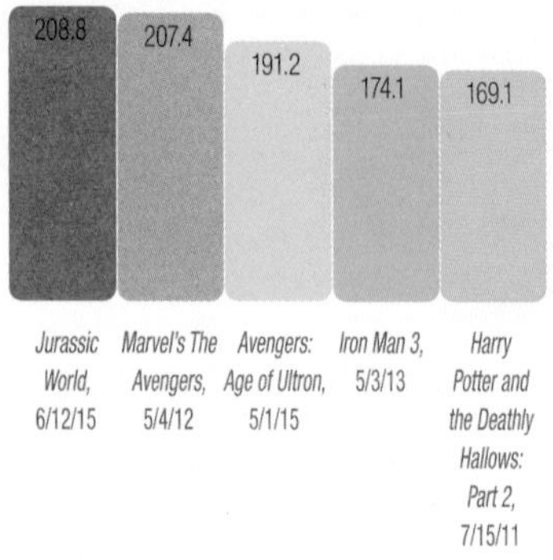

Jurassic World, 6/12/15	*Marvel's The Avengers*, 5/4/12	*Avengers: Age of Ultron*, 5/1/15	*Iron Man 3*, 5/3/13	*Harry Potter and the Deathly Hallows: Part 2*, 7/15/11
208.8	207.4	191.2	174.1	169.1

top-grossing movie

Avatar

Avatar, James Cameron's science-fiction epic, was released in December 2009 and grossed more than $2.78 billion worldwide in less than two months. Starring Sigourney Weaver, Sam Worthington, and Zoe Saldana, *Avatar* cost more than $230 million to make. Cameron began working on the film in 1994, and it was eventually filmed in 3-D, with special cameras made just for the movie. Due to *Avatar*'s overwhelming success, Cameron is planning two sequels.

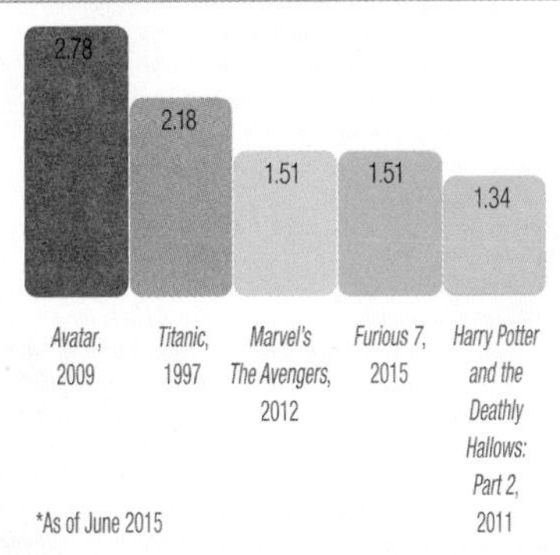
top-grossing movies
total worldwide gross, in billions of US dollars*
2.78
2.18
1.51
1.51
1.34
Avatar, 2009
Titanic, 1997
Marvel's The Avengers, 2012
Furious 7, 2015
Harry Potter and the Deathly Hallows: Part 2, 2011
*As of June 2015

most successful movie franchise

Avengers

The 11 movies in the Avengers franchise have collectively earned $7.98 billion worldwide. The first film in the franchise was *Iron Man* which was released in May 2008, and the most current is *The Avengers: Age of Ultron*, which debuted in May 2015. The most successful movie in the franchise is *The Avengers*, which earned $1.5 billion in 2012. Some of the stars of the franchise include Robert Downey, Jr. as Iron Man, Chris Hemsworth as Thor, Mark Ruffalo as Hulk, Chris Evans as Captain America, Samuel L. Jackson as Nick Fury, and Scarlett Johansson as Black Widow.

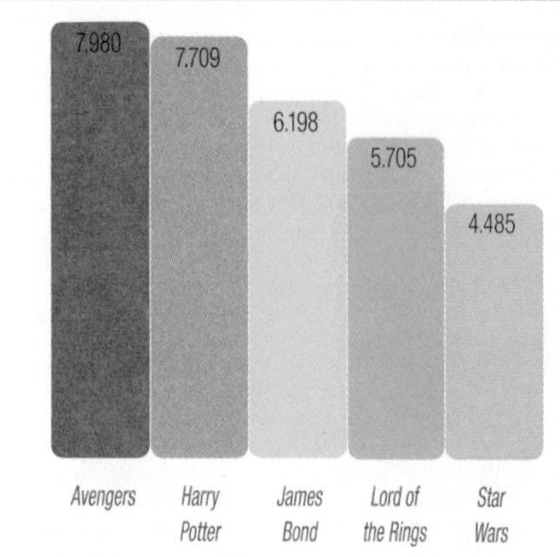
most successful movie franchises
total worldwide gross, in billions of US dollars*
7.980
7.709
6.198
5.705
4.485
Avengers
Harry Potter
James Bond
Lord of the Rings
Star Wars
*As of May 2015

top-earning actor

Robert Downey Jr.

Robert Downey Jr. raked in $75 million in 2014, mostly due to the great success of *Iron Man 3*. In the movie, Downey plays Tony Stark, also known as the superhero Iron Man. It was released in May 2013 and earned $1.21 billion worldwide. The prequel, *Marvel's The Avengers*, was released a year earlier and brought in $1.5 billion around the globe. In 2015, Downey resumed his role in *Avengers: Age of Ultron* and will be one of the highest-paid actors on the set since he renegotiated his deal with Marvel. Downey also has another successful movie franchise—*Sherlock Holmes*. Between 2009 and 2011, the actor completed two of these films, which earned a combined total of $1 billion worldwide.

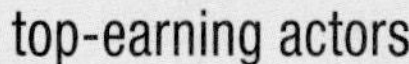
top-earning actors

2014 earnings, in millions of US dollars

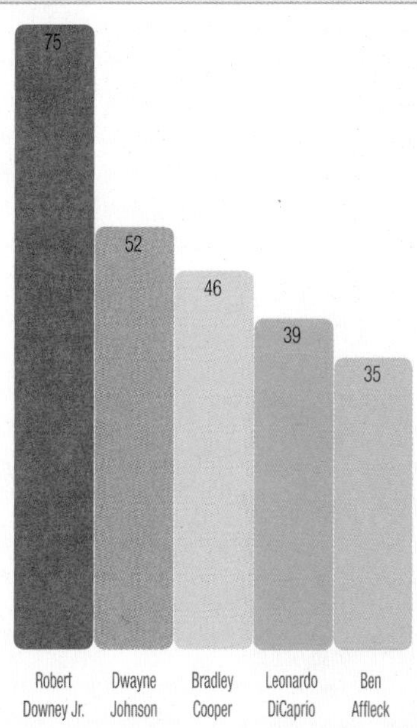
75
52
46
39
35
Robert Downey Jr.
Dwayne Johnson
Bradley Cooper
Leonardo DiCaprio
Ben Affleck

top-earning actress

Sandra Bullock

Blockbuster actress Sandra Bullock earned $51 million in 2014. Much of her success was due to her role as Dr. Ryan Stone in the thriller *Gravity*. In the film, Bullock portrays a medical engineer on her first space mission. *Gravity* grossed more than $716 million worldwide at the box office and won seven Oscars. During her career, Bullock has appeared in more than 35 films, which combined have earned more than $3.84 billion worldwide. Most recently, Bullock provided the voice for Scarlett Overkill in *Minions*, the latest film in the Despicable Me franchise, which was released July 2015.

top-earning actresses

2014 earnings, in millions of US dollars

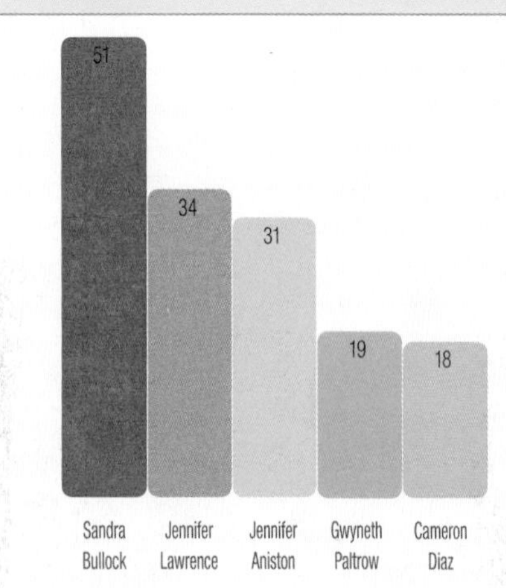
51
34
31
19
18
Sandra Bullock
Jennifer Lawrence
Jennifer Aniston
Gwyneth Paltrow
Cameron Diaz

actor with the highest box office gross in 2014

Jennifer Lawrence

Jennifer Lawrence commanded the box office in 2014, with her films bringing in $1.4 billion. Lawrence starred in two blockbusters released in 2014—*The Hunger Games: Mockingjay - Part 1* and *X-Men: Days of Future Past*. In *Mockingjay*, Lawrence reprised her role as Katniss Everdeen in the first part of the Hunger Games trilogy's two-part finale. It earned $751.4 million internationally. In the seventh installment of the X-Men series, Lawrence portrayed Mystique, a role she first took on in 2011. It brought in $748.1 million worldwide.

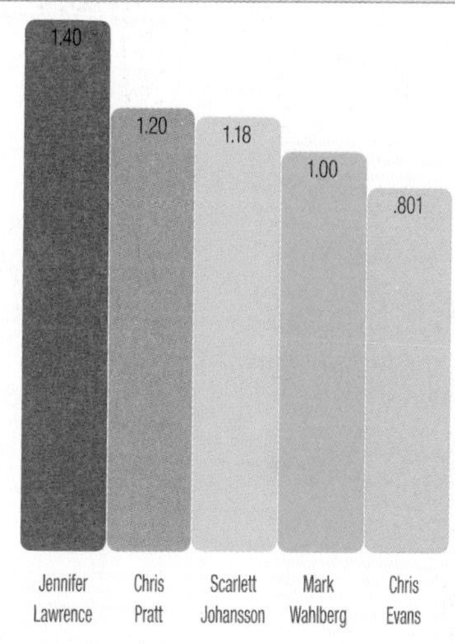

actors with the highest box office gross in 2014
combined box office gross from 2014, in billions of US dollars
1.40
1.20
1.18
1.00
.801
Jennifer Lawrence
Chris Pratt
Scarlett Johansson
Mark Wahlberg
Chris Evans

top-grossing movie of 2014

Transformers: Age of Extinction

Transformers: Age of Extinction ruled the international box office in 2014, earning more than $1.10 billion. The movie pulled in $245.4 million in the US, and another $835.7 million worldwide. The fourth installment of the Transformers franchise tells what happen as people struggle to recover after the Battle of Chicago that almost destroyed the world. Some of the stars that headlined this summer blockbuster include Mark Wahlberg as Cade Yeager, Stanley Tucci as Joshua Joyce, and Kelsey Grammer as Harold Attinger. Michael Bay directed the film, and Steven Spielberg was the executive director.

top-grossing movies of 2014

worldwide gross,
in millions and billions of US dollars

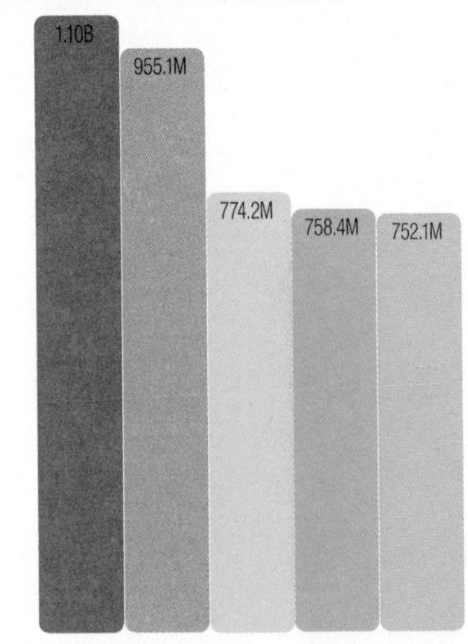
1.10B
955.1M
774.2M
758.4M
752.1M
Transformers: Age of Extinction
The Hobbit: The Battle of the Five Armies
Guardians of the Galaxy
Maleficent
The Hunger Games: Mockingjay - Part 1

movie that earned the most in a single day

Harry Potter and the Deathly Hallows: Part 2

On July 15, 2011, fans rushed to theaters to see *Harry Potter and the Deathly Hallows: Part 2*, spending $91 million in a single day. It was released in 4,375 theaters and earned an average of $20,816 per location. The final film in the wizard franchise went on to earn $1.3 billion worldwide—making it the fourth-highest-grossing movie of all time. It also holds the film record for earning $150 million in the shortest amount of time. *Harry Potter and the Deathly Hallows: Part 2* was nominated for three Academy Awards: Art Direction, Visual Effects, and Makeup.

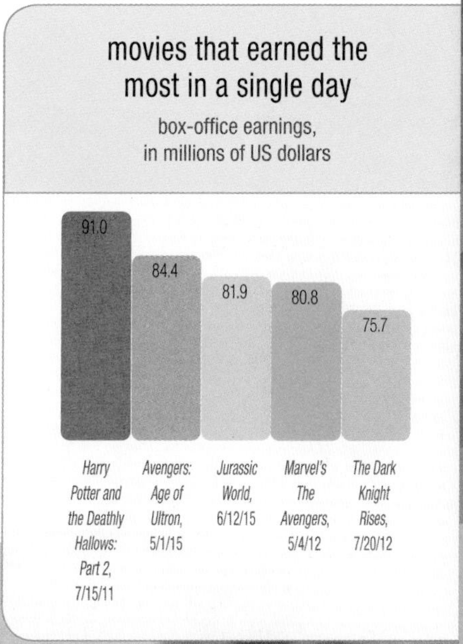

movies that earned the most in a single day

box-office earnings, in millions of US dollars

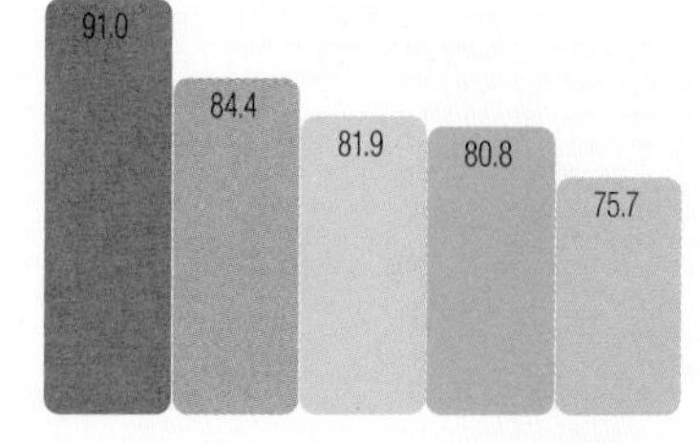
91.0
84.4
81.9
80.8
75.7
Harry Potter and the Deathly Hallows: Part 2, 7/15/11
Avengers: Age of Ultron, 5/1/15
Jurassic World, 6/12/15
Marvel's The Avengers, 5/4/12
The Dark Knight Rises, 7/20/12

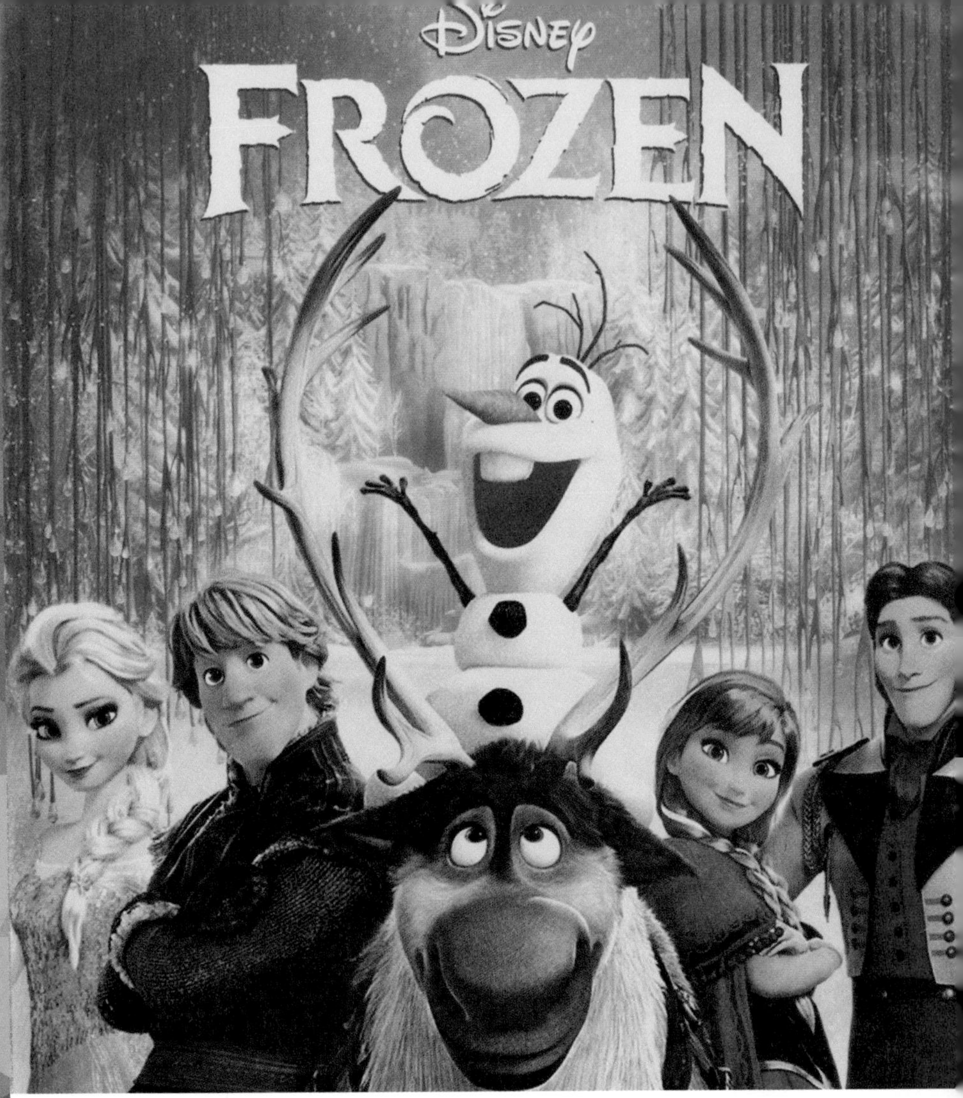

top-selling DVD of 2014

Frozen

Disney's *Frozen* continued its success in the DVD market, selling more than 11 million copies in 2014. That's more than the next three top-selling DVDs combined. *Frozen* DVD sales totaled $185.5 million. The movie has made more than $1.27 billion internationally and is the fifth highest-grossing movie ever. *Frozen* stars Kristen Bell as Anna, Idina Menzel as Elsa, and Jonathan Groff as Kristoff. The movie was released in November 2013.

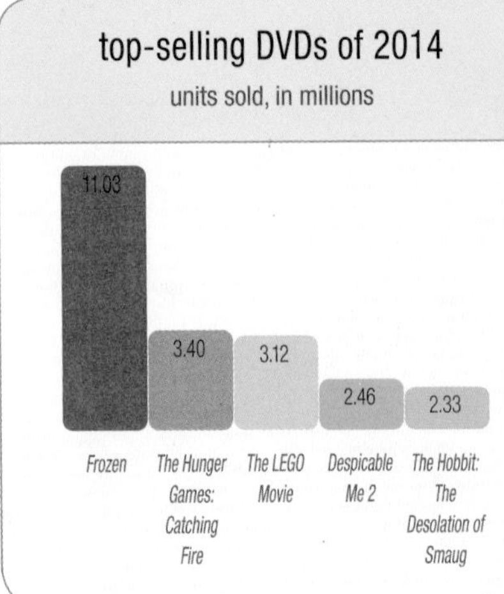
top-selling DVDs of 2014
units sold, in millions
11.03
3.40
3.12
2.46
2.33
Frozen
The Hunger Games: Catching Fire
The LEGO Movie
Despicable Me 2
The Hobbit: The Desolation of Smaug

United States' bestselling recording group

The Beatles

The Beatles have sold 178 million copies of their albums in the United States since their first official recording session in September 1962. In the two years that followed, they had 26 Top 40 singles. John Lennon, Paul McCartney, George Harrison, and Ringo Starr made up the "Fab Four," as the Beatles were known. Together they recorded many albums that are now considered rock masterpieces, such as *Rubber Soul, Sgt. Pepper's Lonely Hearts Club Band,* and *The Beatles* (The White Album). The group broke up in 1969. In 2001, however, their newly released greatest hits album—*The Beatles 1*—reached the top of the charts. One of their best-known songs—"Yesterday"—is the most-recorded song in history, with about 2,500 different artists recording their own versions.

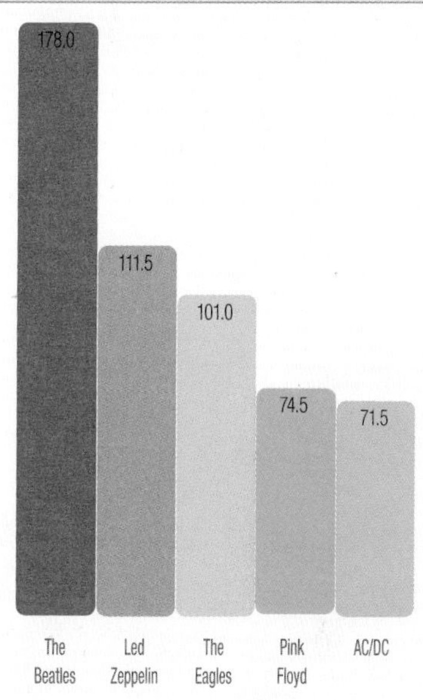
United States' bestselling recording groups
albums sold, in millions
178.0
111.5
101.0
74.5
71.5
The Beatles
Led Zeppelin
The Eagles
Pink Floyd
AC/DC

MUSIC

top-earning deceased celebrity

Michael Jackson

Even though Michael Jackson passed away in June 2009, he's still earning a ton of cash. In fact, in the 12 months following his death, he sold 35 million albums worldwide. In 2014, Xscape—an album of Jackson's previously unreleased work—was released and reached number 2 on the charts. He also made an appearance on stage at the Billboard Music Awards that year, in hologram form. In 2013, Cirque du Soleil created a show called *Michael Jackson: One* in Las Vegas. During his impressive career, Jackson made 10 solo albums, including *Thriller*—the bestselling album of all time. He also won 13 Grammy Awards and 26 American Music Awards.

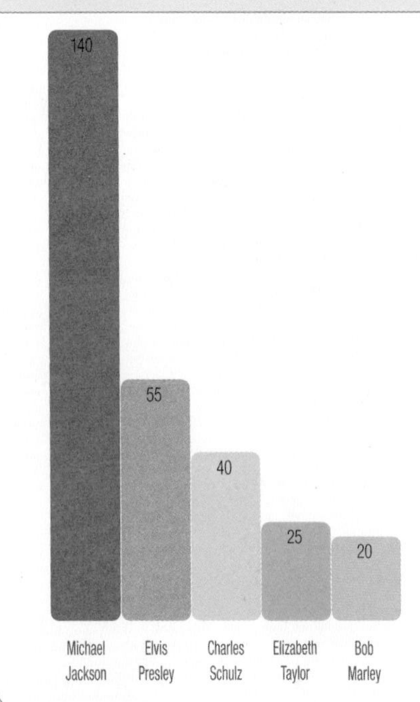
top-earning deceased celebrities
earnings in 2014, in millions of US dollars
140
55
40
25
20
Michael Jackson
Elvis Presley
Charles Schulz
Elizabeth Taylor
Bob Marley

top-earning country artist

Toby Keith

During 2014, country superstar Toby Keith earned $65 million, mostly due to his entrepreneurial ventures and a hit record in 2013. In October 2013, Keith released his seventeenth studio album called *Drinks After Work*. The following year, he released a song off his upcoming album entitled *35 MPH Town*. The song, called "Drunk Americans," sold 15,000 downloads in its first week. In April 2015, Keith released the second song off the album, also called "35 MPH Town." Keith hit the road with the *Hammer Down Under Tour 2014* with Kellie Pickler and the Eli Young Band.

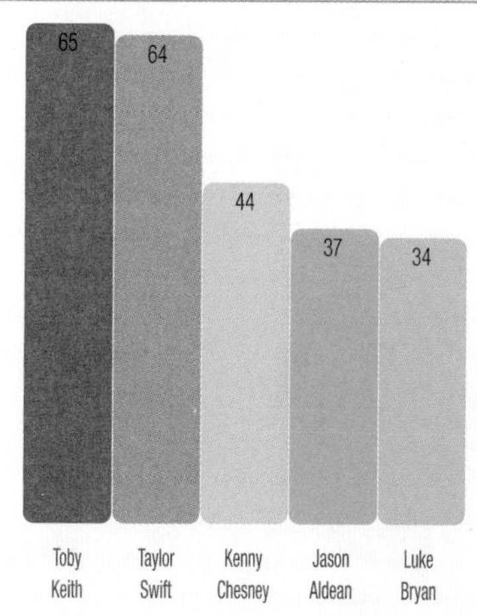
top-earning country artists
earnings in 2014, in millions of US dollars
65
64
44
37
34
Toby Keith
Taylor Swift
Kenny Chesney
Jason Aldean
Luke Bryan

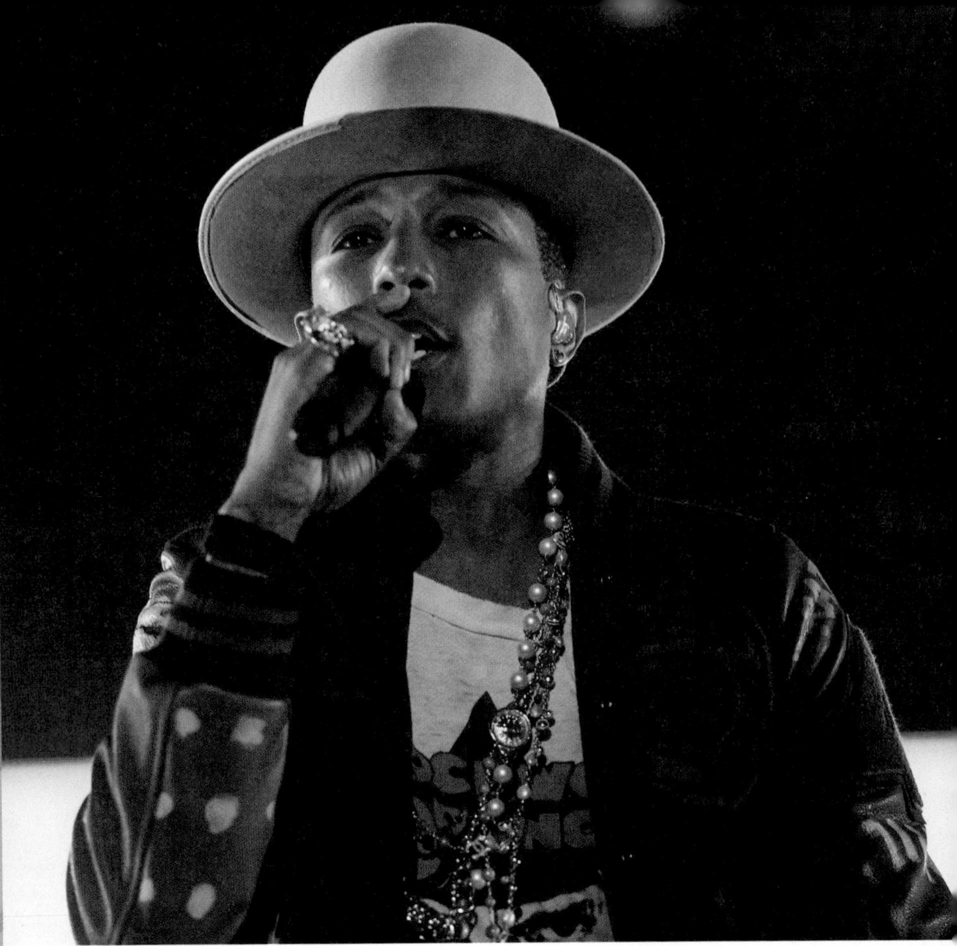

most downloaded song of 2014

"Happy"

Pharrell Williams's bouncy smash hit "Happy" was by far the most downloaded song of 2014 with 6.45 million purchases. Williams wrote the song for the 2013 movie *Despicable Me 2*, and this is only the fourth time in history that a movie theme became the year's best seller. "Happy" was also the lead single on Williams's second album, *Girl*. The song reached number one on the charts in the US, the UK, Canada, and twenty-one other countries. It also picked up two Grammy Awards in 2015 for Best Pop Solo Performance and Best Music Video.

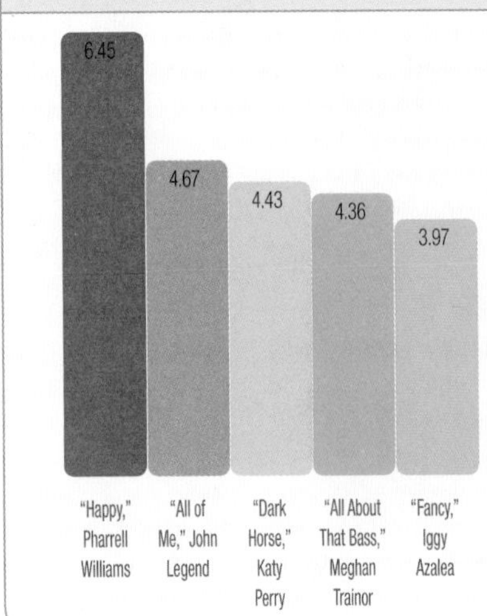
most downloaded songs of 2014
copies downloaded, in millions
6.45
4.67
4.43
4.36
3.97
"Happy," Pharrell Williams
"All of Me," John Legend
"Dark Horse," Katy Perry
"All About That Bass," Meghan Trainor
"Fancy," Iggy Azalea

most-streamed music video of 2014

"All About That Bass"

Meghan Trainor's song "All About That Bass" was the most on-demand streamed video in 2014 with 188.7 million streams. This was Trainor's debut song, and it came off her studio album *Title*. The track's catchy doo-wop style is about positive body image and inner beauty. The song spent eight consecutive weeks at number one on the Billboard Hot 100 and reached number one in fifty-eight other countries. The song was also nominated for two Grammy Awards, including Song of the Year and Record of the Year.

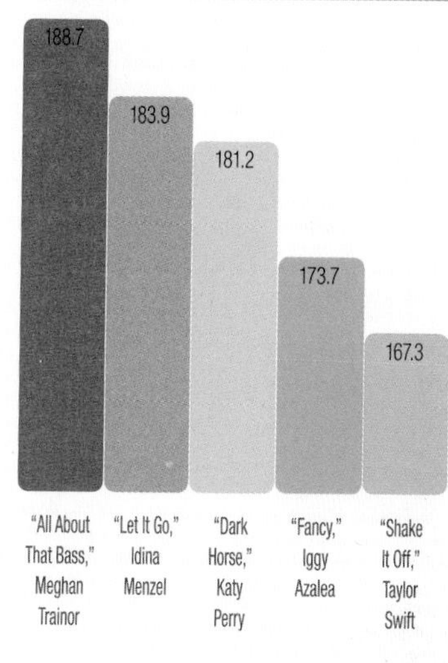
most-streamed music videos of 2014
on-demand video streams, in millions
188.7
183.9
181.2
173.7
167.3
"All About That Bass," Meghan Trainor
"Let It Go," Idina Menzel
"Dark Horse," Katy Perry
"Fancy," Iggy Azalea
"Shake It Off," Taylor Swift

top-selling digital album of all time

21

Adele's *21* is the bestselling digital album of all time, with a total of 3 million downloads. The album debuted at number one on the Billboard 200 and stayed in the top five for 39 consecutive weeks. Some of the album's most-successful songs include "Rolling in the Deep," "Someone Like You," "Set Fire to the Rain," and "Rumour Has It." In 2012, Adele won seven Grammy Awards for *21*, including Album of the Year and Best Pop Vocal Album. It also won the BRIT Award for British Album of the Year. This was the singer's second studio album, and it was released in January 2011.

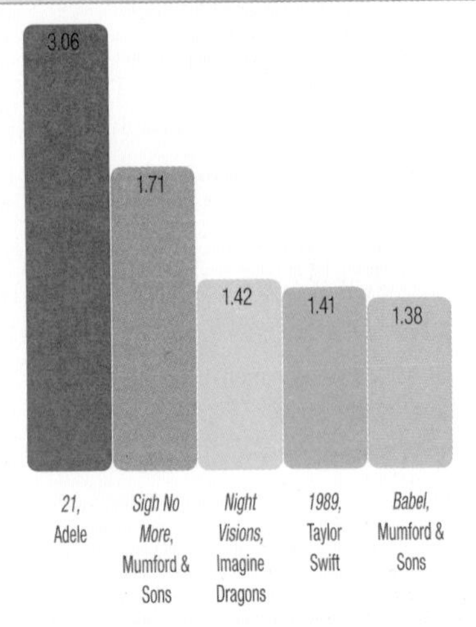
top-selling digital albums of all time
units downloaded, in millions
3.06
1.71
1.42
1.41
1.38
21, Adele
Sigh No More, Mumford & Sons
Night Visions, Imagine Dragons
1989, Taylor Swift
Babel, Mumford & Sons

artist with the most digital singles

Taylor Swift

Taylor Swift is the queen of digital singles, having sold more than 84 million songs since she hit it big in 2006. Since that time, Swift has released five albums: *Taylor Swift* (2006), *Fearless* (2008), *Speak Now* (2010), *Red* (2012), and *1989* (2014). Some of her most popular tracks include "I Knew You Were Trouble," "Love Story," "Shake It Off," and "22." During her impressive career, Swift has won seven Grammy Awards and is the youngest recipient of Billboard's Woman of the Year award.

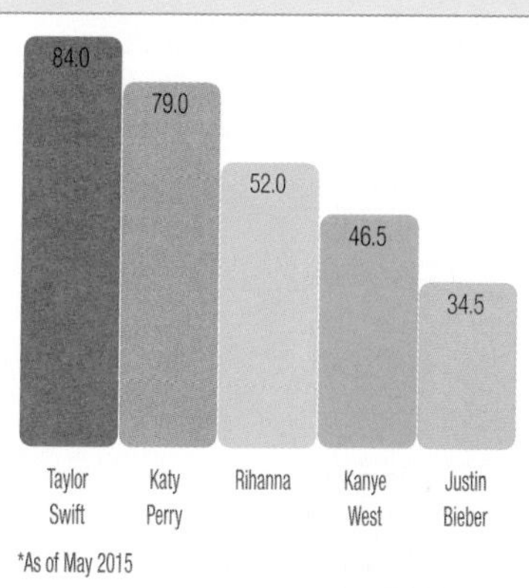
artists with the most digital singles
units downloaded, in millions*
84.0
79.0
52.0
46.5
34.5
Taylor Swift
Katy Perry
Rihanna
Kanye West
Justin Bieber
*As of May 2015

bestselling movie soundtrack

The Bodyguard

The soundtrack of *The Bodyguard* has sold more than 17 million copies since it was released in November 1992. The movie starred Kevin Costner as a former secret service agent in charge of a pop singer, played by Whitney Houston. Houston produced the soundtrack, along with Clive Davis, and it features three of Houston's biggest hits—"I Will Always Love You," "I Have Nothing," and "I'm Every Woman." The album picked up a Grammy for Album of the Year and reached number one on music charts worldwide, including Australia, Canada, France, Germany, and Japan.

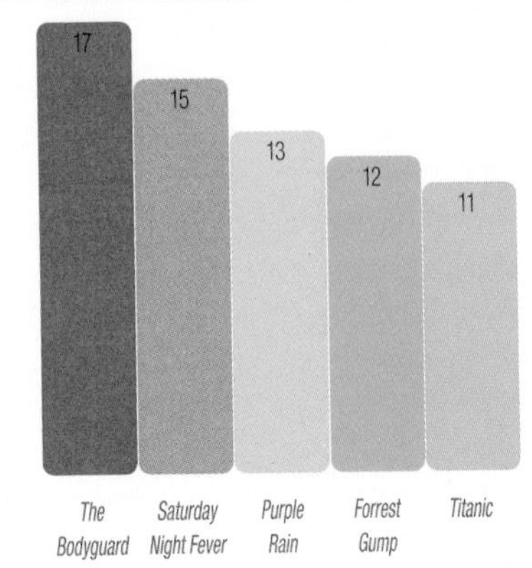
bestselling movie soundtracks
units sold, in millions
17
15
13
12
11
The Bodyguard
Saturday Night Fever
Purple Rain
Forrest Gump
Titanic

bestselling album of 2014

1989

Taylor Swift's *1989* beat out the competition in 2014 and sold more than 3.66 million copies in the United States. About 2.25 million of those were CDs, and the other 1.41 million were digital albums. *1989* was Swift's fifth studio album and debuted at number one on the Billboard 200 chart. Some hit songs from the album include "Shake It Off," "Blank Space," and "Style." *Rolling Stone* magazine ranked it at number ten on their list of best albums of 2014, and *Time* ranked it at number four on their best albums of 2014 list.

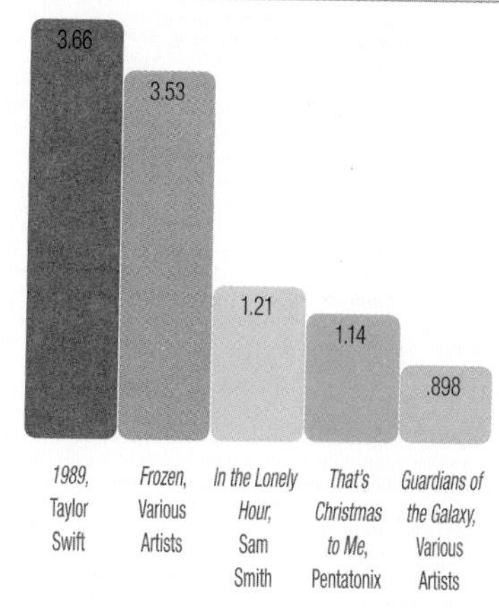
bestselling albums of 2014
albums sold, in millions
3.66
3.53
1.21
1.14
.898
1989, Taylor Swift
Frozen, Various Artists
In the Lonely Hour, Sam Smith
That's Christmas to Me, Pentatonix
Guardians of the Galaxy, Various Artists

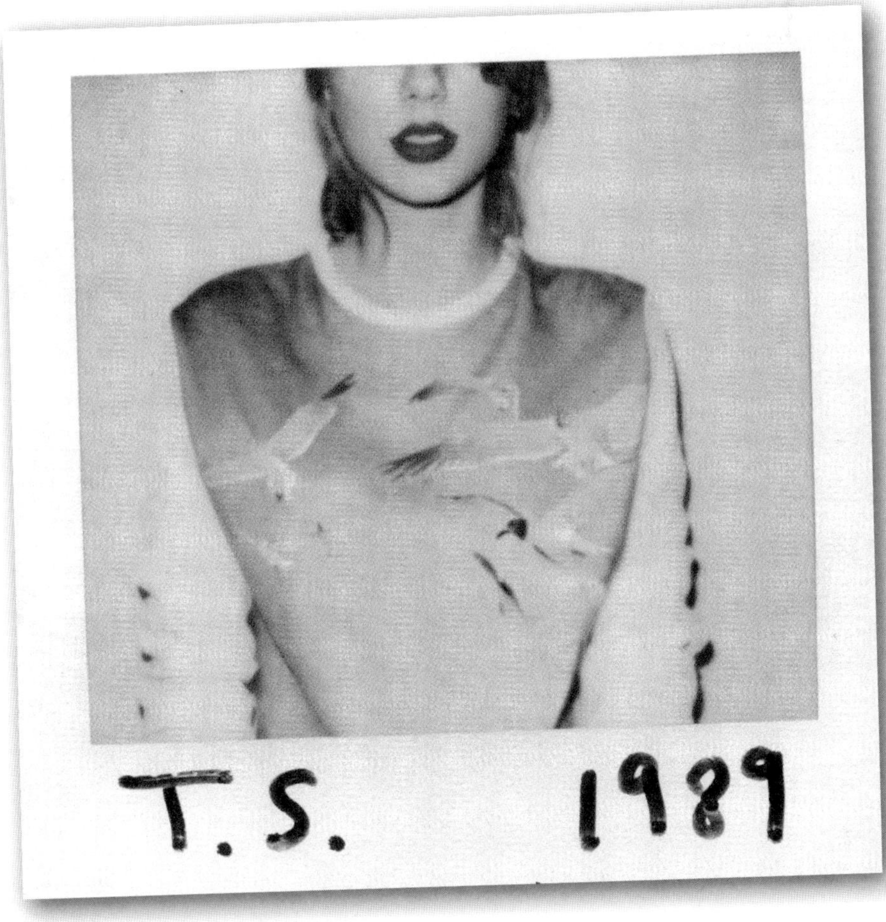

most-watched music video ever on YouTube

"Gangnam Style"

YouTube ranked the most-watched music video of all time, and PSY's "Gangnam Style" came in at number one. The South Korean singer achieved international fame with his hit, which debuted June 2012, and since then has entertained more than 2.3 billion YouTube viewers with his signature dance moves. The video was the first ever to surpass 2,147,483,647 views, the site's original maximum views, causing YouTube to rebuild its view counter in 2014. Now a video can be viewed up to 9,223,372,036,854,775,808 times!

most-watched music videos ever on YouTube

views in billions*

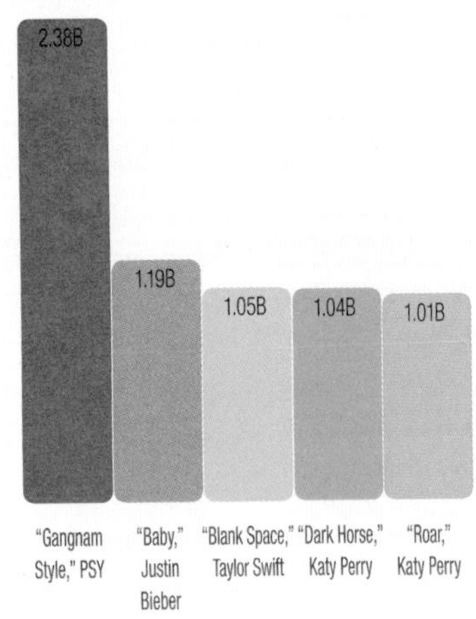
2.38B
1.19B
1.05B
1.04B
1.01B
"Gangnam Style," PSY
"Baby," Justin Bieber
"Blank Space," Taylor Swift
"Dark Horse," Katy Perry
"Roar," Katy Perry

*As of July, 2015

top-earning male singer

Dr. Dre

Dr. Dre earned more than $620 million in 2014—more than the other top four male singers combined. In addition to being a rapper, Dr. Dre is also a record producer and an entrepreneur. He's the CEO of Aftermath Entertainment, a label that counts Eminem and Kendrick Lamar as two of its artists. He also founded Beats Electronics—an audio products company that Apple purchased in 2014 for $3 billion. This purchase price also includes Beats Music—a subscription streaming music service.

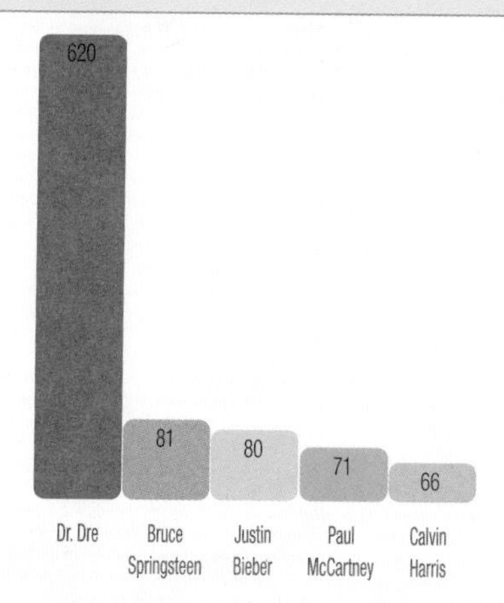
top-earning male singers
earnings in 2014, in millions of US dollars
620
81
80
71
66
Dr. Dre
Bruce Springsteen
Justin Bieber
Paul McCartney
Calvin Harris

top-earning female singer

Beyoncé

Beyoncé, also known as Queen B, earned some serious cash in 2014, bringing in $115 million. The main source of income for the pop star was her huge *On the Run* tour with husband, Jay-Z. They played twenty-one shows and took in about $2.4 million per stop. She also released her fifth studio album, entitled *Beyoncé*, on iTunes in December 2013, which debuted at number one on the Billboard 200 chart. This was her fifth consecutive number one album in the United States. It features the hits "Drunk in Love" and "Pretty Hurts."

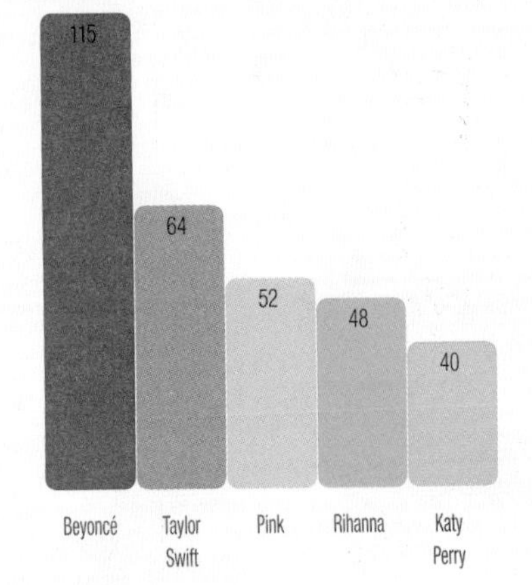
top-earning female singers
earnings in 2014, in millions of US dollars
115
64
52
48
40
Beyoncé
Taylor Swift
Pink
Rihanna
Katy Perry

most played song on radio stations of 2014

"All of Me"

John Legend's "All of Me" ruled the radio in 2014, registering approximately 816,000 plays during the year. The song, which was part of Legend's fourth studio album, *Love in the Future*, was released in August 2013. "All of Me" became Legend's first number one single in May 2014 when it peaked on the Billboard Hot 100 chart. It also topped the charts in seven other countries. He performed the song at the 56th Grammy Awards in 2014.

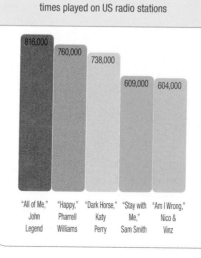

most played songs of 2014

times played on US radio stations

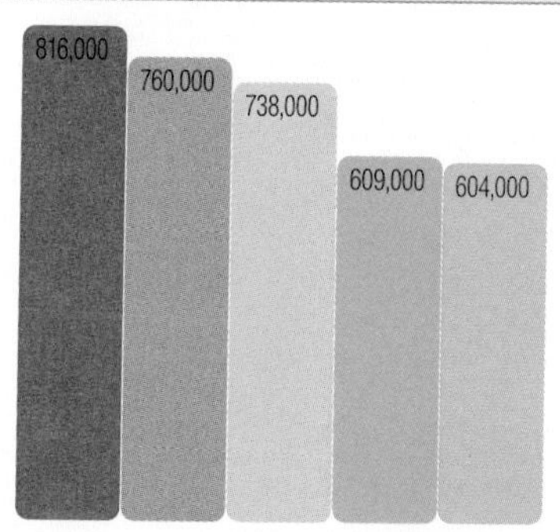
816,000
760,000
738,000
609,000
604,000
"All of Me," John Legend
"Happy," Pharrell Williams
"Dark Horse," Katy Perry
"Stay with Me," Sam Smith
"Am I Wrong," Nico & Vinz

musician with the most MTV Video Music Awards

Madonna

Madonna has won 20 MTV Video Music Awards since the ceremony was first held in 1984. She has won four Cinematography awards, three Female Video awards, three Directing awards, two Editing awards, and two Art Direction awards. She also picked up single awards for Video of the Year, Choreography, Special Effects, and Long Form Video, as well as a Viewer's Choice and a Video Vanguard Award. Madonna's award-winning videos include "Papa Don't Preach," "Like a Prayer," "Express Yourself," "Vogue," "Rain," "Take a Bow," "Ray of Light," and "Beautiful Stranger."

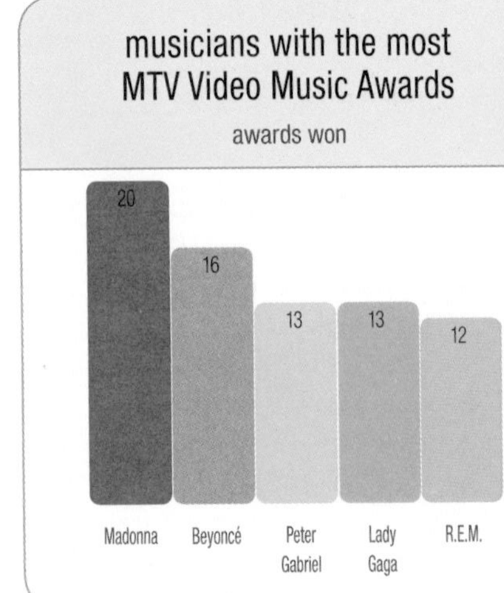
musicians with the most
MTV Video Music Awards
awards won
20
16
13
13
12
Madonna
Beyoncé
Peter Gabriel
Lady Gaga
R.E.M.

top-earning tour of 2014

One Direction

One Direction dominated the 2014 tour scene, bringing in more than $282 million. The *Where We Are* tour covered sixty-nine stops between April and October 2014, and about 3.4 million tickets were sold. The tour promoted the band's third album, *Midnight Memories*. One Direction's members include Niall Horan, Liam Payne, Harry Styles, and Louis Tomlinson. The English/Irish band came together in 2010 after each auditioned for *The X Factor*. In April 2015, Zayn Malik shocked fans and left the band to pursue other interests.

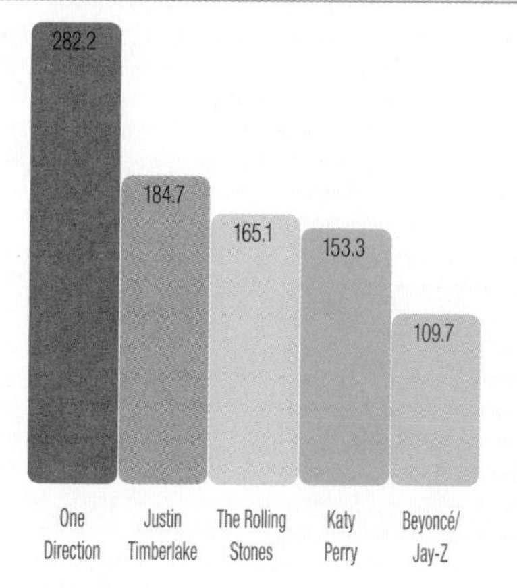
top-earning tours of 2014
earnings, in millions of US dollars
282.2
184.7
165.1
153.3
109.7
One Direction
Justin Timberlake
The Rolling Stones
Katy Perry
Beyoncé/ Jay-Z

act with the most Country Music Awards

George Strait

George Strait has won a whopping 23 Country Music Awards and has been nicknamed the "King of Country" for all of his accomplishments in the business. He won his first CMA in 1985 and his most recent in 2013. In addition to his many awards, Strait holds the record for the most number one hits on the Billboard Hot Country Songs with 44. He also has 38 hit albums, including 13 multiplatinum and 33 platinum records. He was inducted into the Country Music Hall of Fame in 2006.

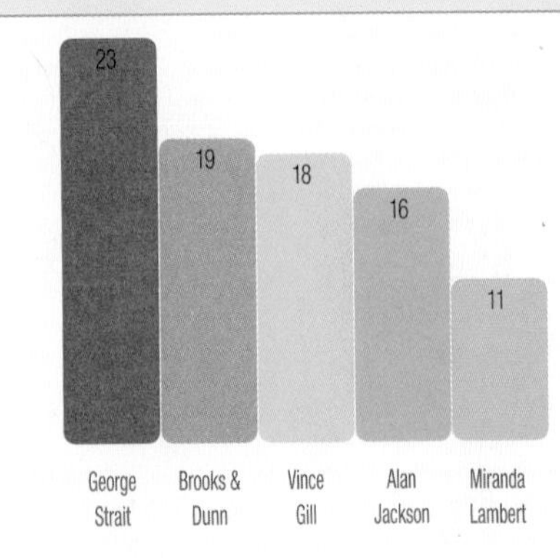
acts with the most
Country Music Awards
awards won
23
19
18
16
11
George Strait
Brooks & Dunn
Vince Gill
Alan Jackson
Miranda Lambert

longest-running Broadway show

The Phantom of the Opera

The Phantom of the Opera has been performed well over 11,000 times since it opened in January 1988. The show tells the story of a disfigured musical genius who terrorizes the performers of the Paris Opera House. More than 130 million people have seen a performance in 145 cities and 27 countries. The show won seven Tony Awards in 1988, including Best Musical. The musical drama is performed at the Majestic Theatre.

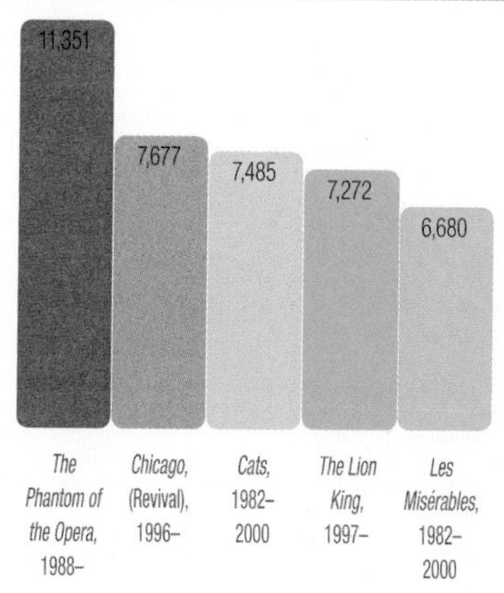
longest-running
Broadway shows
total performances*
11,351
7,677
7,485
7,272
6,680
The Phantom of the Opera, 1988–
Chicago, (Revival), 1996–
Cats, 1982–2000
The Lion King, 1997–
Les Misérables, 1982–2000
*As of May 1, 2015

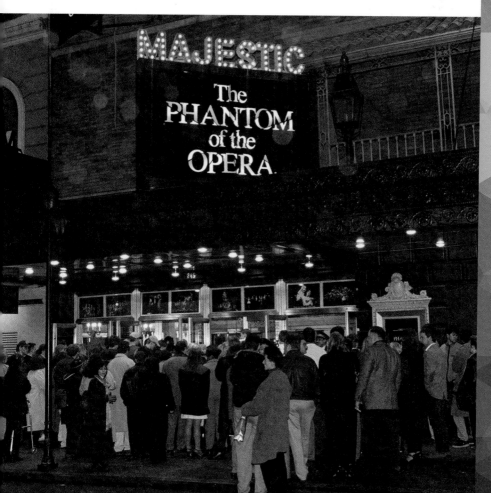

musical with the most Tony Awards

The Producers

In March 2001, *The Producers* took home 12 of its record-breaking 15 Tony Award nominations. The Broadway smash won awards for Best Musical, Original Score, Book, Direction of a Musical, Choreography, Orchestration, Scenic Design, Costume Design, Lighting Design, Actor in a Musical, Featured Actor in a Musical, and Actress in a Musical. *The Producers*, which originally starred Nathan Lane and Matthew Broderick, is a stage adaptation of Mel Brooks's 1968 movie of the same name. Brooks wrote the lyrics and music for the 16 new songs featured in the stage version.

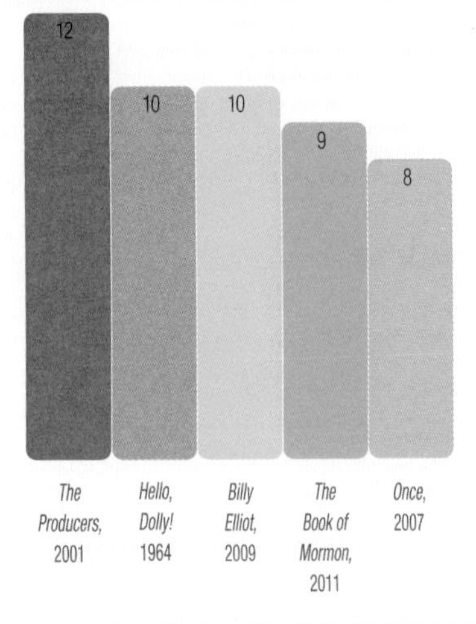
musicals with the most Tony Awards
awards won
12
10
10
9
8
The Producers, 2001
Hello, Dolly! 1964
Billy Elliot, 2009
The Book of Mormon, 2011
Once, 2007

NATURE RECORDS

- EPIC FAILS
- NATURAL FORMATIONS
- ANIMALS
- ENVIRONMENT
- WEATHER
- PLANTS
- DISASTERS

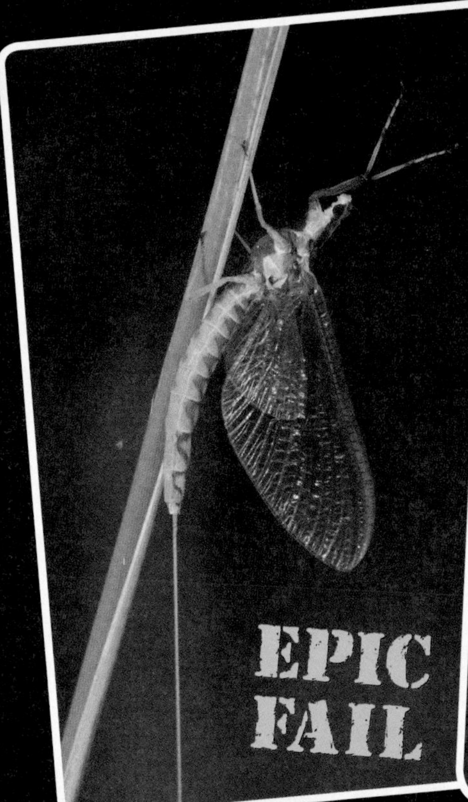

EPIC FAIL

SHORTEST-LIVED INSECT

With its adult life ranging from 1 to 48 hours, the mayfly is one of the shortest-lived insects on Earth. There are about 2,500 different species of these aquatic insects, and some females can produce approximately 10,000 eggs at one time. Since members of a mayfly population often reach the adult stage at once, it is common to see mayflies flying in large groups, clogging gutters or covering all surfaces in an area.

EPIC FAIL

LONGEST MAMMAL PREGNANCY

African elephant mothers carry their babies for a record 22 months. That's about 660 days, or almost 2.5 times as long as a normal human pregnancy. Elephant babies weigh about 200 pounds (91 kg) at birth, and measure about 3 feet (1 m) tall. Female adult elephants live in small herds with their young.

SLOWEST-MOVING MAMMAL

The top speed of a three-toed sloth is just 0.15 miles per hour (0.24 km/hr). In fact, these treetop-dwelling mammals are so slow, algae actually grows on them! Each day, sloths only move about 125 feet (38 m) and spend about 15 to 20 hours sleeping.

EPIC
FAIL

EPIC
FAIL

LEAST POPULAR DOG BREED

The English foxhound is the least popular dog breed in North America, according to the American Kennel Association. These hounds were originally bred in the early 1700s to hunt foxes, but since the sport isn't very popular these days, the dogs have become fairly rare.

EPIC
FAIL

MOST POISONOUS FISH

The stonefish is the most poisonous fish in the sea, and its venom can kill a human in just two hours. Sitting on the bottom of the ocean, the stonefish is so well camouflaged that it is easily stepped on. It has thirteen spikes on its back that pierce the skin and transfer the venom into its victim. Stonefish are found in the Red Sea and the Indian and Pacific Oceans.

ILLEGALLY TRADED MAMMAL

Pangolins—cat-sized mammals that are covered in scales—are coveted in countries such as China for their blood, meat, and scales. About 10,000 are known to be illegally trafficked each year, but only about 10% of incidents are reported. Native to Asia and sub-Saharan Africa, a pangolin eats small insects but has no teeth for chewing. It swallows its meal whole, and the insects are ground up in the animal's stomach by pebbles and sand that are ingested along with the bugs.

EPIC
FAIL

EPIC
FAIL

HIBERNATING BIRDS

Common poorwills are the only birds that need to hibernate. During bad weather, these little birds nestle under loose rock or rotten wood and sleep for up to 5 months—that's 150 days at a time! Poorwills only need about 93% of their normal energy at this time. Once out of hibernation, they need about 7 hours to restore their normal body temperature.

EPIC FAIL

BAD ANIMAL EYESIGHT

A rhinoceros cannot clearly see objects that are more than 15 feet (4.5 m) away. In fact, these giant mammals often charge rocks because they mistake them for predators. However, rhinos do have excellent hearing and a strong sense of smell to help make up for their poor eyesight.

MOST DESTRUCTIVE INSECT

Desert locusts are the most destructive insects, capable of eating their own weight in vegetation each day. These creatures, which are found in Africa, the Middle East, and India, travel in large swarms containing millions of locusts. Such a swarm can consume 211,000 tons of food daily.

EPIC FAIL

EPIC FAIL

SMALLEST LAKE

Benxi Lake, in the Liaoning province of China, measures just 161 square feet (15 sq m), making it the smallest lake in the world. In comparison, an Olympic-sized swimming pool measures about 13,400 square feet (1,245 sq m). This natural lake is located within a cave, and though small is considered a place of beauty.

MOST POLLUTED RIVER

Citarum River in Indonesia has so much trash in it, you can't actually see the water's surface. About 5 million people live at the river's basin, and the Citarum is used for agriculture irrigation, water supply, fishing, and sewage. In addition to the trash, about 2,000 factories and industries dump lead, mercury, arsenic, and other toxins into the 186-mile (300-km) river.

EPIC FAIL

U.S. STATE WITH THE MOST EARTHQUAKES

Alaska leads the United States in earthquakes, accounting for more than 50% of the country's total. In fact, during a 30-year period, Alaskans felt about 12,000 rumbles rating a 3.5 magnitude or greater. The largest earthquake in Alaska occurred in 1964 and had a magnitude of 9.2.

EPIC FAIL

PIONEER
LOANS
BAR
D&D
CAFE
TV SHOW
ARCADE
AMUSEMENTS
PIONEER LOAN CO
LOANS
LOANS

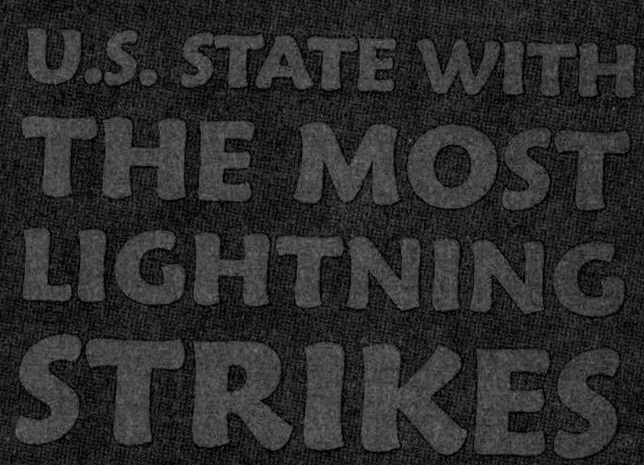

U.S. STATE WITH THE MOST LIGHTNING STRIKES

Floridians see more than 1.41 million lightning strikes each year, with an average of 24.7 per square mile. The state's location between the Gulf of Mexico and the Atlantic Ocean is a prime spot for thunderstorms to blow in from the sea. Central Florida experiences about 90 days with thunderstorms each year.

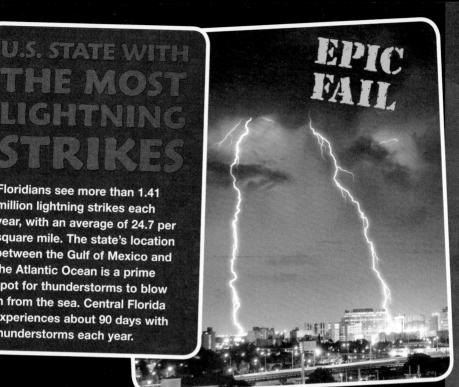

EPIC
FAIL

UGLIEST DOG

The Chinese Crested has won the World's Ugliest Dog Contest a record seven times since the competition began in 2000! The breed has two varieties—hairless and powderpuff. Both are small dogs with friendly, social personalities. However, the breed tends to lose teeth easily, which adds to their unique appearance.

EPIC FAIL

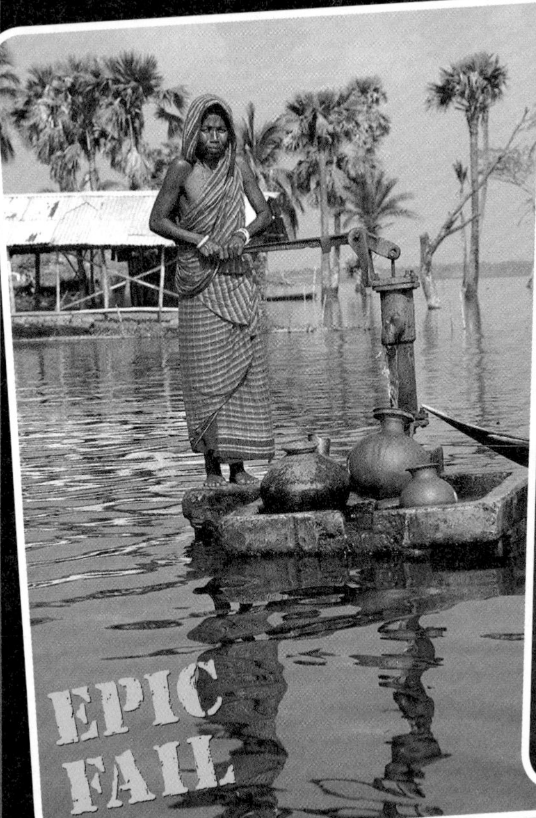
EPIC
FAIL

MOST FLOODED AREA

India faces the greatest risk of river flooding in the world, with about 4.84 million citizens affected by high waters each year. The country has 15 major rivers that are very susceptible to flash floods after torrential rain. The three areas most likely to flood in India include the Ganges basin, the Brahmaputra and Barak basins, and the Deccan River basin.

MOST HURRICANES

The spot in the world most likely to get hit with a hurricane is Cape Hatteras, North Carolina. The town experiences a hurricane every 1.36 years. The most recent hurricane to affect the area came in July 2014, when Hurricane Arthur hit with 100-mile-per-hour (161-kph) winds that knocked out power to about 41,000 people.

EPIC
FAIL

SULFUR SKUNK SPRAY

A skunk's spray doesn't just stink, it's strong enough to choke an enemy and cause temporary blindness. The spray contains sulfur, which is the same chemical in onions that can cause tears. A skunk can accurately hit targets 12 feet (3.6 m) away and can shoot its stinky spray six times with little hesitation.

EPIC FAIL

SHORT MAMMAL LIFESPAN

The shrew has a life expectancy of approximately 1 year, giving it one of the shortest mammal lifespans. One reason is because it has so many predators, including cats, weasels, foxes, stoats, and birds of prey. Even so, a female shrew still usually manages to have 3–4 litters of 5–7 young in her short life.

EPIC FAIL

EPIC FAIL

BIGGEST FLOATING GARBAGE DUMP

The world's largest collection of trash is located in the North Pacific Ocean. The Great Pacific Garbage Patch is located in the waters between California and Japan. Garbage makes its way from the coasts of North America and Asia into a slow-moving current that deposits debris in the North Pacific. Most of the millions of pounds of garbage is plastic, but don't expect to see it on a satellite image. Much of the plastic isn't visible to the naked eye. Plastic debris can be deadly to marine life such as sea turtles and seals. The tiny bits of plastic can also block the sun and prevent algae and plankton from growing.

WORST SHORT-TERM MEMORY

Bees have one of the worst short-term memories in the animal kingdom and are unable to recall things after 2.4 seconds. And, similar to humans, bees can sometimes merge two past memories to create an incorrect new one. On average, the short-term memory span of an animal is 27 seconds.

EPIC FAIL

EPIC
FAIL

STINKIEST FLOWER

Native to Indonesia, the corpse flower smells like rotting flesh when it blooms. Luckily, the flower lasts less than a day, and the plant may not even bloom for the first time until it is about 10 years old. The corpse flower's terrible odor attracts flies that pollinate the plant.

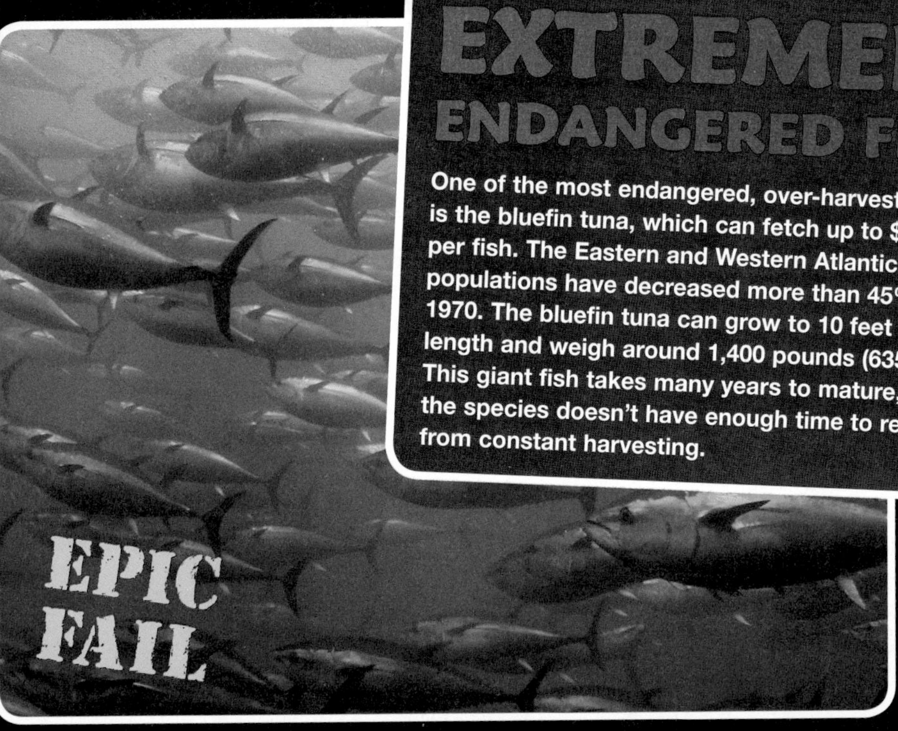
EPIC
FAIL

EXTREMELY ENDANGERED FISH

One of the most endangered, over-harvested fish is the bluefin tuna, which can fetch up to $100,000 per fish. The Eastern and Western Atlantic populations have decreased more than 45% since 1970. The bluefin tuna can grow to 10 feet (3 m) in length and weigh around 1,400 pounds (635 kg). This giant fish takes many years to mature, and the species doesn't have enough time to recover from constant harvesting.

EPIC FAIL

LONGEST HIBERNATING MAMMAL

Belding's ground squirrels hibernate between 7 and 9 months a year. After spending the summer feeding in order to double their weight, males begin hibernation in August, and females begin a month later. They do not store food in their burrows, so they must live on stored body fat until they emerge the following spring.

DANGEROUS WEED

The giant hogweed can top out at about 15 feet (4.5 m). If you see one, don't touch! The fast-growing plant's large, umbrella-like flowers contain a powerful sap that can cause burns, blisters, and even blindness. Native to Asia, the invasive plant has been reported in the Northeast and mid-Atlantic regions of the United States.

EPIC FAIL

EPIC
FAIL

DEADLIEST INSECT

Mosquitoes are the deadliest insect in the world because of the diseases they spread to people. Each year, mosquito bites infect more than a billion people with illnesses such as yellow fever, malaria, dengue fever, and West Nile virus. Although most mosquito-borne illnesses can be treated or prevented, 1 million people worldwide die from these diseases annually.

MOST ENDANGERED CORAL REEF

The Great Barrier Reef has lost 50% of its coral cover in the last 27 years. Threats to the reef and its inhabitants include climate change, illegal fishing, pollution, and coastal development. The reef is home to 1,625 species of fish, about 600 species of coral, and more than 3,000 species of mollusks.

EPIC
FAIL

ANIMAL WITH THE WORST SENSE OF SMELL

With only 296 smell genes, an orangutan's sense of smell is pretty weak. By comparison, elephants, which top the list with the best sense of smell, have about 2,000 smell genes. Scientists think orangutans may have lost some of their sense of smell because they rely more heavily on sight.

EPIC FAIL

EPIC
FAIL

SMALLEST ISLAND

Bishop Rock, located just west of the Isles of Scilly in southwest England, is the world's smallest island. At low tide, it measures about 150 feet (46 m) wide by 52 feet (16 m) long—roughly the size of three tennis courts. The island's first lighthouse was completed in 1858 to help prevent shipwrecks, and the only inhabitants of the island were the lighthouse keepers. In 1991, the lighthouse became automated, and the last keeper left the island a short time later.

SLOWEST-FLYING BIRD

An American woodcock is the slowest-flying bird, with a recorded flight speed of just 5 miles (8 km) per hour. The short-legged woodland bird blends in very well on the forest floor and spends most of its time on the ground looking for food. However, males do fly high into the air and spiral slowly downward while looking for mates each spring and summer.

EPIC
FAIL

ON TO THE
EPIC WINS!

largest diamond

Golden Jubilee

The Golden Jubilee is the world's largest faceted diamond, with a weight of 545.65 carats. This gigantic gem got its name when it was presented to the king of Thailand in 1997 for the Golden Jubilee—or 50th anniversary celebration—of his reign. The diamond weighed 755.5 carats when it was discovered in a South African mine in 1986. Once it was cut, the diamond featured 148 perfectly symmetrical facets. The process took almost a year because of the diamond's size and multiple tension points.

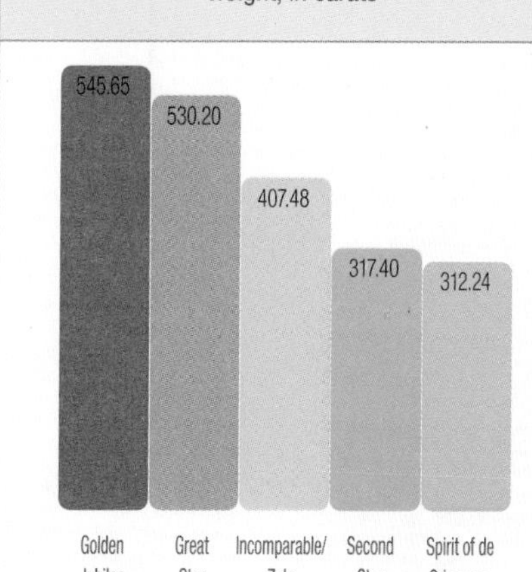

largest diamonds
weight, in carats
545.65
530.20
407.48
317.40
312.24
Golden Jubilee
Great Star of Africa
Incomparable/ Zale
Second Star of Africa
Spirit of de Grisogono

tallest mountain

Mount Everest

Mount Everest's tallest peak towers 29,035 feet (8,850 m) into the air, and it is the highest point on Earth. This peak is an unbelievable 5.5 miles (8.8 km) above sea level. Mount Everest is located in the Himalayas, on the border between Nepal and Tibet. The mountain got its official name from surveyor Sir George Everest. In 1953, Sir Edmund Hillary and Tenzing Norgay were the first people to reach the peak. In April 2015, a giant earthquake rocked Nepal, and scientists are currently investigating if Everest actually lost about 1 inch (2.54 cm) when the earth shifted.

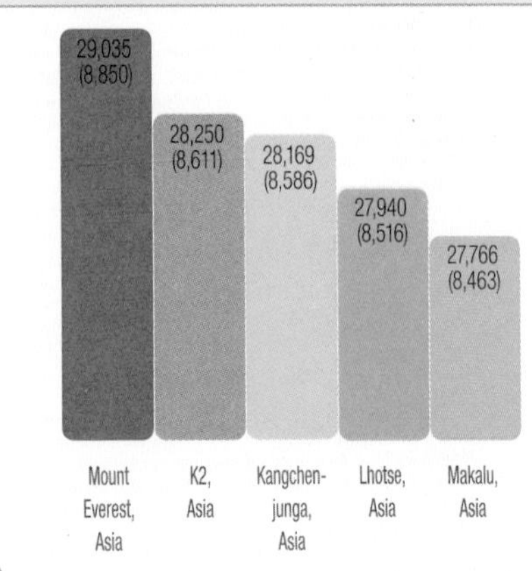
tallest mountains
highest point, in feet (meters)
29,035 (8,850)
28,250 (8,611)
28,169 (8,586)
27,940 (8,516)
27,766 (8,463)
Mount Everest, Asia
K2, Asia
Kangchen-junga, Asia
Lhotse, Asia
Makalu, Asia

largest lake

Caspian Sea

This giant inland body of salt water stretches for almost 750 miles (1,207 km) from north to south, with an average width of about 200 miles (322 km). Altogether, it covers 143,200 square miles (370,901 sq km). The Caspian Sea is located east of the Caucasus Mountains in central Asia. It is bordered by Iran, Russia, Kazakhstan, Azerbaijan, and Turkmenistan. The Caspian Sea has an average depth of about 550 feet (170 m). It is an important fishing resource, with species including sturgeon, salmon, perch, herring, and carp. Other animals living in the Caspian Sea include porpoises, seals, and tortoises. The sea is estimated to be 30 million years old and became landlocked 5.5 million years ago.

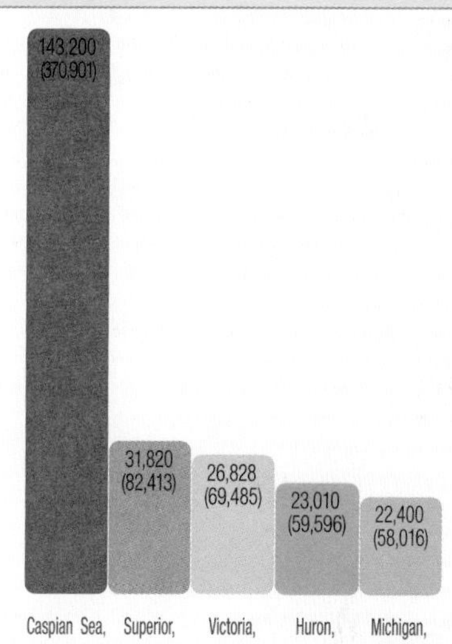
largest lakes
approximate area, in square miles (square kilometers)
143,200 (370,901)
31,820 (82,413)
26,828 (69,485)
23,010 (59,596)
22,400 (58,016)
Caspian Sea, Asia
Superior, N. America
Victoria, Africa
Huron, N. America
Michigan, N. America

largest desert

Sahara

Located in northern Africa, the Sahara desert covers approximately 3.5 million square miles (9.1 million sq km). It stretches for 5,200 miles (8,372 km) through the countries of Morocco, Algeria, Tunisia, Libya, Egypt, Mauritania, Mali, Niger, Chad, and Sudan. The Sahara gets very little rainfall—less than 8 inches (20 cm) per year. Even with its harsh environment, some 2.5 million people—mostly nomads—call the Sahara home. Date palms and acacias grow near oases. Some of the animals that live in the Sahara include gazelles, antelopes, jackals, foxes, and badgers.

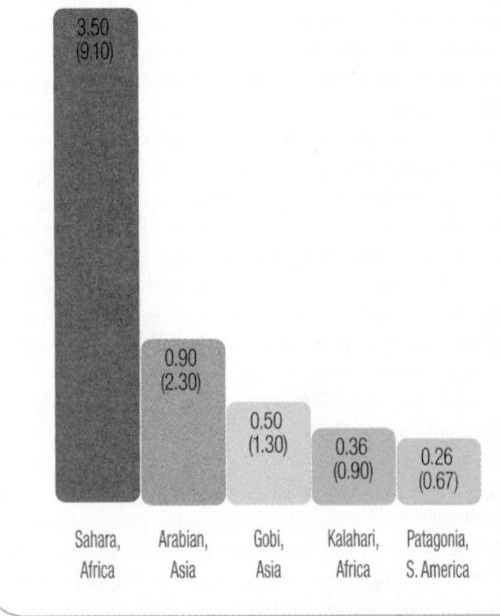
largest deserts
area, in millions of square miles (square kilometers)
3.50 (9.10)
0.90 (2.30)
0.50 (1.30)
0.36 (0.90)
0.26 (0.67)
Sahara, Africa
Arabian, Asia
Gobi, Asia
Kalahari, Africa
Patagonia, S. America

longest river

Nile

The Nile River in Africa stretches 4,145 miles (6,671 km) from the tributaries of Lake Victoria in Tanzania and Uganda out to the Mediterranean Sea. Because of varying depths, ships can sail on only about 2,000 miles (3,217 km) of the river. The Nile flows through Rwanda, Uganda, Sudan, and Egypt. The river's water supply is crucial to the existence of these African countries. The Nile's precious water is used to irrigate crops and to generate electricity. The Aswan Dam and the Aswan High Dam—both located in Egypt—are used to store the autumn floodwater for later use. The Nile is also used to transport goods from city to city along the river.

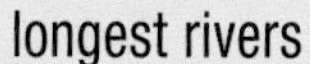
longest rivers

total length, in miles (kilometers)

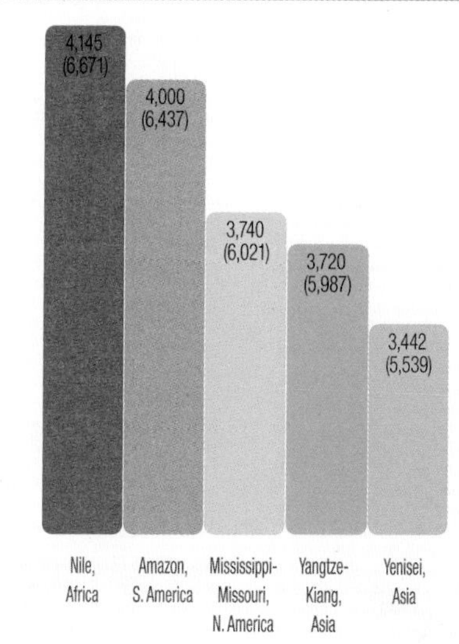
4,145
(6,671)
4,000
(6,437)
3,740
(6,021)
3,720
(5,987)
3,442
(5,539)
Nile, Africa
Amazon, S. America
Mississippi-Missouri, N. America
Yangtze-Kiang, Asia
Yenisei, Asia

largest ocean

Pacific

The Pacific Ocean covers almost 64 million square miles (166 million sq km) and reaches 36,200 feet (11,000 m) below sea level at its greatest depth—the Mariana Trench (south of Japan). In fact, this ocean is so large that it covers about one-third of the planet (more than all of Earth's land put together) and holds more than half of all the seawater on Earth. The United States could fit inside this ocean 18 times! Some of the major bodies of water included in the Pacific are the Bering Sea, the Coral Sea, the Philippine Sea, and the Gulf of Alaska.

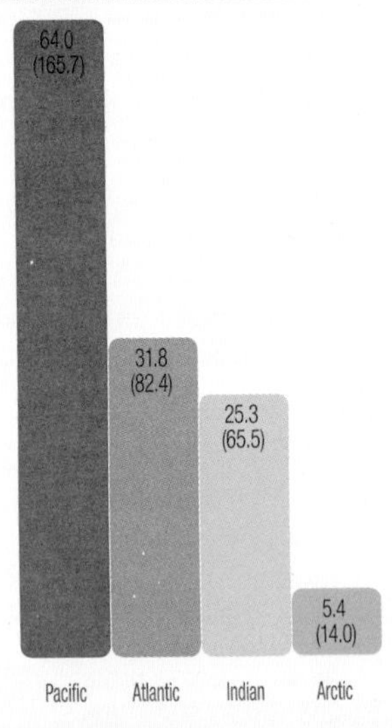
largest oceans
approximate area, in millions of square miles (square kilometers)
64.0 (165.7)
31.8 (82.4)
25.3 (65.5)
5.4 (14.0)
Pacific
Atlantic
Indian
Arctic

largest coral reef

Great Barrier Reef

The Great Barrier Reef stretches for some 1,429 miles (2,300 km) in the Coral Sea along the coast of Australia. It's larger than the Great Wall of China, and it's the only living thing that can be seen from space. More than 3,000 individual reef systems and coral cays make up this intricate structure. A large part of the reef makes up Great Barrier Reef Marine Park, which helps to preserve the area by limiting fishing, tourism, and human use. Thousands of animal species are supported by the reef, including 1,625 species of fish, 450 species of hard coral, and about 30 species of dolphins and whales. The Great Barrier Reef is considered a World Heritage Site, and one of the Seven Natural Wonders of the World.

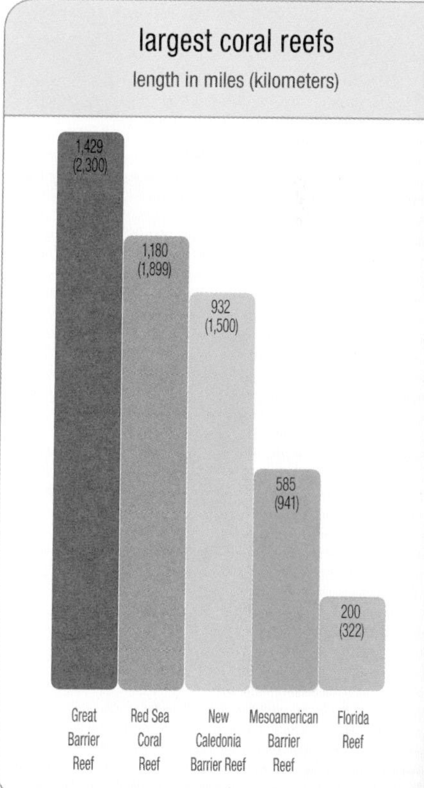
largest coral reefs
length in miles (kilometers)
1,429 (2,300)
1,180 (1,899)
932 (1,500)
585 (941)
200 (322)
Great Barrier Reef
Red Sea Coral Reef
New Caledonia Barrier Reef
Mesoamerican Barrier Reef
Florida Reef

deepest sea trench

Mariana Trench

Located in the Pacific Ocean near Japan, the Mariana Trench is the deepest opening in Earth's crust at 35,787 feet (10,907 m)—that's almost 7 miles (11.2 km) deep! Mount Everest—the world's tallest mountain at 29,035 feet (8,850 m)—could easily fit inside. The deepest point in the trench is called Challenger Deep, named after the Royal Navy vessel the "HMS Challenger," which first measured the trench in 1951. In 1960, Swiss oceanographer Jacques Piccard and U.S. Navy Lt. Don Walsh were the first people to explore the trench after an almost five-hour descent to reach the ocean floor. The two were the only people to reach that depth until March 2012, when filmmaker James Cameron became the first human to complete a solo journey to the bottom of the trench to collect samples and video. The trench is home to many types of crabs and fish, as well as more than 200 different types of microorganisms.

deepest sea trenches
deepest point, in feet (meters)
35,787 (10,907)
35,702 (10,881)
34,580 (10,540)
34,449 (10,500)
32,963 (10,047)
Mariana Trench
Tonga Trench
Philippine Trench
Kuril-Kamchatka Trench
Kermadec Trench

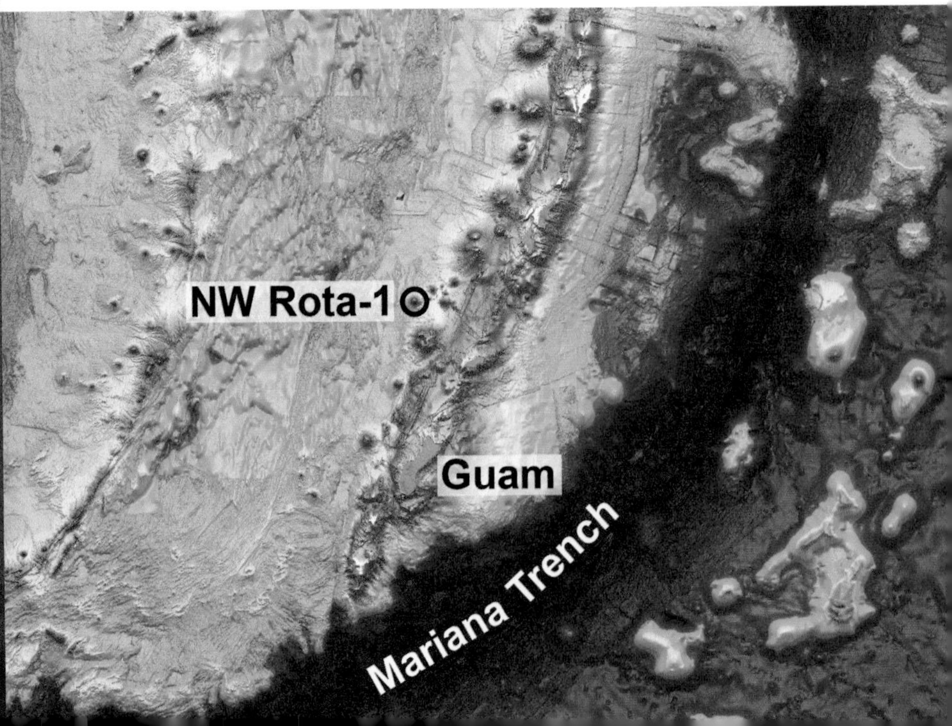

largest crustacean

Giant Spider Crab

The giant spider crab has up to a 12-foot (3.7 m) leg span. That's almost wide enough to take up two parking spaces! The crab's body measures about 15 inches (38.1 cm) wide. Its ten long legs are jointed, and the first pair has large claws at the end. The giant sea creature can weigh 35–44 pounds (16–20 kg). It feeds on dead animals and shellfish it finds on the ocean floor. Giant spider crabs live in the deep water of the Pacific Ocean off southern Japan.

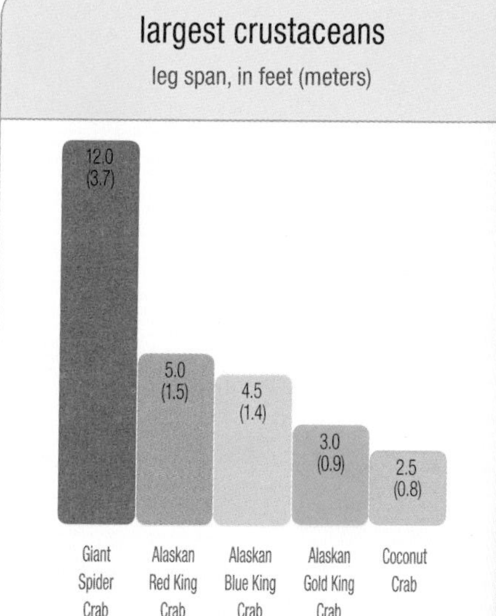
largest crustaceans
leg span, in feet (meters)
12.0 (3.7)
5.0 (1.5)
4.5 (1.4)
3.0 (0.9)
2.5 (0.8)
Giant Spider Crab
Alaskan Red King Crab
Alaskan Blue King Crab
Alaskan Gold King Crab
Coconut Crab

largest cephalopod

Colossal Squid

Living up to 6,000 feet (1,829 m) deep in the Antarctic Ocean, the colossal squid can grow to a length of 46 feet (14 m). That's about the same size as three SUVs! The squid, which is very rarely seen by people, can weigh about 1,500 pounds (681 kg). Its eyes are the size of dinner plates, and are the largest eyes in the animal kingdom. The colossal squid uses its 20-foot (6 m)-long tentacles to catch its prey. In addition to the two tentacles, this giant cephalopod has eight arms. In the center of its body, the squid has a razor-sharp beak that it uses to shred its prey before eating it.

largest cephalopods

length, in feet (meters)

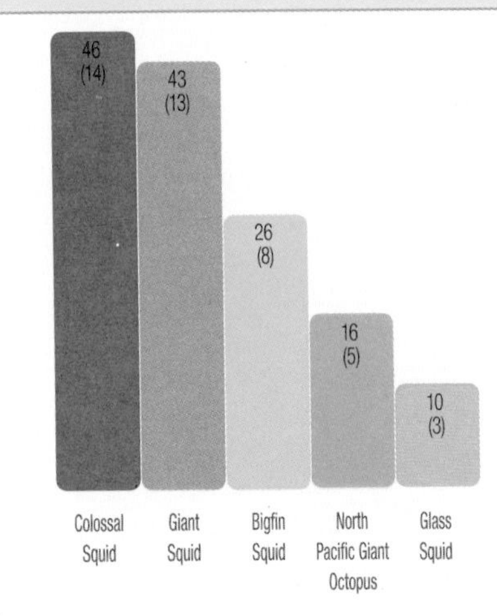
46
(14)
43
(13)
26
(8)
16
(5)
10
(3)
Colossal Squid
Giant Squid
Bigfin Squid
North Pacific Giant Octopus
Glass Squid

most dangerous shark

Great White

With a total of 279 known unprovoked attacks on humans since the early 1900s, great white sharks are the most dangerous predators in the sea. A great white can measure up to 20 feet (6.1 m) in length—that's a few feet longer than a pickup truck—and weigh 5,000 pounds (2,268 kg) or more. Because of the sharks' size, they can feed on large prey, including seals, dolphins, and even small whales. Often, when a human is attacked by a great white, it is because the shark has mistaken the person for its typical prey. Even though shark attacks may appear on the news frequently, they are pretty rare. In 2014, only 3 people died from unprovoked attacks. The sharks make their homes in waters throughout the world, but are most frequently found off the coasts of Australia, South Africa, California, Florida, and Mexico.

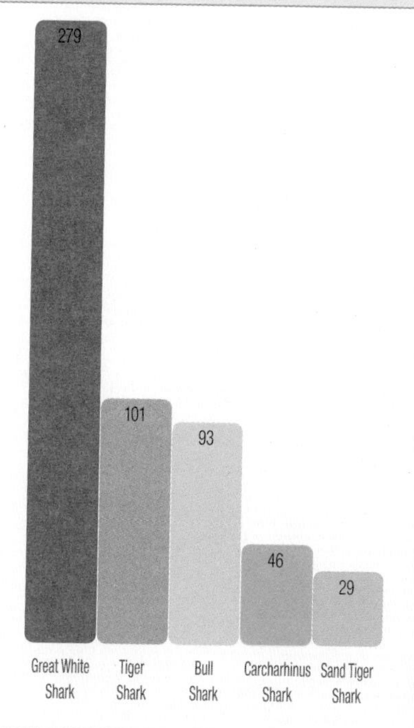
most dangerous sharks
number of unprovoked attacks
279
101
93
46
29
Great White Shark
Tiger Shark
Bull Shark
Carcharhinus Shark
Sand Tiger Shark

biggest fish

Whale Shark

Although the average length of a whale shark is 30 feet (9 m), many have been known to reach up to 60 feet (18 m) long. That's the same length as two school buses! Whale sharks also weigh an average of 50,000 pounds (22,680 kg). As with most sharks, the females are larger than the males. Their mouths measure about 5 feet (1.5 m) wide and contain about 3,000 teeth. Amazingly, these gigantic fish eat only microscopic plankton and tiny fish. They float near the surface looking for food.

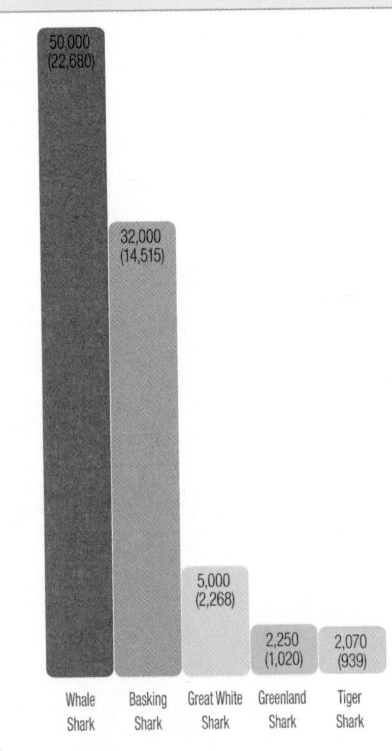
biggest fish
average weight, in pounds (kilograms)
50,000 (22,680)
32,000 (14,515)
5,000 (2,268)
2,250 (1,020)
2,070 (939)
Whale Shark
Basking Shark
Great White Shark
Greenland Shark
Tiger Shark

fastest fish

Sailfish

A sailfish once grabbed a fishing line and dragged it 300 feet (91 m) away in just three seconds. That means it was swimming at an average speed of 69 miles (109 km) per hour—higher than the average speed limit on a highway! Sailfish are very large—they average 6 feet (1.8 m) long, but can grow up to 11 feet (3.4 m). They eat squid and surface-dwelling fish, and sometimes several sailfish will work together to catch their prey. They are found in both the Atlantic and Pacific Oceans and prefer a water temperature of about 80°F (27°C).

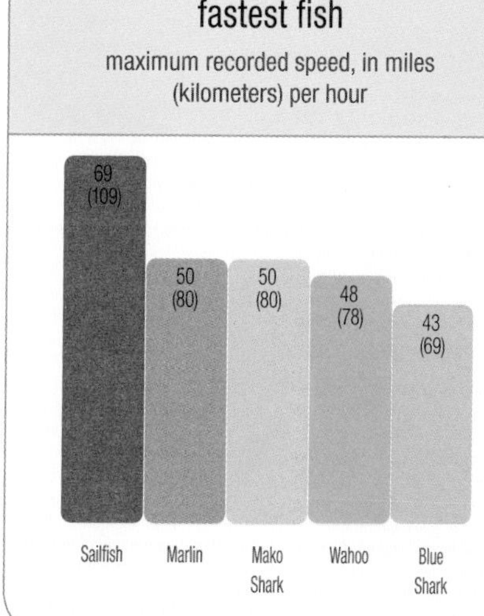
fastest fish
maximum recorded speed, in miles (kilometers) per hour
69 (109)
50 (80)
50 (80)
48 (78)
43 (69)
Sailfish
Marlin
Mako Shark
Wahoo
Blue Shark

biggest dolphin

Orca

Although it is known as a *killer whale*, the orca is actually a member of the dolphin family and can measure up to 32 feet (9.7 m) in length and weigh up to 6 tons (5.4 t). These powerful marine mammals are carnivores with 4-inch (1.6 cm)-long teeth, and they feed mainly on seals, sea lions, and small whales. Orcas live in pods of up to 40 other whales, and pod members help one another round up prey. Orcas can live for up to 80 years and are highly intelligent.

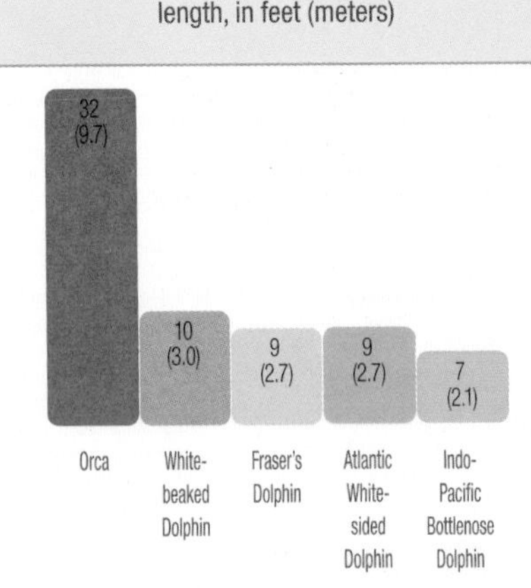
biggest dolphins
length, in feet (meters)
32 (9.7)
10 (3.0)
9 (2.7)
9 (2.7)
7 (2.1)
Orca
White-beaked Dolphin
Fraser's Dolphin
Atlantic White-sided Dolphin
Indo-Pacific Bottlenose Dolphin

ANIMALS

heaviest marine mammal

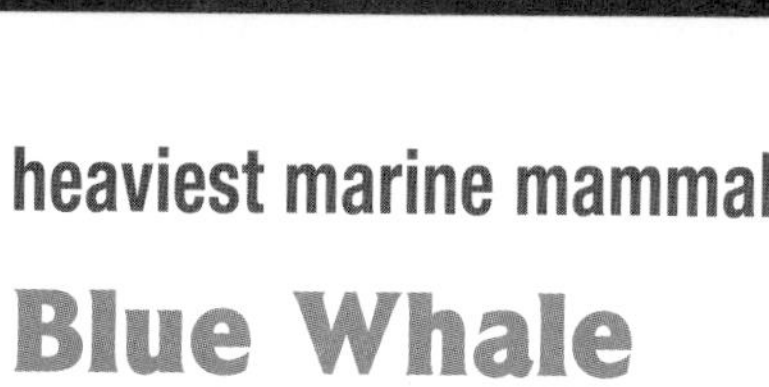

Blue Whale

Blue whales are the largest animals that have ever inhabited Earth. They can weigh more than 143.3 tons (130 t) and measure over 100 feet (30 m) long. Amazingly, these gentle giants only eat krill—small shrimplike animals. A blue whale can eat about 4 tons (3.6 t) of krill each day in the summer, when food is plentiful. To catch the krill, a whale gulps as much as 17,000 gallons (64,600 L) of seawater into its mouth at one time. Then it uses its tongue—which can be as big as a car—to push the water back out. The krill get caught in hairs on the whale's baleen (a keratin filtering structure that hangs down from the roof of the whale's mouth).

heaviest marine mammals

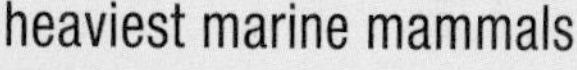

weight, in tons (metric tons)

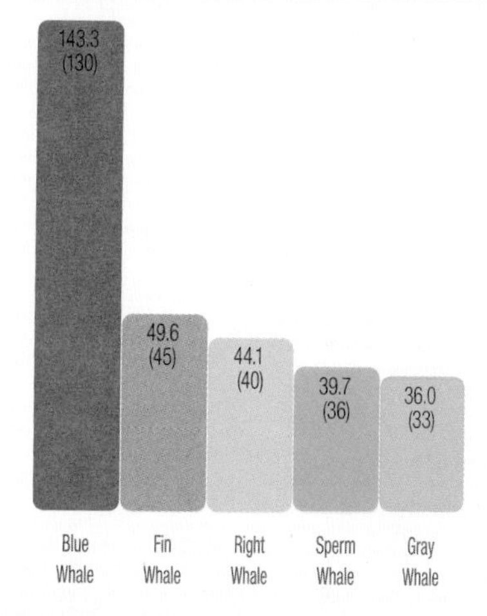
143.3
(130)
49.6
(45)
44.1
(40)
39.7
(36)
36.0
(33)
Blue Whale
Fin Whale
Right Whale
Sperm Whale
Gray Whale

marine mammal with the largest brain

Sperm Whale

The sperm whale's brain is the largest marine mammal brain in the world, weighing more than 17 pounds (7.7 kg). That's more than five times the size of a human brain. Sperm whales can grow to about 60 feet (18 m) long and weigh up to 45 tons (41 t). The head makes up about one-third of the animal's body. Sperm whales can also dive deeper than any other whale, reaching depths of 3,300 feet (1,006 m) in search of squid. They can eat about 1 ton (0.9 t) of fish and squid daily. Sperm whales can be found in all oceans, and they generally live in pods of about a dozen adults and their offspring.

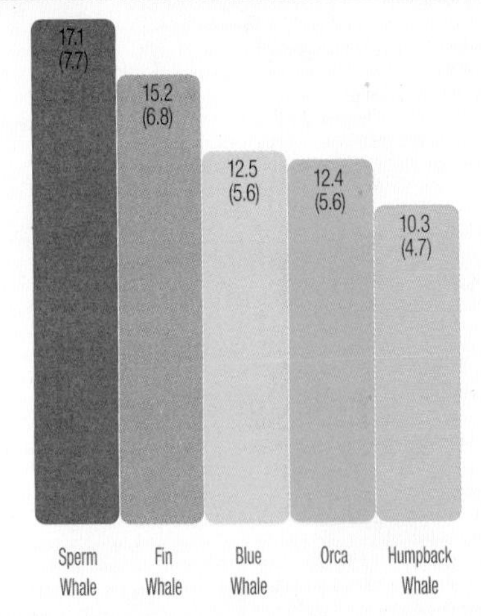
marine mammals with the largest brains
brain weight, in pounds (kilograms)
17.1 (7.7)
15.2 (6.8)
12.5 (5.6)
12.4 (5.6)
10.3 (4.7)
Sperm Whale
Fin Whale
Blue Whale
Orca
Humpback Whale

largest bird wingspan

Marabou Stork

With a wingspan that can reach up to 13 feet (4 m), the marabou stork has the largest wingspan of any bird. These large storks weigh up to 20 pounds (9 kg) and can grow up to 5 feet (150 cm) tall. Their long leg bones and toe bones are actually hollow. This adaptation is very important for flight because it makes the bird lighter. Although marabous eat insects, small mammals, and fish, the majority of their food is carrion—meat that is already dead. In fact, the stork's head and neck do not have any feathers. This helps the bird stay clean as it sticks its head into carcasses to pick out scraps of food.

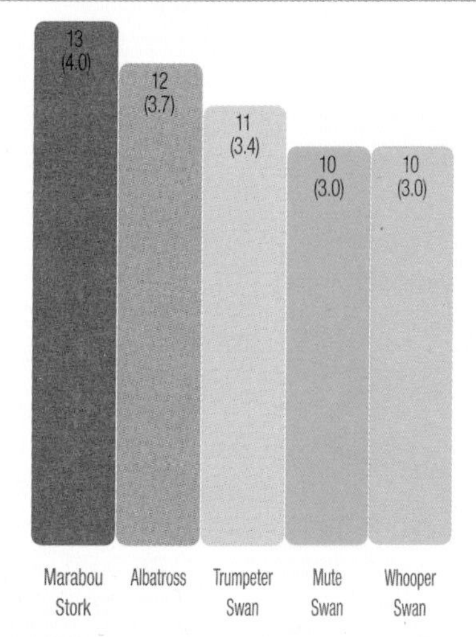
largest bird wingspans
wingspan, in feet (meters)
13 (4.0)
12 (3.7)
11 (3.4)
10 (3.0)
10 (3.0)
Marabou Stork
Albatross
Trumpeter Swan
Mute Swan
Whooper Swan

biggest penguin

Emperor Penguin

Emperor penguins are giants among their species, growing to a height of 44 inches (111.7 cm) and weighing up to 80 pounds (37 kg). These penguins are the only animals that spend the entire winter on the open ice in Antarctica, withstanding temperatures as low as -75°F (-60°C). The female penguin lays a 1-pound (0.5 kg) egg on the ice and then goes off to hunt for weeks at a time. The male penguin scoops up the egg and keeps it warm on his feet below his toasty belly. When the eggs hatch, the females return with food.

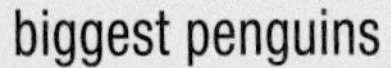

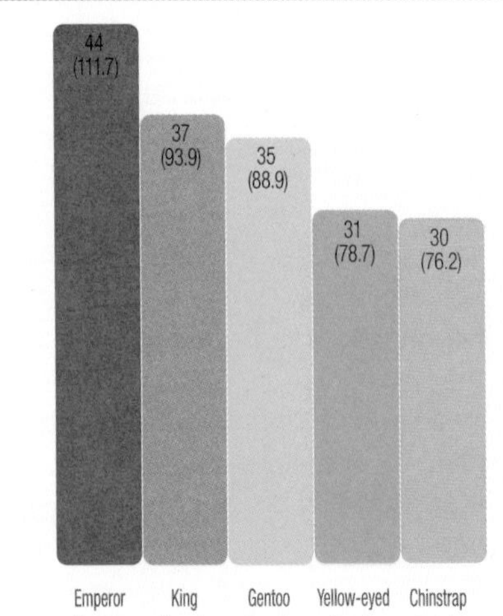
biggest penguins
height in inches (centimeters)
44 (111.7)
37 (93.9)
35 (88.9)
31 (78.7)
30 (76.2)
Emperor Penguin
King Penguin
Gentoo Penguin
Yellow-eyed Penguin
Chinstrap Penguin

largest owl

Blakiston's Fish Owl

A female Blakiston's fish owl can measure up to 3 feet (.9 m) high, weigh up to 10 pounds (4.5 kg), and have a 6-foot (1.8 m) wingspan. Females are larger than males. As its name suggests, the Blakiston's fish owl primarily eats fish—including pike, trout, and salmon—and can catch a meal that weighs almost as much as the owl itself. These birds live and nest in old-growth forests along coastlines throughout Japan and Russia. However, due to forest clearing and other threats to its habitat, the Blakiston's fish owl is endangered.

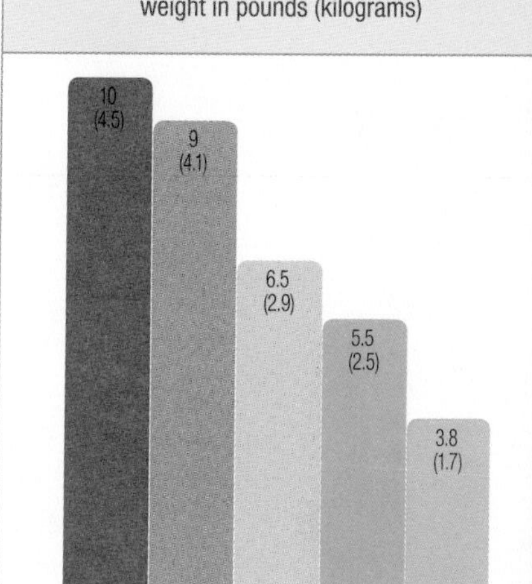
largest owls
weight in pounds (kilograms)
10 (4.5)
9 (4.1)
6.5 (2.9)
5.5 (2.5)
3.8 (1.7)
Blakiston's Fish Owl
Eurasian Eagle Owl
Snowy Owl
Great Horned Owl
Great Grey Owl

bird that builds the largest nest

Bald Eagle

With a nest that can measure 8 feet (2.4 m) wide—the diameter—and 16 feet (4.9 m) deep, bald eagles have plenty of room to move around. These birds of prey have wingspans of up to 7.5 feet (2.3 m) and need a home that they can nest in comfortably. By carefully constructing their nest with sticks, branches, and plant material, a pair of bald eagles can balance their home—which can weigh up to 4,000 pounds (1,814 kg)—on the top of a tree or cliff. These nests are usually located by rivers or coastlines, the birds' watery hunting grounds. Called an aerie, this home will be used for the rest of the eagles' lives.

birds that build the largest nests

nest diameter, in feet (meters)

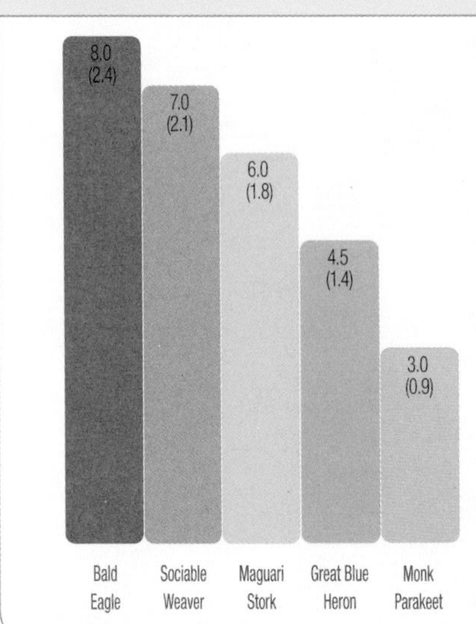
8.0 (2.4)
7.0 (2.1)
6.0 (1.8)
4.5 (1.4)
3.0 (0.9)
Bald Eagle
Sociable Weaver
Maguari Stork
Great Blue Heron
Monk Parakeet

largest bird egg

Ostrich Egg

Ostriches—the world's largest birds—can lay eggs that measure 5 inches by 6 inches (13 cm by 16 cm) and weigh up to 4 pounds (1.8 kg). In fact, just one ostrich egg weighs as much as 24 chicken eggs! The egg yolk makes up one-third of the volume. Although the eggshell is only 0.08 inches (2 mm) thick, it is tough enough to withstand the weight of a 345-pound (157 kg) ostrich. An ostrich hen can lay from 10 to 70 eggs each year. Females are usually able to recognize their own eggs, even when they are mixed in with those of other females in their shared nest.

largest bird eggs

weight, in pounds (kilograms)

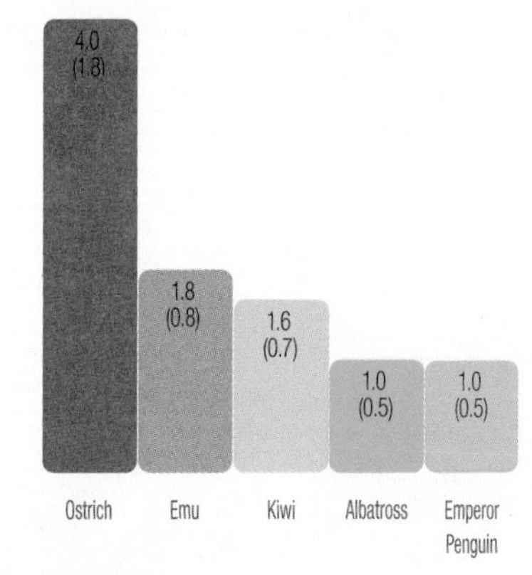
4.0
(1.8)
1.8
(0.8)
1.6
(0.7)
1.0
(0.5)
1.0
(0.5)
Ostrich
Emu
Kiwi
Albatross
Emperor Penguin

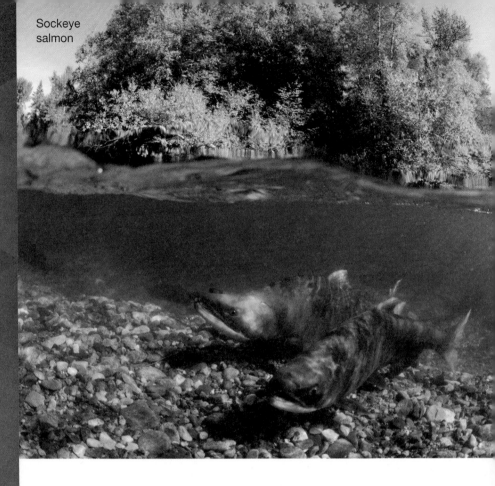

Sockeye salmon

most endangered US animal group

Fish

There are 93 species of fish that are currently endangered in the United States. A species is considered endangered if it is at risk of becoming extinct. In addition, there are another 70 fish species that are considered threatened. Out of the 163 endangered and threatened fish species, there is a recovery plan in place for 103 of them. The main reasons for the decline in some species' populations are overfishing, water pollution, and loss of habitat. Some of the most well-known endangered fish include the Atlantic salmon, the steelhead trout, the sockeye salmon, and the Atlantic sturgeon.

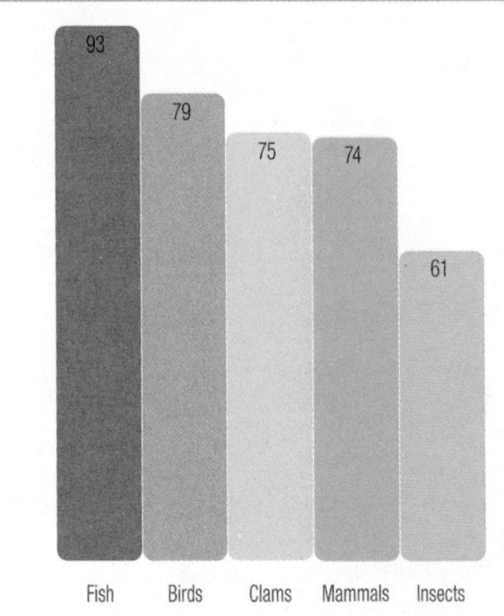
most endangered US animal groups
by number of endangered species
93
79
75
74
61
Fish
Birds
Clams
Mammals
Insects

sleepiest animal

Koala

Awake for just 2 hours a day, the koala is the sleepiest animal on earth. This means that the marsupial is asleep for about 8,000 hours a year! Koalas are found in eastern Australia, and spend most of the day snoozing and feeding in eucalyptus trees. They eat about 2.5 pounds (1.1 kg) of leaves a day. Koalas rarely need to drink because they get most of their water from the trees' juicy leaves. Although eucalyptus leaves cannot be eaten by humans, koalas have a special digestive system that allows them to easily digest the toxic oil in the foliage. In the wild, these mammals can live for up to 20 years.

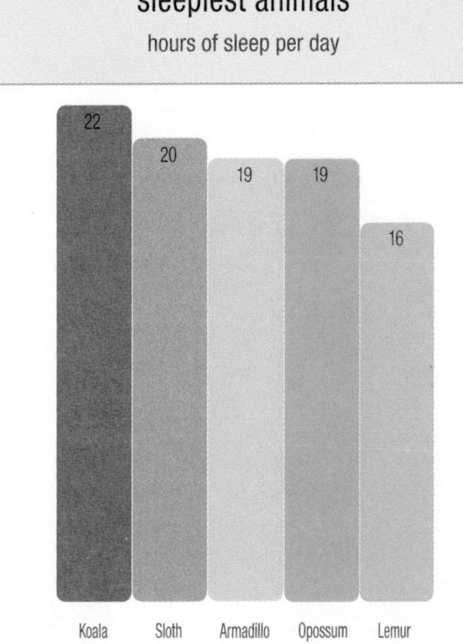
sleepiest animals
hours of sleep per day
22
20
19
19
16
Koala
Sloth
Armadillo
Opossum
Lemur

heaviest land mammal

African Elephant

Weighing up to 17,637 pounds (8,000 kg) and measuring approximately 24 feet (7.3 m) long, African elephants are truly humongous. Even at their great size, they are strictly vegetarian. They will, however, eat up to 500 pounds (226 kg) of vegetation a day! Their two tusks—which are actually elongated teeth—grow continuously during their lives and can reach about 9 feet (2.7 m) in length. Elephants live in small groups of 8 to 15 family members with one female (called a cow) as the leader.

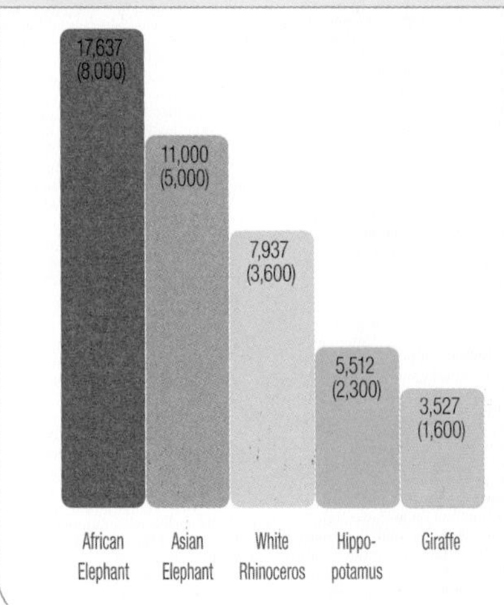
heaviest land mammals
weight, in pounds (kilograms)
17,637 (8,000)
11,000 (5,000)
7,937 (3,600)
5,512 (2,300)
3,527 (1,600)
African Elephant
Asian Elephant
White Rhinoceros
Hippopotamus
Giraffe

fastest land mammal

Cheetah

For short spurts, these sleek mammals can reach a speed of 71 miles (114 km) per hour. They can accelerate from 0 to 40 miles (64 km) per hour in just three strides. Their quickness easily enables these large African cats to outrun their prey. All other African cats can only stalk their prey because they lack the cheetah's amazing speed. Unlike the paws of all other cats, cheetah paws do not have skin sheaths (thin protective coverings). Their claws, therefore, cannot be retracted.

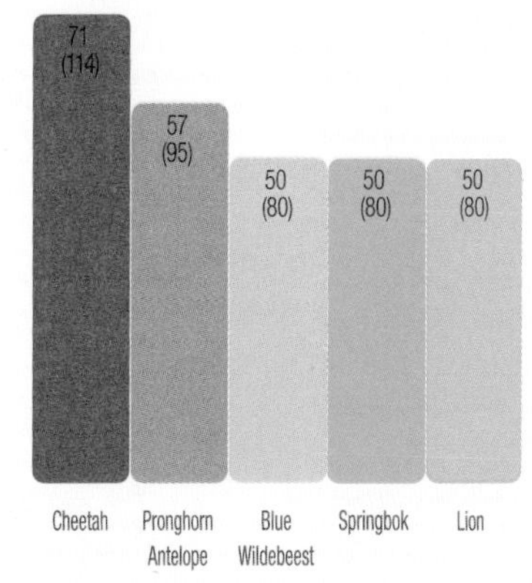
fastest land mammals
speed, in miles (kilometers) per hour
71 (114)
57 (95)
50 (80)
50 (80)
50 (80)
Cheetah
Pronghorn Antelope
Blue Wildebeest
Springbok
Lion

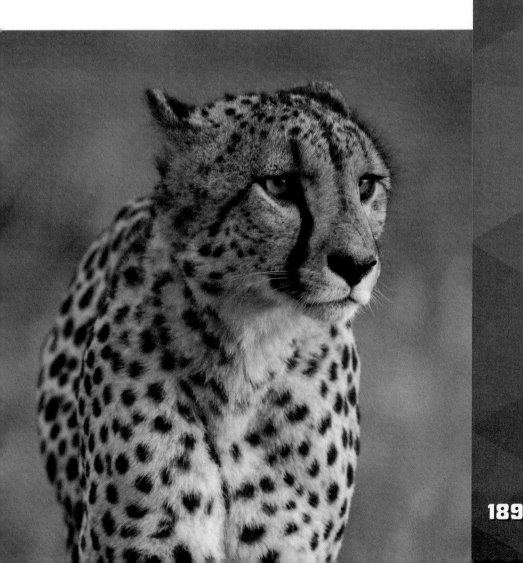

heaviest cat

Tiger

Although tigers average about 448 pounds (203 kg), some of these big cats can grow to 725 pounds (300 kg) and measure 6 feet (1.8 m) long—not including a 3-foot (0.9 m) tail. Tigers that live in colder habitats are usually larger than ones that live in warmer areas. These giant cats hunt at night and can easily bring down a full-grown antelope alone. One tiger can eat about 60 pounds (27 kg) of meat in just one night. The six types of tigers are Bengal, Indochinese, Malayan, South China, Sumatran, and Siberian. All tiger species are endangered, mostly because of overhunting and loss of habitat due to farming and logging.

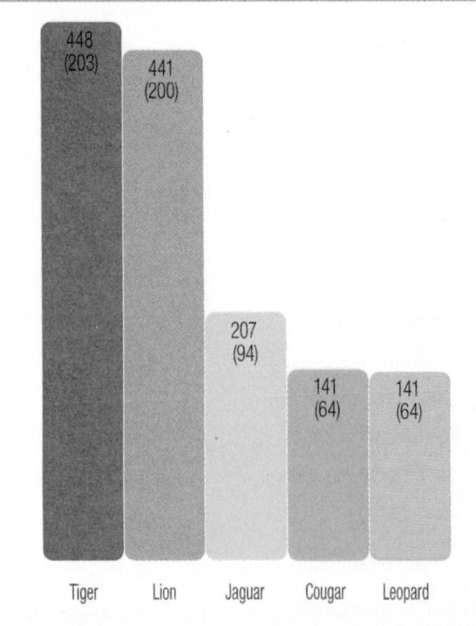
heaviest cats
average weight, in pounds (kilograms)
448 (203)
441 (200)
207 (94)
141 (64)
141 (64)
Tiger
Lion
Jaguar
Cougar
Leopard

largest rodent

Capybara

Capybaras reach an average length of 4 feet (1.2 m), stand about 20 inches (51 cm) tall, and weigh 75–150 pounds (34–68 kg)! That's about the same size as a Labrador retriever. Also known as water hogs and carpinchos, capybaras are found in South and Central America, where they spend much of their time in groups, looking for food. They are strictly vegetarian and have been known to raid gardens for melons and squash. Their partially webbed feet make capybaras excellent swimmers. They can dive down to the bottom of a lake or river to find plants and stay there for up to five minutes.

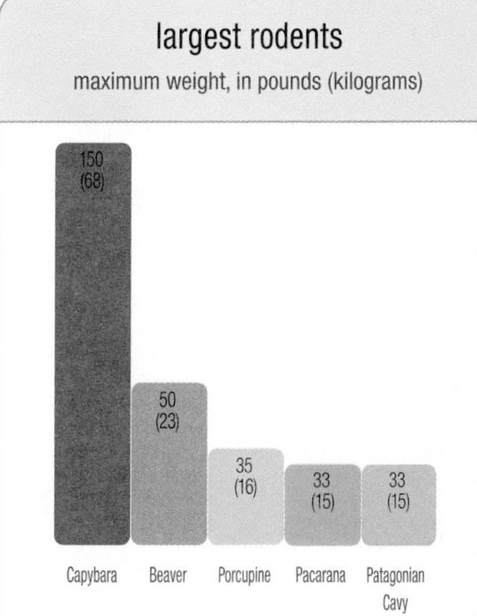
largest rodents
maximum weight, in pounds (kilograms)
150 (68)
50 (23)
35 (16)
33 (15)
33 (15)
Capybara
Beaver
Porcupine
Pacarana
Patagonian Cavy

animal with the longest teeth

African Elephant

An African elephant has two teeth that measure up to 118 inches (300 cm), or 9.8 feet (2.9 m) each. Also known as tusks, they are actually enlarged incisor teeth that are made of ivory. About two-thirds of the tusk can be seen, and the rest reaches back and attaches to the skull. Both male and female African elephants have tusks, and they are mainly used for defense, digging, lifting, stripping tree bark, gathering food, and protecting the animal's sensitive trunk. While an elephant will grow six sets of molars, or chewing teeth, during its lifetime, it will only grow one set of tusks.

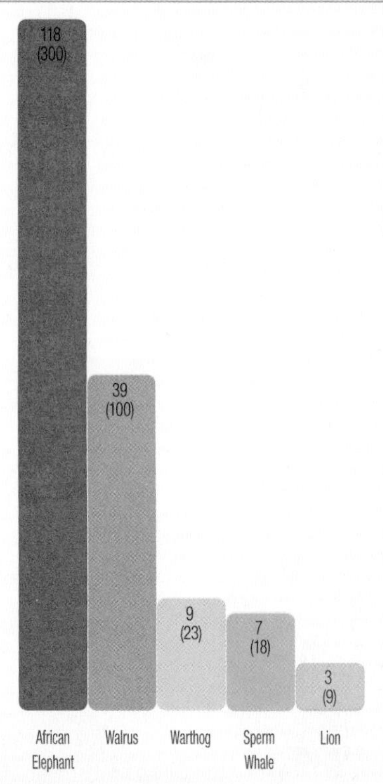
animals with the longest teeth
length in inches (cm)
118 (300)
39 (100)
9 (23)
7 (18)
3 (9)
African Elephant
Walrus
Warthog
Sperm Whale
Lion

largest bat

Giant Flying Fox

The giant flying fox—a member of the megabat family—can have a wingspan of up to 6 feet (1.8 m). These furry mammals average just 7 wing beats per second, but can travel more than 40 miles (64 km) a night in search of food. Unlike smaller bats, which use echolocation, flying foxes rely on their acute vision and sense of smell to locate fruit, pollen, and nectar. Flying foxes got their name because their faces resemble a fox's face. Megabats live in the tropical areas of Africa, Asia, and Australia.

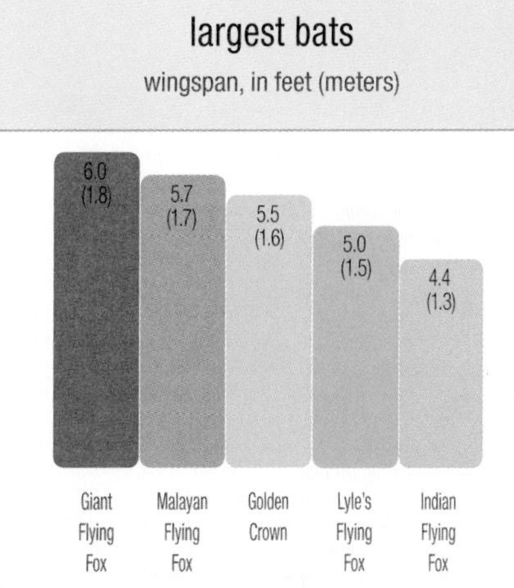
largest bats
wingspan, in feet (meters)
6.0 (1.8)
5.7 (1.7)
5.5 (1.6)
5.0 (1.5)
4.4 (1.3)
Giant Flying Fox
Malayan Flying Fox
Golden Crown
Lyle's Flying Fox
Indian Flying Fox

tallest land animal

Giraffe

Giraffes are the giants among mammals, growing up to 18 feet (5.5 m) in height. That means an average giraffe could look through the window of a two-story building! A giraffe's neck is 18 times longer than a human's, but both mammals have exactly the same number of neck bones. A giraffe's long legs enable it to outrun most of its enemies. When cornered, giraffes have the strength to kill a lion with a single kick to the head.

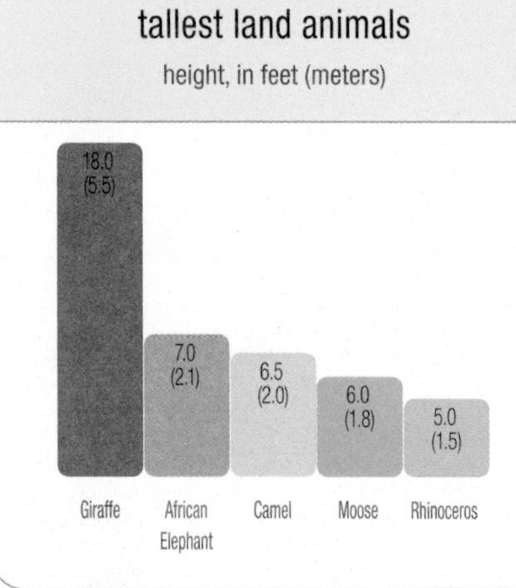
tallest land animals
height, in feet (meters)
18.0 (5.5)
7.0 (2.1)
6.5 (2.0)
6.0 (1.8)
5.0 (1.5)
Giraffe
African Elephant
Camel
Moose
Rhinoceros

largest domestic rabbit

Flemish Giant

The Flemish giant rabbit can weigh up to 20 pounds (9 kg) and measure about 2.5 feet (.7 m) long—about two and a half times the size of the average house cat. These rabbits are believed to have been first bred in Belgium in the 16th century, mostly for their meat and fur. In the early 20th century, Flemish giants became very popular in pet shows because of their large size and dense fur. The fur can be black, blue, fawn, light gray, sandy, steel gray, or white. Many Flemish giants are also owned as pets because they are very gentle animals. In captivity, they can live for up to ten years.

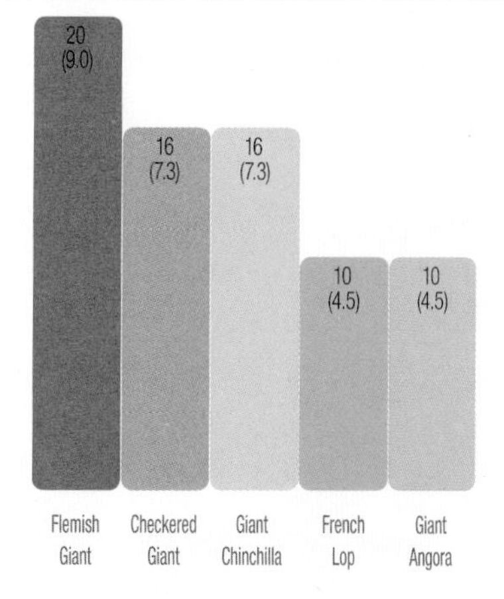
largest domestic rabbits
maximum weight in pounds (kilograms)
20 (9.0)
16 (7.3)
16 (7.3)
10 (4.5)
10 (4.5)
Flemish Giant
Checkered Giant
Giant Chinchilla
French Lop
Giant Angora

largest primate

Gorilla

Gorillas are the kings of the primate family, weighing in at up to 400 pounds (181 kg). The eastern lowland gorilla is the largest of the four subspecies of gorillas, which also include western lowland, Cross River, and mountain. All gorillas are found in Africa, and all but mountain gorillas live in tropical forests. They are mostly plant-eaters, but will occasionally eat small animals. An adult male gorilla can eat up to 45 pounds (32 kg) of food in a day. Gorillas live in groups of about 4 to 12 family members, and can live for about 35 years in the wild.

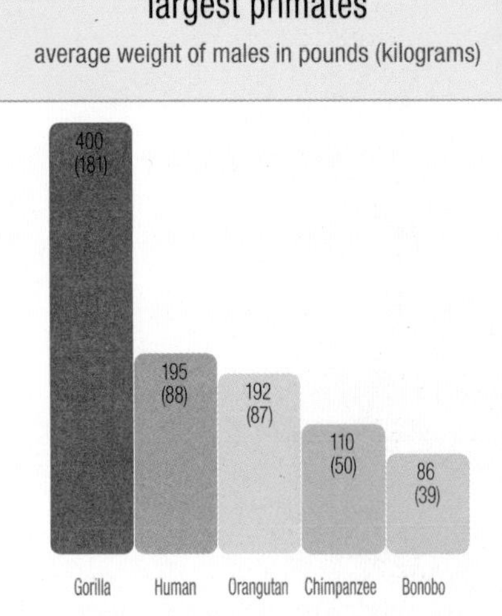
largest primates
average weight of males in pounds (kilograms)
400 (181)
195 (88)
192 (87)
110 (50)
86 (39)
Gorilla
Human
Orangutan
Chimpanzee
Bonobo

deadliest amphibian

Poison Dart Frog

Poison dart frogs are found mostly in the tropical rain forests of Central and South America, where they live on the moist land. These lethal amphibians have enough poison to kill up to 20 humans. A dart frog's poison is so effective that native Central and South Americans sometimes coat their hunting arrows or hunting darts with it. These brightly colored frogs can be yellow, orange, red, green, blue, or any combination of these colors. They measure only 0.5–2.6 inches (12–19 mm) long. There are more than 100 different species of poison dart frogs.

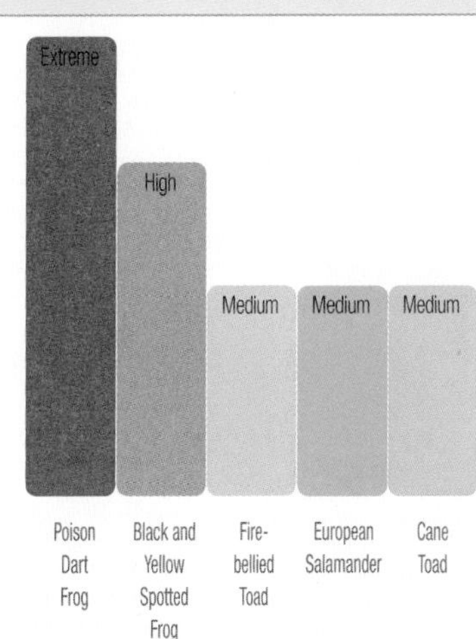

deadliest amphibians
risk of fatality
Extreme
High
Medium
Medium
Medium
Poison Dart Frog
Black and Yellow Spotted Frog
Fire-bellied Toad
European Salamander
Cane Toad

ANIMALS

longest snake

Reticulated Python

Some adult reticulated pythons can grow to 27 feet (8.2 m) long, but most reach an average length of 17 feet (5 m). That's about the length of a van! These pythons live mostly in Asia, from Myanmar to Indonesia to the Philippines. Pythons have teeth that curl backward to hold their prey, and they hunt mainly at night for mammals and birds. Reticulated pythons are slow-moving creatures that kill their prey by constriction, or strangulation.

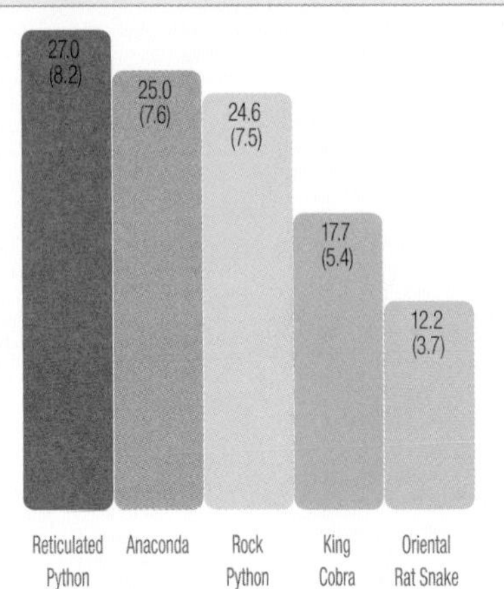
longest snakes
maximum length, in feet (meters)
27.0 (8.2)
25.0 (7.6)
24.6 (7.5)
17.7 (5.4)
12.2 (3.7)
Reticulated Python
Anaconda
Rock Python
King Cobra
Oriental Rat Snake

snake with the longest fangs

Gaboon Viper

The fangs of a Gaboon viper measure 2 inches (5.1 cm) in length! These giant fangs fold up against the snake's mouth so it does not pierce its own skin. When it is ready to strike its prey, the fangs snap down into position. The snake can grow up to 7 feet (2 m) long and weigh 18 pounds (8 kg). It is found in Africa and is perfectly camouflaged for hunting on the ground beneath leaves and grasses. The Gaboon viper's poison is not as toxic as some other snakes', but it is quite dangerous because of the amount of poison it can inject at one time. The snake is not very aggressive, however, and usually attacks only when bothered.

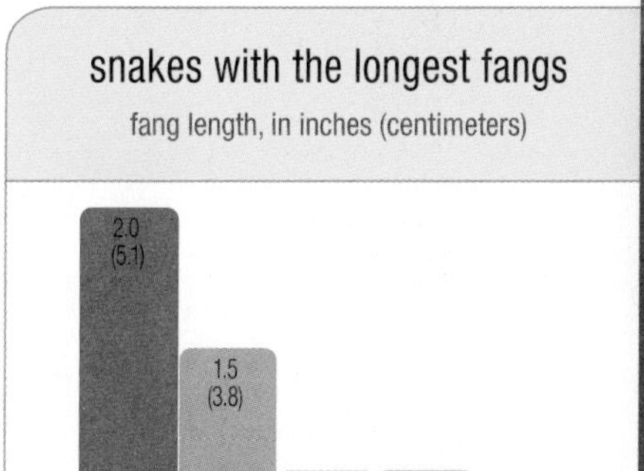

snakes with the longest fangs

fang length, in inches (centimeters)

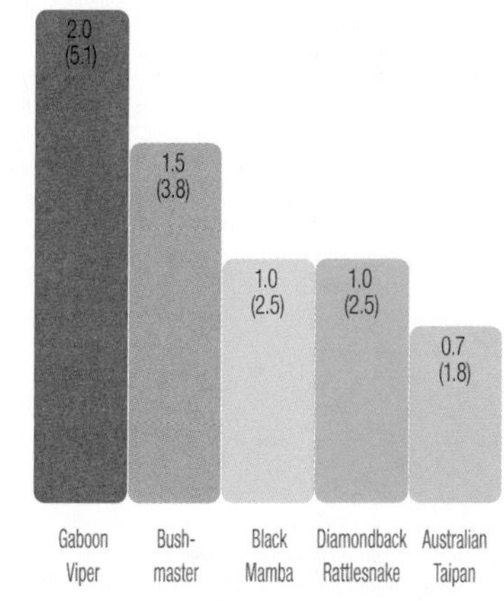
2.0 (5.1)
1.5 (3.8)
1.0 (2.5)
1.0 (2.5)
0.7 (1.8)
Gaboon Viper
Bush-master
Black Mamba
Diamondback Rattlesnake
Australian Taipan

country with the most reptile species

Australia

There are at least 987 reptile species living throughout the continent of Australia. Lizards account for the most with 737 species, including the unique frilled lizard, followed by snakes with more than 200 different species. Australia also has more species of venomous snakes than any other continent. Among the deadliest Australian snakes are the common death adder, the lowlands copperhead, and several types of taipans. Many reptiles thrive in the hot, dry desert climate of Australia. The world's largest reptile—the saltwater crocodile—is also found there. Some of the other well-known reptile residents include sea and freshwater turtles, which nest and lay eggs along Australia's shoreline.

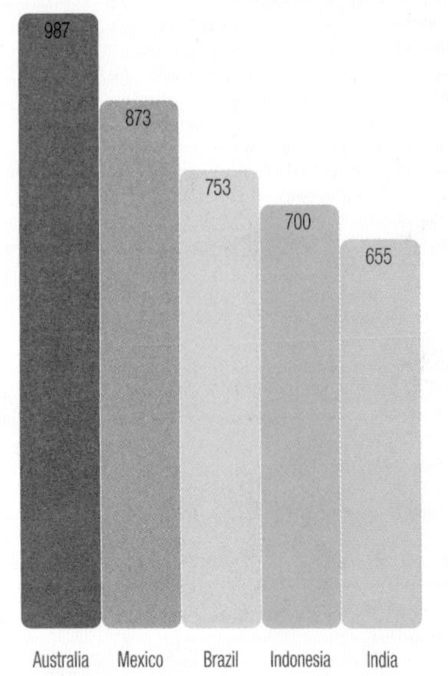
countries with the most reptile species
number of different reptile species
987
873
753
700
655
Australia
Mexico
Brazil
Indonesia
India

Australian frilled lizard

largest amphibian

Chinese Giant Salamander

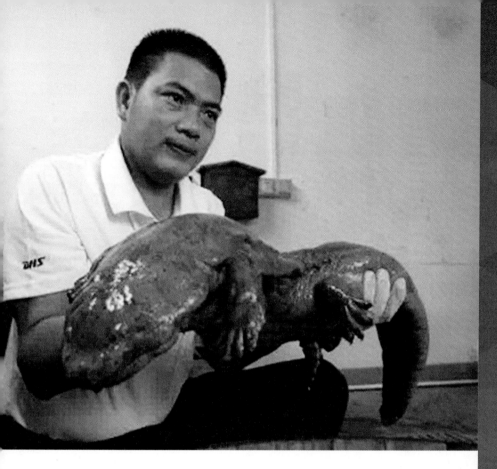

With a length of 6 feet (1.8 m) and a weight of 55 pounds (25 kg), Chinese giant salamanders rule the amphibian world. This salamander has a large head, but its eyes and nostrils are small. It has short legs, a long tail, and very smooth skin. This large creature can be found in the streams of northeastern, central, and southern China. It feeds on fish, frogs, crabs, and snakes. The Chinese giant salamander will not hunt its prey. It waits until a potential meal wanders too close and then grabs it in its mouth. Because many people enjoy the taste of the salamander's meat, it is often hunted and its population is shrinking.

largest amphibians

maximum length, in feet (meters)

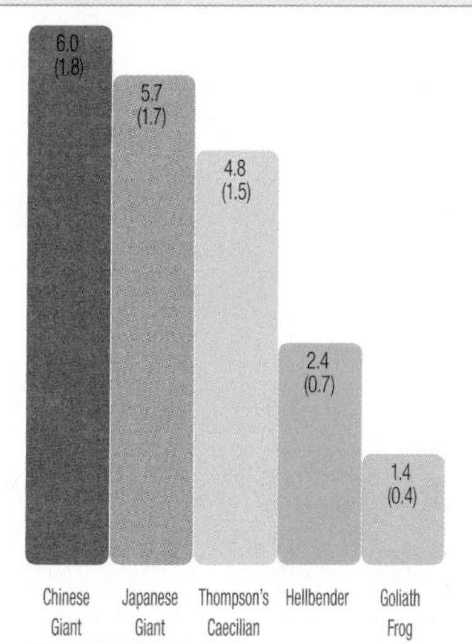
6.0 (1.8)
5.7 (1.7)
4.8 (1.5)
2.4 (0.7)
1.4 (0.4)
Chinese Giant Salamander
Japanese Giant Salamander
Thompson's Caecilian
Hellbender
Goliath Frog

largest frog

Goliath Frog

The Goliath frog has a body that measures 13 inches (33 cm) long, but when its legs are extended, its total body length can increase to more than 2.5 feet (0.76 m). These gigantic frogs can weigh around 7 pounds (3 kg). Oddly enough, the eggs and tadpoles of this species are the same size as those of smaller frogs. Goliath frogs are found only in the western African countries of Equatorial Guinea and Cameroon. They live in rivers that are surrounded by dense rain forests. These huge amphibians are becoming endangered, mostly because their rain-forest homes are being destroyed.

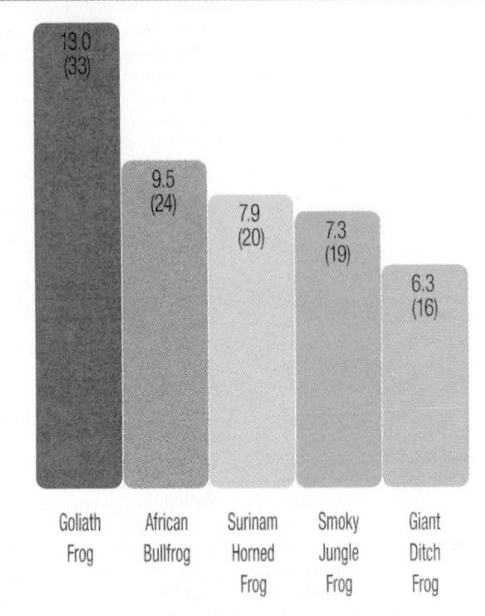
largest frogs
size, in inches (centimeters), excluding legs
13.0 (33)
9.5 (24)
7.9 (20)
7.3 (19)
6.3 (16)
Goliath Frog
African Bullfrog
Surinam Horned Frog
Smoky Jungle Frog
Giant Ditch Frog

largest lizard

Komodo Dragon

With a length of 10 feet (3 m) and a weight of 300 pounds (136 kg), Komodo dragons are the largest lizards roaming the earth. A Komodo dragon has a long neck and tail, and strong legs. These members of the monitor family are found mainly on Komodo Island, located in the Lesser Sunda Islands of Indonesia. Komodos are dangerous and have even been known to attack and kill humans. A Komodo uses its sense of smell to locate food, using its long, yellow tongue. A Komodo can consume 80 percent of its body weight in just one meal!

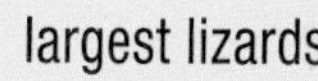
largest lizards

length, in feet (meters)

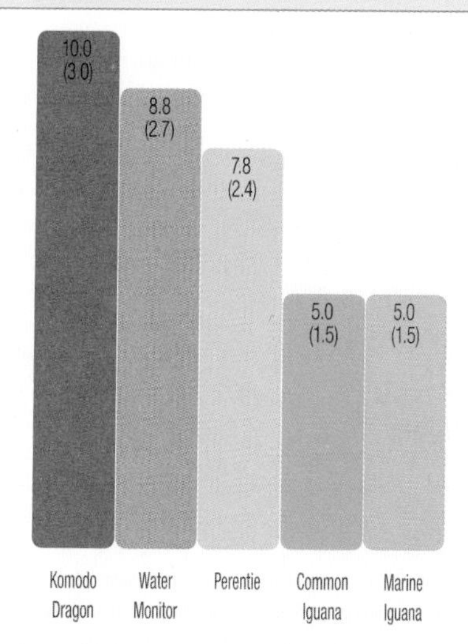
10.0 (3.0)
8.8 (2.7)
7.8 (2.4)
5.0 (1.5)
5.0 (1.5)
Komodo Dragon
Water Monitor
Perentie
Common Iguana
Marine Iguana

largest reptile

Saltwater Crocodile

Saltwater crocodiles can grow to 22 feet (6.7 m) long. That's about twice the length of the average car! However, males usually measure only about 17 feet (5 m) long, and females normally reach about 10 feet (3 m) in length. A large adult will feed on buffalo, monkeys, cattle, wild boar, and other large mammals. Saltwater crocodiles are found throughout the East Indies and Australia. Despite their name, saltwater crocodiles can also be found in freshwater and swamps. Some other common names for this species are the estuarine crocodile and the Indo-Pacific crocodile.

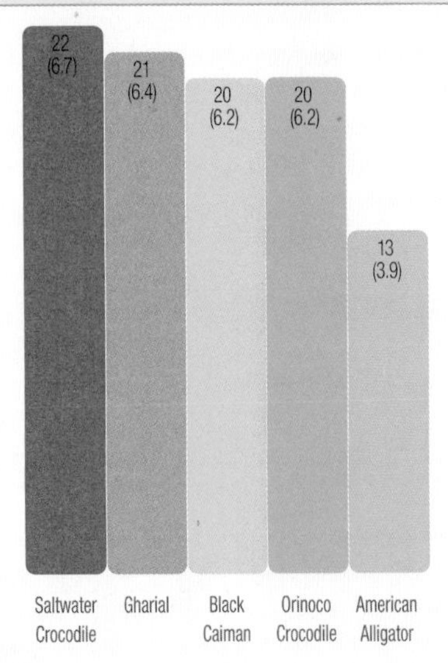
largest reptiles
maximum length, in feet (meters)
22 (6.7)
21 (6.4)
20 (6.2)
20 (6.2)
13 (3.9)
Saltwater Crocodile
Gharial
Black Caiman
Orinoco Crocodile
American Alligator

largest spider

Goliath Birdeater

A Goliath birdeater is about the same size as a dinner plate—it can grow to a total length of 12 inches (30 cm) and weigh about 6 ounces (170 g). A Goliath's spiderlings are also big—they can have a 6-inch (15 cm) leg span just one year after hatching. These giant tarantulas are found mostly in the rain forests of Guyana, Suriname, Brazil, and Venezuela. The Goliath birdeater's name is misleading—they commonly eat insects and small reptiles. Similar to other tarantula species, the Goliath birdeater lives in a burrow. The spider will wait by the opening to ambush prey that gets too close.

largest spiders

length, in inches (centimeters)

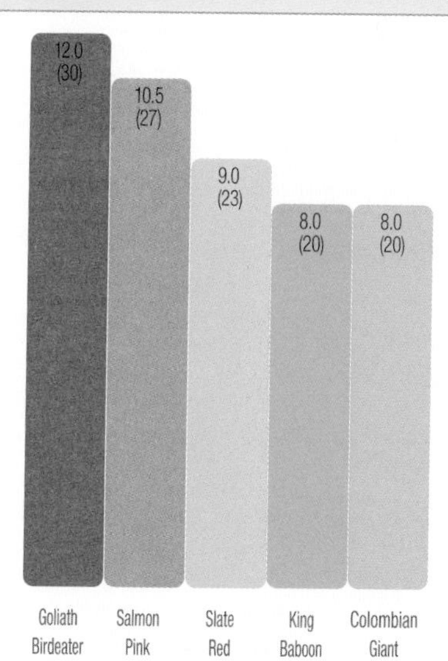
12.0 (30)
10.5 (27)
9.0 (23)
8.0 (20)
8.0 (20)
Goliath Birdeater
Salmon Pink Birdeater
Slate Red Ornamental
King Baboon
Colombian Giant Redleg

fastest-flying insect

Hawk Moth

The average hawk moth—which got its name from its swift and steady flight—can cruise along at speeds over 33 miles (53.6 km) per hour. That's faster than the average speed limit on most city streets! Hawk moths, also known as the sphinx moth and the hummingbird moth, are found throughout the world. This large insect can have a wingspan that reaches up to 2–2.3 inches (5–5.8 cm). Hawk moths also have good memories, may return to the same flowers at the same time each day, and have the longest tongues of any other moth or butterfly (some up to 14 inches long).

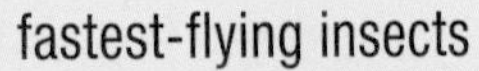
fastest-flying insects

speed, in miles (kilometers) per hour

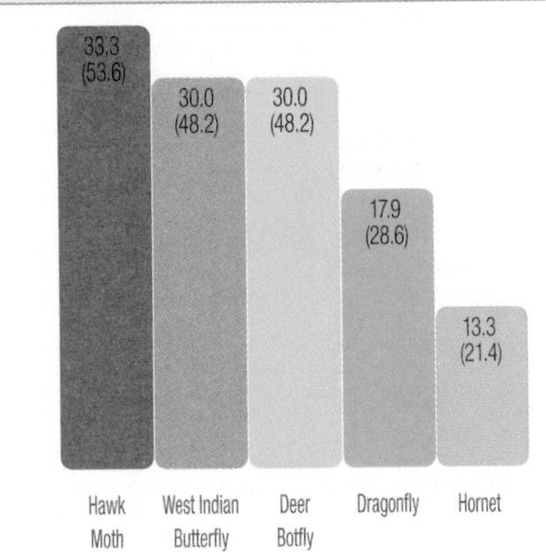
33.3 (53.6)
30.0 (48.2)
30.0 (48.2)
17.9 (28.6)
13.3 (21.4)
Hawk Moth
West Indian Butterfly
Deer Botfly
Dragonfly
Hornet

most common insect

Beetle

There are more than 350,000 different types of beetles crawling around in the world. Beetles make up about 25 percent of all life-forms on Earth, and about 40 percent of all insects are beetles. They come in all shapes, colors, and sizes. The most common types of insects in this order are weevils and rove beetles. Some of the most well-known include ladybugs, fireflies, and dung beetles. Beetles are found in all climates except cold polar regions. Fossils indicate that beetles may have been around for about 300 million years.

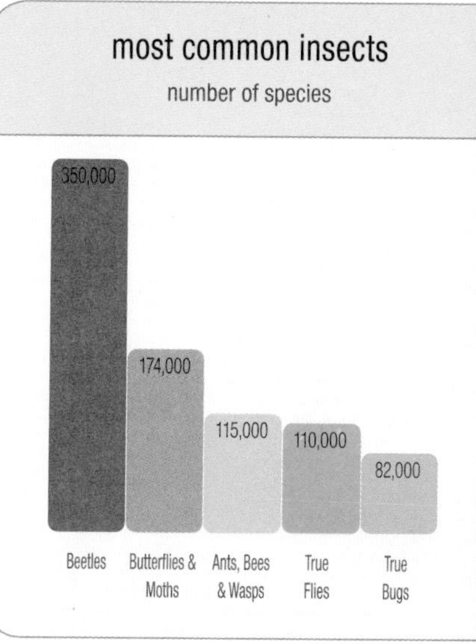
most common insects
number of species
350,000
174,000
115,000
110,000
82,000
Beetles
Butterflies & Moths
Ants, Bees & Wasps
True Flies
True Bugs

Ladybug

longest insect migration

Monarch Butterfly

Millions of monarch butterflies travel to Mexico from all parts of North America every fall, flying as far as 2,700 miles (4,345 km). Once there, they will huddle together in the trees and wait out the cold weather. In spring and summer, most butterflies only live four or five weeks as adults, but in the fall, a special generation of monarchs is born. These butterflies will live for about seven months and participate in the great migration to Mexico. Scientists are studying these butterflies in the hope of learning how the insects know where and when to migrate to a place they have never visited before.

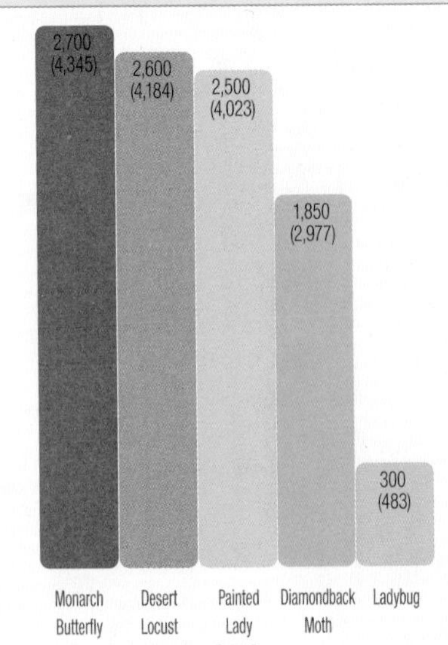
longest insect migrations
migration, in miles (kilometers)
2,700 (4,345)
2,600 (4,184)
2,500 (4,023)
1,850 (2,977)
300 (483)
Monarch Butterfly
Desert Locust
Painted Lady Butterfly
Diamondback Moth
Ladybug

most common pet in the United States

Dog

More than 43.3 million households across the United States own one or more dogs. Approximately 69.9 million dogs live in the country. When it comes to finding a dog, approximately 21 percent of families head to a shelter to adopt one. Those who prefer purebreds tend to choose Labrador retrievers, German shepherds, and Golden retrievers. Some of the most popular dog names include Bella, Max, Daisy, and Buddy. In the United States, about 68 percent of households own at least one type of pet. Fish are the most common pets in the country with 142 million kept as pets, followed by cats with 88.3 million.

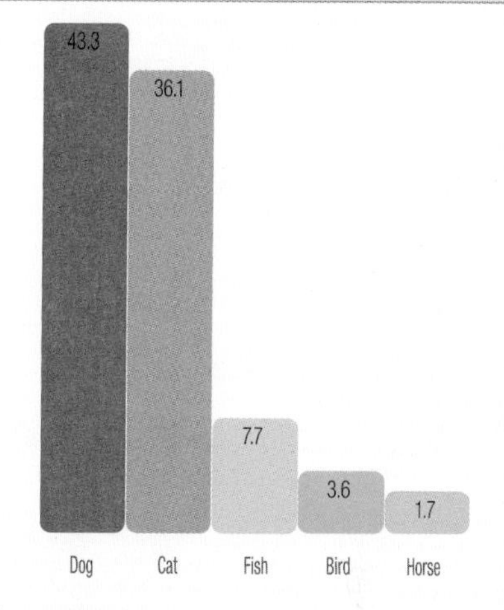
most common pets in the United States
number of US households that own pets, in millions
43.3
36.1
7.7
3.6
1.7
Dog
Cat
Fish
Bird
Horse

most popular dog breed in the United States

Labrador Retriever

Labrador retrievers are top dog in the United States! In 2014, the American Kennel Club recorded more purebred dog registrations for Labs than any other dog in the United States. Labs are very popular with families because of their gentle nature, and they are popular with hunters because of their retrieving skills. A very intelligent breed, Labrador retrievers can be trained to work in law enforcement or as guide dogs. They come in three colors—yellow, black, and brown—and are medium-size athletic dogs. They are considered by the American Kennel Club to be part of the sporting class.

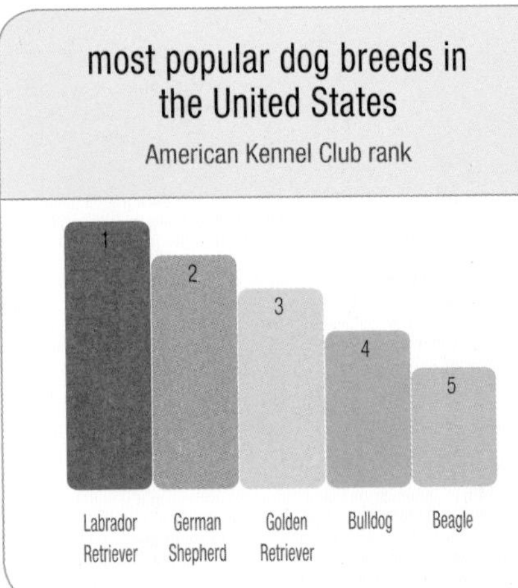
most popular dog breeds in the United States
American Kennel Club rank
1
2
3
4
5
Labrador Retriever
German Shepherd
Golden Retriever
Bulldog
Beagle

most popular cat breed in the world

Exotic

The Cat Fanciers' Association—the world's largest registry of purebred cats—ranks the Exotic as the most popular cat in the world. The breed looks similar to its extremely popular Persian ancestors but has shorter hair. The Exotic also has the same gentle personality as the Persian, but it requires much less grooming and maintenance. Playful and active, Exotics come in many colors. The most popular include black, tortoiseshell, red tabby, brown tabby, and bicolor. These cats, like most other cat breeds, can live about fifteen years.

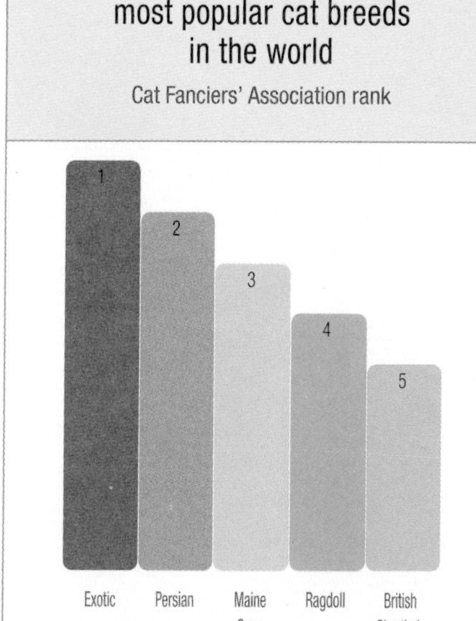

most popular cat breeds in the world
Cat Fanciers' Association rank
1
2
3
4
5
Exotic
Persian
Maine Coon
Ragdoll
British Shorthair

ANIMALS

country that uses the most wind power

China

China produces 44 percent of the world's wind power. Wind is the country's third-largest energy source though China still produces about 80 percent of its energy by burning coal, which creates heavy pollution. However, China plans to increase its wind turbines to increase its production by about 17 gigawatts each year. Currently, there are about 480 wind farms in the country. China has enough turbines to generate about 75 gigawatts of power, or 2.8% of the country's total energy. There are about 15 Chinese companies that produce wind turbines, and the three largest are Goldwind, United Power, and Ming Yang.

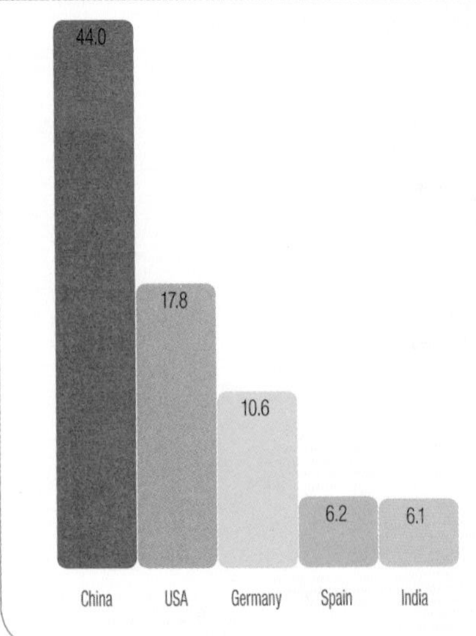
countries that use the most wind power
percentage of worldwide use
44.0
17.8
10.6
6.2
6.1
China
USA
Germany
Spain
India

country with the most solar power

Germany

Germany generates about 35,411 megawatts of solar power each year. Solar power in Germany is slightly cheaper than traditional power sources, which have some of the highest rates in the world. Germany decommissioned its nuclear power plants in 2012 and turned to solar power plants. These plants now produce about 50 percent of the nation's power. Germany hopes to have 80 percent of its energy coming from solar plants by 2050. Solar power is much cleaner than fossil fuels, and therefore considered a "greener" option.

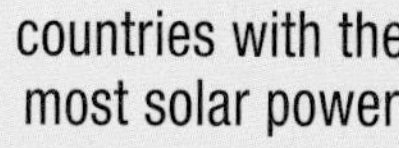
countries with the most solar power
capacity in megawatts

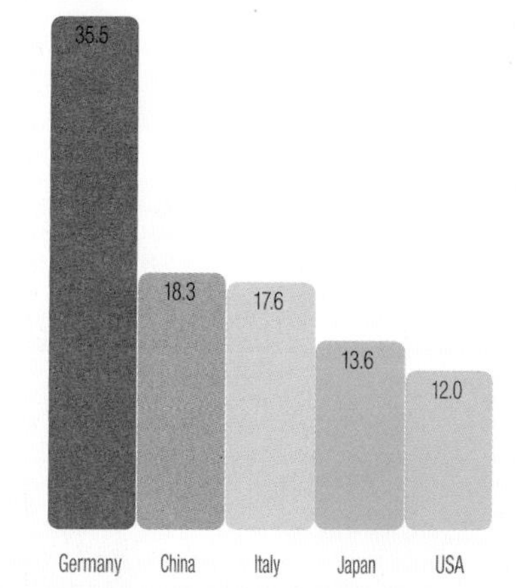
35.5
18.3
17.6
13.6
12.0
Germany
China
Italy
Japan
USA

coldest inhabited place

Resolute

The residents of Resolute, Canada, have to bundle up—the average temperature is just -13°F (-25°C). Located on the northeast shore of Resolute Bay on the south coast of Cornwallis Island, the community is commonly the starting point for expeditions to the North Pole. In the winter it can stay dark for 24 hours, and in the summer it can stay light during the entire night. Only about 200 people brave the climate year-round, but the area is becoming quite popular with tourists.

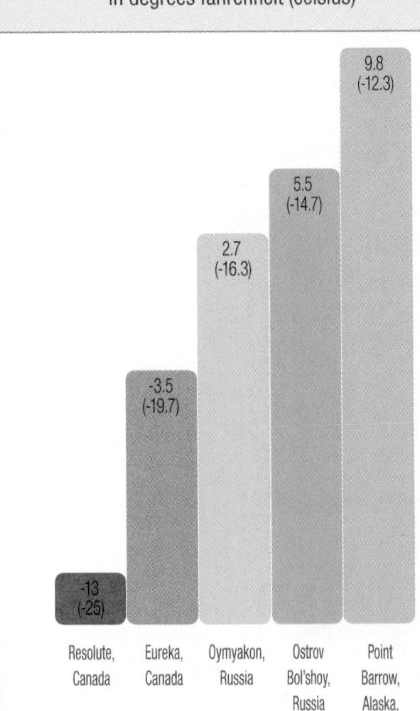
coldest inhabited places
average temperature,
in degrees fahrenheit (celsius)
-13 (-25)
-3.5 (-19.7)
2.7 (-16.3)
5.5 (-14.7)
9.8 (-12.3)
Resolute, Canada
Eureka, Canada
Oymyakon, Russia
Ostrov Bol'shoy, Russia
Point Barrow, Alaska, USA

wettest inhabited place

Mawsynram

Located in the Meghalaya State of India, Mawsynram receives about 467.3 inches (11,871 mm) of rain annually. One of the main reasons that the area gets so much rain is its close proximity to the Bay of Bengal. When moisture gathers above the body of water, it then falls as rain over the nearby village. The heavy monsoon season brings landslides that can cover main roads, and flooding that reaches inside homes. In an effort to block out the loud noise of the driving rain, many villagers line the roofs of their huts with grass.

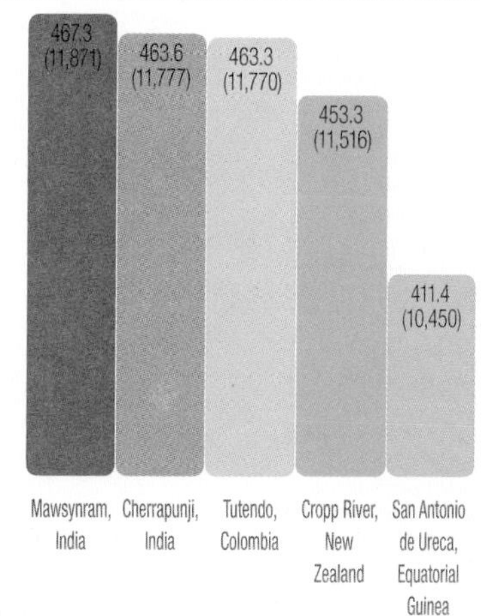
wettest inhabited places
annual rainfall, in inches (mm)
467.3 (11,871)
463.6 (11,777)
463.3 (11,770)
453.3 (11,516)
411.4 (10,450)
Mawsynram, India
Cherrapunji, India
Tutendo, Colombia
Cropp River, New Zealand
San Antonio de Ureca, Equatorial Guinea

driest inhabited place

Aswan

Each year, only 0.02 inches (0.5 mm) of rain falls on Aswan, Egypt. In the country's sunniest and southernmost city, summer temperatures can reach a blistering 114°F (46°C). Aswan is located on the west bank of the Nile River, and it has a very busy marketplace that is also popular with tourists. The Aswan High Dam, at 12,565 feet (3,830 m) long, is the city's most famous landmark. It produces the majority of Egypt's power in the form of hydroelectricity.

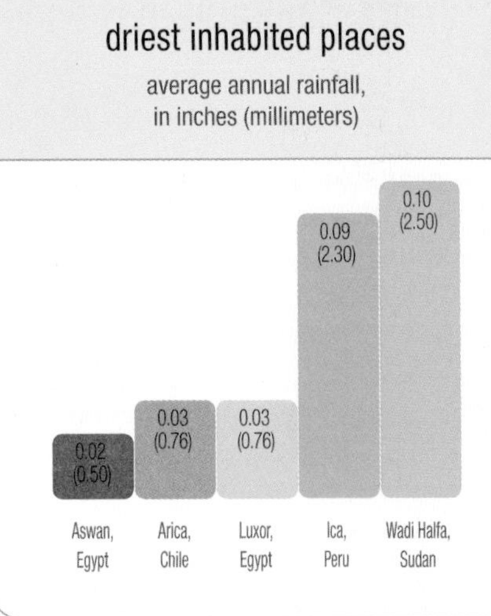
driest inhabited places
average annual rainfall, in inches (millimeters)
0.02 (0.50)
0.03 (0.76)
0.03 (0.76)
0.09 (2.30)
0.10 (2.50)
Aswan, Egypt
Arica, Chile
Luxor, Egypt
Ica, Peru
Wadi Halfa, Sudan

place with the fastest winds

Barrow Island

On April 10, 1996, Cyclone Olivia blew through Barrow Island in Australia and created a wind gust that reached 253 miles (408 km) an hour. Barrow Island is about 31 miles (50 km) off the coast of Western Australia and is home to many endangered species, such as dugongs and green turtles. The dry, sandy land measures about 78 square miles (202 sq km) and is the second-largest island in Western Australia. Barrow Island also has hundreds of oil wells and is a top source of oil for the country. The island has produced more than 300 million barrels of oil since 1967.

places with the fastest winds

speed of strongest winds, in miles (kilometers) per hour

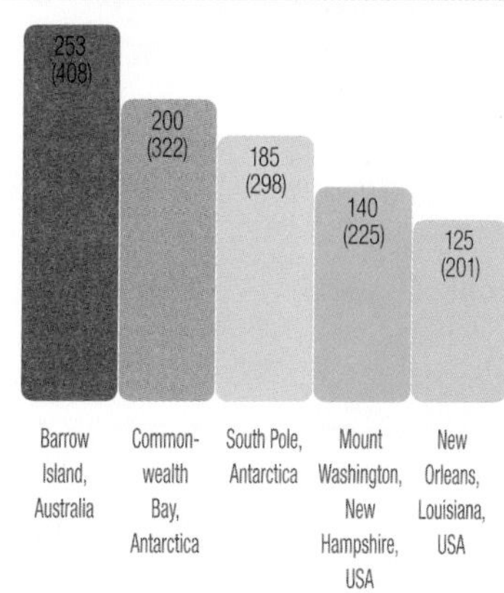
253 (408)
200 (322)
185 (298)
140 (225)
125 (201)
Barrow Island, Australia
Common-wealth Bay, Antarctica
South Pole, Antarctica
Mount Washington, New Hampshire, USA
New Orleans, Louisiana, USA

the place with the hottest recorded temperature

Death Valley, California

On July 10, 1913, thermometers in Furnace Creek Ranch in Death Valley, California, reached 134°F (56.7°C)! This was part of quite a heat wave, since temperatures in this region reached at least 129°F (53.9°C) or higher for 5 straight days. In 2001, the area had 154 consecutive days with temperatures in the triple digits. Death Valley is just 300 feet (100 m) above sea level and has a very dry climate. Just about 2.4 inches (6.1 cm) of rain fall annually. With little rain on the ground, the sun's energy is used only for heating the air and not evaporation.

some of the places with the hottest recorded temperatures

degrees in fahrenheit (celsius)

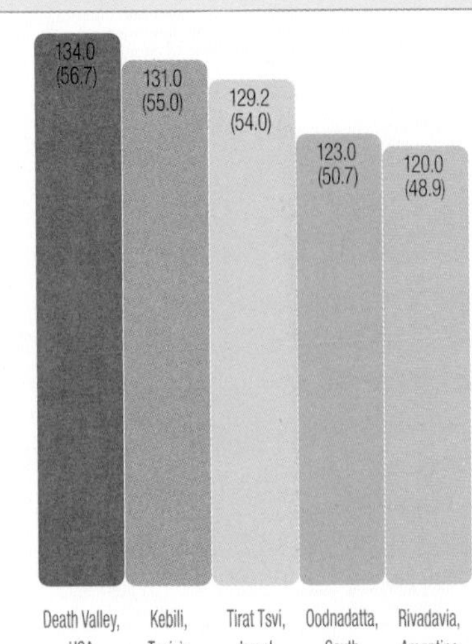
134.0 (56.7)
131.0 (55.0)
129.2 (54.0)
123.0 (50.7)
120.0 (48.9)
Death Valley, USA 7/10/1913
Kebili, Tunisia 7/7/1931
Tirat Tsvi, Israel 6/21/1942
Oodnadatta, South Australia 1/2/1960
Rivadavia, Argentina 12/11/1905

tallest tree

California Redwood

Growing in both California and southern Oregon, California redwoods can reach a height of 385 feet (117 m). Their trunks can grow up to 25 feet (8 m) in diameter. The tallest redwood on record is more than 60 feet (18 m) taller than the Statue of Liberty. Amazingly, this giant tree grows from a seed the size of a tomato. Some redwoods are believed to be more than 2,000 years old. The trees' thick bark and foliage protect them from natural hazards, such as insects and fires.

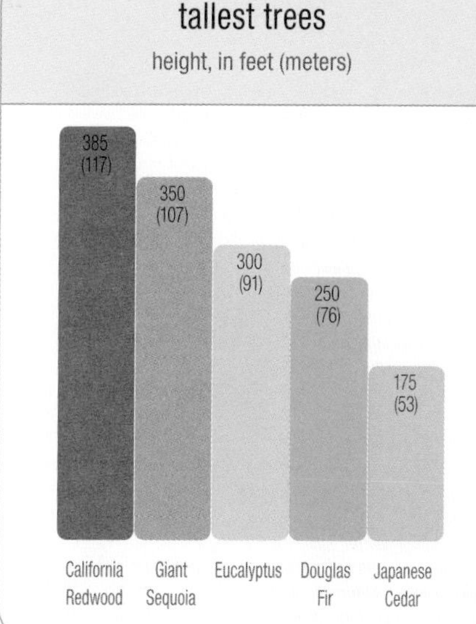
tallest trees
height, in feet (meters)
385 (117)
350 (107)
300 (91)
250 (76)
175 (53)
California Redwood
Giant Sequoia
Eucalyptus
Douglas Fir
Japanese Cedar

most poisonous mushroom

Death Cap

Death cap mushrooms are members of the Amanita family, which are among the most dangerous mushrooms in the world. The death cap contains deadly peptide toxins that cause rapid loss of bodily fluids and intense thirst. Within six hours, the poison shuts down the kidneys, liver, and central nervous system, causing coma and—in more than 50 percent of cases—death. Estimates of the number of poisonous mushroom species range from 80 to 2,000. Most experts agree, however, that at least 100 varieties will cause severe symptoms and even death if eaten.

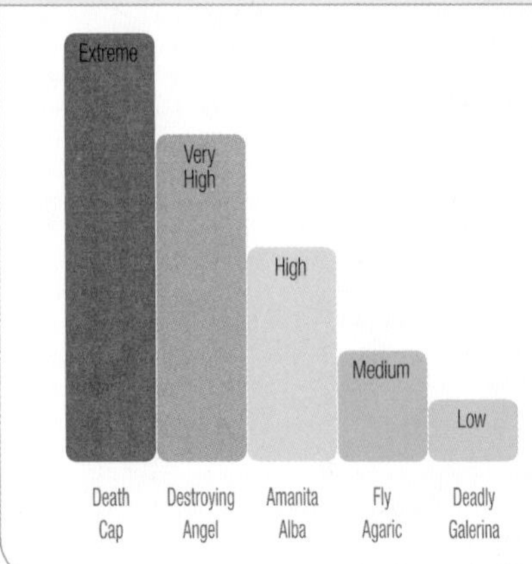
most poisonous mushrooms
risk of fatality if consumed
Extreme
Very High
High
Medium
Low
Death Cap
Destroying Angel
Amanita Alba
Fly Agaric
Deadly Galerina

largest flower

Rafflesia

The blossoms of the giant rafflesia—or stinking corpse lily—can reach 36 inches (91 cm) in diameter and weigh up to 25 pounds (11 kg). Its petals can grow 1.5 feet (0.5 m) long and 1 inch (2.5 cm) thick. There are 16 different species of rafflesia. This endangered plant is found only in the rain forests of Borneo and Sumatra. It lives inside the bark of host vines and is noticeable only when its flowers break through to blossom. The large, reddish-purple flowers give off a smell similar to rotting meat, which attracts insects that help spread the rafflesia's pollen.

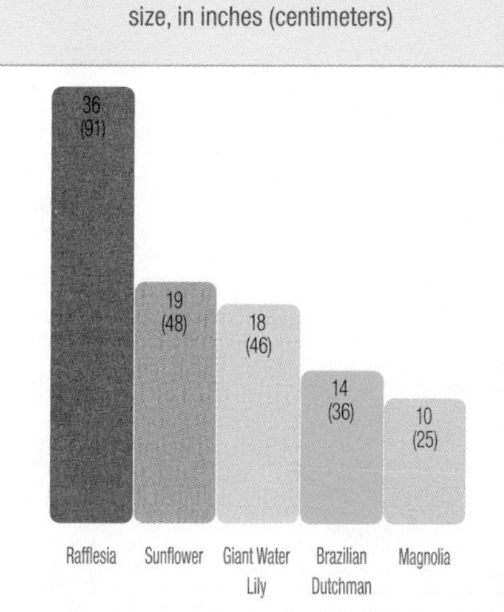
largest flowers
size, in inches (centimeters)
36 (91)
19 (48)
18 (46)
14 (36)
10 (25)
Rafflesia
Sunflower
Giant Water Lily
Brazilian Dutchman
Magnolia

tallest cactus

Saguaro

Many saguaro cacti grow to a height of 50 feet (15 m), but some have actually reached 75 feet (23 m). That's taller than a seven-story building! Saguaros start out quite small and grow very slowly. A saguaro reaches only about 1 inch (2.5 cm) high during its first 10 years. It will not bloom until it is between 50 and 75 years old. By this time, the cactus has a strong root system that can support about 9–10 tons (8–9 t) of growth. Its spines can measure up to 2.5 inches (5 cm) long. Saguaro cacti live for about 170 years. The giant cacti can be found from southeastern California to southern Arizona.

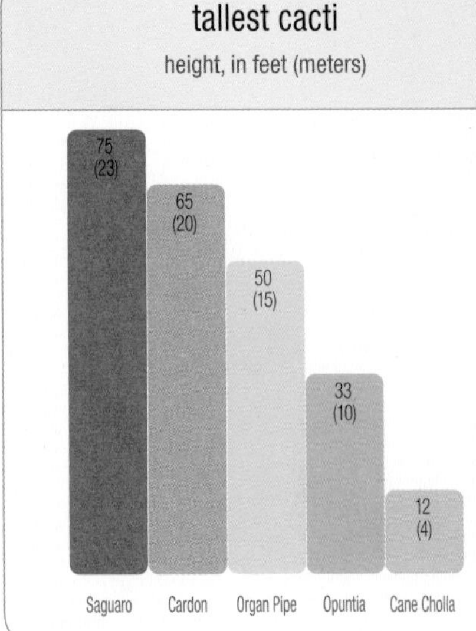
tallest cacti
height, in feet (meters)
75 (23)
65 (20)
50 (15)
33 (10)
12 (4)
Saguaro
Cardon
Organ Pipe
Opuntia
Cane Cholla

most intense earthquake since 1900

Chile

An explosive earthquake measuring 9.5 on the Richter scale rocked the coast of Chile on May 22, 1960. This is equal to the intensity of about 60,000 hydrogen bombs. Some 2,000 people were killed and another 3,000 injured. The death toll was fairly low because the foreshocks frightened people into the streets. When the massive jolt came, many of the buildings that collapsed were already empty. The coastal towns of Valdivia and Puerto Montt suffered the most damage because they were closest to the epicenter—located about 100 miles (161 km) offshore. On April 1, 2014, an 8.2-magnitude quake hit northern Chile, causing a tsunami with 7-foot (2-m) waves. More than 900,000 people in lowland areas had to evacuate, and many came back to find their homes destroyed.

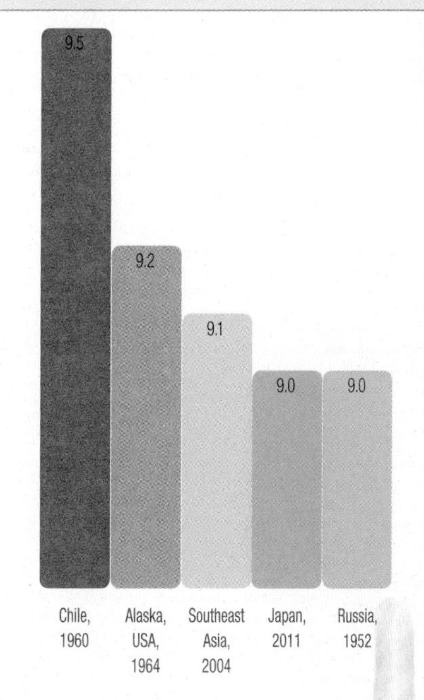
most intense
earthquakes since 1900
magnitude per Richter scale
9.5
9.2
9.1
9.0
9.0
Chile, 1960
Alaska, USA, 1964
Southeast Asia, 2004
Japan, 2011
Russia, 1952

DISASTERS

most destructive flood since 1900

Hurricane Katrina

The pounding rain and storm surges of Hurricane Katrina resulted in catastrophic flooding that cost about $108 billion. The storm formed in late August 2005 over the Bahamas, moved across Florida, and finally hit Louisiana on August 29 as a category-3 storm. The storm surge from the Gulf of Mexico flooded the state, as well as neighboring Alabama and Mississippi. Many levees could not hold back the massive amounts of water, and entire towns were destroyed. In total, some 1,800 people lost their lives.

most destructive floods since 1900

cost of damages, in billions of US dollars

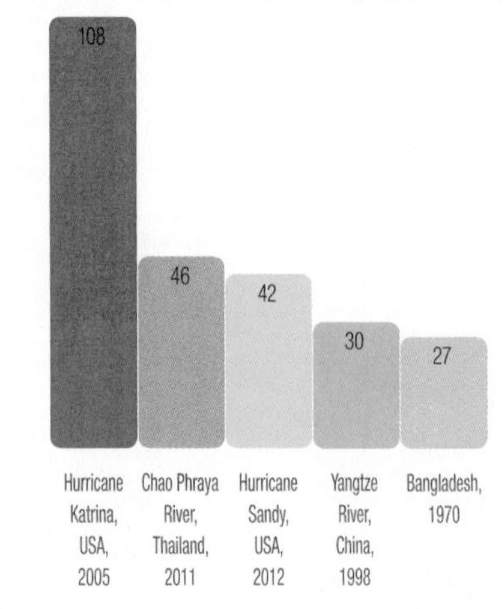
108
46
42
30
27
Hurricane Katrina, USA, 2005
Chao Phraya River, Thailand, 2011
Hurricane Sandy, USA, 2012
Yangtze River, China, 1998
Bangladesh, 1970

worst oil spill

Gulf War

During the Gulf War in 1991, Iraqi troops opened valves of oil wells in Kuwait, releasing more than 300 million gallons (1,136 million liters) of oil into the Persian Gulf. At its worst, the spill measured 101 miles by 42 miles (163 km by 68 km) and was about 5 inches (13 cm) thick. Some of the oil eventually evaporated, another 1 million barrels were collected out of the water, and the rest washed ashore. Although much of the oil can no longer be seen, most of it remains, soaked into the deeper layers of sand along the coast. Amazingly, the wildlife that lives in these areas was not immediately harmed as much as was initially feared. However, salt marsh areas without strong currents were hit the hardest, as oil collected there and killed off entire ecosystems.

worst oil spills

oil spilled, in millions of gallons (liters)

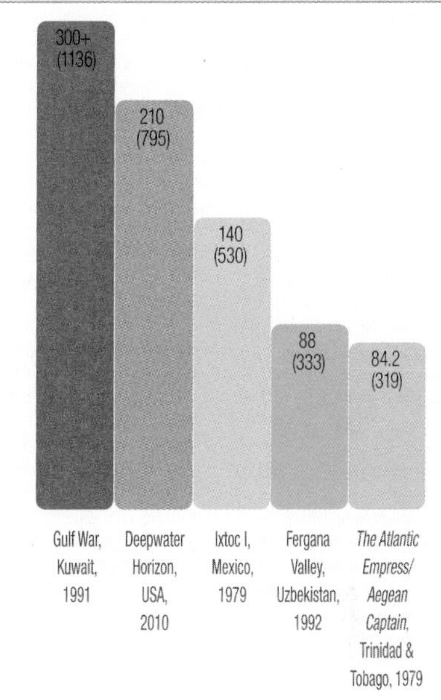
300+
(1136)
210
(795)
140
(530)
88
(333)
84.2
(319)
Gulf War, Kuwait, 1991
Deepwater Horizon, USA, 2010
Ixtoc I, Mexico, 1979
Fergana Valley, Uzbekistan, 1992
The Atlantic Empress/ Aegean Captain, Trinidad & Tobago, 1979

most destructive tornado since 1900

Joplin, Missouri

On May 22, 2011, a category EF5 tornado ripped through Joplin, Missouri, and destroyed about 8,000 buildings, or 30 percent of the small Midwest town. The devastating storm caused damage totaling $2.8 billion and killed 158 people. The tornado measured up to a mile (1.6 km) wide, and was part of a large outbreak of storms during that week, which affected Arkansas, Kansas, and Oklahoma. A category-5 tornado on the Enhanced Fujita (EF) scale is the most intense, capable of producing winds greater than 200 miles (322 km) per hour. With more than 1,000 storms popping up across the country, 2011 was the deadliest year for tornadoes in fifty years.

most destructive tornadoes since 1900

cost of damages, in millions and billions of US dollars

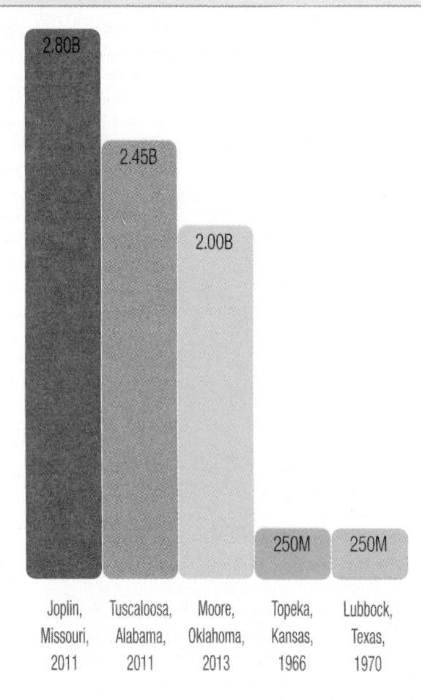
2.80B
2.45B
2.00B
250M
250M
Joplin, Missouri, 2011
Tuscaloosa, Alabama, 2011
Moore, Oklahoma, 2013
Topeka, Kansas, 1966
Lubbock, Texas, 1970

world's most intense hurricane since 1900

Super Typhoon Haiyan

With winds reaching a top speed of 195 miles per hour (314 kph), Super Typhoon Haiyan was the most intense hurricane in the last 115 years. The category-5 storm, also known as Typhoon Yolanda, made landfall in the Philippines on November 8, 2013. The raging storm destroyed more than 600,000 people's homes, and caused $14 billion in damage. More than 6,200 people lost their lives. The most devastating effect of the typhoon was from the storm surge that caused widespread flooding. Regions of Micronesia, Palau, southern China, and Vietnam were also affected.

world's most intense hurricanes since 1900

highest sustained wind speeds, in miles (kilometers) per hour

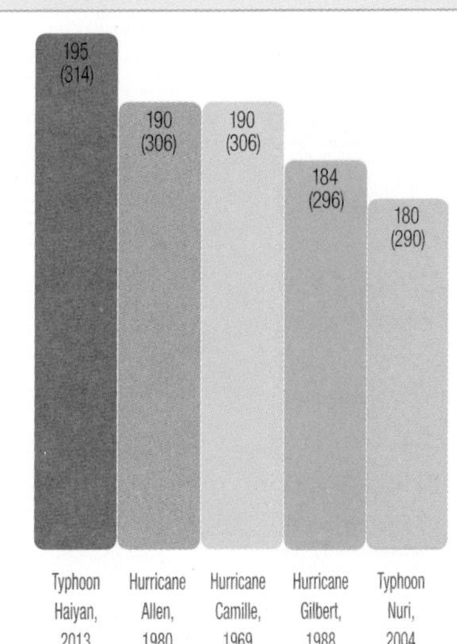
195 (314)
190 (306)
190 (306)
184 (296)
180 (290)
Typhoon Haiyan, 2013
Hurricane Allen, 1980
Hurricane Camille, 1969
Hurricane Gilbert, 1988
Typhoon Nuri, 2004

highest tsunami wave since 1900

Lituya Bay

A 1,720-foot (524-m) tsunami wave crashed down in Lituya Bay, Alaska, on July 10, 1958. Located in Glacier Bay National Park, the tsunami was caused by a massive landslide that was triggered by a 7.7-magnitude earthquake. The water from the bay covered 5 square miles (13 sq km) of land and traveled inland as far as 3,600 feet (1,097 m). Millions of trees were washed away. Amazingly, because the area was very isolated and the coastline was sheltered by coves, only five people died when their fishing boat sank.

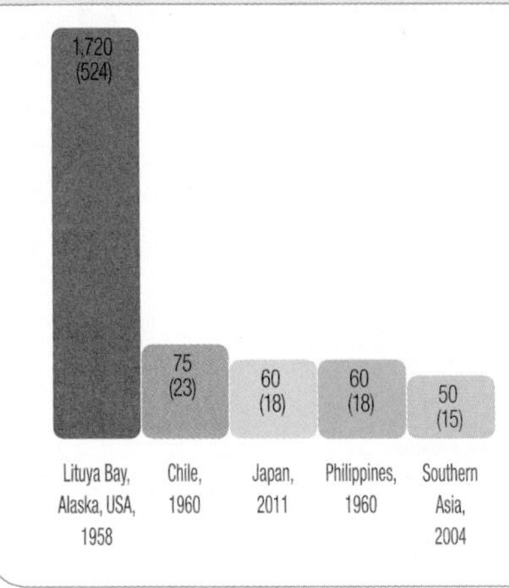
highest tsunami waves since 1900
height of wave, in feet (meters)
1,720 (524)
75 (23)
60 (18)
60 (18)
50 (15)
Lituya Bay, Alaska, USA, 1958
Chile, 1960
Japan, 2011
Philippines, 1960
Southern Asia, 2004

SPORTS RECORDS

- EPIC FAILS
- OLYMPICS
- BASKETBALL
- FOOTBALL
- SPORTING EVENTS
- GOLF
- BASEBALL
- TRACK & FIELD
- TENNIS
- SOCCER
- CAR RACING
- MOTORCYCLING
- HORSE RACING
- HOCKEY

EPIC FAIL
AMERICAN

MLB CAUGHT STEALING LEADER

Rickey Henderson has been caught stealing bases 335 times during his MLB career. He also holds the record for unsuccessful stolen bases for the season with 42 in 1982. Ironically, Henderson also holds the record for the most career stolen bases with 1,406. During his career, Henderson played for nine Major League teams including the Oakland A's and the New York Yankees.

HONDA
ELEVEN
Michael Andretti

DRIVER WITH THE MOST INDY 500 LEADING LAPS WITHOUT WINNING

Michael Andretti has led 431 laps of the Indy 500 car race during his career without a win. Andretti dropped out of the race after holding the lead in 1989, 1991, 1992, 1995, and 2003. This became known as the "Andretti Curse."

EPIC FAIL

MLB PLAYER MOST HIT BY A PITCH

MLB Hall-of-Famer Hughie Jennings was hit by a pitch 287 times during his career. Once he was even hit in the head, but kept on playing. After that game, Jennings passed out and was unconscious for three days! He was a shortstop and played in the majors between 1891 and 1918.

EPIC FAIL

MLB PITCHER WITH THE MOST WALKS

Baseball pitching legend Nolan Ryan walked 2,795 players between 1966 and 1993. He also holds the record for the most grand slams allowed with 10. However, Ryan has the most no-hitter games with 7 and is one of the only MLB players to have his number retired by at least three teams—the Rangers, the Astros, and the Angels.

EPIC FAIL

MLB PLAYER WITH THE MOST STRIKEOUTS

MLB Hall-of-Famer Reggie Jackson is the all-time strikeouts leader, recording 2,597 during his 21-year career—even so, he still achieved a career slugging average of .490. Nicknamed "Mr. October" for his postseason performances, Jackson played for the A's, Orioles, Yankees, and Angels. He graduated from Arizona State and was a first-round draft pick at the age of 21.

EPIC FAIL

EPIC FAIL

PROFESSIONAL BASEBALL TEAM WITH THE MOST LOSSES

Since Philadelphia's baseball franchise began in 1883, they have lost a total of 10,551 games up through the 2014 season. They lost 10,127 games as the Philadelphia Phillies (1890–present) and 424 games as the Philadelphia Quakers (1883–1889). Their worst season came in 1941 when they lost 111 of the 155 games they played.

MLB TEAM CAUGHT IN THE MOST DOUBLE PLAYS

In 1990, the Boston Red Sox grounded out into double plays 174 times. However, they had a win-loss record of 88–74 and finished first in the American League East. Some of the players on the team included catcher Tony Peña, third baseman Wade Boggs, short stop Luis Rivera, and first baseman Carlos Quintana.

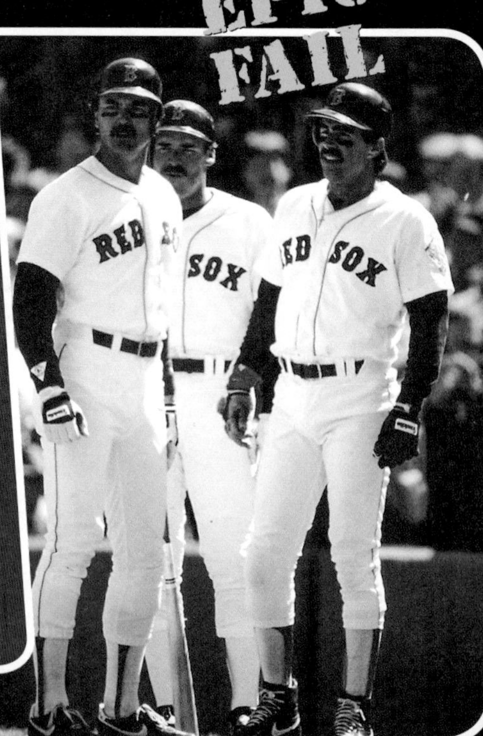
EPIC FAIL
RED SOX
RED SOX

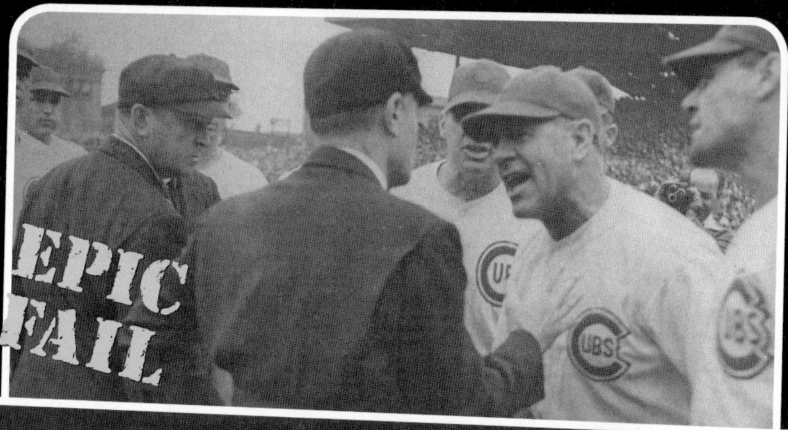
EPIC
FAIL

MLB TEAM WITH THE MOST PLAYERS THROWN OUT OF THE WORLD SERIES

The Chicago Cubs have had the most players thrown out of World Series games. Between 1910 and 1935, a total of 6 players were tossed, mostly for taunting umpires and opposing players from the bench. These players include Frank Chance, Tom Needham, Ray Schalk, Charlie Grimm, Woody English, and Tuck Stainback.

NFL QUARTERBACK WHO HAS BEEN SACKED THE MOST

Between 1991 and 2010, quarterback Brett Favre was sacked 525 times. Favre played for the Atlanta Falcons, Green Bay Packers, New York Jets, and Minnesota Vikings. Denver Broncos quarterback John Elway was just behind Favre with 516 takedowns.

EPIC
FAIL

EPIC FAIL

FAVRE
4
4

NFL QUARTERBACK WITH THE MOST INTERCEPTIONS

With 336 career interceptions, Brett Favre missed his target more times than any other quarterback in the NFL. He attempted 10,169 passing yards during his career and had a 62.0% completion rate. Favre was a second-round draft pick by the Atlanta Falcons in 1991.

NFL PLAYER WITH THE MOST FUMBLES

Both Daunte Culpepper and Kerry Collins hold the record for the most fumbles in an NFL season with 23 each—Culpepper while playing for the Minnesota Vikings in 2002 and Collins for the New York Giants in 2001.

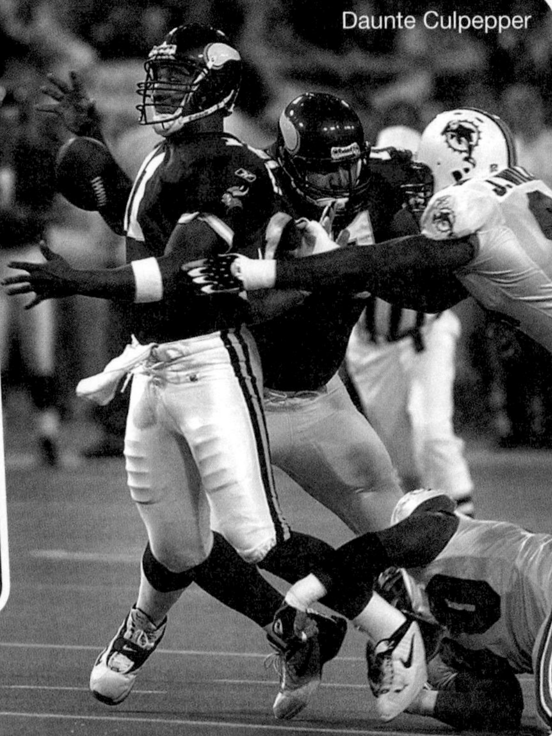
Daunte Culpepper

EPIC FAIL

EPIC
FAIL

NFL TEAM WITH THE WORST OVERALL RECORD

The Tampa Bay Buccaneers have the worst overall record in the NFL with a winning percentage of just .385. Between 1976 and 2014, the team won 241 games and lost 385, including 9 losses in the postseason.

NFL COACH WITH THE WORST WIN-LOSS PERCENTAGE

From 1928 to 1929, NFL coach Fay Abbott won none of his games, giving him a win-loss percentage of 0%! During his very short career, he coached the Dayton Triangles.

EPIC
FAIL

MILWAUKEE
33
EPIC
FAIL

NBA PLAYER WITH THE MOST FOULS

Kareem Abdul-Jabbar leads the NBA in career fouls with 4,657. That's an average of almost 3 fouls per game. Abdul-Jabbar, who played from 1969 to 1989, spent his first 6 seasons with the Milwaukee Bucks and finished his career with the LA Lakers.

EPIC
FAIL

NBA PLAYER WHO MISSED THE MOST FIELD GOALS

In November 2014, Los Angeles Lakers star Kobe Bryant became the NBA all-time leader in missed field goal shots with 13,421. He's missed at least 20 shots in 44 games—the fourth highest in NBA history. Bryant signed with the Lakers in 1996 and has remained with the team throughout his impressive career.

NBA TEAM WITH THE WORST SEASON

During the 1972-1973 regular NBA season, the Philadelphia 76ers had a win-loss percentage of just .110. They won only 9 of their 73 games! During this time, the team was coached by Roy Rubin, until he was replaced by Kevin Loughery in January 1973.

EPIC
FAIL
Sixers
25

EPIC
FAIL
8
MILTON-JONES

WNBA PLAYER WITH THE MOST FOULS

With 1,544, DeLisha Milton-Jones leads the WNBA in career fouls. The forward joined the league in 1999 with the Los Angeles Sparks and later went on to play for the Washington Mystics, the San Antonio Stars, the New York Liberty, and the Atlanta Dream.

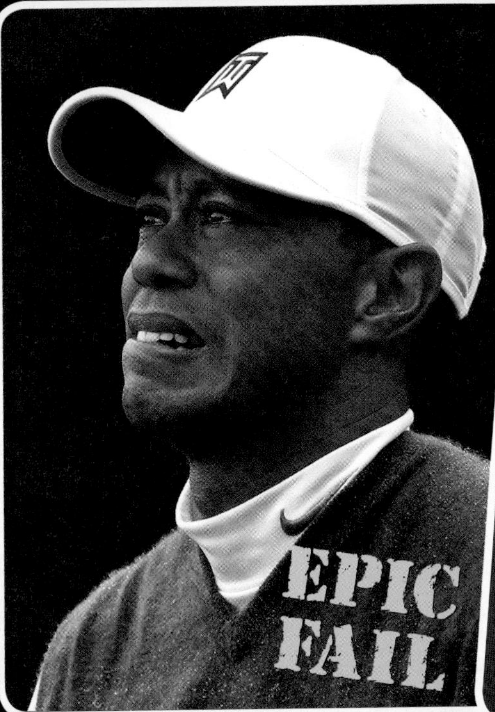
EPIC
FAIL

BAD DAYS FOR TIGER WOODS

In January 2015, Tiger Woods had one of the worst games of his professional career at the Phoenix Open in Arizona. He finished with an 82 and missed making the cut. It was the first time he'd missed making the cut in two consecutive PGA events. Then, in June 2015, Woods hit a new low at the Memorial Tournament in Ohio. He scored an 85, which was 13 strokes over par. He only hit onto the fairways and greens half the time, and had to putt 32 times.

EPIC
FAIL

GOALIE WITH THE MOST PENALTY MINUTES

Even though penalty minutes for NHL goalies are unusual, Ron Hextall recorded 100+ minutes a season for three seasons in a row (1986–1989) while playing for the Philadelphia Flyers. He is the NHL's all-time leader in goalie penalty minutes with 584.

ATP PLAYER WITH THE MOST DOUBLE FAULTS IN A ROW

ATP player Greg Rusedski holds the record for the most double faults in a row with five during a 2006 match against Mikhail Youzhny of Russia. Rusedski was on the ATP circuit between 1992 and 2007, and played for both Canada and Britain. After retirement, he worked as a sportscaster and commentator.

EPIC
FAIL

EPIC FAIL

ATP PLAYER WITH THE MOST TIE BREAK LOSSES IN A ROW

Robin Haase set the record for the most lost tie breaks in a row with 17 between 2012 and 2013. Haase is a right-handed player from the Netherlands who turned pro in 2005. During his career, he's had 1,597 aces and 703 double faults. Haase has won two career singles titles.

NHL GOALIE WHO HAS ALLOWED THE MOST GOALS

Martin Brodeur has allowed more goals than any other player in the NHL. During his 22-season career, the Montreal native gave up 2,781 points. He allowed the most goals during the 1995-1996 season with 173. Widely considered one of the NHL's greatest goalies, Brodeur won three Stanley Cups and four Vezina Trophies with the New Jersey Devils, where he played for most of his career. Brodeur retired in January 2015 after a brief stint with the St. Louis Blues.

RUPP
30

EPIC FAIL

MOST EXPENSIVE MISSED PUTT

During the Masters Tournament in 2013, Angel Cabrera missed a 15-foot (4.5-m) putt causing him to lose about $576,000. That's one of the costliest missed putts in history. In 2009, Cabrera had been in a similar situation but managed to sink that putt to win.

EPIC
FAIL

TAYLOR
19
EPIC
FAIL

MLS TEAM WITH THE WORST SEASONAL ATTENDANCE

Chivas USA suffered Major League Soccer's worst average home game attendance with an average of just 6,942 people per game in 2014—far short of the stadium's 27,000-seat capacity. Not surprisingly, the club stopped operating at the end of the season. It will be reorganized under new ownership. The previous record holder was the Miami Fusion, with an average of 7,460 people per game in 2000.

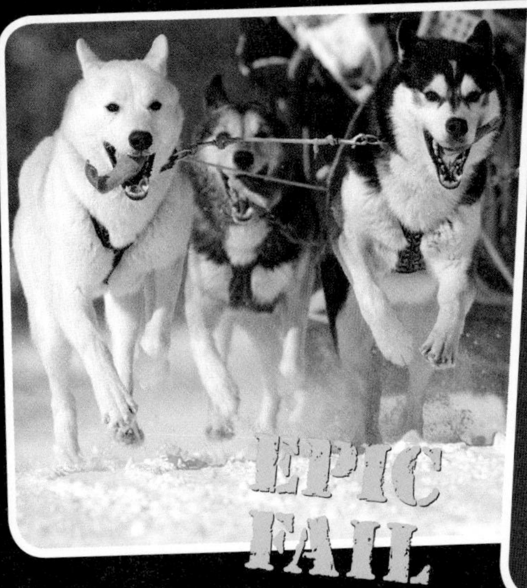
EPIC
FAIL

SLOWEST IDITAROD WINNER

In 1974, Carl Huntington mushed into the record books when he became the slowest winner of Alaska's Iditarod dog-sled race with a time of 20 days, 15 hours, 2 minutes, and 7 seconds. By comparison, the fastest race was in 2002 when Martin Buser won in just under 9 days.

DRIVER WHO LEAD THE DAYTONA 500 FOR THE MOST LAPS BUT DIDN'T WIN

Racecar driver Fireball Roberts led for 170 laps of the Daytona 500 in 1961 but failed to win the race. That's the most laps led without scoring the trophy. He did manage to win the race the following year.

EPIC
FAIL

EPIC
FAIL

WORLD'S WORST NATIONAL SOCCER TEAM

The Bhutan soccer team is the worst in the world, losing every game they played between 2009 and 2014. Because of this, they had 0 points. However, in 2015, they managed to win a qualifying game for the 2018 World Cup.

SLOWEST OLYMPIC SWIMMING FREESTYLE TIME

Eric Moussambani, an Olympic swimmer from Equatorial Guinea, finished with the slowest Olympic time in history in the 100-meter freestyle at the 2000 Sydney Olympics, with a time of about 1 minute, 52 seconds. The winner (Pieter van den Hoogenband) finished in just over 48 seconds. Moussambani—the only person who volunteered to swim for his country—was entered into the race as a wildcard. He had never even swum in an Olympic-sized pool before the trip!

EPIC FAIL

DALLAS
STARS
ALL STAR

EPIC FAIL

WORST NHL FIRST-ROUND DRAFT PICK

Patrik Stefan was the first pick of the 1999 NHL draft, but he went on to score just 64 goals in 455 games—an average of 1 every 7 games. While playing for the Dallas Stars in 2007, he even missed scoring a goal on an empty net!

ON TO THE EPIC WINS!

fastest Olympic 100-meter dash

Usain Bolt

Jamaican sprinter Usain Bolt flew into the record books yet again when he ran the 100-meter dash in just 9.63 seconds at the 2012 Olympic Games in London, England. In 2008, Bolt had become the first man ever to win the 100-meter and 200-meter dashes at the Olympics while setting world records in both races. Four years later, he became the first man to win gold medals in both races for two consecutive Olympics. With two additional wins with the Jamaican relay team, Bolt has a total of 6 Olympic gold medals. He also set the world record for the 100-meter dash when he ran the race in just 9.58 seconds at the World Championships in Berlin, Germany, in 2009.

fastest Olympic
100-meter dash
time in seconds

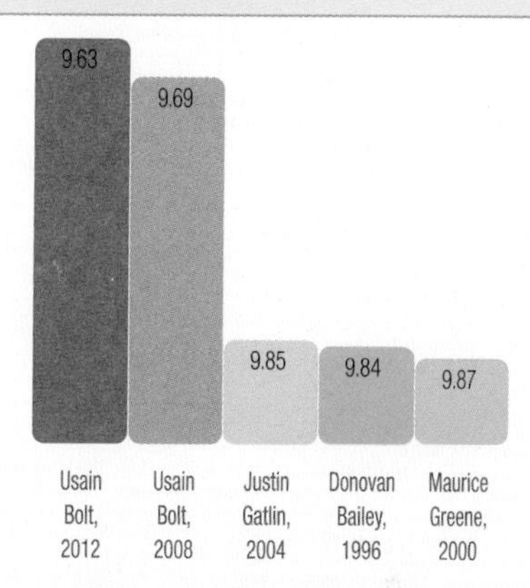
9.63
9.69
9.85
9.84
9.87
Usain Bolt, 2012
Usain Bolt, 2008
Justin Gatlin, 2004
Donovan Bailey, 1996
Maurice Greene, 2000

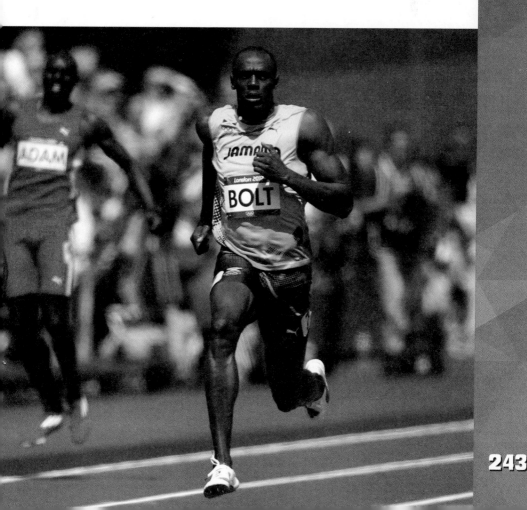

Shaun White

country with the most Olympic snowboarding medals

United States

With a total of 24 Olympic medals, US athletes are tops in snowboarding. The nation's impressive collection includes 10 gold, 5 silver, and 9 bronze medals. The most successful US snowboarder is Kelly Clark, who won a total of 3 medals—more than any other snowboarder in the world. Shaun White and Seth Wescott are the only two US athletes who have won two gold medals. Snowboarding first appeared in the winter Olympics in 1998, and the US has been in each of the competitions since then. The country's most successful year was 2006 in Torino, Italy, when athletes brought home a total of 7 medals.

countries with the most Olympic snowboarding medals

total medals won

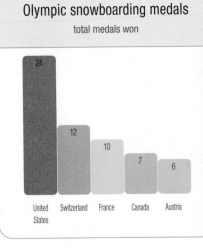

Country	Total medals
United States	24
Switzerland	12
France	10
Canada	7
Austria	6

country with the most Olympic figure skating medals

United States

The United States has dominated Olympic figure skating, picking up a total of 48 medals since the event was first featured in 1908. The medal collection includes 15 gold, 16 silver, and 17 bronze. The US has competed in 24 of the 26 Olympic skating competitions, and had its most successful year in 1956, when athletes picked up 5 medals. Men's and ladies' singles have been included in the winter Games since it began, while ice dancing was added in 1976. A new competition—mixed team—was added in 2014. Some of the US's recent medal winners include Meryl Davis and Charlie White, an ice-dancing team that won gold in Sochi in 2014.

countries with the most
Olympic figure skating medals
total medals won
48
26
25
24
20
United States
Russia
Canada
Soviet Union
Austria

Meryl Davis and Charlie White

country with the most Olympic swimming medals

United States

United States' swimmers have brought home a grand total of 519 Olympic Medals—230 gold, another 164 silver, and 125 bronze. Some of the country's most successful swimmers include Michael Phelps, Ryan Lochte, Mark Spitz, Jenny Thompson, Amy Van Dyken, and Dara Torres. During the 2012 games in London, the US picked up 31 medals—more than three times as many as the swimming medal count of China, the next highest country. Together, Michael Phelps, Missy Franklin, and Allison Schmitt contributed more than half of the medals that year.

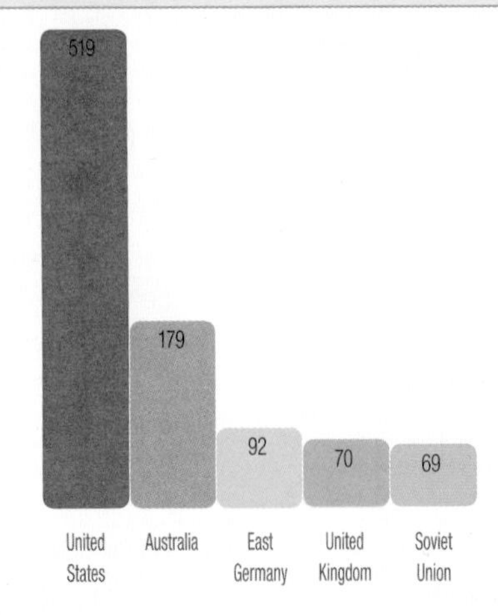
countries with the most
Olympic swimming medals
total medals won
519
179
92
70
69
United States
Australia
East Germany
United Kingdom
Soviet Union

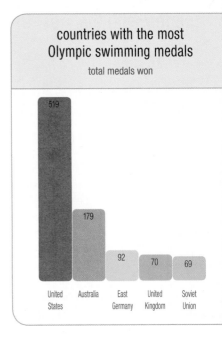

(L-R) US swimmers Conor Dwyer, Michael Phelps, Ryan Lochte, Ricky Berens

Paul Pierce

NBA team with the most championship titles

Boston Celtics

The Boston Celtics are the most successful team in the NBA with 17 championship wins. The first win came in 1957, and the team went on to win the next seven consecutive titles—the longest streak of consecutive championship wins in the history of US sports. The most recent championship title came in 2008. The Celtics entered the Basketball Association of America in 1946, which later merged into the NBA in 1949. The Celtics made the NBA play-offs for four consecutive seasons from 2001 to 2005, but they were eliminated in early rounds each time. They also made the playoffs from 2009 through 2013, and 2015, but were not able to bring home another title.

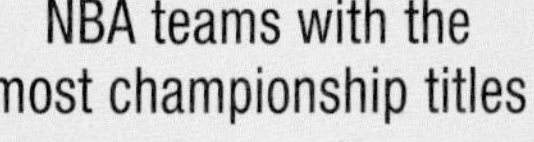
NBA teams with the
most championship titles
number of championship titles

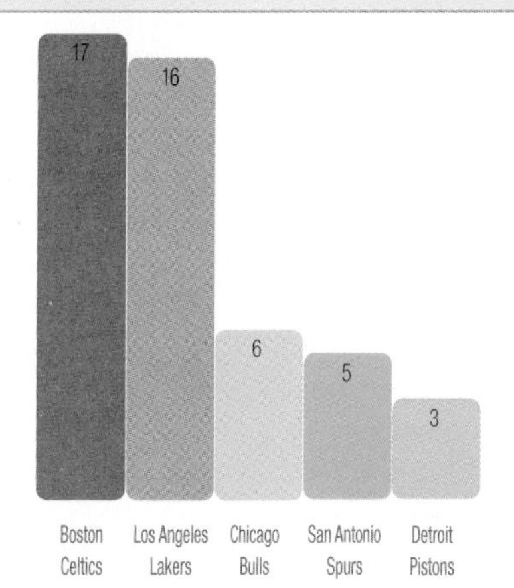
17
16
6
5
3
Boston Celtics
Los Angeles Lakers
Chicago Bulls
San Antonio Spurs
Detroit Pistons

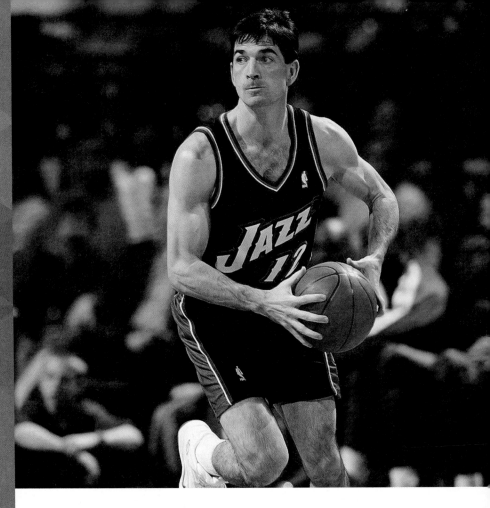

NBA player with the most steals

John Stockton

As an NBA point guard from 1984 to 2003, John Stockton recorded a staggering 3,265 steals. A first-round draft pick by the Utah Jazz, Stockton remained with the team throughout his career. During this time, he also scored 19,711 points and an NBA-leading 15,806 assists in 1,504 games. Stockton was an NBA All-Star ten times, and he picked up Olympic gold medals in 1992 and 1996. He was also named one of the 50 Greatest Players in NBA history in 1996. Stockton was inducted into the Basketball Hall of Fame in 2009.

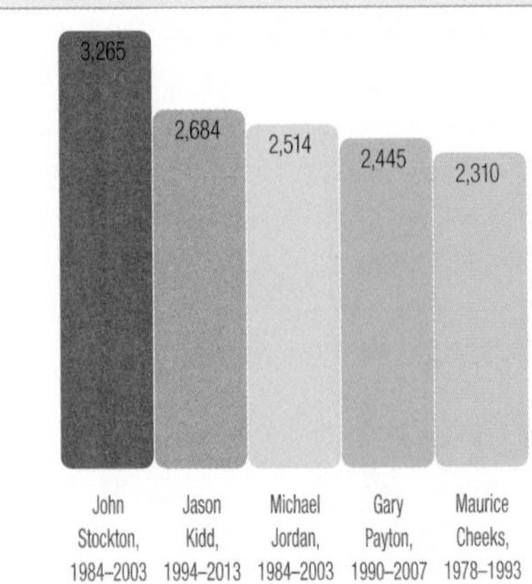
NBA players with the most steals
career steals
3,265
2,684
2,514
2,445
2,310
John Stockton, 1984–2003
Jason Kidd, 1994–2013
Michael Jordan, 1984–2003
Gary Payton, 1990–2007
Maurice Cheeks, 1978–1993

NBA player with the highest career scoring average

Michael Jordan

Michael Jordan averaged an amazing 30.12 points during his legendary career. He was a first-round draft pick in 1984 for the Chicago Bulls, and played with them until 1998. Jordan led the league in scoring for seven years. During the 1986 season, he became the second player ever to score 3,000 points in a single season. Following a three-year retirement after leaving the Bulls, Jordan came back to the NBA to play for the Washington Wizards in 2001. He stayed with the team for two seasons before retiring again in 2003. During his career, Jordan scored 32,292 points.

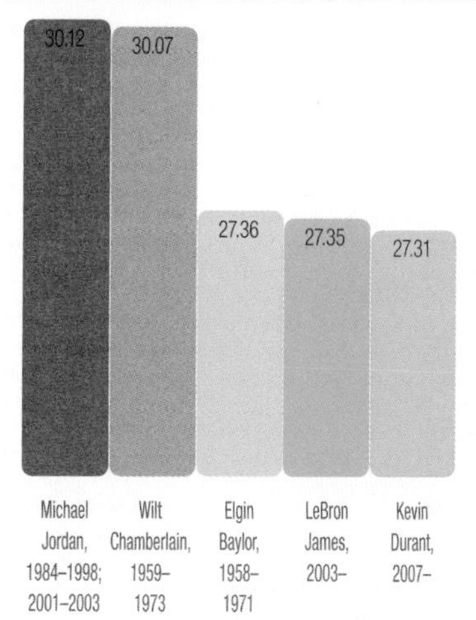
NBA players with the highest career scoring averages
average points per game
30.12
30.07
27.36
27.35
27.31
Michael Jordan, 1984–1998; 2001–2003
Wilt Chamberlain, 1959–1973
Elgin Baylor, 1958–1971
LeBron James, 2003–
Kevin Durant, 2007–

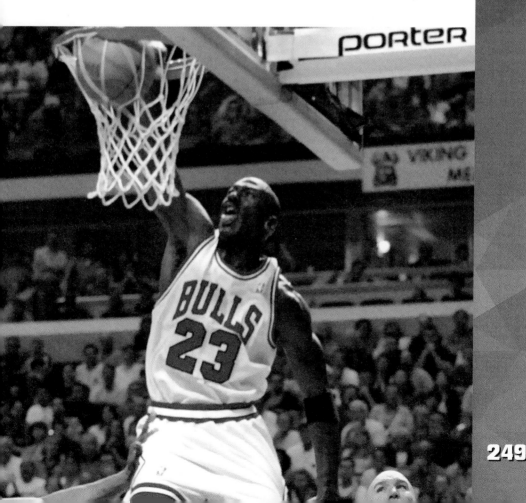

NBA's highest-scoring game

Detroit Pistons

On December 13, 1983, the Detroit Pistons beat the Denver Nuggets with a score of 186–184 at McNichols Arena in Denver, Colorado. The game was tied at 145 at the end of regular play, and three overtime periods were needed to determine the winner. During the game, both the Pistons and the Nuggets each had six players who scored in the double digits. Four players scored more than 40 points each, which was an NBA first. The Pistons scored 74 field goals that night, claiming another NBA record that still stands today.

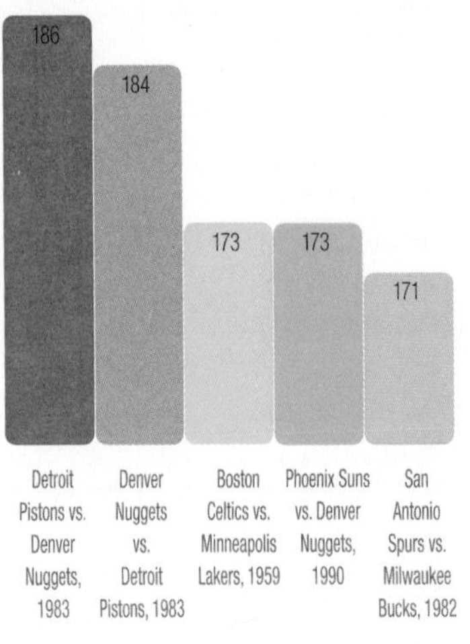
NBA's highest-scoring games
points scored by a team in one game
186
184
173
173
171
Detroit Pistons vs. Denver Nuggets, 1983
Denver Nuggets vs. Detroit Pistons, 1983
Boston Celtics vs. Minneapolis Lakers, 1959
Phoenix Suns vs. Denver Nuggets, 1990
San Antonio Spurs vs. Milwaukee Bucks, 1982

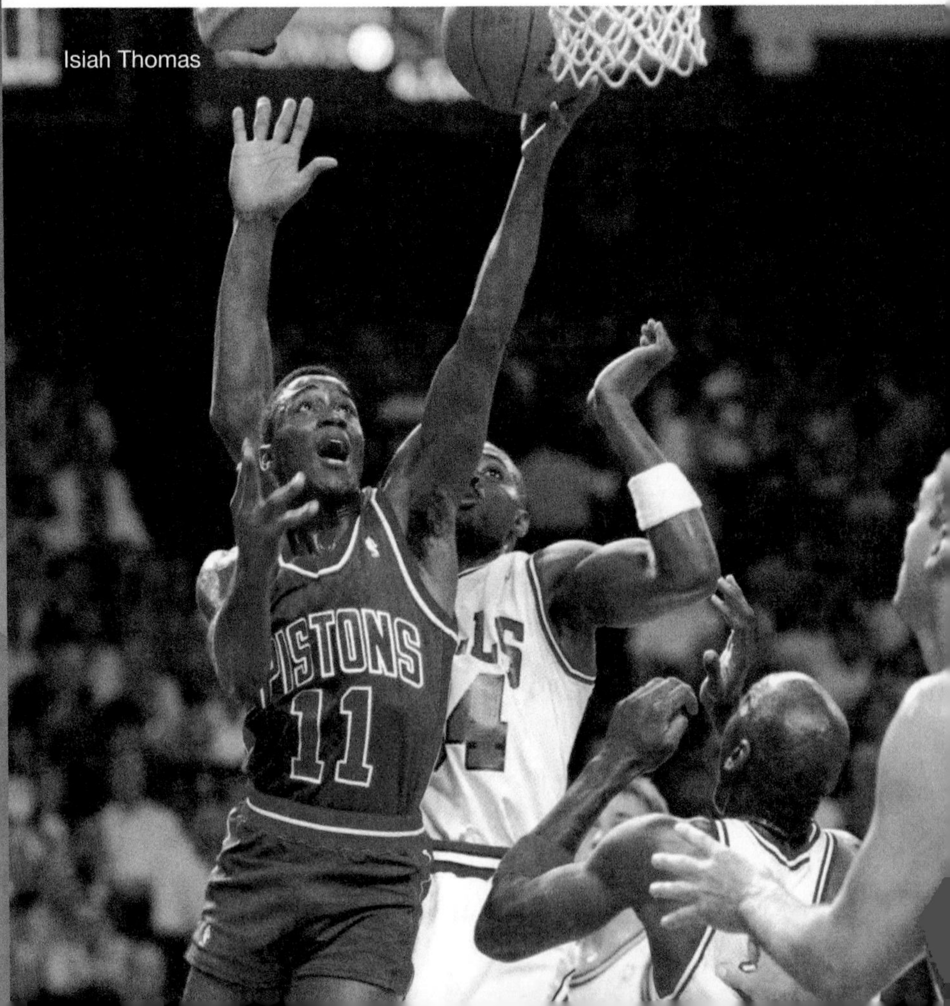

Isiah Thomas

NBA player with the highest earnings

LeBron James

NBA superstar LeBron James earned $64.6 million in 2014–2015, including $20.6 million in salary and $44 million in endorsements. In 2014, he signed a two-year contract with the Cleveland Cavaliers worth $42.1 million. Some of the products James pitches include Kia, McDonald's, Nike, Coca-Cola, Samsung, and Beats by Dre. James was the first overall draft pick in 2003 with the Cavaliers, and although he played for the Miami Heat between 2010 and 2014, he headed back to Cleveland in 2014. He has played in every NBA All-Star Game since 2005, and he won two championships with Miami in 2012 and 2013. In 2015, James lead his team to the NBA finals, though they lost to the Golden State Warriors.

NBA players with the highest earnings

2014–2015 earnings, in millions of US dollars

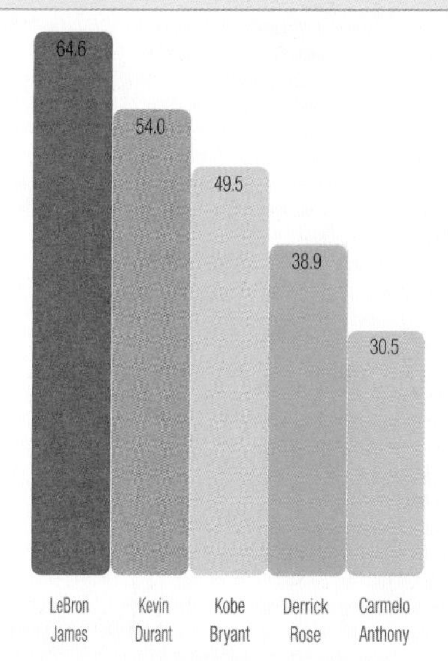
64.6
54.0
49.5
38.9
30.5
LeBron James
Kevin Durant
Kobe Bryant
Derrick Rose
Carmelo Anthony

NBA player with the highest field goal percentage

DeAndre Jordan

DeAndre Jordan sinks 66.4% of all field goals (any shot not made on the free throw line). Jordan was a second-round draft pick by the Los Angeles Clippers in 2008 and has remained with the team. During his NBA career, he has played 13,454 minutes and scored 4,142 points—or a point every 3.2 minutes. He's also grabbed 4,644 rebounds and racked up 307 steals. During the 2014–2015 season, Jordan started all 82 games and averaged 11.5 points and 15.0 rebounds per game.

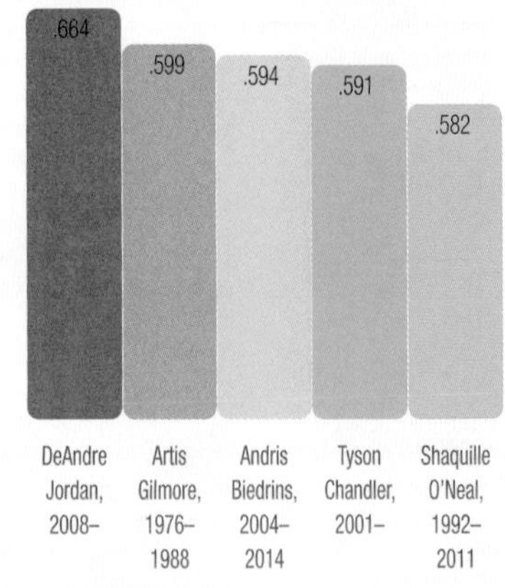
NBA players with the highest field goal percentages
career field goal percentages
.664
.599
.594
.591
.582
DeAndre Jordan, 2008–
Artis Gilmore, 1976–1988
Andris Biedrins, 2004–2014
Tyson Chandler, 2001–
Shaquille O'Neal, 1992–2011

NBA player with the most career points

Kareem Abdul-Jabbar

During his highly successful career, Kareem Abdul-Jabbar scored a total of 38,387 points. In 1969, Abdul-Jabbar began his NBA tenure with the Milwaukee Bucks. He was named Rookie of the Year in 1970. The following year he scored 2,596 points and helped the Bucks win the NBA championship. He was traded to the Los Angeles Lakers in 1975, and with his new team, Abdul-Jabbar won the NBA championship in 1980, 1982, 1985, 1987, and 1988. He retired from basketball in 1989 and was inducted into the Basketball Hall of Fame in 1995.

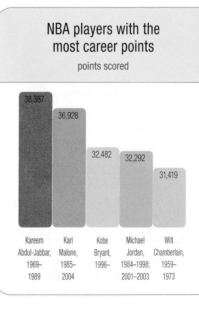

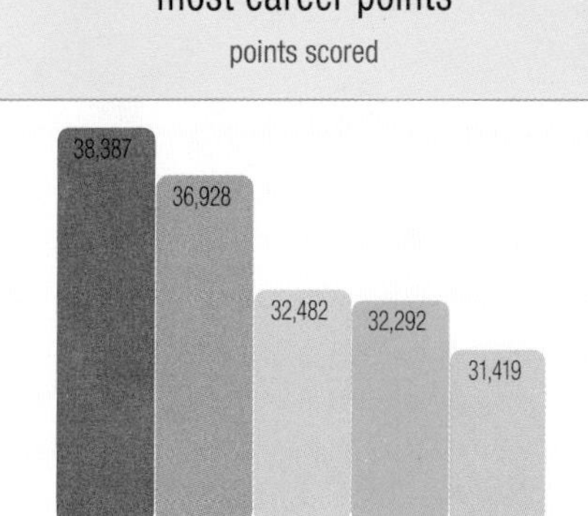
NBA players with the most career points
points scored
38,387
36,928
32,482
32,292
31,419
Kareem Abdul-Jabbar, 1969–1989
Karl Malone, 1985–2004
Kobe Bryant, 1996–
Michael Jordan, 1984–1998; 2001–2003
Wilt Chamberlain, 1959–1973

WNBA player with the highest career PPG average

Cynthia Cooper

Cynthia Cooper has the highest scoring average in the WNBA with 21 points per game. During the play-offs, she averaged 23.3 points per game. Cooper joined the league in 1997 as a Houston Comet and remained there for four years. After a two-year hiatus, she returned for a year and then retired in 2003. During her five years in the WNBA, she scored a total of 2,601 points. Cooper has a career high of 44 points in one game versus Sacramento in 1997. She won a gold medal in the 1988 summer Olympics in Seoul, the 1987 Pan American Games, and the 1990 FIBA World Championship. Cooper is currently the head coach for the women's basketball team at the University of Southern California.

WNBA players with the highest career PPG average

average points per game

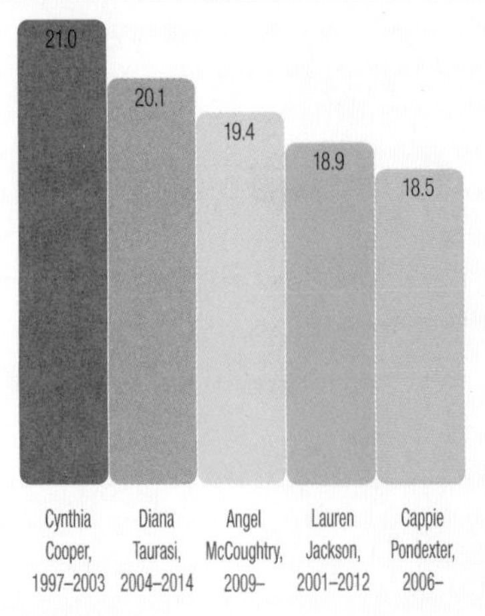
21.0
20.1
19.4
18.9
18.5
Cynthia Cooper, 1997–2003
Diana Taurasi, 2004–2014
Angel McCoughtry, 2009–
Lauren Jackson, 2001–2012
Cappie Pondexter, 2006–

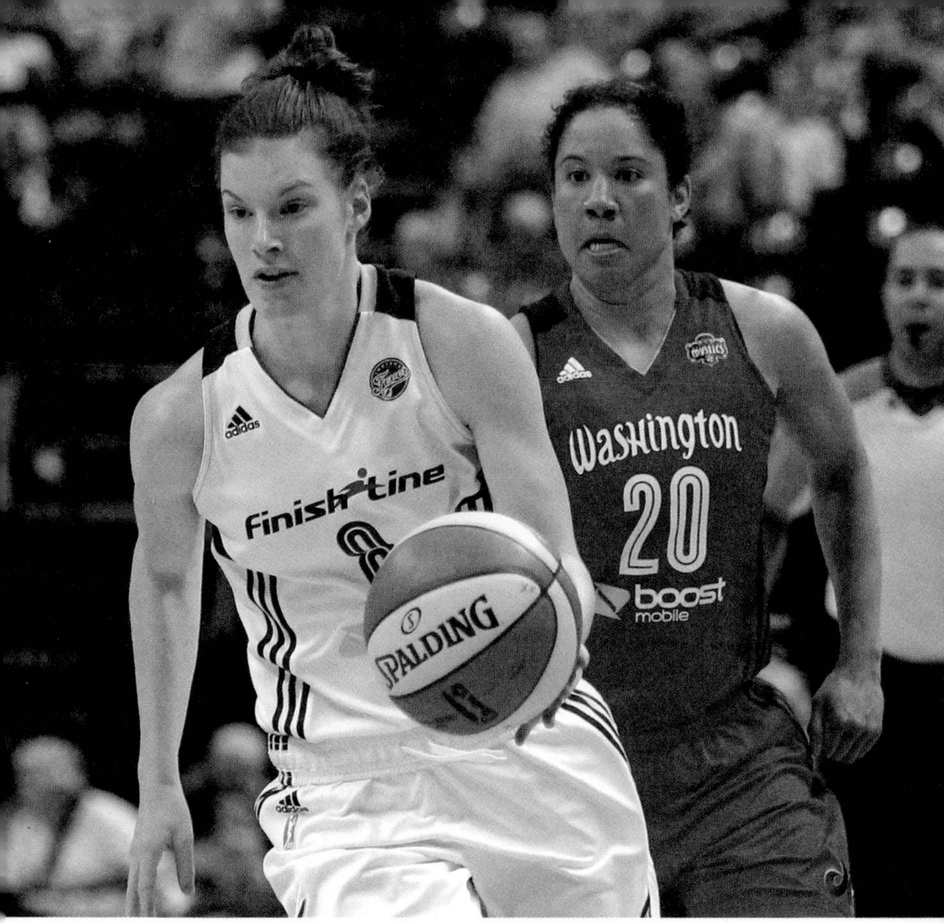

WNBA player with the highest free-throw percentage

Maggie Lucas

You don't want to foul Maggie Lucas—she has the highest free-throw percentage in the WNBA with .957. Lucas was a second-round draft pick by the Phoenix Mercury in 2014, but she made her league debut with the Indiana Fever after a training camp trade. As a guard, Lucas played in 30 games that year and scored 110 points. She also had 20 assists, 8 steals, and 26 rebounds. Before turning pro, Lucas played for Penn State and was a two-time Big Ten Player of the Year. She also holds the Big Ten and Penn State records for three-point baskets with 365 sunk.

WNBA players with the highest free-throw percentages

free-throw percentage*

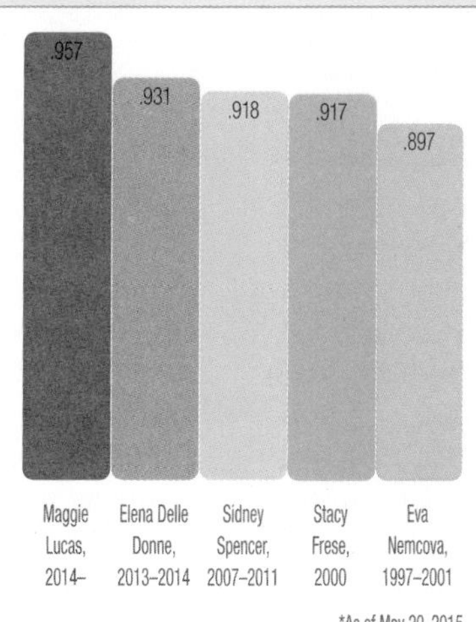
.957
.931
.918
.917
.897
Maggie Lucas, 2014–
Elena Delle Donne, 2013–2014
Sidney Spencer, 2007–2011
Stacy Frese, 2000
Eva Nemcova, 1997–2001

*As of May 20, 2015

WNBA player with the most career points

Tina Thompson

A nine-time WNBA All-Star, Tina Thompson has scored 7,488 points during her 17-year career. The Los Angeles Sparks forward began her WNBA career in 1997 with the Houston Comets. She was the first draft pick in WNBA history. During her first four years with the Comets, she helped the team win the WNBA Championship each season and was the 2000 All-Star MVP. She joined the Los Angeles Sparks in 2009 and has a points-per-game average of 15.1. At the 2004 and 2008 summer Olympic Games, Thompson picked up gold medals for her role in helping Team USA dominate the competition.

WNBA players with the most career points

career points

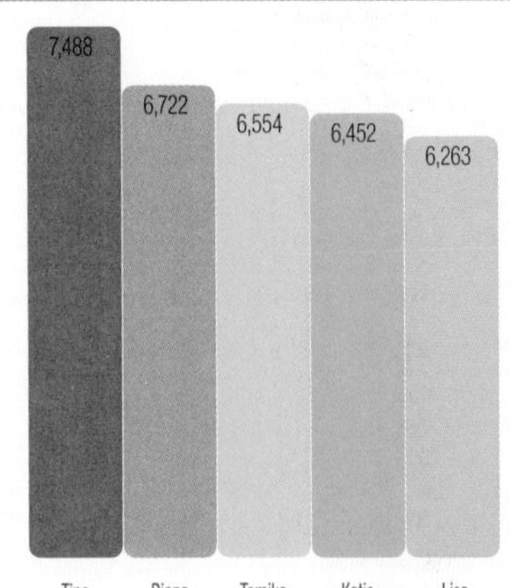
7,488
6,722
6,554
6,452
6,263
Tina Thompson, 1997–2013
Diana Taurasi, 2004–2014
Tamika Catchings, 2002–2013
Katie Smith, 1999–2003
Lisa Leslie, 1997–2009

WNBA player with the most career rebounds

Lisa Leslie

Lisa Leslie grabbed 3,307 rebounds during her 12-year career in the WNBA. Leslie joined the league during its inaugural season in 1997 when she was signed by the Los Angeles Sparks, and she remained with the team throughout her career. A three-time WNBA MVP and eight-time WNBA All-Star, Leslie became the first woman to dunk in the league in 2002. In 2009, she again made history by becoming the first woman to score 6,000 points. Leslie won four Olympic gold medals between 1996 and 2008.

WNBA players with the most career rebounds

career rebounds*

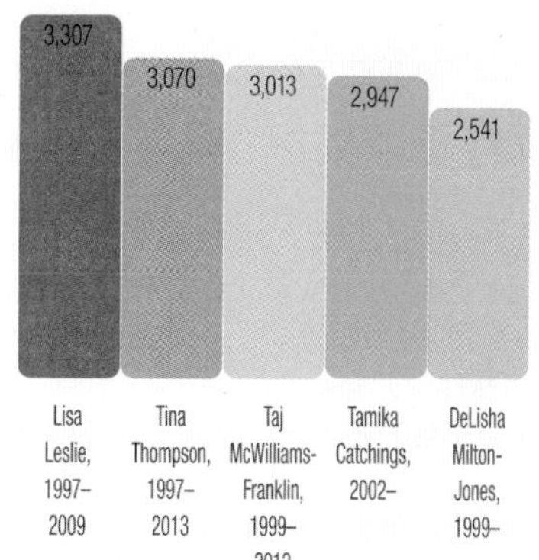
3,307
3,070
3,013
2,947
2,541
Lisa Leslie, 1997–2009
Tina Thompson, 1997–2013
Taj McWilliams-Franklin, 1999–2012
Tamika Catchings, 2002–
DeLisha Milton-Jones, 1999–

*As of June 13, 2015

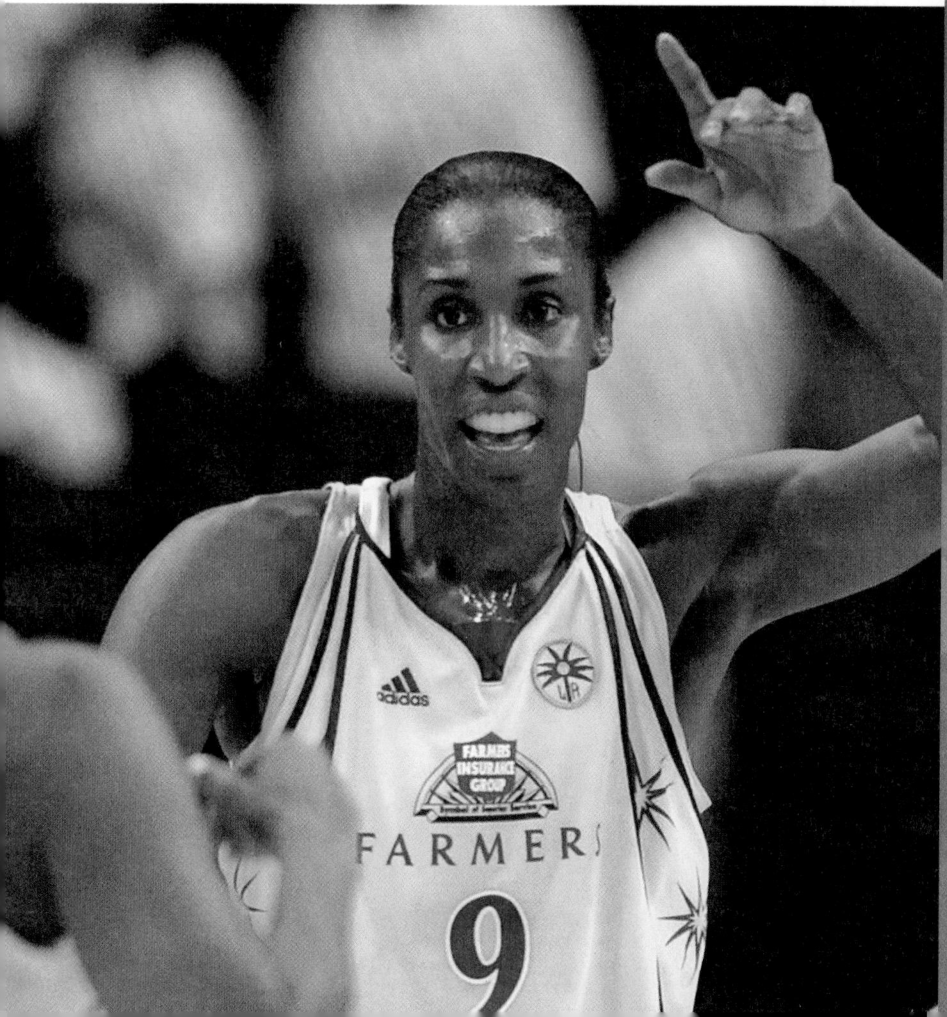

women's basketball team with the most NCAA championships

UCONN

The UCONN Huskies have won the NCAA basketball championship 10 times. All 10 championships were celebrated between 1995 and 2015 under the leadership of Geno Auriemma. The team has qualified for the Final Four 16 times and has won the Big East Tournament Championship 19 times. The Huskies have sent more than 20 players to the WNBA. Connecticut also holds the record for the most consecutive games won in the NCAA with 90 between April 2005 and December 2010. In 2013–2014, the Huskies had a perfect season, winning all 40 games.

women's basketball teams with the most NCAA championships

wins

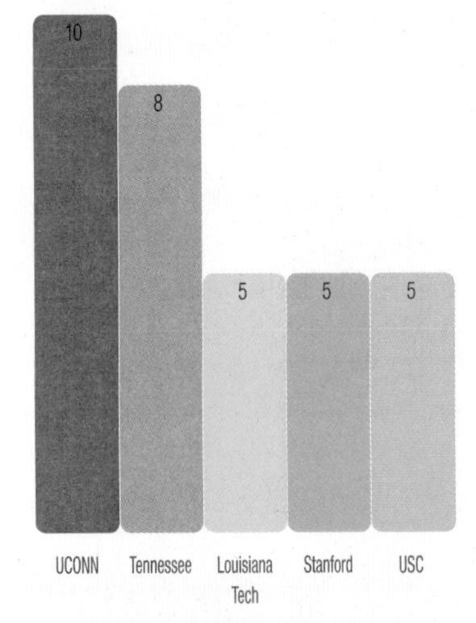
10
8
5
5
5
UCONN
Tennessee
Louisiana Tech
Stanford
USC

Isaac Hamilton

men's basketball team with the most NCAA championships

UCLA

With 11 titles, the University of California, Los Angeles (UCLA) has the most NCAA basketball championship wins. The Bruins won their 11th championship in 1995. The school has won 23 of their last 41 league titles and has been in the NCAA play-offs for 35 of the last 41 years. UCLA did make it to the Elite Eight of the NCAA championship in 2015, but they lost to Gonzaga with a score of 62–74. Not surprisingly, UCLA has produced some basketball legends, including Kareem Abdul-Jabbar, Reggie Miller, and Baron Davis. For the last 50 years, the Bruins have called Pauley Pavilion home.

men's basketball teams with the most NCAA championships

wins

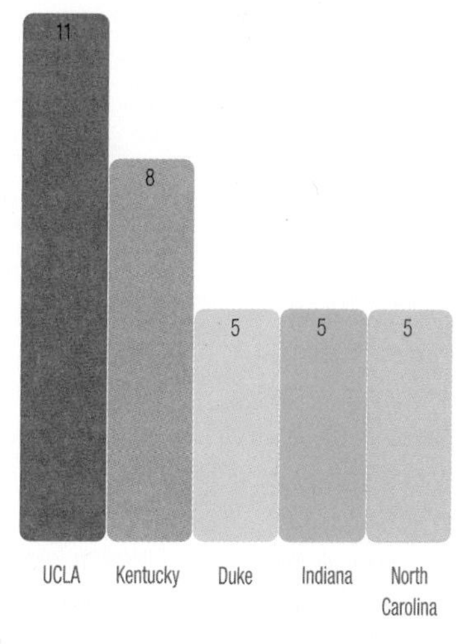
11
8
5
5
5
UCLA
Kentucky
Duke
Indiana
North Carolina

NFL player with the most passing yards

Brett Favre

Quarterback Brett Favre knew how to hit his receivers: He completed 71,838 passing yards during his amazing career. He had a completion rate of 62 percent and connected for 508 touchdowns. Favre was also the NFL's all-time leader in passing touchdowns (508), completions (6,300), and attempts (10,169). Favre began his career with the Atlanta Falcons in 1991. He was traded to the Green Bay Packers the next season and played for them until 2007. Favre joined the New York Jets for a season and was then signed by the Minnesota Vikings for the 2009 season. Favre retired in 2010, and the Green Bay Packers retired his jersey number and inducted him into their Hall of Fame in 2015.

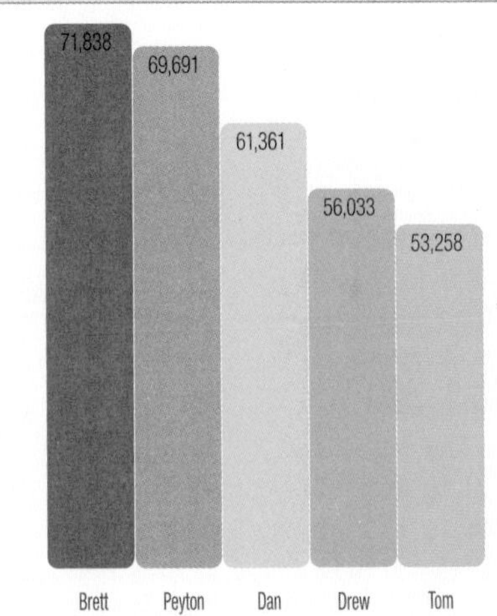
NFL players with the most passing yards
yards
71,838
69,691
61,361
56,033
53,258
Brett Favre, 1991–2010
Peyton Manning, 1998–
Dan Marino, 1983–2000
Drew Brees, 2001–
Tom Brady, 2000–

NFL player with the most career touchdowns

Jerry Rice

Jerry Rice has scored a record 208 touchdowns. He is widely considered to be one of the greatest wide receivers to ever play in the National Football League. Rice holds a total of 14 NFL records, including career receptions (1,549), receiving yards (22,895), receiving touchdowns (197), most games with 100 receiving yards (75), and many others. He was named NFL Player of the Year twice, *Sports Illustrated* Player of the Year four times, and NFL Offensive Player of the Year once. Rice retired from the NFL in 2005.

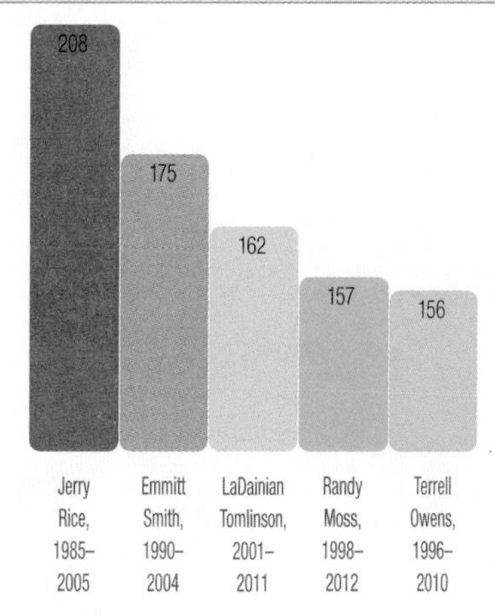
NFL players with the most career touchdowns
touchdowns scored
208
175
162
157
156
Jerry Rice, 1985–2005
Emmitt Smith, 1990–2004
LaDainian Tomlinson, 2001–2011
Randy Moss, 1998–2012
Terrell Owens, 1996–2010

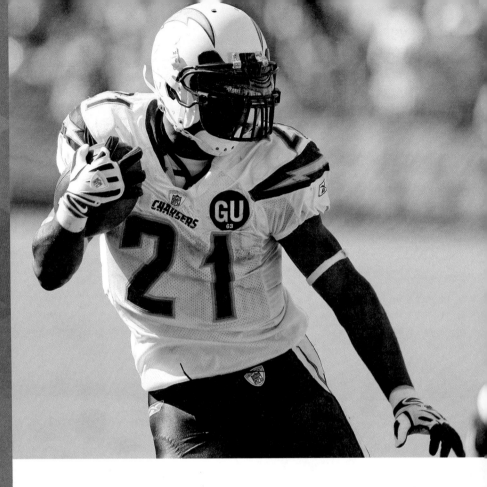

NFL player with the most single-season touchdowns

LaDainian Tomlinson

Running back LaDainian Tomlinson scored 31 touchdowns during the 2006 season. He was also named NFL Most Valuable Player that season for his outstanding performance. During his pro career, he scored a total of 138 touchdowns. Tomlinson was selected fifth overall in the 2001 draft by the San Diego Chargers but was traded to the New York Jets in 2010. He holds several Chargers records, including 372 rushing attempts (2002), 100 receptions (2003), and 1,815 rushing yards in a season (2006). Tomlinson was named to five Pro Bowls before retiring in 2012.

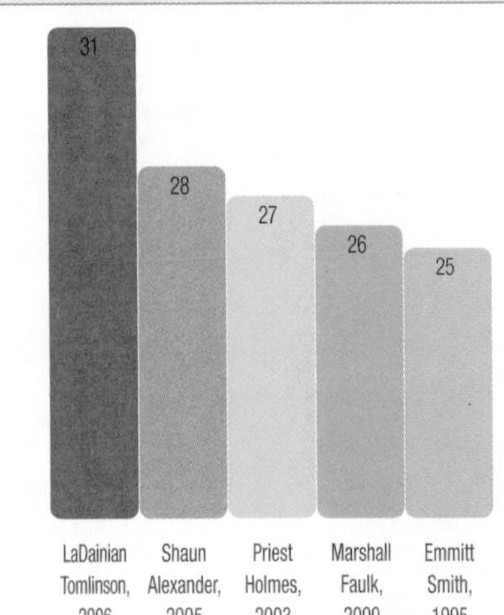
NFL players with the most single-season touchdowns
touchdowns scored
31
28
27
26
25
LaDainian Tomlinson, 2006
Shaun Alexander, 2005
Priest Holmes, 2003
Marshall Faulk, 2000
Emmitt Smith, 1995

NFL player with the highest career scoring total

Morten Andersen

Morten Andersen led the NFL in scoring with a career total of 2,544 points. He made 565 field goals out of 709 attempts, giving him a 79.7 percent completion rate. He scored 849 extra points out of 859 attempts, resulting in a 98.8 percent success rate. Andersen, a placekicker who began his career in 1982 with the New Orleans Saints, retired in 2008 after playing for the Atlanta Falcons. Known as the Great Dane, partly because of his birthplace of Denmark, Andersen played 382 professional games. His most successful season was in 1995, when he scored 122 points.

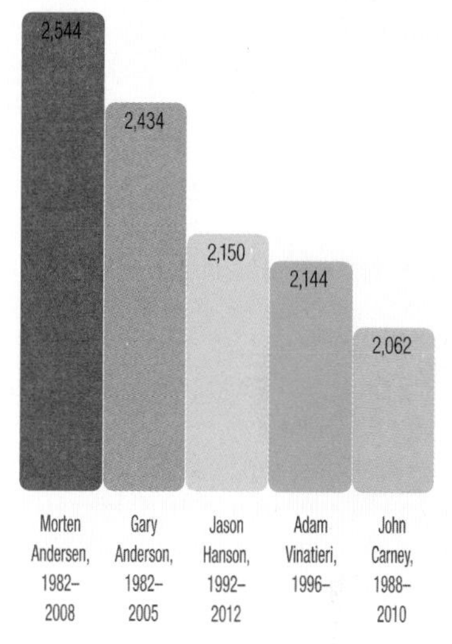
NFL players with the highest career scoring totals
points scored
2,544
2,434
2,150
2,144
2,062
Morten Andersen, 1982–2008
Gary Anderson, 1982–2005
Jason Hanson, 1992–2012
Adam Vinatieri, 1996–
John Carney, 1988–2010

NFL coach with the most wins

Don Shula

Don Shula led his teams to a remarkable 347 wins during his 33 years as a head coach in the National Football League. When Shula became head coach of the Baltimore Colts in 1963, he became the youngest head coach in football history. He stayed with the team until 1969 and reached the play-offs four times. Shula became the head coach for the Miami Dolphins in 1970 and coached them until 1995. During this time, the Dolphins reached the play-offs 20 times and won at least 10 games a season 21 times. After leading them to Super Bowl wins in 1972 and 1973, Shula became one of only five coaches to win the championship in back-to-back years.

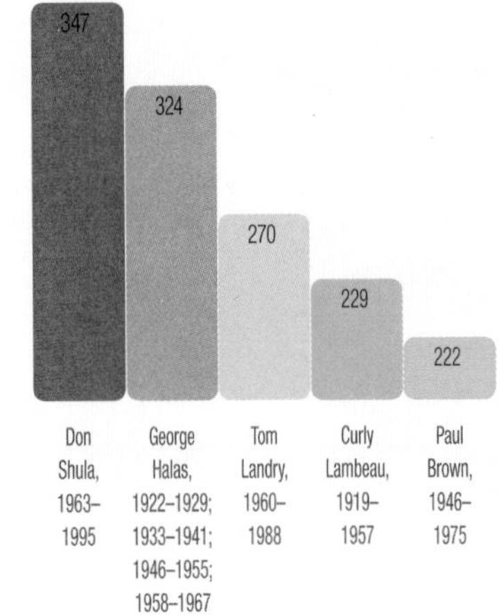
NFL coaches
with the most wins
games won
347
324
270
229
222
Don Shula, 1963–1995
George Halas, 1922–1929; 1933–1941; 1946–1955; 1958–1967
Tom Landry, 1960–1988
Curly Lambeau, 1919–1957
Paul Brown, 1946–1975

NFL player with the highest salary

Jay Cutler

In 2014, quarterback Jay Cutler had the top NFL salary with $17.5 million for the season—part of a seven-year contract worth $126.7 million. The base salary was $22.5 million for the year, but $5 million was converted into a signing bonus. Cutler began his NFL career with the Denver Broncos in 2006, but he moved to the Chicago Bears in 2009. During his career, he has completed 27,749 passing yards and thrown 183 touchdown passes. He also played in the Pro Bowl in 2008.

NFL players with the highest salaries

annual salary, in millions of US dollars

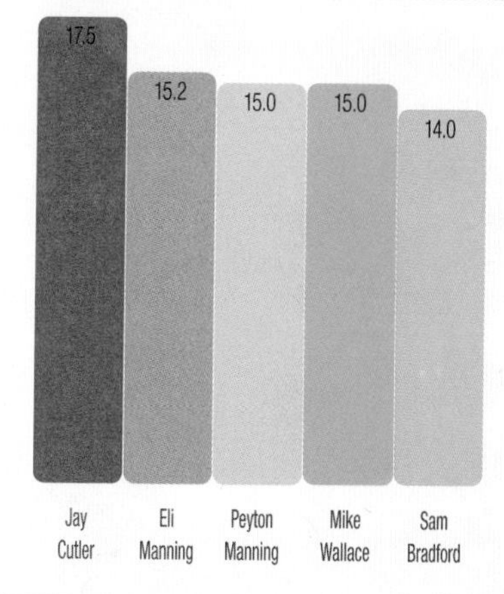
17.5
15.2
15.0
15.0
14.0
Jay Cutler
Eli Manning
Peyton Manning
Mike Wallace
Sam Bradford

NFL quarterback with the highest seasonal rating

Tony Romo

With a rating of 82.7, Tony Romo was the top quarterback of the 2014 NFL season. The seasonal quarterback rating factors in how much the player's actions contributed to the team winning a game. Romo, who has played his entire career with the Dallas Cowboys since signing with them in 2003, saw his rating jump 23.2 points from 2013. During the 2014 season, he threw for 3,705 yards, completed 34 touchdown passes, and had a completion percentage of 69.9%. Romo has been selected for the Pro Bowl four times and holds the NFL record for the most consecutive road games with at least one touchdown pass (41).

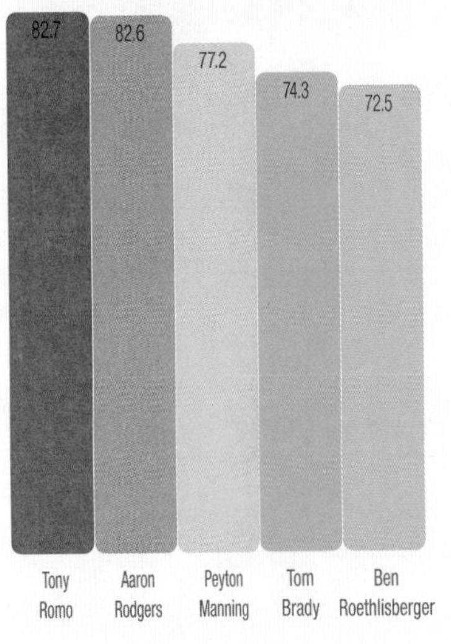
NFL quarterbacks with the highest seasonal rating
total quarterback rating in 2014
82.7
82.6
77.2
74.3
72.5
Tony Romo
Aaron Rodgers
Peyton Manning
Tom Brady
Ben Roethlisberger

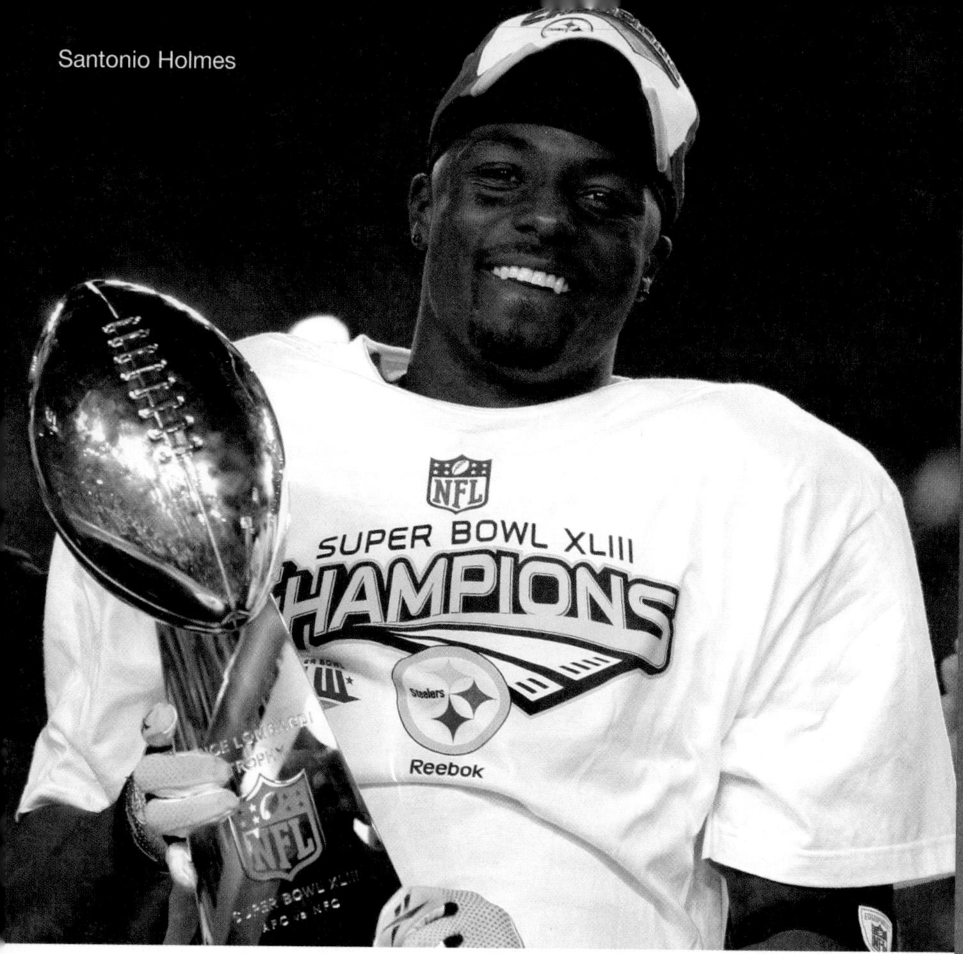

Santonio Holmes

NFL team with the most Super Bowl wins

Pittsburgh Steelers

With six championship wins between 1974 and 2009, the Pittsburgh Steelers have won more Super Bowls than any other team in NFL history. The Steelers have also played and won more AFC championship games than any other team in the conference. The Steelers were founded in 1933 and are the fifth-oldest franchise in the league. Twenty-six retired Steelers have been inducted into the Pro Football Hall of Fame, including Franco Harris, Chuck Noll, Terry Bradshaw, and Jerome Bettis.

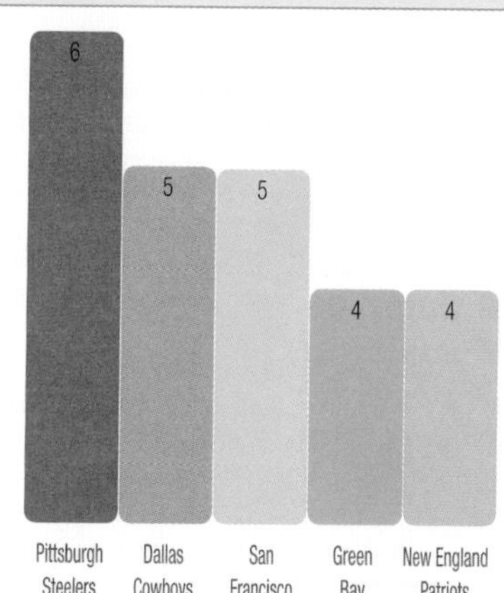
NFL teams with the most Super Bowl wins
Super Bowls won
6
5
5
4
4
Pittsburgh Steelers
Dallas Cowboys
San Francisco 49ers
Green Bay Packers
New England Patriots

world's highest-paid athlete of 2015

Floyd Mayweather

Floyd Mayweather earned a whopping $300 million in 2015. About $285 million was from salary and winnings, and another $15 million came from endorsements from Hublot, FanDuel, and Burger King. His record is currently 48 wins and no losses. In 2013, Mayweather signed a deal with Showtime to compete in six fights within 30 months. On May 2, 2015, Mayweather fought Manny Pacquiao, and the fight set several financial records, including pay-per-view buys at $4.4 million, total gate revenue at $73 million, and sponsorships at $13 million. Once Mayweather completes his last contracted fight in late 2015, he plans to retire.

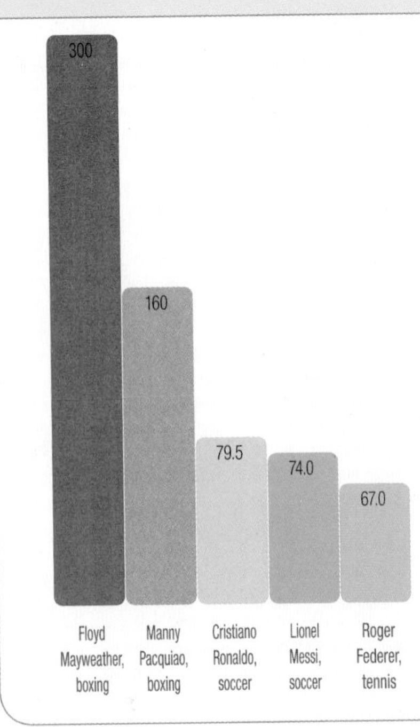
world's highest-paid athletes of 2015
earnings in 2015, in millions
300
160
79.5
74.0
67.0
Floyd Mayweather, boxing
Manny Pacquiao, boxing
Cristiano Ronaldo, soccer
Lionel Messi, soccer
Roger Federer, tennis

PGA golfer with the lowest seasonal average

Rory McIlroy

In 2014, Rory McIlroy had the lowest seasonal average in the PGA with 68.827. During the season, McIlroy played 17 PGA tournaments and finished in the top 25 in each one. He won 3 tournaments and earned $8.28 million in prize money. McIlroy entered the PGA in 2007 and has won 9 events and earned more than $26 million since then. He formed the Rory Foundation in 2010 to support children's charities around the world.

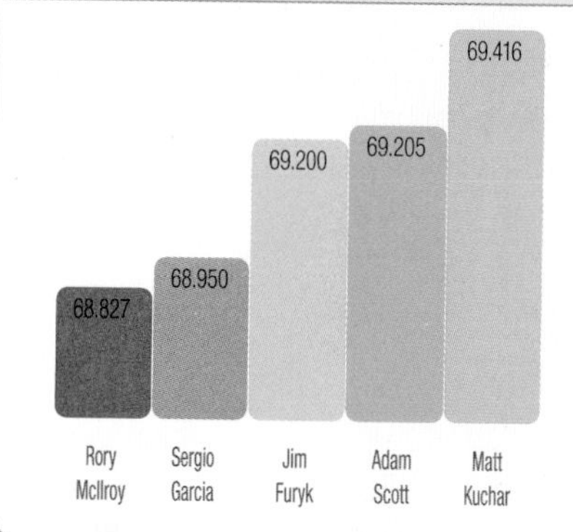

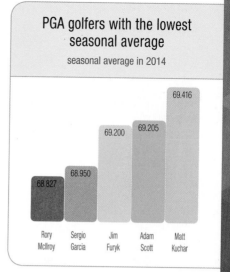

PGA golfers with the lowest seasonal average
seasonal average in 2014
68.827
68.950
69.200
69.205
69.416
Rory McIlroy
Sergio Garcia
Jim Furyk
Adam Scott
Matt Kuchar

LPGA golfer with the lowest seasonal average

Stacy Lewis

American golfer Stacy Lewis had a seasonal average of 69.53, which was the lowest in the LPGA during 2014. During the year, she played 28 events and was named Rolex Player of the Year. Lewis also led the LPGA in birdies and eagles. She turned pro in 2008 and joined the LPGA the following year. Since then, she's won two major championships—the 2011 Kraft Nabisco Championship and the 2013 British Open. She was named the LPGA Player of the Year in 2012. Lewis's career earnings total more than $9.3 million.

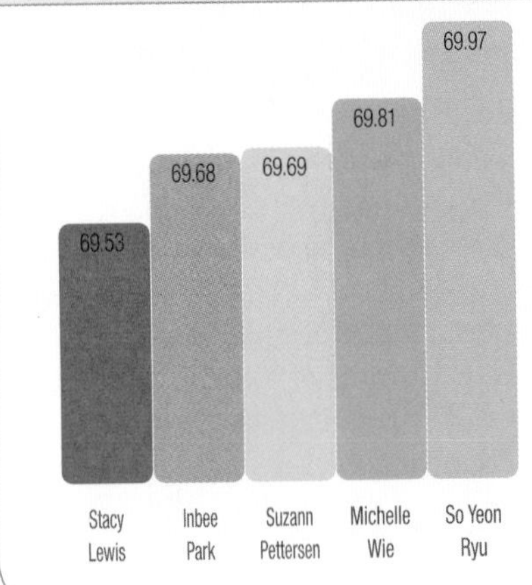
LPGA golfers with the lowest seasonal average
seasonal average in 2014
69.53
69.68
69.69
69.81
69.97
Stacy Lewis
Inbee Park
Suzann Pettersen
Michelle Wie
So Yeon Ryu

LPGA's highest-paid golfer

Annika Sorenstam

Annika Sorenstam earned $22.5 million during her 15-year LPGA career and she had 72 career victories, including ten majors. In 2005, Sorenstam received her eighth Rolex Player of the Year award—the most in LPGA history. She also became the first player to sweep Rolex Player of the Year honors, the Vare Trophy, and the ADT Official Money List title five times. Sorenstam won her fifth consecutive Mizuno Classic title in 2005, making her the first golfer in LPGA history to win the same event five years in a row. Sorenstam retired at the end of the 2008 season.

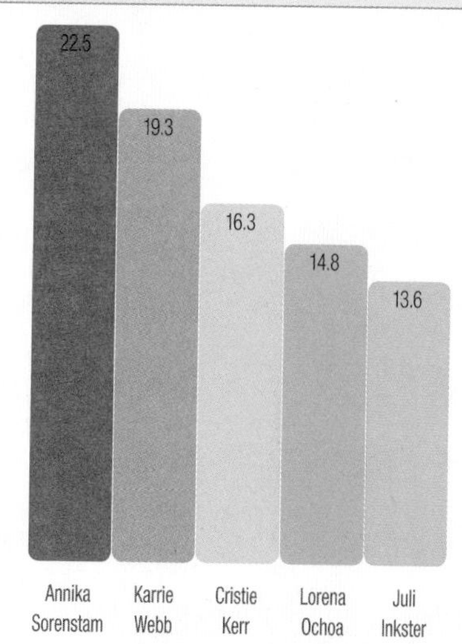
LPGA's highest-paid golfers
career earnings, in millions of US dollars
22.5
19.3
16.3
14.8
13.6
Annika Sorenstam
Karrie Webb
Cristie Kerr
Lorena Ochoa
Juli Inkster

golfer with the most major tournament wins

Jack Nicklaus

Golfing great Jack Nicklaus won a total of 18 major championships. His wins include six Masters, five PGAs, four US Opens, and three British Opens. Nicklaus was named PGA Player of the Year five times. He was a member of the winning US Ryder Cup team six times and was an individual World Cup winner a record three times. He was inducted into the World Golf Hall of Fame in 1974, just 12 years after he turned professional. He joined the US Senior PGA Tour in 1990. In addition to playing the game, Nicklaus has designed close to 200 golf courses and has written a number of popular books about the sport.

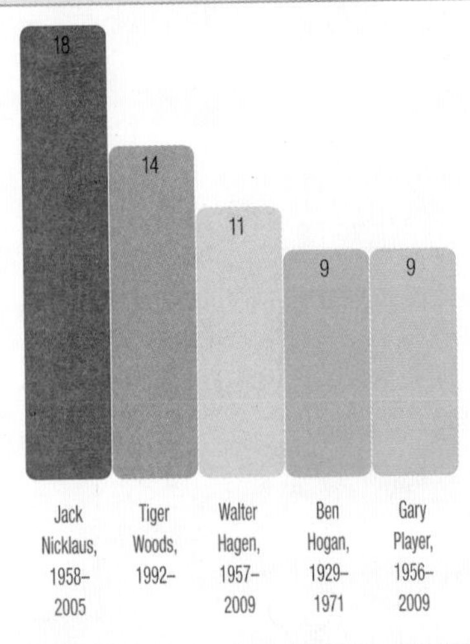
golfers with the most major tournament wins
major tournament wins
18
14
11
9
9
Jack Nicklaus, 1958–2005
Tiger Woods, 1992–
Walter Hagen, 1957–2009
Ben Hogan, 1929–1971
Gary Player, 1956–2009

MLB player with the most stolen bases

Rickey Henderson

Rickey Henderson is known as the "Man of Steal" because he holds the record for the most stolen bases in a career with 1,406. The left fielder played in 3,081 games during his time in the majors, and got 3,055 hits during his 10,961 at bats. He won the Silver Slugger Award in 1981, 1985, and 1990. Henderson was selected for 10 All-Star games, and played in 7 of them. He was named MLB Player of the week 5 times between 1982 and 1991. Henderson retired from the game in 2003. He was inducted into the MLB Hall of Fame in 2009.

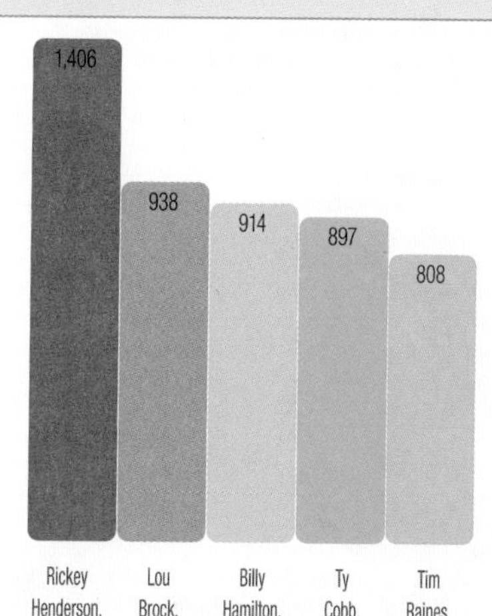
MLB players with the most stolen bases
total stolen bases
1,406
938
914
897
808
Rickey Henderson, 1979–2003
Lou Brock, 1961–1979
Billy Hamilton, 1888–1901
Ty Cobb, 1905–1928
Tim Raines, 1979–2002

MLB team with the highest payroll

Los Angeles Dodgers

During the 2015 season, the Los Angeles Dodgers dished out more than $276.3 million for its payroll. That's a 17 percent increase from the previous season. The largest salaries went to first baseman Adrian Gonzales with $21 million, pitcher Zack Greinke with $23 million, and pitcher Clayton Kershaw with $30 million. In all, 10 Dodgers earned $10 million or more during the season. About 51 percent of the payroll went to hitters, almost 42 percent went to pitchers, and nearly 7 percent went to people who didn't play.

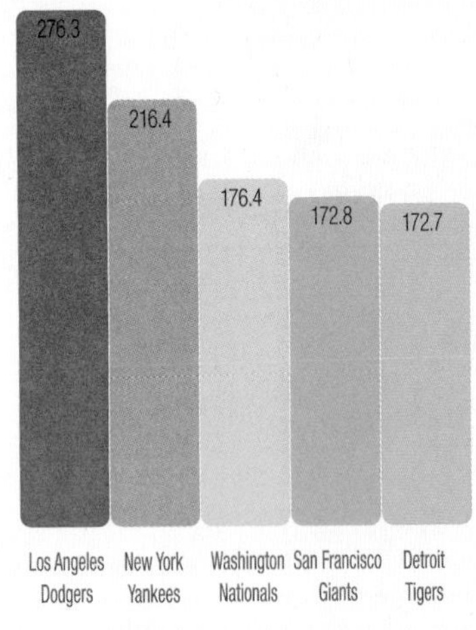
MLB teams with the highest payrolls
payroll in 2015,
in millions of US dollars
276.3
216.4
176.4
172.8
172.7
Los Angeles Dodgers
New York Yankees
Washington Nationals
San Francisco Giants
Detroit Tigers

Clayton Kershaw

MLB player with the most home runs

Barry Bonds

Barry Bonds hit more home runs than anyone who ever played in the MLB, cracking 762 balls over the wall during his career. Bonds hit more than 30 home runs in a season 14 times—another MLB record. During his impressive career, Bonds won 8 Gold Gloves, and 12 Silver Slugger awards, and played in 14 All-Star games. Bonds began his career with the Pittsburgh Pirates in 1986; he was transferred to the San Francisco Giants in 1993 and played for the team until he retired. He is one of only three players to join the 700 Home Run Club.

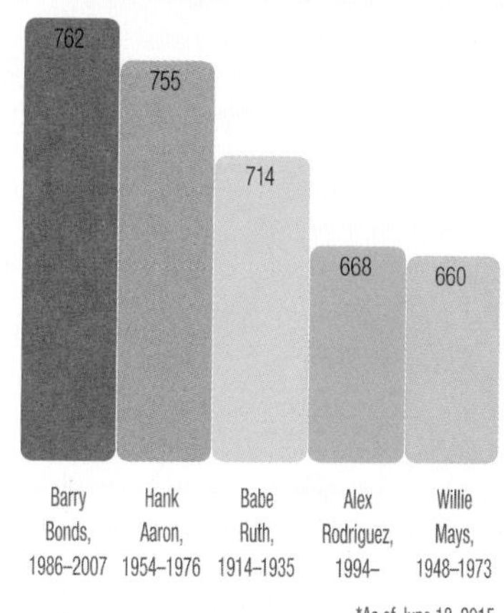
MLB players with the most home runs
number of home runs*
762
755
714
668
660
Barry Bonds, 1986–2007
Hank Aaron, 1954–1976
Babe Ruth, 1914–1935
Alex Rodriguez, 1994–
Willie Mays, 1948–1973
*As of June 13, 2015

MLB pitcher with the most career strikeouts

Nolan Ryan

Nolan Ryan leads Major League Baseball with an incredible 5,714 career strikeouts. In his impressive 27-season career, he played for the New York Mets, the California Angels, the Houston Astros, and the Texas Rangers. The right-handed pitcher from Refugio, Texas, led the American League in strikeouts ten times. In 1989, at the age of 42, Ryan became the oldest pitcher ever to lead the Major Leagues in strikeouts. Ryan set another record in 1991 when he pitched his seventh career no-hitter.

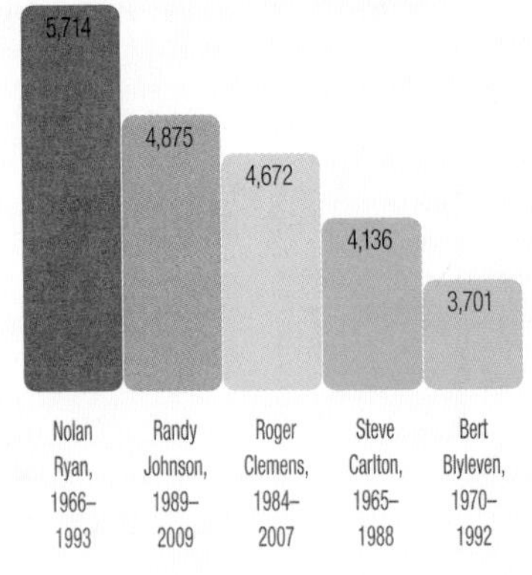
MLB pitchers with the most career strikeouts
number of strikeouts
5,714
4,875
4,672
4,136
3,701
Nolan Ryan, 1966–1993
Randy Johnson, 1989–2009
Roger Clemens, 1984–2007
Steve Carlton, 1965–1988
Bert Blyleven, 1970–1992

MLB player with the most career hits

Pete Rose

Pete Rose belted an amazing 4,256 hits during his 23 years of professional baseball. He made his record-setting hit in 1985, when he was a player-manager for the Cincinnati Reds. By the time Rose retired as a player from Major League Baseball in 1986, he had set several other career records. Rose holds the Major League records for the most career games (3,562), the most times at bat (14,053), and the most seasons with more than 200 hits (10). During his career, he played for the Cincinnati Reds, the Philadelphia Phillies, and the Montreal Expos.

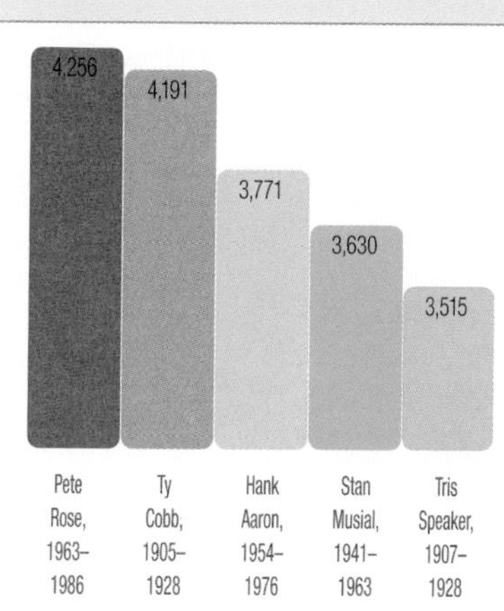
MLB players with the most career hits
number of hits
4,256
4,191
3,771
3,630
3,515
Pete Rose, 1963–1986
Ty Cobb, 1905–1928
Hank Aaron, 1954–1976
Stan Musial, 1941–1963
Tris Speaker, 1907–1928

MLB player with the highest batting average

Ty Cobb

Baseball legend Ty Cobb had a batting average of .367 during his 23-year career, and it has remained the highest average in MLB history for more than 80 years. Known as the "Georgia Peach," the American League outfielder set 90 different MLB records during his outstanding career. He won 12 batting titles, including 9 consecutive wins between 1907 and 1915. Cobb began his career with the Detroit Tigers in 1905 and later moved to the Philadelphia Athletics in 1927. Cobb was voted into the Baseball Hall of Fame in 1936 with 98.2 percent of the votes.

MLB players with the highest batting average

highest career scoring average

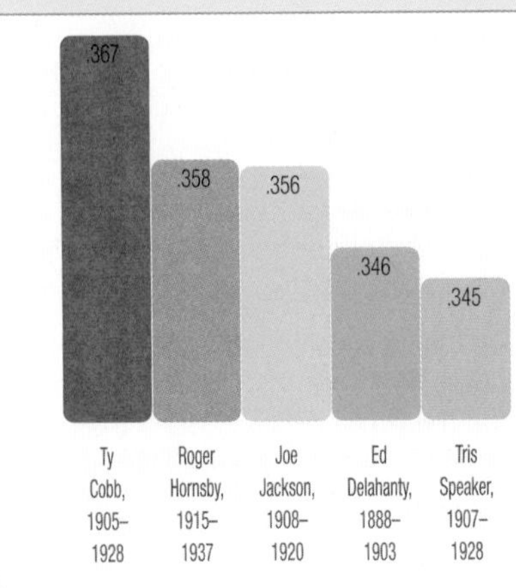
.367
.358
.356
.346
.345
Ty Cobb, 1905–1928
Roger Hornsby, 1915–1937
Joe Jackson, 1908–1920
Ed Delahanty, 1888–1903
Tris Speaker, 1907–1928

MLB player with the most career runs

Rickey Henderson

During his 25 years in the majors, baseball great Rickey Henderson boasts the most career runs with 2,295. Henderson got his start with the Oakland Athletics in 1979 and went on to play for the New York Yankees, the Toronto Blue Jays, the San Diego Padres, the Anaheim Angels, the New York Mets, the Seattle Mariners, the Boston Red Sox, and the Los Angeles Dodgers. Henderson won a Gold Glove award in 1981, and the American League MVP award in 1989 and 1990.

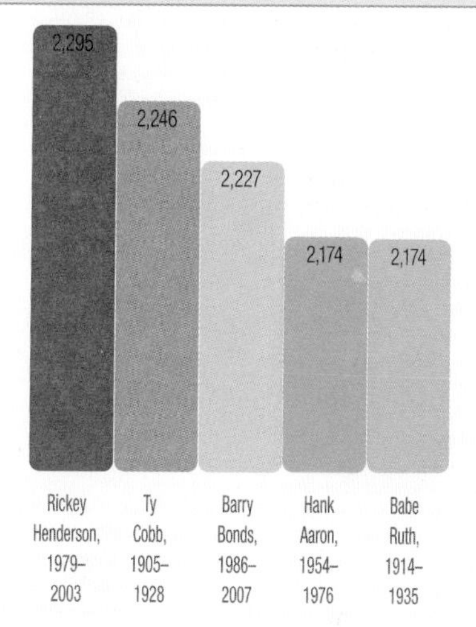
MLB players with the most career runs
number of career runs
2,295
2,246
2,227
2,174
2,174
Rickey Henderson, 1979–2003
Ty Cobb, 1905–1928
Barry Bonds, 1986–2007
Hank Aaron, 1954–1976
Babe Ruth, 1914–1935

Yogi Berra

most MVP awards in the American League

Yogi Berra, Joe DiMaggio, Jimmie Foxx, Mickey Mantle, & Alex Rodriguez

With three honors each, Yogi Berra, Joe DiMaggio, Jimmie Foxx, Mickey Mantle, and Alex Rodriguez all hold the record for the most Most Valuable Player awards during their professional careers. Berra, DiMaggio, Mantle, and Rodriguez were all New York Yankees. Foxx played for the Athletics, the Cubs, and the Phillies. The player with the biggest gap between wins was DiMaggio, who won his first award in 1939 and his last in 1947. Also nicknamed "Joltin' Joe" and the "Yankee Clipper," DiMaggio began playing in the Major Leagues in 1936. The following year, he led the league in home runs and runs scored. He was inducted into the Baseball Hall of Fame in 1955.

MLB players with the most American League MVP awards

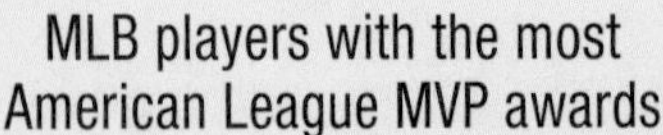

number of MVP awards

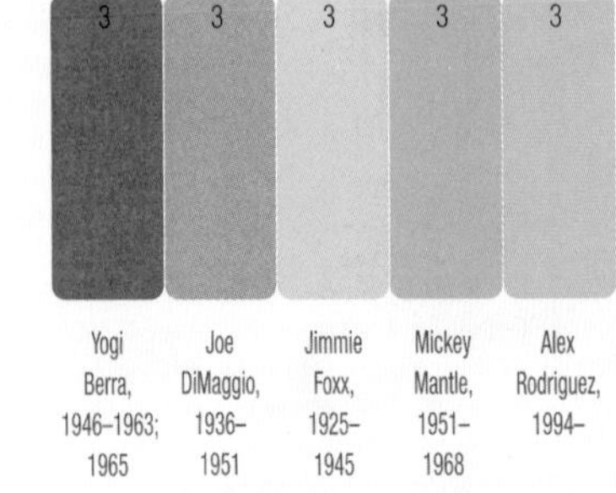
3
3
3
3
3
Yogi Berra, 1946–1963; 1965
Joe DiMaggio, 1936–1951
Jimmie Foxx, 1925–1945
Mickey Mantle, 1951–1968
Alex Rodriguez, 1994–

most MVP awards in the National League

Barry Bonds

During his illustrious 22-year career, Barry Bonds earned seven Most Valuable Player awards for his achievements in the National League and fourteen All-Star selections. He received his first two MVP awards in 1990 and 1992 while playing for the Pittsburgh Pirates. The next five awards came while wearing the San Francisco Giants uniform in 1993, 2001, 2002, 2003, and 2004. Bonds is the first player to win an MVP award three times in consecutive seasons. In fact, Bonds is the only baseball player in history to have won more than three MVP awards. He retired in 2007.

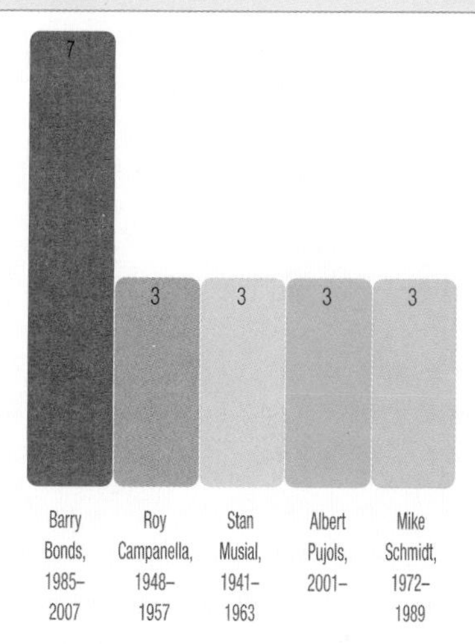
MLB players with the most National League MVP awards
number of MVP awards
7
3
3
3
3
Barry Bonds, 1985–2007
Roy Campanella, 1948–1957
Stan Musial, 1941–1963
Albert Pujols, 2001–
Mike Schmidt, 1972–1989

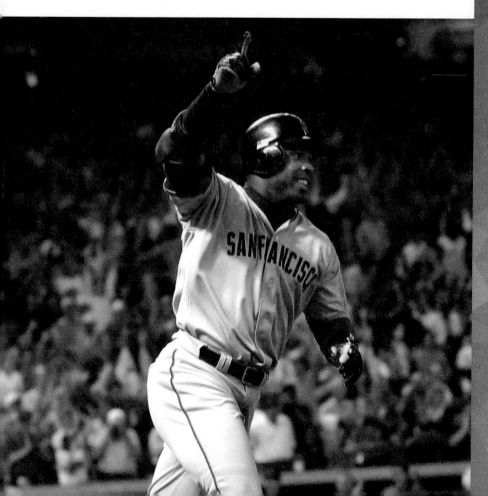

MLB team with the most World Series wins

New York Yankees

Between 1923 and 2010, the New York Yankees were the World Series champions a record 27 times. The team picked up their latest win in October 2009 when they beat the Philadelphia Phillies. The Yankees beat the Phillies 4 games to 2 to get their first win in nine years. Since their early days, the team has included some of baseball's greatest players, including Babe Ruth, Lou Gehrig, Yogi Berra, Joe DiMaggio, and Mickey Mantle.

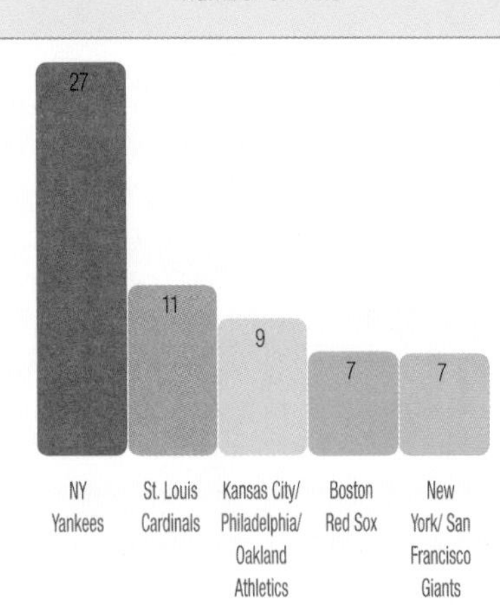
MLB teams with the most World Series wins
number of wins
27
11
9
7
7
NY Yankees
St. Louis Cardinals
Kansas City/ Philadelphia/ Oakland Athletics
Boston Red Sox
New York/ San Francisco Giants

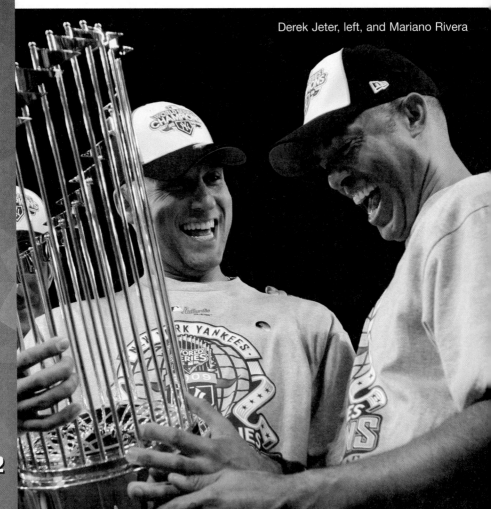

Derek Jeter, left, and Mariano Rivera

MLB pitcher with the most Cy Young awards

Roger Clemens

Roger Clemens earned a record seven Cy Young Awards during his 23-year career pitching in the MLB. He set a Major League record in April 1986, when he struck out 20 batters in one game. He later tied this record in September 1996. In September 2001, Clemens became the first Major League pitcher to win 20 of his first 21 decisions in one season. In June 2003, he became the first pitcher in more than a decade to win his 300th game. He also struck out his 4,000th batter that year.

MLB pitchers with the most Cy Young awards

number of Cy Young awards

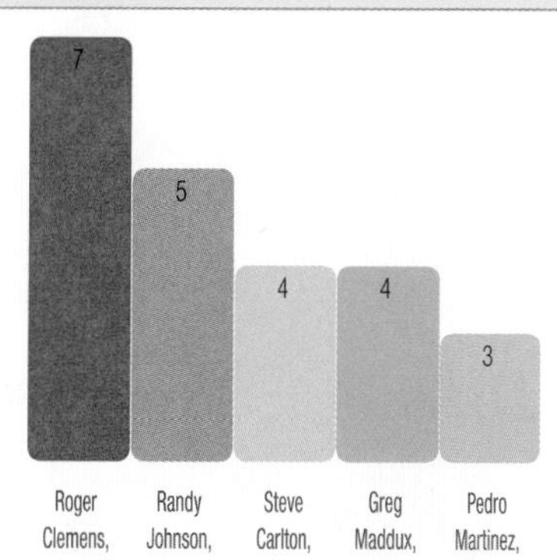
7
5
4
4
3
Roger Clemens, 1984–2007
Randy Johnson, 1988–2010
Steve Carlton, 1965–1988
Greg Maddux, 1986–2008
Pedro Martinez, 1992–2011

MLB player with the most at bats

Pete Rose

Pete Rose stood behind the plate for 14,053 at bats—more than any other Major League player. Rose signed with the Cincinnati Reds after graduating from high school in 1963 and played second base. During his impressive career, Rose set several other records, including the most singles in the major leagues (3,315), most seasons with 600 or more at bats in the major leagues (17), most career doubles in the National League (746), and most career runs in the National League (2,165). He was also named World Series MVP, *Sports Illustrated*'s Sportsman of the Year, and the *Sporting News* Man of the Year.

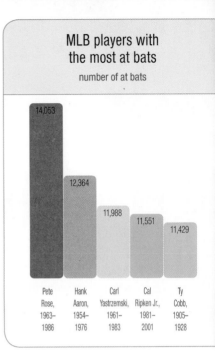

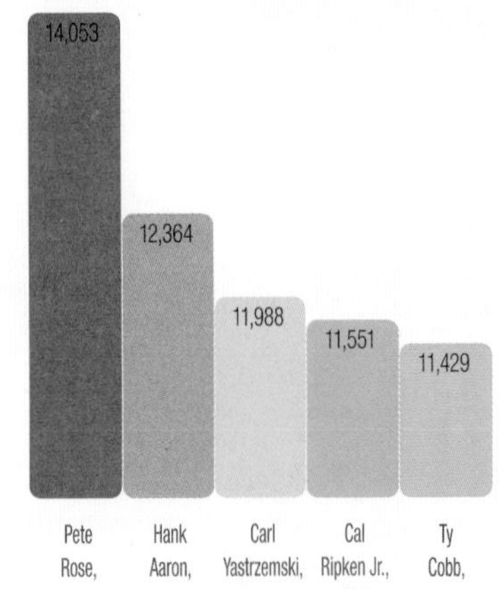
MLB players with the most at bats
number of at bats
14,053
12,364
11,988
11,551
11,429
Pete Rose, 1963–1986
Hank Aaron, 1954–1976
Carl Yastrzemski, 1961–1983
Cal Ripken Jr., 1981–2001
Ty Cobb, 1905–1928

MLB player with the most career RBIs

Hank Aaron

During his 23 years in the major leagues, right-handed Hank Aaron batted in an incredible 2,297 runs. Aaron began his professional career with the Indianapolis Clowns, a team in the Negro American League, in 1952. He was traded to the Milwaukee Braves in 1954 and won the National League batting championship with an average of .328. He was named the league's Most Valuable Player a year later when he led his team to a World Series victory. Aaron retired as a player in 1976 and was inducted into the Baseball Hall of Fame in 1982.

MLB players with the most career RBIs

number of runs batted in*

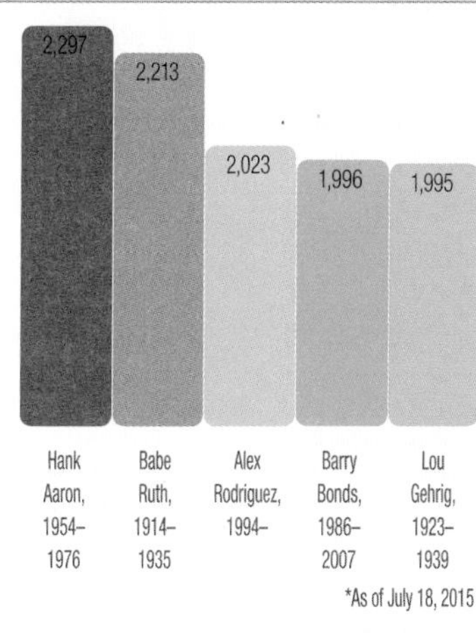
2,297
2,213
2,023
1,996
1,995
Hank Aaron, 1954–1976
Babe Ruth, 1914–1935
Alex Rodriguez, 1994–
Barry Bonds, 1986–2007
Lou Gehrig, 1923–1939

*As of July 18, 2015

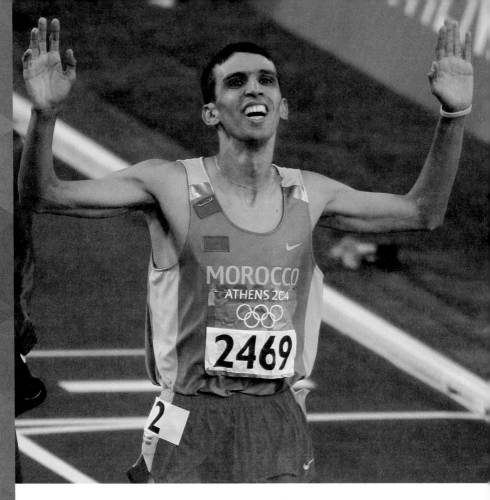

runner with the fastest mile

Hicham El Guerrouj

Moroccan runner Hicham El Guerrouj is super speedy—he ran a mile in just over 3 minutes and 43 seconds in July 1999 while racing in Rome. He also holds the record for the fastest mile in North America with a time just short of 3 minutes and 50 seconds. El Guerrouj is an Olympian with gold medals in the 1,500-meter and 5,000-meter races. With this accomplishment at the 2004 Athens Games, he became the first runner in more than 75 years to win both races at the same Olympics. El Guerrouj returned to the Olympics in 2006 as a torchbearer in Torino, Italy.

runners with the fastest mile

time, in minutes and seconds

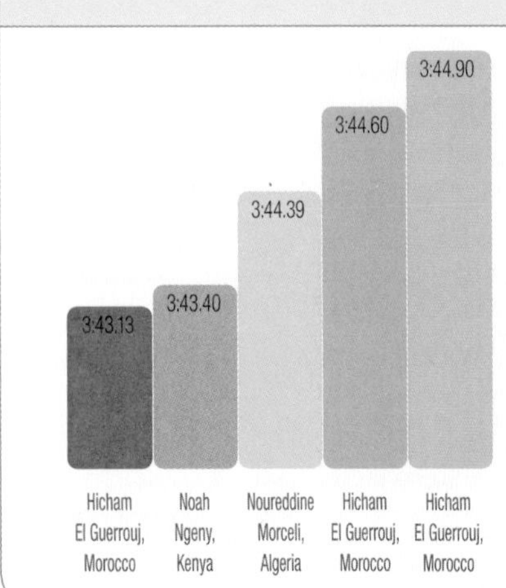
3:43.13
3:43.40
3:44.39
3:44.60
3:44.90
Hicham El Guerrouj, Morocco
Noah Ngeny, Kenya
Noureddine Morceli, Algeria
Hicham El Guerrouj, Morocco
Hicham El Guerrouj, Morocco

top-earning female tennis player

Serena Williams

Serena Williams has earned more than $72 million since she began playing professional tennis in 1995. During her amazing career, Williams has won 67 singles championships and 22 doubles championships, as well as four gold medals in the 2000, 2008, and 2012 summer Olympics. She has also won all four of the Grand Slam championships and holds 20 of those titles. Williams has won many impressive awards, including AP's Female Athlete of the Year, the BBC's Sports Personality of the Year, and two ESPY Awards.

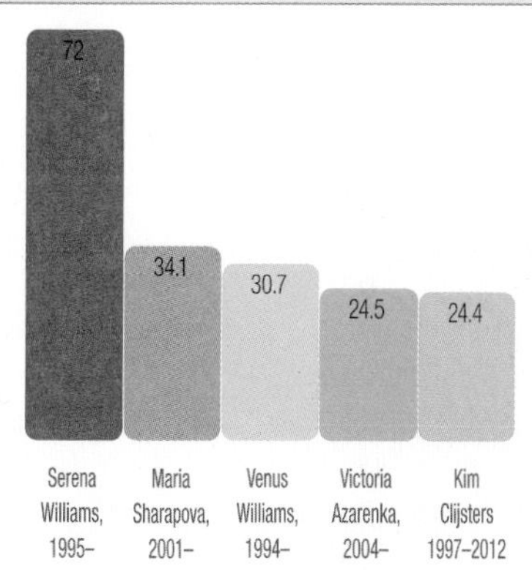
top-earning female tennis players
career earnings, in millions of US dollars
72
34.1
30.7
24.5
24.4
Serena Williams, 1995–
Maria Sharapova, 2001–
Venus Williams, 1994–
Victoria Azarenka, 2004–
Kim Clijsters 1997–2012

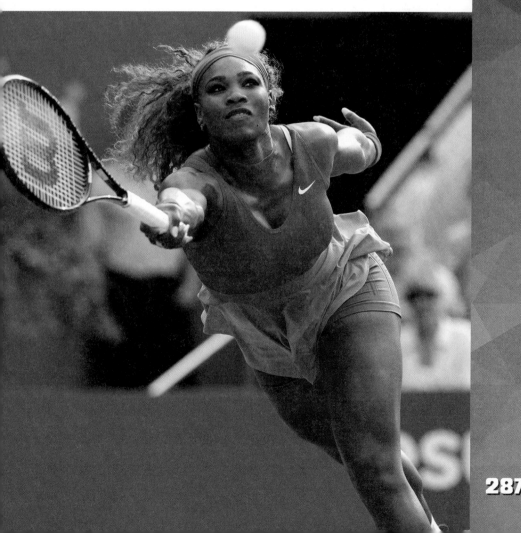

TENNIS

top-earning male tennis player

Roger Federer

Tennis great Roger Federer has earned $90.5 million since his career began in 1998. He has won 85 singles titles and 8 doubles titles, including 17 Grand Slams. His major victories include four Australian Opens, one French Open, six Wimbledon titles, and five US Opens. From February 2, 2004, to August 17, 2008, Federer was ranked first in the world for 237 consecutive weeks. He is also the only player in history to win five consecutive titles at two different Grand Slam tournaments (Wimbledon and US Open).

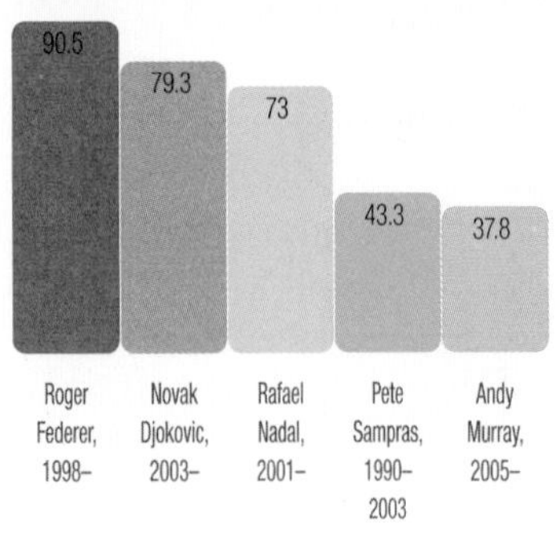
top-earning male tennis players
career earnings, in millions of US dollars
90.5
79.3
73
43.3
37.8
Roger Federer, 1998–
Novak Djokovic, 2003–
Rafael Nadal, 2001–
Pete Sampras, 1990–2003
Andy Murray, 2005–

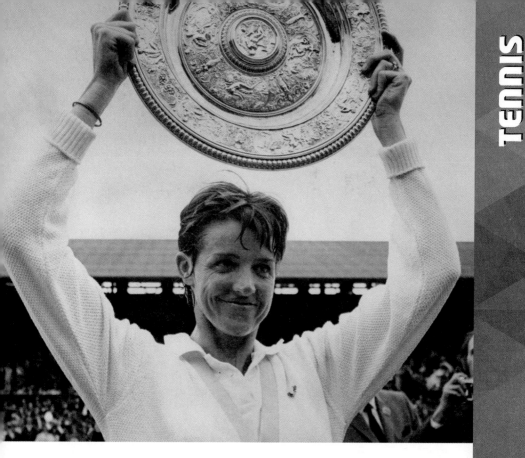

woman with the most Grand Slam singles titles

Margaret Court Smith

Margaret Court Smith won 24 Grand Slam singles titles between 1960 and 1975. She is the only woman ever to win the French, British, US, and Australian titles during one year in both the singles and doubles competitions. She was only the second woman to win all four singles titles in the same year. During her amazing career, she won a total of 64 Grand Slam championships—more than any other woman. Court was the world's top-seeded female player from 1962 to 1965, 1969 to 1970, and 1973. She was inducted into the International Tennis Hall of Fame in 1979.

women with the most Grand Slam singles titles

number of titles won

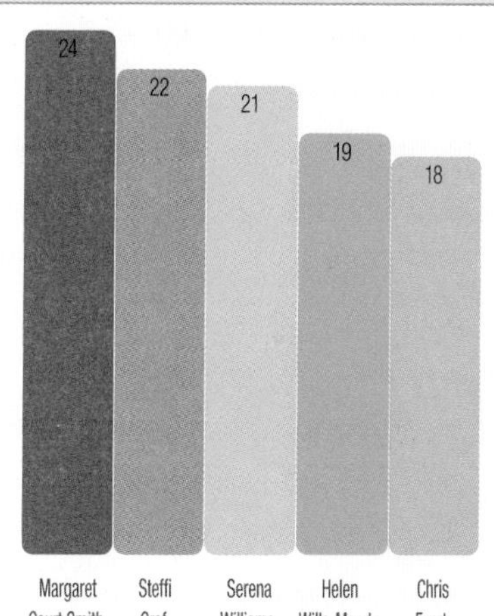
24
22
21
19
18
Margaret Court Smith, 1960–1975
Steffi Graf, 1987–1999
Serena Williams, 1995–
Helen Wills-Moody, 1923–1938
Chris Evert, 1974–1986

man with the most Grand Slam singles titles

Roger Federer

Swiss tennis great Roger Federer has won a record 17 Grand Slam championship titles. He has four Australian Open wins, one French Open win, seven Wimbledon wins, and five US Open wins. Federer is also one of only two players to win the Golden Slam—winning all four Grand Slam championships and an Olympic gold medal in the same year (2008). Federer achieved his 17th Grand Slam title when he defeated Andy Murray at the Wimbledon gentlemen's final in 2012. In 2015, Federer made it to the finals at Wimbledon, but lost to Novak Djokovic in four sets.

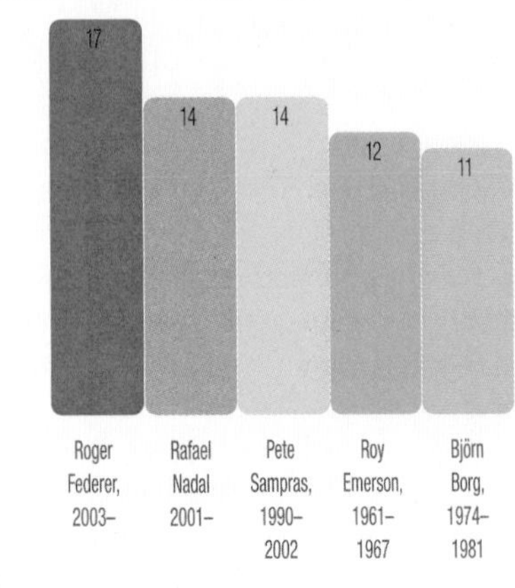
men with the most Grand Slam singles titles
number of titles won
17
14
14
12
11
Roger Federer, 2003–
Rafael Nadal 2001–
Pete Sampras, 1990–2002
Roy Emerson, 1961–1967
Björn Borg, 1974–1981

MLS player with the most goals

Landon Donovan

Midfielder Landon Donovan has scored more goals than any other player in Major League Soccer with 144. He is also the all-time leading scorer for the US national team with 57 goals and 58 assists. He has won the Fútbol de Primera Player of the Year award (formerly Honda Player of the Year) seven times, and he's won the US Soccer Male Athlete of the Year four times. Donovan made his MLS debut with the San Jose Earthquakes in 2001 and moved to the Los Angeles Galaxy in 2005. In the MLS, he played 28,665 minutes during his career and had 365 shots on goal. In December 2014, Donovan retired from the game after helping his team win a record fifth MLS title.

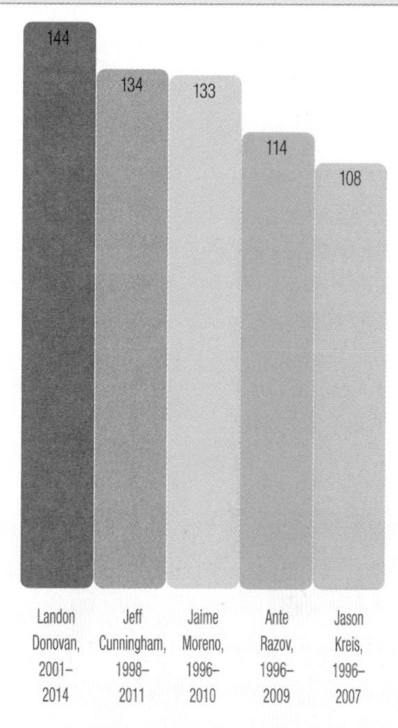
MLS players with the most goals
goals scored
144
134
133
114
108
Landon Donovan, 2001–2014
Jeff Cunningham, 1998–2011
Jaime Moreno, 1996–2010
Ante Razov, 1996–2009
Jason Kreis, 1996–2007

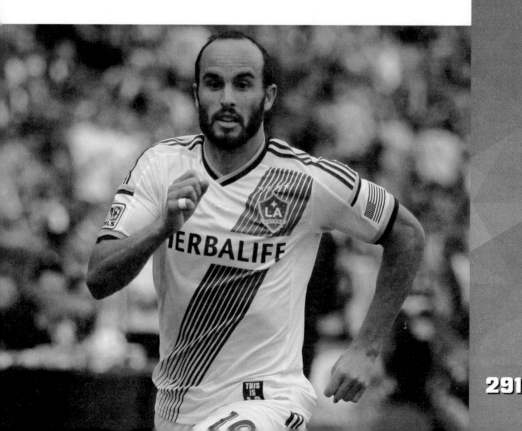

woman with the most caps

Kristine Lilly

With a total of 352, Kristine Lilly holds the world record for the most international games played, or caps. This is the highest number of caps in both the men's and women's international soccer organizations. She has a career total of 130 international goals—the second highest in the world. In 2004, Lilly scored her 100th international goal, becoming one of only five women to ever accomplish that feat. Lilly was named US Soccer's Female Athlete of the Year three times (1993, 2005, 2006). She retired in January 2011.

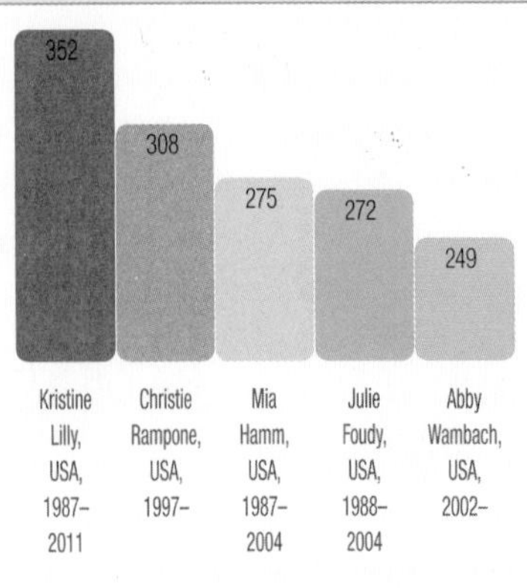
women with the most caps
number of career caps
352
308
275
272
249
Kristine Lilly, USA, 1987–2011
Christie Rampone, USA, 1997–
Mia Hamm, USA, 1987–2004
Julie Foudy, USA, 1988–2004
Abby Wambach, USA, 2002–

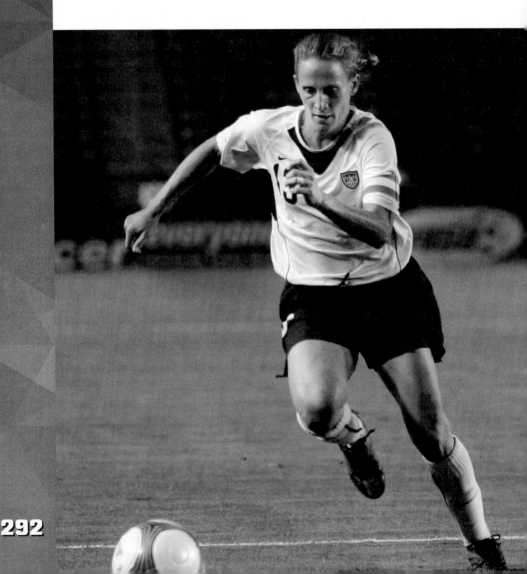

man with the most caps

Ahmed Hassan

Ahmed Hassan, the captain for the Egyptian national soccer team and a midfielder for the Egyptian Premier League's Zamalek SC, has the most caps—or international games—with 184 appearances. He made his international debut in 1995. Hassan helped the National team win four CAF Africa Cup of Nations between 1998 and 2010, and was named the tournament's best player twice. He has also played in the Belgium Cup, the Turkish Cup, and the CAF Championship League. In 2010, Hassan was voted Best African-Based Player of the Year.

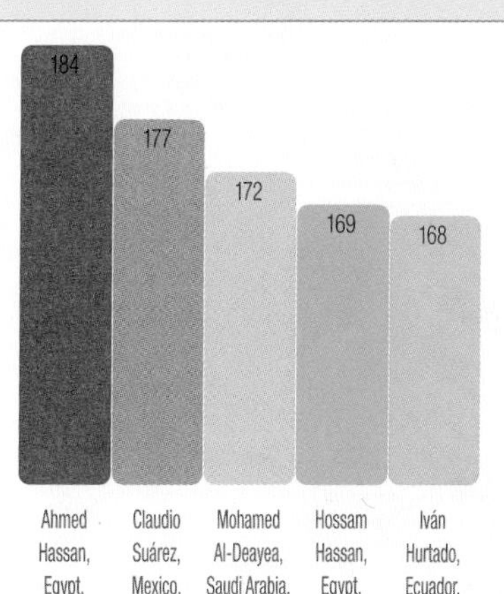
men with the most caps
number of career caps
184
177
172
169
168
Ahmed Hassan, Egypt, 1995–2012
Claudio Suárez, Mexico, 1992–2010
Mohamed Al-Deayea, Saudi Arabia, 1990–2006
Hossam Hassan, Egypt, 1985–2007
Iván Hurtado, Ecuador, 1992–2014

country with the most World Cup points

Germany

Germany has accumulated a total of 37 points during World Cup soccer competition. A win is worth 4 points, runner-up is worth 3 points, third place is worth 2 points, and fourth place is worth 1 point. Germany won the World Cup four times between 1954 and 2014. Most recently, Germany earned 4 points for a first-place finish in 2014. The World Cup is organized by the Fédération Internationale de Football Association (FIFA) and is played every four years.

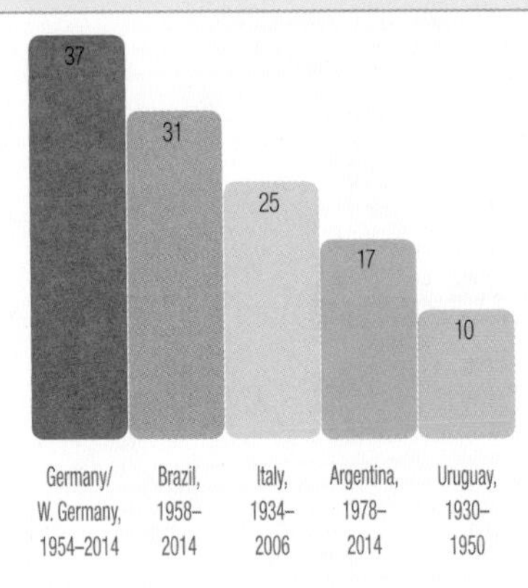
countries with the most World Cup points
total number of points
37
31
25
17
10
Germany/ W. Germany, 1954–2014
Brazil, 1958–2014
Italy, 1934–2006
Argentina, 1978–2014
Uruguay, 1930–1950

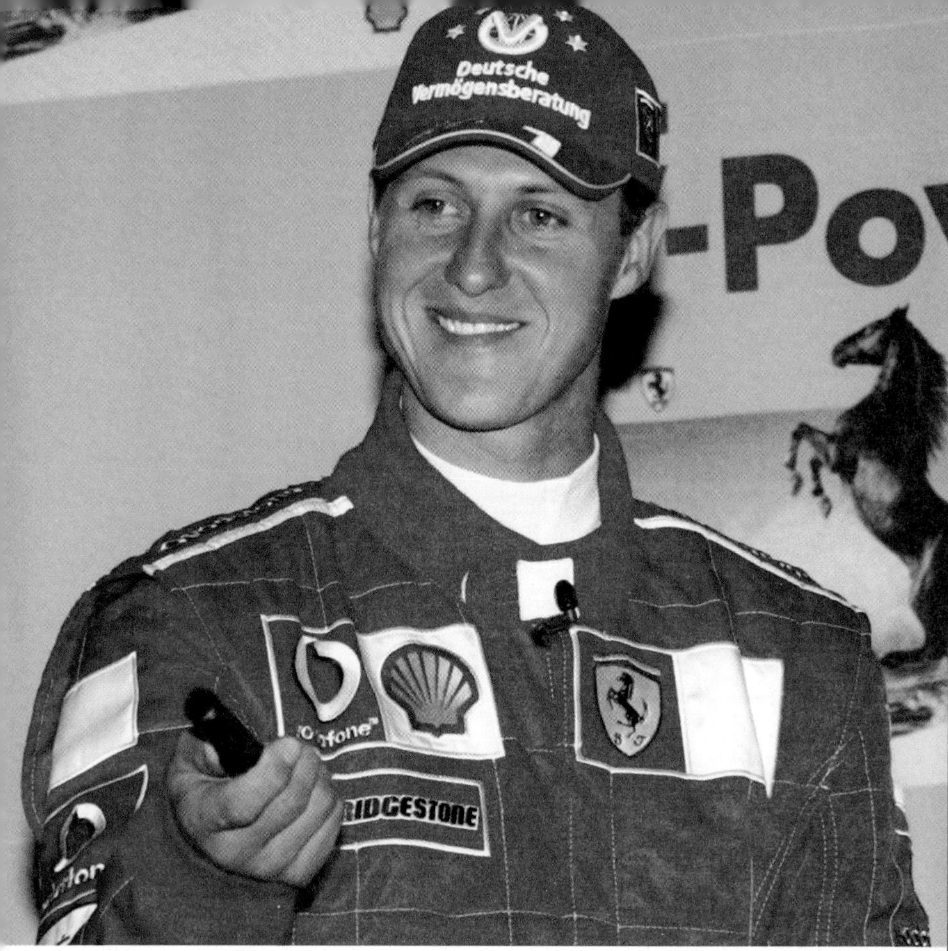

driver with the most Formula One wins

Michael Schumacher

Race-car driver Michael Schumacher won 91 Formula One races in his professional career, which began in 1991. Out of the 250 races he competed in, he reached the podium 154 times. In 2002, Schumacher became the only Formula One driver to have a podium finish in each race in which he competed that season. He won seven world championships between 1994 and 2004. Schumacher, who was born in Germany, began his career with Benetton but later switched to Ferrari. He retired from racing in 2006.

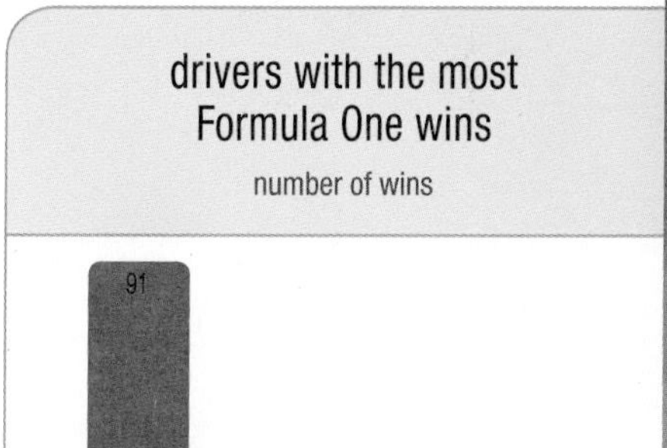

drivers with the most Formula One wins

number of wins

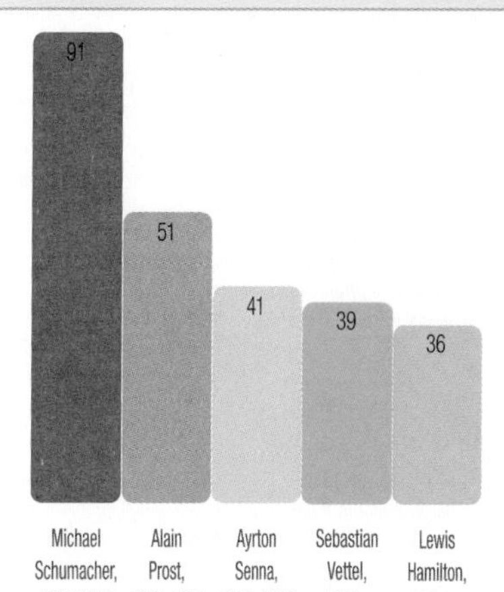
91
51
41
39
36
Michael Schumacher, 1991–2012
Alain Prost, 1985–1993
Ayrton Senna, 1983–1994
Sebastian Vettel, 2006–
Lewis Hamilton, 2007–

driver with the fastest Daytona 500 win

Buddy Baker

Race-car legend Buddy Baker dominated the competition at the 1980 Daytona 500 with an average speed of over 177 miles (285 km) per hour. It was the first Daytona 500 race run in under three hours. Baker had a history of speed before this race—he became the first driver to race more than 200 miles (322 km) per hour on a closed course in 1970. During his amazing career, Baker competed in 688 Winston Cup races—he won 19 of them and finished in the top five in 198 others. He also won more than $3.6 million. He was inducted into the International Motorsports Hall of Fame in 1997.

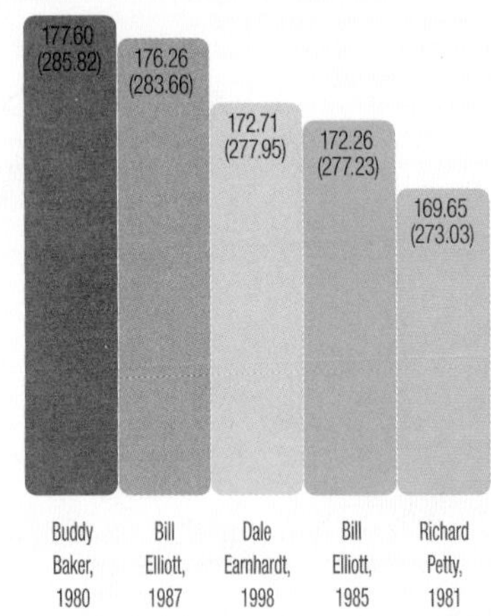
drivers with the fastest Daytona 500 wins
average speed, in miles (kilometers) per hour
177.60 (285.82)
176.26 (283.66)
172.71 (277.95)
172.26 (277.23)
169.65 (273.03)
Buddy Baker, 1980
Bill Elliott, 1987
Dale Earnhardt, 1998
Bill Elliott, 1985
Richard Petty, 1981

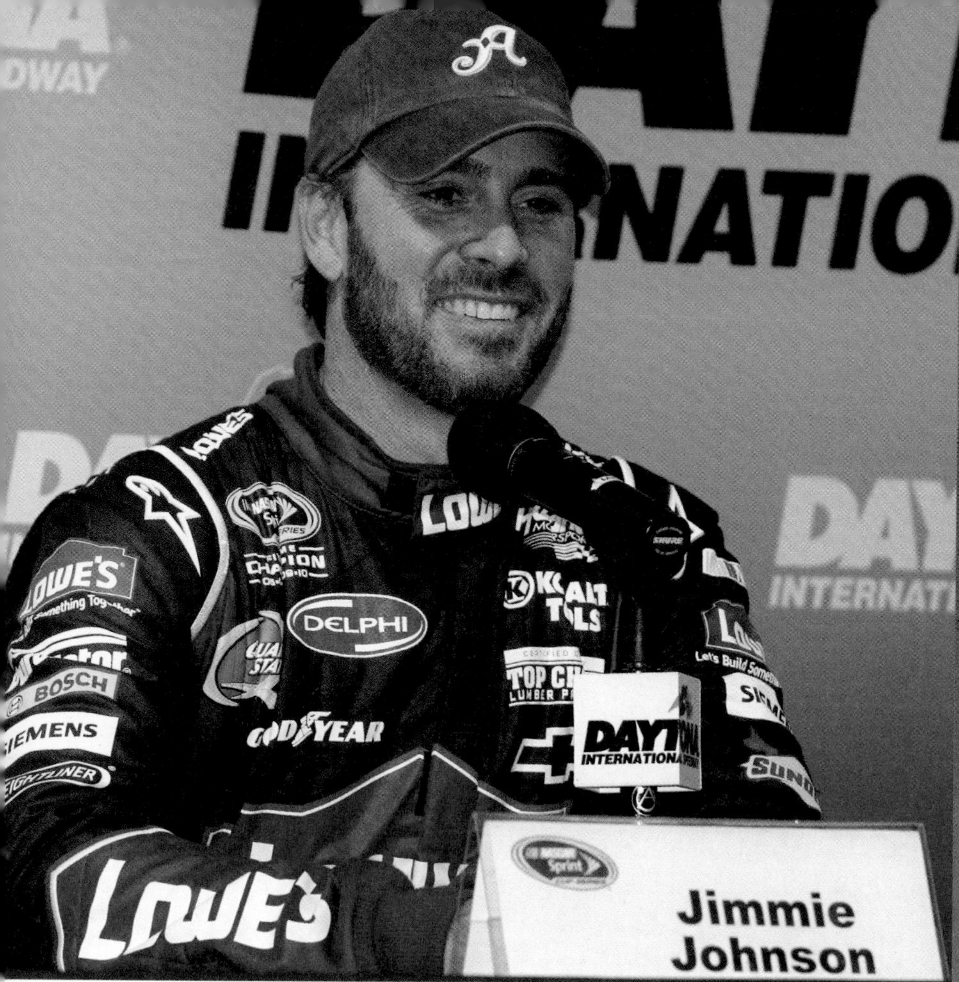

driver with the most consecutive Sprint Cup Championships

Jimmie Johnson

Johnson won five consecutive Sprint Cup Championships between 2006 and 2010. With his 54 series wins, he is ranked 10th in career victories. During his career, Johnson has also had 138 top-five finishes and 208 top-ten finishes. He has been named Driver of the Year four times, which is a record he holds with teammate Jeff Gordon. Johnson joined the Hendrick Motorsports team in 2002, and drives a Chevrolet owned by Gordon. In addition to his Sprint Cup victories, Johnson has won the Daytona 500 one time and the Coca-Cola 500 and the Allstate 400 three times each.

drivers with the most consecutive Sprint Cup Championships
consecutive wins

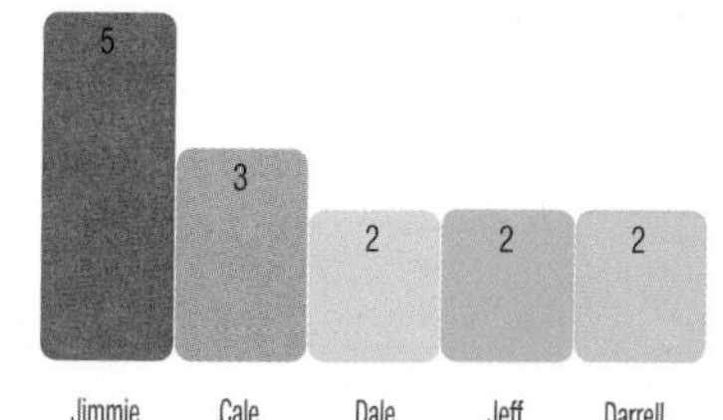
5
3
2
2
2
Jimmie Johnson, 2006–2010
Cale Yarborough, 1976–1978
Dale Earnhardt 1993–1994
Jeff Gordon, 1997–1998
Darrell Waltrip 1981–1982

highest-paid NASCAR driver

Dale Earnhardt Jr.

In 2014, NASCAR driver Dale Earnhardt Jr. earned $23.8 million. This total includes race winnings, as well as income earned for several endorsements including Wrangler, Chevrolet, and eBay. During his career, he has made more than $100 million. Earnhardt drives the number 88 Chevy Impala for Hendrick Motors in the NASCAR Sprint Cup Series. He's competed in more than 450 NASCAR Sprint Cup races during his 16-year career. Earnhardt Jr. has 24 career wins and 134 top-five finishes. He won the Daytona 500 in 2004 and the Busch Series Championship in 1998 and 1999. In May 2015, Earnhardt Jr. won the Geico 500 at the Talladega Speedway.

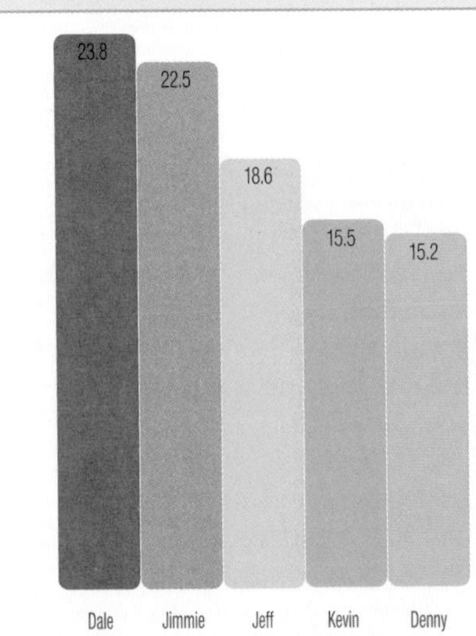
highest-paid NASCAR drivers
earnings in 2014, in millions of US dollars
23.8
22.5
18.6
15.5
15.2
Dale Earnhardt Jr.
Jimmie Johnson
Jeff Gordon
Kevin Harvick
Denny Hamlin

rider with the most superbike race points

Sylvain Guintoli

Sylvain Guintoli topped the superbike leaderboard in 2014 with 416 points. Drivers earn points based on what position they are in when they finish the race. During the season, he competed in 24 races for Aprilia, coming in first 5 times, second 8 times, and third 3 times. The French rider signed to race for the Pata Honda World Superbike team in 2015. Since he began racing in 2009, he has reached the podium 40 times and won 9 of his 139 races. Before racing in the World Superbike Championships, Guintoli raced the 250cc and MotoGP series, as well as the British Superbike Championship.

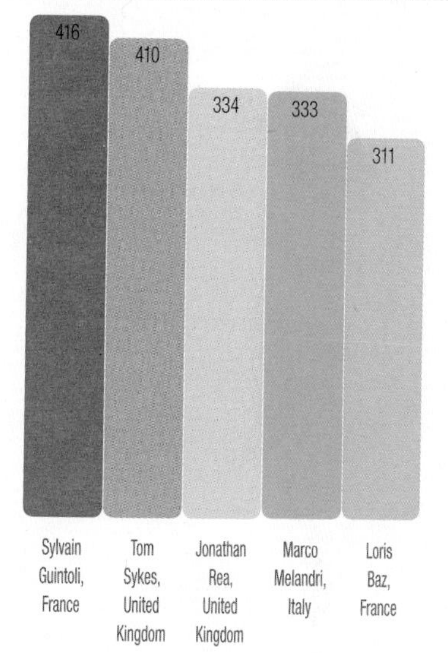
riders with the most superbike race points
total points in 2014
416
410
334
333
311
Sylvain Guintoli, France
Tom Sykes, United Kingdom
Jonathan Rea, United Kingdom
Marco Melandri, Italy
Loris Baz, France

rider with the most motocross world titles

Stefan Everts

Stefan Everts is the king of motocross with a total of ten world titles. He won twice on a 500cc bike, seven more times on a 250cc bike, and once on a 125cc bike. During his 18-year career, he had 101 Grand Prix victories. Everts was named Belgium Sportsman of the Year five times. He retired after his final world title in 2006 and is now a consultant and coach for the riders who compete for the KTM racing team.

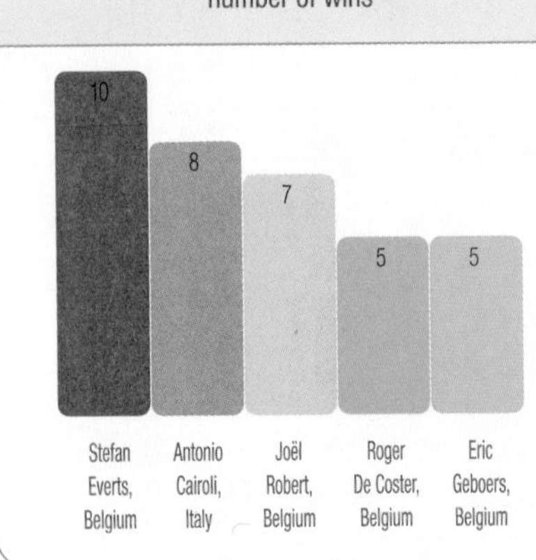
riders with the most
motocross world titles
number of wins
10
8
7
5
5
Stefan Everts, Belgium
Antonio Cairoli, Italy
Joël Robert, Belgium
Roger De Coster, Belgium
Eric Geboers, Belgium

jockey with the most Triple Crown wins

Eddie Arcaro

Between 1938 and 1961, jockey Eddie Arcaro won a total of 17 Triple Crown races. Nicknamed "the Master," Arcaro won the Kentucky Derby five times, the Preakness six times, and the Belmont six times. He holds the record for the most Preakness wins and is tied for the most Kentucky Derby and Belmont wins. He was also horse racing's top money winner six times between 1940 and 1955. During his career, Arcaro competed in 24,092 races and won 4,779 of them.

jockeys with the most Triple Crown wins

number of wins

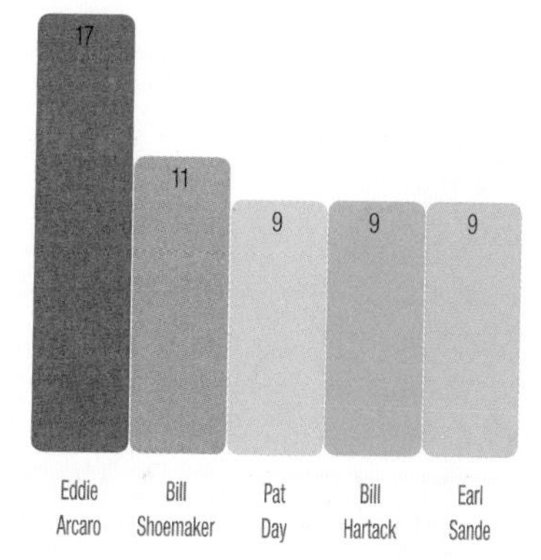
17
11
9
9
9
Eddie Arcaro
Bill Shoemaker
Pat Day
Bill Hartack
Earl Sande

NHL team with the most Stanley Cup wins

Montreal Canadiens

The Montreal Canadiens, also known as the Habs, won an amazing 24 Stanley Cup victories between 1916 and 1993. That's almost one-quarter of all the Stanley Cup championships ever played. The Canadiens were created in December 1909 by J. Ambrose O'Brien to play for the National Hockey Association (NHA). They eventually made the transition into the National Hockey League. Over the years, the Canadiens have included such great players as Maurice Richard, George Hainsworth, Jacques Lemaire, Saku Koivu, and Emile Bouchard. The Canadiens started strong in the 2014 NHL Playoffs but were defeated in Eastern Conference finals. They had a repeat trip to the Eastern Conference playoffs in 2015, but lost to the Tampa Bay Lightning.

NHL teams with the most Stanley Cup wins

number of Stanley Cup wins

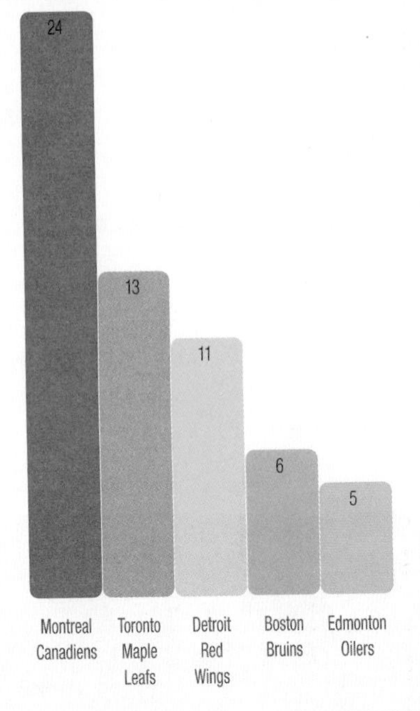
24
13
11
6
5
Montreal Canadiens
Toronto Maple Leafs
Detroit Red Wings
Boston Bruins
Edmonton Oilers

The Stanley Cup winners, 1993

NHL player with the most career points

Wayne Gretzky

Wayne Gretzky scored an unbelievable 2,857 points and 894 goals during his 20-year career. Gretzky was the first person in the NHL to average more than two points per game. Many people consider Canadian-born Gretzky to be the greatest player in the history of the National Hockey League. In fact, he is called "The Great One." He officially retired from the sport in 1999 and was inducted into the Hockey Hall of Fame that same year. After his final game, the NHL retired his jersey number (99). In 2005, Gretzky became the head coach of the Phoenix Coyotes.

NHL players with the most career points

number of points scored

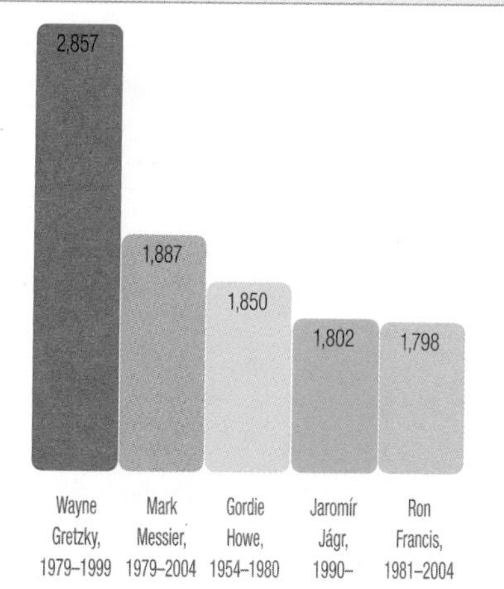
2,857
1,887
1,850
1,802
1,798
Wayne Gretzky, 1979–1999
Mark Messier, 1979–2004
Gordie Howe, 1954–1980
Jaromír Jágr, 1990–
Ron Francis, 1981–2004

NHL goalie with the most career wins

Martin Brodeur

Not much got by goalie Martin Brodeur—he's won 691 games since he was drafted by the New Jersey Devils in 1990. While playing with the Devils, Brodeur helped the team win three Stanley Cup championships. He is also the only goalie in NHL history to complete seven seasons with 40 or more wins. Brodeur has been an NHL All-Star ten times. He has received the Vezina Trophy four times and the Jennings Trophy five times. After playing with the St. Louis Blues for a season, Brodeur retired in 2015.

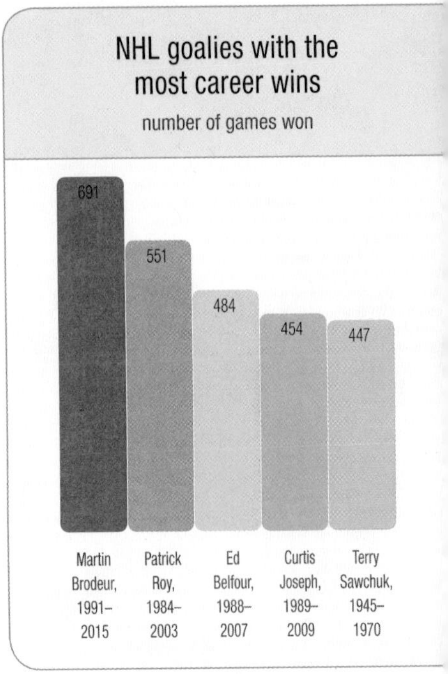

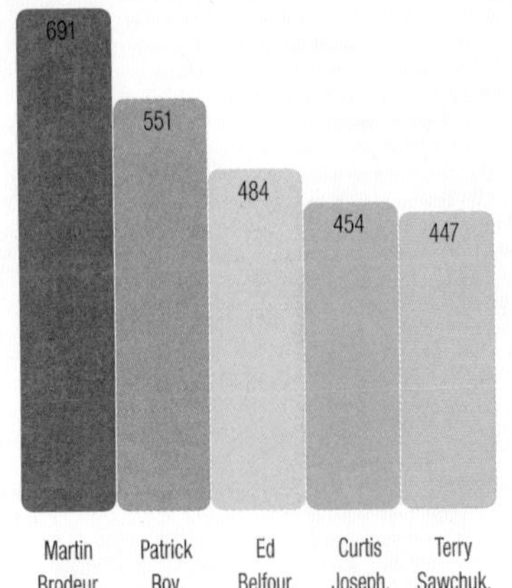
NHL goalies with the most career wins
number of games won
691
551
484
454
447
Martin Brodeur, 1991–2015
Patrick Roy, 1984–2003
Ed Belfour, 1988–2007
Curtis Joseph, 1989–2009
Terry Sawchuk, 1945–1970

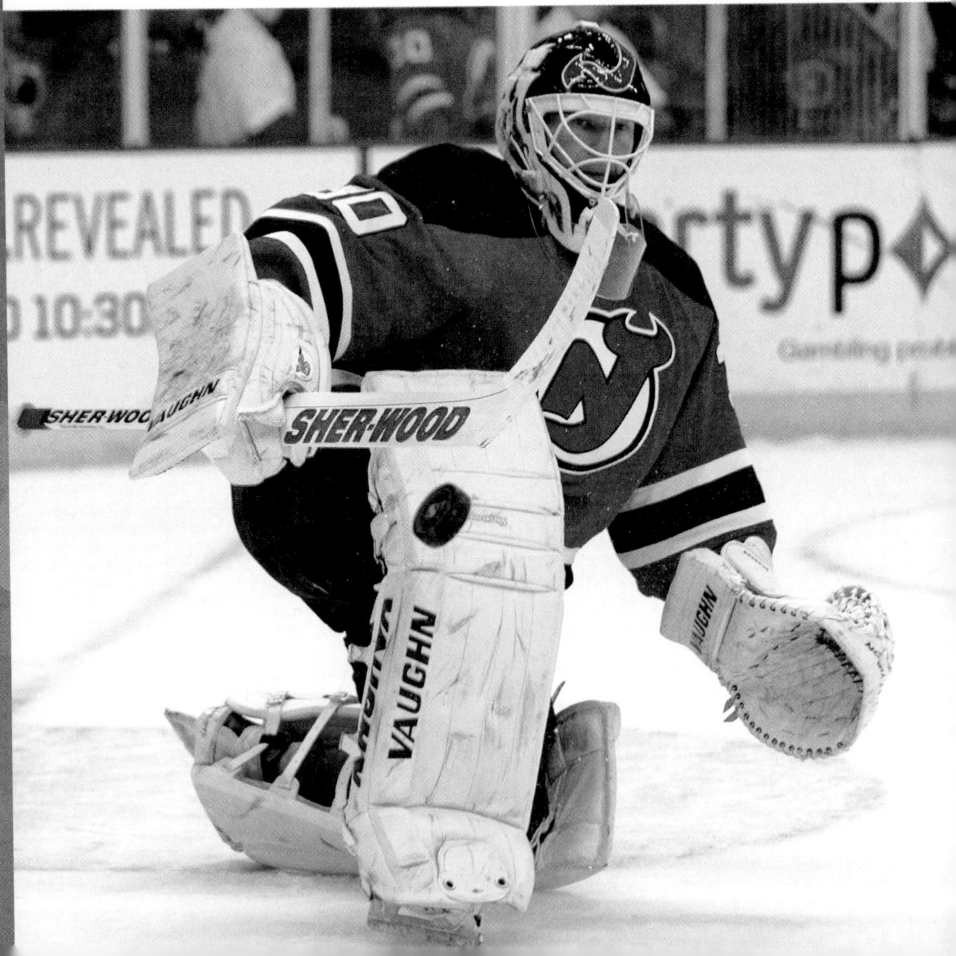

NHL player with the most power play goals

Dave Andreychuk

Dave Andreychuk has scored more power play goals than any other player in NHL history with 274. A power play occurs when one team has all five players on the ice and the other team has at least one player in the penalty box. The full-strength team has a huge advantage to score with the extra player on the ice. Andreychuk was in the NHL from 1982 to 2006, and played for the Buffalo Sabres, the Toronto Maple Leafs, the New Jersey Devils, the Boston Bruins, the Colorado Avalanche, and the Tampa Bay Lightning. With a total of 1,338 points, he is one of the highest-scoring left wings in NHL history.

NHL players with the most power play goals

power play goals

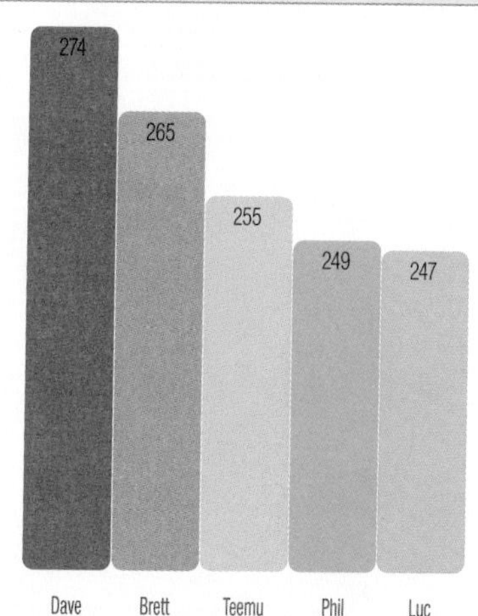
274
265
255
249
247
Dave Andreychuk, 1982– 2006
Brett Hull, 1985–2006
Teemu Selänne, 1988–2014
Phil Esposito, 1964–1981
Luc Robitaille, 1986–2006

NHL player with the most winning goals

Jaromír Jágr

Jaromír Jágr works well under pressure—he has 129 winning goals during his 25-year NHL career. He has a career point total of 1,802 and was the fifth overall draft pick in 1990. Currently a Florida Panther, Jágr has also played for the Pittsburgh Penguins, the Washington Capitals, the New York Rangers, the Philadelphia Flyers, the Boston Bruins, and the Dallas Stars. He also has two Olympic medals, and—in 1991 and 1992—he helped the Penguins win the Stanley Cup.

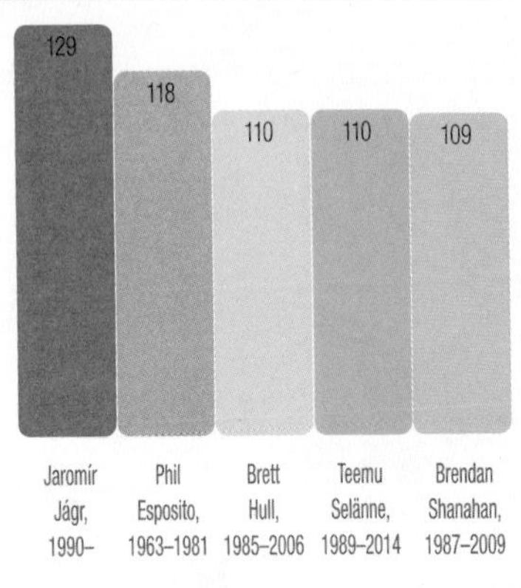
NHL players with the most winning goals
goals
129
118
110
110
109
Jaromír Jágr, 1990–
Phil Esposito, 1963–1981
Brett Hull, 1985–2006
Teemu Selänne, 1989–2014
Brendan Shanahan, 1987–2009

highest-paid hockey player

Sidney Crosby

In 2014, Sidney Crosby earned $16.5 million through his NHL salary, endorsements, and memorabilia. The Pittsburgh Penguins pay Crosby $12 million per year, and he banked another $4.5 million in endorsements for Reebok, Gatorade, and Tim Horton's. The Canadian center was the first overall draft pick in 2005 and was the captain of the gold-medal-winning Team Canada at the 2010 winter Olympic Games. He holds several NHL records, which include being the youngest player voted to the starting lineup in an All-Star Game, and the youngest player to reach 200 career points.

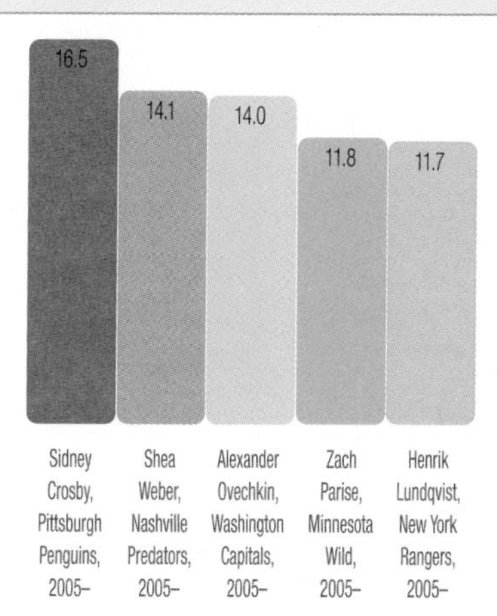
highest-paid hockey players
salary and endorsements in 2014, in millions of US dollars
16.5
14.1
14.0
11.8
11.7
Sidney Crosby, Pittsburgh Penguins, 2005–
Shea Weber, Nashville Predators, 2005–
Alexander Ovechkin, Washington Capitals, 2005–
Zach Parise, Minnesota Wild, 2005–
Henrik Lundqvist, New York Rangers, 2005–

Index

Photo Credits

Photographs ©:

Photos ©: 3 top left: Al Bello/Getty Images; 3 bottom left: 2nix Studio/Shutterstock Inc.; 3 right: Jordan Strauss/AP Images; 4: Car Collection/Alamy Images; 5 top: bunhill/iStockphoto; 5 bottom: Chalabala/Thinkstock; 6 top: tomeng/iStockphoto; 6 bottom: robas/iStockphoto; 7 top: EdStock/iStockphoto; 7 bottom: BDphoto/iStockphoto; 8 top: Alex Brandon/AP Images; 8 center: R.D. Burchfield; 8 bottom: Afflamen/Dreamstime; 9 top: digitaldreamland.co.uk/Alamy Images; 9 bottom: bunhill/iStockphoto; 10 top: Benkrut/Dreamstime; 10 bottom: Jordan Strauss/Getty Images; 11 top: Press Association via AP Images; 11 bottom: Mark Lennihan/AP Images; 12 top: Imaginechina via AP Images; 12 bottom: Brett Critchley/Dreamstime; 13 top: Bloomberg/Getty Images; 13 bottom: AFP/Getty Images; 14 top: Ric Tapia/AP Images; 14 center: Bebeto Matthews/AP Images; 14 bottom: Steven Franczek/Shutterstock, Inc.; 15 top: Ed Jones/Getty Images; 15 bottom: Kamran Jebreili/AP Images; 16 top: LornaWu/Thinkstock; 16 bottom: Scholastic Inc.; 17 top: Ted S. Warren/AP Images; 17 bottom: ymgerman/iStockphoto; 18 left: Scholastic Inc.; 18 right: Scholastic Inc.; 19: Antonio Jodice/Dreamstime; 20: Ellen DeGeneres/Twitter via Getty Images; 21: Eric Carr/Alamy Images; 22-23: Alex Segr/Alamy Images; 24, 25: Scholastic Inc.; 26: ChinaFotoPress/ChinaFotoPress via Getty Images; 27: Prykhodo/ Dreamstime; 28: razorpi/Alamy Images; 29: Jaguarps/Dreamstime; 30: MorelSO/iStockphoto; 31: Marcel De Grijs/Dreamstime; 32: Courtesy Twitter; 33: Chrishowey/Dreamstime; 34: Paul White/AP Images; 35: Eagleflying/Dreamstime; 36 left, 36 right: Courtesy Samsung Mobile; 37: Rosie Hallam/Nokia; 38: Radub85/Dreamstime; 39: 2nix Studio/Shutterstock Inc.; 40: Bosca78/iStockphoto; 41: Sallyeva/Dreamstime; 42: Laszlo Halasi/Shutterstock, Inc.; 43: AFP/Getty Images; 44: Bigfoot 4x4, Inc, 2011; 45: Shelley Mays/AP Images; 46: Getty Images; 47: Alan Diaz/AP Images; 48: MWA/ZOJ/Michael Wright/Wenn.com/Newscom; 49: Gonzalo Fuentes/Reuters; 50: Danjaq/Eon/UA/The Kobal Collection; 51: NASA; 52: Mike Derer/AP Images; 53: Courtesy of Cedar Point; 54: Ferrari World, Abu Dhabi; 55: Leung Cho Pan/Dreamstime; 56: Kamran Jebreili/AP Images; 57: Walter Bibikow/age Fotostock; 58: Korean Central News Agency via Korea News Service/AP Images; 59: Barry Williams/Getty Images; 60: Hu guolin/AP Images; 61: Bjorn Svensson/Science Source; 62: selensergen/Thinkstock; 63 top: Goodluz/Dreamstime; 63 bottom: Manuel-F-O/Thinkstock; 64 top: Rocky Widner/Getty Images; 64 center: Michael Thomas/Getty Images; 64 bottom: Cal Sport Media via AP Images; 65 top: Jeff Whyte/Dreamstime; 65 bottom: Frank Gunn/The Canadian Press via AP; 66 top: Eliot J. Schechter/Getty Images; 66 bottom: Icon Sportswire via AP Images; 67 top: James Devaney/Getty Images; 67 bottom: Rebius/Dreamstime; 68 top: scyther5/Thinkstock; 68 bottom: Justin Sullivan/Getty Images; 69 top: Douglas C. Pizac/AP Images; 69 center: Spencer Platt/Getty Images; 69 bottom: Imageegami/Dreamstime; 70 top: Mikael Damkier/Dreamstime; 70 bottom: Michael Cohen/Getty Images; 71 top: Bloomberg/Getty Images; 71 bottom: Wrangel/Dreamstime; 72 top: Bloomberg/Getty Images; 72 bottom: Darren Abate/AP Images; 73 top: Timothy A. Clary/Getty Images; 73 bottom: Yevgenia Gorbulsky/Dreamstime; 74 top: AF archive/Alamy Images; 74 center: Jupiterimages/Thinkstock; 74 bottom: Ambientideas/Dreamstime; 75 top: John Leyba/Getty Images; 75 bottom: New York Daily News Archive/Getty Images; 76: John Barr/Getty Images; 77: President Wilson Hotel, Geneva; 78: Georgios Kefalas/AP Images; 79: Chris Pizzello/AP Images; 80: Sipa via AP Images; 81: Gene Blevins/Polaris/Newscom; 82: Glenn Chapman/Getty Images; 83: Jonathan Newton/The Washington Post via Getty Images; 84: Brian Babineau/NHLI via Getty Images; 85: Javier Soriano/Getty Images; 86: Catherine Steenkeste/Getty Images; 87: Cal Sport Media via AP Images; 88: Carlos Osorio/AP Images; 89: Robert Convery/Alamy Images; 90: Bloomberg/Getty Images; 91: Jaguarps/Dreamstime; 92 top: Featureflash/Dreamstime; 92 bottom: Tracy Bennett/©Columbia Pictures/Everett Collection; 93 top: Debby Wong/Shutterstock, Inc.; 93 bottom: Luca Bruno/AP Images; 94 top: Featureflash/Shutterstock, Inc.; 94 bottom: John Shearer/Invision for iHeartRadio/AP Images; 95 top: 247PAPS.TV/Corbis Images; 95 bottom: Helga Esteb/Shutterstock, Inc.; 96 top: Jeff Vespa/Getty Images; 96 bottom: Kevork Djansezian/Getty Images; 97 top: Jason Merritt/Getty Images; 97 center: Victoria Will/Invision/AP Images; 97 bottom: Janet Van Ham/©HBO/Everett Collection; 98 top: Kevin Winter/Getty Images; 98 bottom: Michael Albright/Dreamstime; 99 top: Mark J. Terrill/AP Images; 99 bottom: Mark J. Terrill/AP Images; 100 top: Scott Suchman; 100 bottom: Frederick M. Brown/Getty Images; 101 top: Moviestore collection Ltd/Alamy Images; 101 bottom: New Line/Everett Collection; 102 top: Sbukley/Dreamstime; 102 bottom: Damian Dovarganes/AP Images; 103 top: Pictorial Press Ltd/Alamy Images; 103 center: Helga Esteb/Shutterstock, Inc.; 103 bottom: Frederick M. Brown/Getty Images; 104 top: Adam Taylor/Getty Images; 104 bottom: Elise Amendola/AP Images; 105: Jordan Strauss/AP Images; 106: Frazer Harrison/Getty Images; 107: Kevin Mazur/Getty Images; 108: NBC Universal/Getty Images; 109: Jason Merritt/Getty Images; 110: Frederick M. Brown/Getty Images; 111: Jordan Strauss/AP Images; 112: CBS Photo Archive/Getty Images; 113: Jeff Kravitz/FilmMagic/Getty Images; 114: Todd Williamson/Invision/AP Images; 115: Tracy Bennett/©Columbia Pictures/Everett Collection; 116: Mike Marsland/Getty Images; 117: Jaguarps/Dreamstime; 118: Kevork Djansezian/AP Images; 119: Matt Sayles/AP Images; 120: Jason Merritt/Getty Images; 121: Mark J. Terrill/AP Images; 122: Press Association via AP Images; 123: Frazer Harrison/Getty Images; 124: Universal Pictures/Everett Collection; 125: Twentieth Century Fox Film Corporation/Photofest; 126: Pictorial Press Ltd/Alamy Images; 127: Paul Drinkwater/AP Images; 128: Steve Granitz/Getty Images; 129: Jordan Strauss/Invision/AP Images; 130: Andrew

Cooper/©Paramount Pictures/Everett Collection; 131: Everett Collection; 132: urbanbuzz/iStockphoto; 133: AF archive/ Alamy Images; 134: NY Daily News via Getty Images; 135: Ethan Miller/Getty Images for ACM; 136: Chelsea Lauren/ Getty Images; 137: Amy Sussman/Invision/AP Images; 138: Armando Arorizo/Zuma Press/Newscom; 139: Michael Stewart/Getty Images; 140: Ben Glass/Warner Bros/ Regency/Canal+/The Kobal Collection; 141: Scholastic Inc.; 142: Kevin Mazur/WireImage/Getty Images; 143: Shareif Ziyadat/Getty Images; 144: Jordan Strauss/Invision/AP Images; 145: Richard Shotwell/Invision/AP Images; 146: Featureflash/Dreamstime; 147: Kobby Dagan/Dreamstime; 148: Mark Humphrey/AP Images; 149: David Karp/AP Images; 150: Greg Wood/Getty Images; 151: rmarnold/ iStockphoto; 152 top: Fuse/Thinkstock; 152 bottom: anek_s/ Thinkstock; 153 top: David McNew/AP Images; 153 bottom: Jodi Jacobson/iStockphoto; 154 top: Moolkum/Shutterstock, Inc.; 154 bottom: All Canada Photos/Alamy Images; 155 top: alaincouillaud/iStockphoto; 155 center: Davemhuntphotography/Dreamstime; 155 bottom: Thomas H. Hahn docu-images; 156 top: Barcroft/Getty Images; 156 bottom: Slade Paul/Getty Images; 157 top: marshalgonz/ Thinkstock; 157 bottom: Olena Savytska/iStockphoto; 158 top: Stockbyte/Thinkstock; 158 bottom: Mark Wilson/Getty Images; 159 top: Comstock/Media Bakery; 159 bottom: Ivan Kuzmin/Thinkstock; 160 top: Smithore/iStockphoto; 160 bottom: boryak/iStockphoto; 161 top: Kevin Britland/Alamy Images; 161 bottom: DeepAqua/iStockphoto; 162 top: Marie Read/Science Source; 162 bottom: Argument/Thinkstock; 163 top: mycteria/Shutterstock, Inc.; 163 center: pniesen/ iStockphoto; 163 bottom: USO/Thinkstock; 164 top: MichaelGrant/Alamy Images; 164 bottom: PaulReevesPhotography/iStockphoto; 165: Borsheim's Jewelry Store/AP Images; 166: TimHesterPhotography/ Thinkstock; 167: Rafael Wiedenmeier/Thinkstock; 168: Ramzi Hachicho/Dreamstime; 169: JudyDillon/Thinkstock; 170: Bruce Whittingham/Dreamstime; 171: Ippei Naoi/Thinkstock; 172: Courtesy of Submarine Ring of Fire 2014 - Ironman, NOAA/PMEL, NSF; 173: Cookelma/Dreamstime; 174: Courtesy Ministry for Primary Industries; 175: Sergey Uryadnikov/Dreamstime; 176: Krzysztof Odziomek/ Thinkstock; 177: Ronald C. Modra/Getty Images; 178: Ziss/ Dreamstime; 179: MR1805/Thinkstock; 180: Shane Gross/ Thinkstock; 181: ohn Carnemolla/Thinkstock; 182: Silver/ Fotolia; 183: Jeremy Woodhouse/Media Bakery; 184: Jeanro/ Dreamstime; 185: Elizabeth Hoffmann/Dreamstime; 186: Darryl Leniuk/Media Bakery; 187: John Carnemolla/ Thinkstock; 188: Lourens Lee/Thinkstock; 189: Hilton Kotze/ Dreamstime; 190: Jo Ann Crebbin/Thinkstock; 191: Dave Morton/Dreamstime; 192: Robert Hardholt/Dreamstime; 193: Craig Dingle/iStockphoto; 194: Anagramm/Thinkstock; 195: Dlhoward/Dreamstime; 196: Wendell Clendennen/ Dreamstime; 197: Kenneth Kohn/Thinkstock; 198: Scott Delony/Dreamstime; 199: mgkuijpers/Fotolia; 200: Matt Cornish/Shutterstock, Inc.; 201: Europics/Newscom; 202: Renaud Fulconis/Biosphoto; 203: Driverjcs/Dreamstime; 204: mikewi/Thinkstock; 205: Louiseefer/Fotolia; 206: Dave Massey/Dreamstime; 207: Ingram Publishing/Thinkstock; 208: EllaKingston/Thinkstock; 209: Lurin/Thinkstock; 210: brackish_nz/Thinkstock; 211: retrofutur/Thinkstock; 212: Chuyu/Dreamstime; 213: rsester/Thinkstock; 214: Stringer Canada/Reuters; 215: Amos Chapple/Zuma Press/ Newscom; 216: nexusimage/Thinkstock; 217: Archivo GDA Photo Service/Newscom; 218: littleny/Thinkstock; 219: petrenkoua/Fotolia; 220: Filippo Brandini/Thinkstock; 221: Manakin/Thinkstock; 222: raphoto/Thinkstock; 223: AP Images; 224: Andy Levin/Science Source; 225: Michel Gamgme/Getty Images; 226: Kathryn Sidenstricker/ Dreamstime; 227: Jim Edds/Science Source; 228: Lloyd Cluff/Corbis Images; 229: Jae C. Hong/AP Images; 230 top: Tom Strattman/AP Images; 230 bottom: Sports Studio Photos/Getty Images; 231 top: Eric Gay/AP Images; 231 bottom: Jerry Coli/Dreamstime; 232 top: Rusty Kennedy/AP Images; 232 bottom: Jerry Coli/Dreamstime; 233 top: Wallace Kirkland/Getty Images; 233 bottom: Jerry Coli/ Dreamstime; 234 top: Morry Gash/AP Images; 234 bottom: Craig Lassig/Getty Images; 235 top: Jonathan Bachman/AP Images; 235 center: Michael Burr/AP Images; 235 bottom: Focus On Sport/Getty Images; 236 top: Matt York/AP Images; 236 bottom: Focus On Sport/Getty Images; 237 top: Chris Carlson/AP Images; 237 bottom: Sam Greenwood/ Getty Images; 238 top: George Widman/AP Images; 238 bottom: Andrew Medichini/AP Images; 239 top: Vincent Jannink/AP Images; 239 bottom: Julie Jacobson/AP Images; 240 top: Andrew Redington/Getty Images; 240 bottom: Chris Carlson/AP Images; 241 top: Lightcatcherdreamstime/ Dreamstime; 241 center: RacingOne/Getty Images; 241 bottom: Lakruwan Wanniarachchi/Getty Images; 242 top: Greg Wood/Getty Images; 242 bottom: Jeff Vinnick/Getty Images; 243: Marc Serota/AP Images; 244: Richard Bord/ Getty Images; 245: John Berry/Getty Images; 246: Fabrice Coffrini/Getty Images; 247: Charles Krupa/AP Images; 248: The Sporting News/Getty Images; 249: Beth A. Keiser/AP Images; 250: John Swart/AP Images; 251: Jim Mones/AP Images; 252: Jae C. Hong/AP Images; 253: Bob Galbraith/ AP Images; 254: Kellie Landis/Getty Images; 255: Icon Sportswire via AP Images; 256: Elaine Thompson/AP Images; 257: Mark J. Terrill/AP Images; 258: Bill Shettle/AP Images; 259: Cal Sport Media via AP Images; 260: Jeffrey Phelps/AP Images; 261: Greg Trott/AP Images; 262: Denis Poroy/AP Images; 263: Al Behrman/AP Images; 264: Hans Deryk/AP Images; 265: Scott Boehm/AP Images; 266: Paul Jasienskis/AP Images; 267: Mark Humphrey/AP Images; 268: Al Bello/Getty Images; 269: Bob Leverone/AP Images; 270: Scott Halleran/Getty Images; 271: Alan Diaz/AP Images; 272: Al Messerschmidt/AP Images; 273: Alan Greth/AP Images; 274: Icon Sportswire via AP Images; 275: Denis Poroy/AP Images; 276: Ron Heflin/AP Images; 277: AP Images; 278: Transcendental Graphics/Getty Images; 279: MLB Photos via Getty Images; 280: Harry Harris/AP Images; 281: David Phillip/AP Images; 282: David J. Phillip/AP Images; 283: David J. Phillip/AP Images; 284: Bettmann/ Corbis Images; 285: Transcendental Graphics/Getty Images; 286: Francois Xavier-Marit/Getty Images; 287: Zhukovsky/ Dreamstime; 288: Alan Diaz/AP Images; 289: Mike Lawn/Fox Photos/Getty Images; 290: Mike Hewitt/Getty Images; 291: Jae C. Hong/AP Images; 292: Kevork Djansezian/AP Images; 293: Ben Curtis/AP Images; 294: Frank Augstein/AP Images; 295: Fritz Reiss/AP Images; 296: AP Images; 297: Reinhold Matay/AP Images; 298: Jerome Miron/USA Today Sports Images; 299: Mirco Lazzari gp/Getty Images; 300: Gert Eggenberger/AP Images; 301: Jim Wells/AP Images; 302: Bruce Bennett Studios/Getty Images; 303: Paul Chiasson/AP Images; 304: Bill Kostroun/AP Images; 305: Ryan Remiorz/ AP Images; 306: Joel Auerbach/AP Images; 307: Joe Sargent/NHLI via Getty Images.

SCHOLASTIC
SUMMER
READING
CHALLENGE™

WWW.SCHOLASTIC.COM/SUMMER

WHEN MILLIONS TURN INTO BILLIONS

Every summer, Scholastic challenges students from around the world to kick back with a book and read a little bit every day, and those minutes add up quickly! From May 4 to September 4, 2015, students from the US and around the world read a whopping total of **286,611,349 minutes**! But here's the best part: Since kids starting logging their minutes online in 2009, they have read more than **1 billion minutes**—a world record in reading!

CONGRATULATIONS TO ALL STUDENTS WHO PARTICIPATED IN 2015!

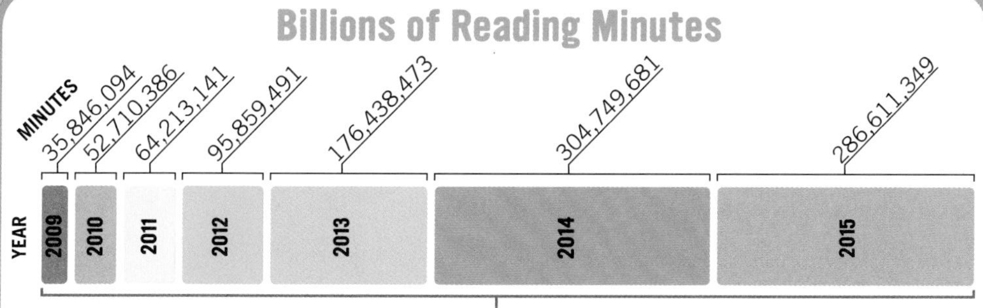
Billions of Reading Minutes
MINUTES
35,846,094
52,710,386
64,213,141
95,859,491
176,438,473
304,749,681
286,611,349
YEAR
2009
2010
2011
2012
2013
2014
2015

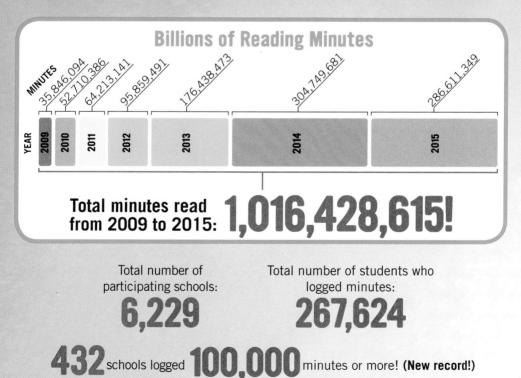

Total minutes read from 2009 to 2015: 1,016,428,615!

Total number of participating schools:
6,229

Total number of students who logged minutes:
267,624

432 schools logged **100,000** minutes or more! **(New record!)**

SCHOLASTIC
SUMMER
READING
CHALLENGE™

CHECK OUT THESE COOL FACTS:

TOP 20 STATES WITH THE MOST MINUTES READ:

	State	Minutes		State	Minutes
1.	Texas	81,347,190	**11.**	Ohio	3,805,032
2.	Florida	61,138,858	**12.**	Kentucky	3,803,566
3.	New York	11,852,419	**13.**	Michigan	3,133,304
4.	New Jersey	10,902,902	**14.**	Rhode Island	2,742,839
5.	North Carolina	9,375,258	**15.**	Nebraska	2,734,337
6.	Louisiana	7,830,208	**16.**	Tennessee	2,637,121
7.	California	7,472,201	**17.**	Wisconsin	2,569,765
8.	Georgia	7,427,993	**18.**	Alabama	2,411,834
9.	Pennsylvania	7,253,968	**19.**	Massachusetts	2,409,934
10.	Illinois	5,004,511	**20.**	Virginia	2,366,806

STATES WITH THE MOST MINUTES READ

Did your state make the top 20?

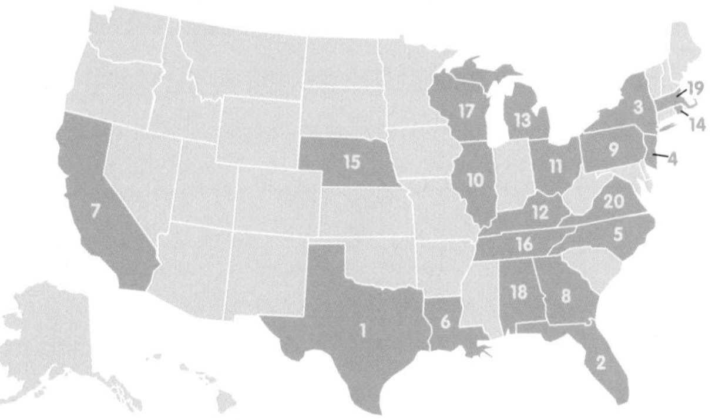
19
3
17
13
14
9
4
15
11
10
12
20
7
5
16
18
8
1
6
2

STUDENTS FROM AROUND THE WORLD PARTICIPATED!

Schools from 28 countries and four territories added minutes to the Summer Reading Challenge. Nine international schools read more than 100,000 minutes, led by Seoul Foreign School, Seoul, South Korea, with 673,118 minutes logged. Top countries included:

Canada	India	South Korea	Puerto Rico
China	Japan	Taiwan	United Arab Emirates
Guam	Nicaragua	Spain	

THE TOP SUMMER READING SCHOOLS IN THE WORLD!

2
1
2
8
5
8
6
3

Top honor in the 2015 Scholastic Summer Reading Challenge goes to Jackson Elementary School in McAllen, Texas, whose students read **21,285,863 minutes** this summer!

6
5
2
6
6
6
2

The top middle school is Lake Nona Middle School, Orlando, FL with **6,526,662 minutes** logged.

ROUNDING OUT THE TOP 20 SUMMER READING SCHOOLS!

These schools round out the top 20 list and are recognized for their outstanding contribution toward the Summer Reading Challenge:

Doedyns Elementary School	San Juan, TX	18,839,499
Boggy Creek Elementary School	Kissimmee, FL	14,844,153
Lake Nona Middle School	Orlando, FL	6,526,662
Carroll Academy	Houston, TX	4,413,046
Newell Elementary School	Allentown, NJ	2,733,841
Heritage Elementary School	Greenacres, FL	2,639,339
Gray Elementary School	Houston, TX	2,579,278
Flora Ridge Elementary School	Kissimmee, FL	2,300,326
Williams Intermediate School	Pell City, AL	2,290,953
Kenner Discovery Health Sciences Academy	Metairie, LA	2,229,072
Odom Elementary School	Houston, TX	2,213,840
Beacon Cove Intermediate School	Jupiter, FL	2,133,452
Ballantyne Elementary School	Charlotte, NC	2,112,954
Lisa Park Elementary School	Houma, LA	2,034,934
George L. Hess Education Complex	Mays Landing, NJ	1,789,298
Warm Springs Elementary School	Fremont, CA	1,717,731
Hill Intermediate School	Houston, TX	1,716,498
Roosevelt Elementary School	McAllen, TX	1,683,033
Etowah Elementary School	Etowah, NC	1,682,225

TOP SCHOOLS IN EACH STATE!

These schools all earned top state school honors by reading the most in their state. Schools with highlights set new summer reading records for their individual states.

Chugiak Elementary School	Chugiak, AK
Williams Intermediate School	Pell City, AL
Eastside Elementary School	Cabot, AR
Horizon Community Learning Center	Phoenix, AZ
Warm Springs Elementary School	Fremont, CA
Jefferson Academy Elementary School	Westminster, CO
Huckleberry Elementary School	Brookfield, CT
Dupont Park Adventist School	Washington, DC
St. Anne's Episcopal School	Middletown, DE
Boggy Creek Elementary School	Kissimmee, FL
McClure Middle School	Kennesaw, GA
Holy Family Catholic Academy	Honolulu, HI
Clayton Ridge Elementary School	Guttenberg, IA
Peregrine Elementary School	Meridian, ID
Western Avenue Elementary School	Flossmoor, IL
Traders Point Christian Academy	Whitestown, IN
St. Thomas Aquinas School	Wichita, KS
Veterans Park Elementary School	Lexington, KY
Kenner Discovery Health Sciences Academy	Metairie, LA
James M. Quinn Elementary School	North Dartmouth, MA
Fallsmead Elementary School	Rockville, MD
Warsaw Middle School	Pittsfield, ME
Rawsonville Elementary School	Ypsilanti, MI
St. Francis Xavier School	Buffalo, MN
Spoede Elementary School	Saint Louis, MO
Annunciation Catholic School	Columbus, MS
Roosevelt Elementary School	Great Falls, MT
Ballantyne Elementary School	Charlotte, NC
Erik Ramstad Middle School	Minot, ND
West Dodge Station Elementary School	Elkhorn, NE
Broken Ground Elementary School	Concord, NH
Newell Elementary School	Allentown, NJ
Aspen Elementary School	Los Alamos, NM
Kirk L. Adams Elementary School	Las Vegas, NV
Village Elementary School	Hilton, NY
Campus Elementary School	Streetsboro, OH
Northeast Elementary School	Owasso, OK
Holy Cross Catholic School	Portland, OR
Bridge Valley Elementary School	Furlong, PA
Marieville Elementary School	North Providence, RI
Crowders Creek Elementary School	Clover, SC
Creek Side Elementary School	Spearfish, SD
Crosswind Elementary School	Collierville, TN
Jackson Elementary School	McAllen, TX
Canyon View Middle School	Cedar City, UT
Ashburn Elementary School	Ashburn, VA
Calais Elementary School	Plainfield, VT
Highlands Elementary School	Renton, WA
Hillcrest Elementary School	Chippewa Falls, WI
North Elementary School	Morgantown, WV
Pronghorn Elementary School	Gillette, WY

MILLION MINUTE READERS CLUB!

Outside of the top 20 schools, students at these schools reached this awesome milestone.

Martin Luther King Elementary School	Edison, NJ	1,671,826
Francis Elementary School	Houston, TX	1,620,216
Bridge Valley Elementary School	Furlong, PA	1,570,073
Liberty Park Elementary School	Greenacres, FL	1,519,678
Raymond Academy	Houston, TX	1,445,796
Village Elementary School	Hilton, NY	1,413,409
Combs Elementary Magnet School	Raleigh, NC	1,377,343
New River Elementary School	Wesley Chapel, FL	1,315,714
Bussey Elementary School	Houston, TX	1,256,610
Veterans Park Elementary School	Lexington, KY	1,238,402
Kujawa Elementary School	Houston, TX	1,234,586
Goodman Elementary School	Houston, TX	1,234,485
Dream Lake Elementary School	Apopka, FL	1,154,384
Timber Trace Elementary School	Palm Beach Gardens, FL	1,079,160
Parker Intermediate School	Houston, TX	1,063,654
St. Aloysius Catholic School	Baton Rouge, LA	1,017,715
Fletcher Elementary School	Fletcher, NC	1,004,464
St. Cloud Elementary School	Saint Cloud, FL	1,000,387